The Fruit of Our Lips

The Transformation of God's Word
into the Speech of Mankind

EUGEN ROSENSTOCK-HUESSY

WIPF & STOCK · Eugene, Oregon

THE FRUIT OF OUR LIPS
The Transformation of God's Word into the Speech of Mankind

Copyright © 2021 the Mariot Huessy Trust.
Translation and apparatus © 2021 Raymond Huessy.
All rights reserved. Except for brief quotations in critical publications or reviews, no part of this book may be reproduced in any manner without prior written permission from the publisher. Write: Permissions, Wipf and Stock Publishers, 199 W. 8th Ave., Suite 3, Eugene, OR 97401.

An ARGO Book

Wipf & Stock
An Imprint of Wipf and Stock Publishers
199 W. 8th Ave., Suite 3
Eugene, OR 97401

www.wipfandstock.com

PAPERBACK ISBN: 978-1-7252-9154-6
HARDCOVER ISBN: 978-1-7252-9153-9
EBOOK ISBN: 978-1-7252-9155-3

01/20/21

For Freya

The Fruit of Our Lips

Contents

Acknowledgments		ix
An Introduction in Four Acts		1
I	In the Cross of Reality from *Soziologie: Die Vollzahl der Zeiten*	23
II	Ichthys: Life, Teaching, and Action as a Reflection of the Trinity from *Das Alter der Kirche*	31
III	The Fruit of Our Lips from *Die Sprache des Menschengeschlechts*	53
Appendices		131
	A. A Letter to Adele Rosenzweig	133
	B. Life, Teaching, and Action	141
	C. "A Letter to an American Friend"	161
	D. Introduction to " Fruit of Lips" (1977)	171
	E. The Fruit of Our Lips	181
	F. Jesus the Illiterate	281
	G. Descent and Assent	295
	H. A Reflection on the 1916 Correspondence	301
	I. Sources and Commentary	313
Bibliography		351

Acknowledgments

IN ONE OF THE codas he composed to "The Fruit of Our Lips," Eugen Rosenstock-Huessy connects the role of the spirit in the Christian era to the theory put forth by his friend, the Swiss zoologist Adolf Portmann, that human beings continue gestation "in the womb of society" for several years after their physical birth.[1] I would like to thank the board of the Eugen Rosenstock-Huessy Fund for its patience with the similarly protracted gestation of this new edition of *The Fruit of Our Lips*.

After the Fund decided to issue a new edition, I had to put the entire project on hold for a number of years. First I was hired to prepare my grandparents' archive for deposit at Dartmouth's Rauner Library, and then I took a "sabbatical" to recover from the six years of chaos that had upended my professional and personal life. Editorial combat delayed the project again. Returning to the project after many years' absence, I have had to rediscover the extent to which the devil is indeed in the details.

The originals of all the manuscripts and typescripts on which this edition is based (including the 183 letters that passed between Adele Rosenzweig and my grandparents) are among the 55,000 pages of letters and other documents now held in the Eugen Rosenstock-Huessy Archive at Rauner, along with fourteen boxes of manuscript material. The library offers open access to the entire collection, and I can only say that scholars so happy as to be working with the staff at Rauner should count their blessings. I must also express my thanks to the staffs at Dartmouth's Baker-Berry library and at the Putney (VT) Public Library; I am deeply grateful for their continuing patience and good humor.

---

1. See Appendix G, 299.

I wish to express my gratitude to Norman Fiering, for his careful copy-editing and more than careful questioning of my editorial decisions; to Frances Bracken Huessy, for her careful comparison of the original 1954 manuscript of "The Fruit of Our Lips" to my Appendix E; to David Bade, Wayne Cristaudo, Otto Kroesen, Lise van der Molen, and the other members of the Eugen Rosenstock-Huessy Society for helping me locate the sources of references in my grandfather's work, and especially to Gottfried Hofmann; to Fritz Herrenbrück and Eckart Wilkens of the Eugen Rosenstock-Huessy Gesellschaft for access to their electronic versions of the printed version of "Ichthys" and the author's correspondence with Georg Müller, respectively; to Richard Drummond and Lloyd Craighill for sharing their knowledge of Christianity in Japan; to Google, for digitizing and so making available to anyone with an internet connection scholarly works and periodicals of a by-gone era, including those of Joseph Wittig; to Marion Davis Battles, in spite of all our disagreements; and last but not least to Elizabeth Margrit Huessy Porter, for her collaboration on the translation of Dom Donatien de Bruyne's essay, and just because she is so utterly and wonderfully herself.

I am especially grateful to Pierre-Maurice Bogaert of *La Revue Bénédictine* for his generous permission to translate and reprint the excerpt from de Bruyne's essay, and to the the monks of Downside Abbey and the Downside Abbey General Trust for their generous permission to reprint the excerpt from John Chapman's *Matthew, Mark and Luke*.

I am grateful to Yuval Lapide, for his permission to quote his father's work; to all those who, like the Berlin-Brandenburgische Akademie der Wissenschaften, declared my sources in the public domain; and to all those who, like Leigh Andersen of the Society of Biblical Literature and Margaret Derbyshire for Hubert Cunliffe-Jones's family, considered my quotations to fall under "fair use."

I am also grateful to the von Moltke family for the dedication photograph, to Dorothea von Haeften for permission to use the portrait of Rosenstock-Huessy that appears on page 352, to Sabine Reichwein for permission to use the portrait of Rosenstock-Huessy that appears on page 57 and on the back cover, to André Stern for permission to use the picture of the Rosenstock-Huessys that appears on page 182, and to Ursula Rosenzweig for permission to use the picture of Adele Rosenzweig that appears on page 136. All other pictures are used by kind permission of Mariot Huessy. None of the pictures printed here may be reproduced without written consent of the owner.

I owe thanks to the Oxford University Press for permission to print the excerpt from Albert J. Clark's *Acts of the Apostles*; to the Aufbau Verlag for permission to reprint the excerpt from Wilhelm Michaelis's *Die Apokryphen*; and to the Reinhardt Verlag and the *Theologische Zeitschrift* of the University of Basel for permission to reprint the excerpt from Lukas Vischer's work. I have been unable to locate the heirs of W.H. Cadman.

—Raymond Huessy

An Introduction in Four Acts

Margrit and Eugen Rosenstock-Huessy in 1917, probably at her parents' home in Säckingen, Germany.

"The Word became flesh." Everything else hangs on that one sentence.
—Eugen Rosenstock-Huessy to Franz Rosenzweig, 1916[1]

We believe that in the beginning the Word was, and that at the end the incarnation will be, because the gift given us in the Word's further birth through Christ in each generation is added to our naked birth. Man the Re-teller, the Passer-on—began as the Son of Man and, as the Word, he perfects us to God's own kind.
—Eugen Rosenstock-Huessy, 1964[2]

I

What makes Eugen Rosenstock-Huessy worth a hearing today? Why should anyone be interested in a man whose time has gone by, even if his prophecies have mostly come true in this world in which we live and move—and which we take for granted?

Thirty years ago, I wrote that my grandfather had been a German soldier who became a dedicated American, a professor who had bitterly attacked his academic colleagues for shirking their responsibility to society at large, and a Christian whose unshakable faith in the power of the word had led him beyond the Church.

Like many others, Rosenstock-Huessy recognized the catastrophe of World War I as a historical watershed; but he set out to make it a watershed in his own life as well, declaring the church, the state, and the university tainted by their willing participation in the making of the catastrophe. Like

---

1. Rosenzweig, *Briefe*, 679. Unless an English-language source is cited, all translations from the German are mine.
2. See 130.

many others, he analyzed and decried the impact of the mechanization of society on the life of the spirit; but he set out to create new social and educational institutions to replace those that had failed German society, and gave that effort fifteen years of his life. Like many others, he recognized the Nazis for what they were; but he refused to teach a single class under Hitler, indeed, he claimed to have proposed in February of 1933 that his law faculty at the University of Breslau vote itself out of existence for the duration of the regime.[3] Like many others, he tried to live out the gospel for his time; but his passionate conviction that the power of the Word was reflected in human speech led him not only to see that power at work in history but to see the necessity of its continuing work if we were to have a truly human future. (The subtitle of this volume captures that conviction in a single phrase.)

He never ceased insisting that faithfulness to the one Spirit required different postures and actions in every generation; he took upon himself the burden of proclaiming the world to come in a world that sought its security in a dream of a world gone by; and he set out to rescue the relevance of the Christian tradition for the twentieth century, to let his "life, work, and teaching" serve as a bridge into a new millennium. In the course of his 1916 correspondence with Franz Rosenzweig, he came to see that each of them had come to the fullness of his own truth only through meeting in friendly opposition. To the end of his life he would continue to quote his friend's crystallization of that insight, that all human truth is polyphonous.[4] Because the Jews were the coals at the heart of the fire that is God and the Christians were the rays that reached out into the world,[5] they could make common cause. Rosenstock-Huessy later reformulated the "one necessary thing" for our time—the recognition that if Man is made in God's image, then Man himself is triune:

> We must all create originally (like the pagans), hope in expectation (like the Jews), and love decisively (like Christians)— that is to say, we must take part in the beginning, end, and middle of life. . . . Franz Rosenzweig was the first to express

---

3. Sixty years later, Prof. Karol Jonca of the University of Wrocław tried to find a record of that meeting. The motion is unlikely to have been minuted, and no record is likely to have survived the creation of "Fortress Breslau" in 1945, which involved razing large sections of the city to create an airstrip and emptying the university library so that the books could be used to help barricade the streets.

4. FR, *Briefe*, 712. Also ERH, *Despite*, 147–48.

5. FR, *Stern*, III.3, 200, 438–39 in the Galli translation. (See also FR, *Stern*, III.1, 48.) I am indebted to Wayne Cristaudo for this reference. See also ERH, *Out*, 221 and the end of "The Four Apostles," 259.

and explain this confounding fact of the openness of the three 'isms' to each other.⁶

Describing their wartime correspondence in 1968, he wrote that "a Jew and a Christian momentarily put aside their insoluble antithesis and united against self-styled humanists of all descriptions," seeing "the swindle of the academic class . . . in its murderous impact on the Western World."⁷ The correspondence had its roots in a day-long discussion the two men had had with Rosenzweig's cousin Rudolf Ehrenberg, the day after Rosenstock-Huessy's twenty-fifth birthday, in the summer of 1913.⁸ The conversation revolved around the last chapter of Selma Lagerlöf's *The Miracles of the Antichrist,* and its last sentence in particular: "No one can save mankind from their sorrows, but much is forgiven to him who brings new courage to bear them."⁹

In a sense, both Rosenstock-Huessy and Rosenzweig took that sentence as their marching orders. They twice attempted to found an institution to embody their recognition of the essential unity of revelation—the necessity for Protestants, Catholics, and Jews to make common cause for revelation against the dead hand of abstract rationalism. The first, the original Patmos Verlag, united Rosenstock-Huessy with Rosenzweig's Christian cousins Hans and Rudolf Ehrenberg, with Werner Picht, Leo Weismantel, and Rosenzweig himself. (Having let Patmos publish his 1920 *Christ in der Gesellschaft* (*The Christian in Society*), Karl Barth later fell out with them over their insistence on rethinking everything in the light of the new historical moment.)¹⁰ Though the friends had imagined three linked publishing houses, "Patmos" was the only one of them to see the light of day and even it survived only a few years. The second attempt, *Die Kreatur* (*The Creature,* 1927–1930), was the first periodical jointly edited by a Catholic, a Protestant, and a Jew; it may also have been the last. The editors were Joseph Wittig, won for the undertaking by Rosenstock-Huessy; Martin Buber, won by Rosenzweig; and Viktor von Weizsäcker, won by Hans Ehrenberg.¹¹ (Both the Patmos Verlag and

---

6. ERH, *Geheimnis,* 54.

7. ERH, *Despite,* 71.

8. See Appendix H, 303–11.

9. See Appendix I, 331–33.

10. Barth knew only that the church and the university existed. . . . For us it was just these buildings and facilities that had forfeited their trustworthiness. . . . We had experienced the World War; he had not. That is not meant as a reproach to Barth. . . . The war had given us a new route to march, a new time-reckoning, a turn away from theology and philosophy in obedience to the path of salvation. . . . For Barth it was only a subject to be handled objectively. ERH, *Ja und Nein,* 81.

11. The complete *Kreatur* is now available at www.compactmemory.de as part of the

Die Kreatur were largely funded by Max Hamburger, Rosenstock-Huessy's childhood friend who had become his brother-in-law.)

Both Rosenzweig and Rosenstock-Huessy fell back on work in adult education with a less expansive view, Rosenzweig in founding the *Freies Jüdisches Lehrhaus* (Free Jewish Study Center) in 1920, Rosenstock-Huessy in founding the *Akademie der Arbeit* (Academy of Labor) in 1921 and the Löwenberg volunteer work camps in 1927. However, the search for common ground despite fundamental differences became both Rosenstock-Huessy's theory and his *modus operandi*: with Paul Riebensahm, Eugen May, Joseph Wittig, and the young men with whom he founded the volunteer labor-camps in both Germany and the U.S. In his first book published in German after 1945, he sought to re-express that truth:

> Augustine spoke truth when he wrote that people are healed by love, faith, and hope. . . . In truly comprehending this sentence, we gain a new category of which sociology needs if it is ever to break the strangle-hold of individualism and socialism: that of mutuality. . . . We speak to each other and live for each other.[12]

Rosenstock-Huessy himself spent his long life re-interpreting the Christian tradition for a world gone deaf to its traditional language.

> Even St. Paul's comparison of the relations between Christ and his church to the relation between man and woman seems to be too high and too far away from the man in the street. The tongue of the Christian faith has been worn out.[13]
>
> We must speak. . . . What has replaced the problem of the Babylonian confusion of tongues is the problem of translation, that is, of healing the former confusion. . . . The true and enormous tension today is whether or not the translation of Christianity, and thereby of Christ's name . . . will succeed or not.[14]

His efforts to overcome the social divisions of post-war Germany in adult education assumed a fundamental break with accepted norms of "education." In 1929 already, Rosenstock-Huessy reported to an international gathering that this work required a new language for a new time, if old truths were ever to become once more "self-evident." He called for a "school of suffering," a "school of events":

Internetarchiv jüdischer Periodika. That it is listed as a *Jewish periodical* is typical of the academic reception of ERH, FR, and their friends.

12. ERH, *Atem*, 292–93. An English translation of this work will appear soon.

13. See Appendix I, 334–35.

14. FR, *Briefe*, 698–99.

> No teacher knows "more" than his students, he can only prepare a solution in patient meditation together with others, acquire the knowledge that solution requires, and receive the impulse to act.... The political school of contemplation we require sees its chief objective in preparing the leisure in which a man may meet a fellow-citizen of a different sort and both may find themselves compelled in the face of common danger to enter, reflect, and exchange opinions.[15]

In response to Rosenzweig's *Der Stern der Erlösung* (*The Star of Redemption*), he wrote that incarnation is the only way spirit can enter the world; that way begins with insight granted in vision, develops in teaching, and ends in action in the world—action that by its very nature is political. The final step is the founding of an institution that can outlast the man whose vision led him to teach and to act.

> Jesus obviously came at the end of one era, and began a new era. He was the first Christian ... and the last Jew, and the Jews came at the end of antiquity.... You can only understand the meaning of Christianity if you connect it with all the beginnings that preceded him, of which he is the fulfillment, and if you put him as the seed, the famous seed of grain that falls into the ground and must die in order to bear fruit.[16]

For Rosenstock-Huessy, time and timing were at the heart of Christianity, as Christ was the heart and hinge-point of history. Had he not denied that Christianity was a religion at all, he could easily have made Abraham Joshua Heschel's statement that his religion was "a *religion of time* aiming at the *sanctification of time*."[17] Instead, he defined Christianity as the "science of timing,"[18] proclaiming that

> the present, whether it be an hour, a day in our life, or a whole era, is not only created, but created by us; it does not simply happen to us, it is not a natural fact like space, not a datum in nature, but a constant social achievement, and neither comes nor lasts except by our own making. There time is not a gift but a task.... The power to live in the fullness of time is something that has to be won arduously and preserved by perpetual vigilance.[19]

---

15. See Appendix I, 335–36.
16. ERH, *Collected Works*, "Universal History 1957," April 9, 1957, 23-002.
17. Heschel, *Sabbath*, 8.
18. ERH, *Collected Works*, "Universal History 1957," April 9, 1957, 23-019.
19. From a speech given May 22, 1940: ERH, *Impure*, 94–114.

For him, creation was an ongoing enterprise until the end of time, and the gospel, with its explicit utterance of truths known to all the ages of man, was the engine that drove the rhythms even of modern history. In *Out of Revolution,* he argued not only that history was rhythmic, as Giuseppe Ferrari had before him, but that the great national revolutions that had made Europe followed each other in succession every 125 to 140 years.[20] In *Das Alter der Kirche* (*The Age of the Church,* 1927–1928),[21] he and Joseph Wittig had found the same rhythm and those same periods in church history, which they set within four longer periods of 500 years.[22] In both books, he declared that an era had come to an end, and that the new in-breaking millennium would require, as the "science of timing" had required in every age, hitherto-unheard-of action, action to be taken at the proper time.

Decades before he wrote about the "secret of the university" (the fifteen-year advance the German system gained by letting a *Privatdozent* teach what he pleased long before he could hope to be called as a full professor),[23] Rosenstock-Huessy had tried to build that same "advance" into his collaboration with his students. In both the Löwenberg volunteer work-camps in Germany and at Camp William James in the United States, "Herr Doktor Professor" stepped back so that the young men whose enthusiasm drove the projects might deal directly with the movers and shakers whose support made the projects possible—giving them an experience of leadership some ten to fifteen years "ahead of time." Norman Fiering has written that Rosenstock-Huessy explicitly told his students at Dartmouth that he was teaching them what they would need to know in twenty or thirty years.[24]

The renewal of war after what he termed a "twenty-year truce" and its terrible aftermath brought the loss of many of his closest earlier collaborators. Helmuth von Moltke was murdered by the Nazis in 1945; Horst von Einsiedel died in Soviet custody in 1947; Carl Dietrich von Trotha, was killed in a senseless speedboat accident in Illinois in 1952. In their deaths, and in the lack of response to his work in the United States, he found cause to consider other thinkers and writers who had come "too soon," whose truths would only find an audience after their death, such as Abelard, Paracelsus, and Saint-Simon.[25] (Rosenstock-Huessy often said that he expected to be discovered only seventy

---

20. ERH, *Out,* 453–82, and particularly 462–63. See ERH, *Geheimnis,* 35–43.

21. A church history whose third chapter is entitled "Marx and Nietzsche."

22. In "The Fruit of Our Lips," Rosenstock-Huessy traced both the idea and the specific period back to Stephen's speech in Acts and its echoes in the gospels of Matthew and Luke. See 88–89 and Appendix E, 224–25.

23. ERH, *Geheimnis,* 22.

24. Cristaudo et al., "Introduction," 9.

25. All three are discussed at length in his *Soziologie* (1956–1958).

years after his death.) Yet during and after the renewed war he also expanded the scope of his teaching of history, following the trail he saw blazed by Matthew's and Luke's gospels, to span history from Adam to the Last Judgment. He lectured on the changing role of the spirit in human society: in its beginnings in tribal ritual and the astrological empires, among the Jews and the Greeks, and in the three millennia of Christian history.

The promise of the third millennium was his "good news." He not only appropriated José Clemente Orozco's image of Christ taking an ax to the cross, but imagined a future counterpart to Michelangelo's image of Adam's creation, in which Adam would be surrounded by the *Elohim* who had once surrounded God—and God would face the Final Man, alone.[26]

II

THE THREE ESSAYS THAT appear here in translation at the front (and as the heart) of this book were printed together in 1968 as *Die Umwandlung vom Wort Gottes in die Sprache des Menschengeschlechtes*, and to honor that book, I have given this one its name as a sub-title.

The three essays bear witness to the understanding of Christianity Rosenstock-Huessy had already begun to formulate in his correspondence with Rosenzweig fifty years earlier. In emending these essays (and in unpublished codas to the last of them)[27] he still articulated and defended his faith in the terms he used in their correspondence.[28] Creation, revelation, and incarnation as on-going processes through the end of time; the rhythms of history; even Marcion's role in forcing the church to formally proclaim Christ's "Father" to be the God of the Old Testament—all appear in the correspondence as they do in "The Fruit of Our Lips."

(The publication of this book brings to an end a long chapter in my own life as well. I first translated the three essays at the front of this book into English thirty years ago, when there was no prospect of a translation being published, and it is a great pleasure to see it happen after all, after all these years.)

Aficionados of Marion Davis Battles' 1978 edition of the title essay will find both the title of this book and most of its content unfamiliar. In 1954, Rosenstock-Huessy named the title essay "The Fruit of Our Lips"; Mrs. Battles chose to translate the German title instead. During his lifetime, he

---

26. See ERH, *Out*, 727–28.
27. Printed here as Appendices F, 283–93, and G, 297–300.
28. See Appendix H, 303–11.

presented the essay to the world in only two ways: in 1964, as the culmination of his collected works on speech, *Die Sprache des Menschengeschlechts* (*The Speech of Mankind*); and in 1968, in this troika of essays. Mrs. Battles' edition of the lone essay appeared after his death.

The title essay exists in two versions in two languages, both of which contain material not found in the other. Four "chapters" of the "finished" English-language typescript are missing from the German version, to which the author added material that did not exist in the English original.[29] (Much of Rosenstock-Huessy's American work was translated into German by others and then edited and expanded by him before publication.) The final 1954 English-language version is the most substantial, but was never prepared for publication during the author's lifetime; the German-language version is the only version he ever approved for publication, but is missing a considerable amount of material. So there is no best or "final" version.

What matters is that between the covers of this book the reader will find *all* the text written under the name "[The] Fruit of [Our] Lips," in its original context. The essay as printed in German, with the material added for *Die Umwandlung*, is in the main body of the text, and the 1954 English-language version is reprinted complete as Appendix E. Anyone interested in either Rosenstock-Huessy's work or the subject of the essay should read the English-language version for the important sections left out of the German version.

Neither of the other two essays at the front of this volume has appeared in English before. The first "new" piece is a brief statement of two claims Rosenstock-Huessy made frequently: that the cross is to be found in every aspect of social reality, and that the truths made explicit in the life of Christ are to be found in all of human history. It is a slightly altered version of the brief coda to the second volume of his sociology, *Die Vollzahl der Zeiten* (*The Full Complement of Times*),[30] which Wayne Cristaudo has said might well be "the key to his entire corpus."[31]

The second essay, "Ichthys: Life, Teaching, and Action," was first published in *Das Alter der Kirche* in 1927. "Ichthys" expresses thoughts central to Rosenstock-Huessy's understanding of Christ and Christianity (more than anything else, it was my desire for this essay to finally appear in English

---

29. See the introduction to Appendix E, 183–88.

30. ERH, *Soziologie II*, 759–60. The title given is in my translation. ERH's translation of the Latin passage from "Hilarius Isaac" contains a near-equivalent, *the plenitude of times* (113, 249). In "Hinge of Generations," he refers to *the full count of the times* (see Appendix D, 173). The first volume of the *Soziologie* has appeared in English as *In the Cross of Reality: The Hegemony of Spaces* (Transaction, 2017). The second volume should appear soon.

31. Cristaudo, *Religion*, 216.

that led me to take on this new edition of *The Fruit of Our Lips*). It gave me great pleasure to discover not only that he had composed the essay in 1923 as a birthday present for his wife, Margrit, but that he had described it both to her and to Franz Rosenzweig's mother, Adele, as his response to the final section of Rosenzweig's *Star of Redemption*. (The hand-written 1923 manuscript opens with a long quotation from the last two pages of *The Star*.) Rosenstock-Huessy included a printed copy of the revised essay from *Das Alter der Kirche* in his 1928 New Year's greeting to "Tante Dele," and introduced it by saying:

> Shakespeare's statement that the benefit of "ill" consists in its tearing up the better, and that renewed love grows in greater beauty, power, and scope, touches on a thought in my *Age of the Church*, in "Life, Teaching, and Action," where I polemicize against Franz. I say there that an adult is no longer capable of walking humbly with his God. He can at most walk humbly once more—just as an adult cannot be a child, but can only become like a child (which is not the same thing as "being" one).[32]

So "Ichthys" is an epilogue to Rosenstock-Huessy's war-time correspondence with Rosenzweig on Judaism and Christianity. In it, he explicitly formulates his "doctrine" of incarnation: how Christ's life bore fruit in His teaching, how Christ lived backwards into life out of the vision granted in "the sanctum that is in the innermost center,"[33] and how his life of action was a third phase quite separate from his teaching. Rosenstock-Huessy proclaims that sequence to be the inescapable conjugation of any fruitful spirit; in laying out the relation between Christ's life, teaching, and actions, he also shows how he had tried to live a life of action "backward" from his own insights.

In *I Am an Impure Thinker*, he relates his decision, on demobilization in 1918, to pass up three attractive offers: to return to his chair at the University of Leipzig, to help draft the constitution of the new republic, or to join Karl Muth as the co-editor of Germany's leading Catholic magazine, *Hochland*.[34] Instead, in a conscious effort to help make peace where management and labor were in open conflict, he went to work for Daimler-Benz in Stuttgart. That decision, his subsequent work in adult education, and his program for the Löwenberg volunteer work camps (what he called attempts to "create new social order" in a country utterly divided by party and class

---

32. Unpublished letter to Adele Rosenzweig dated January 1, 1928. See Appendix A, 137–39.
33. FR, *Stern*, 210. See Appendix B, 145.
34. ERH, *Impure*, 182–90.

hostility), emerge as the clear fruit of this post-war, "post-modern" understanding of the medieval *imitatio Christi*.

In "Ichthys," Rosenstock-Huessy proclaims that "thought creates obligation [to act]." Compare this to Heidegger's ghastly dictum that "thinking acts insofar as it thinks."[35] (Rosenstock-Huessy's fifteen-year commitment to "create new social order" and his immediate recognition of the Nazi threat offer an equally pointed contrast to Heidegger's easy accommodation after 1933.) Here is the full statement of the meaning of his motto "*respondeo etsi mutabor*" and its claim that social truth must be represented in the flesh—or, to use an older term: incarnated. (Cristaudo makes the wonderful comment that "Rosenstock-Huessy is exploring the process of incarnation as a social fact.")[36] Anyone who has listened to the recordings of Rosenstock-Huessy's lectures will recognize how his life informed his "teaching." A more interesting claim is that his life from 1918 to 1941, with its varied attempts to create institutions based on his social and religious insights, shows how he lived out his own declaration that the path from insight to action is always a political path, and that most of those attempts met political opposition and a premature death.

By defending the central importance of "Ichthys" to Rosenstock-Huessy's "life, teaching, and action," I do not by any means seek to diminish the importance of the essay "The Fruit of Our Lips." In 1945, when the essay was still only half-formed, he wrote his young friend Cynthia Harris that it was "the greatest chapter I have ever written. . . . It opens to the human mind another 500 years of meditation, research, reflection."[37] He made a point of setting our title essay as the final word, as the keystone, of his great "speech book," *Die Sprache des Menschengeschlechts*—at one point, he had even planned to name the entire work *Die Frucht der Lippen* (*The Fruit of Lips*).[38] The essay is the final statement of a man who believed so implicitly in the truth of the incarnation that he repeatedly called for the human *body*, in different positions dictated by the spirit, to be used as new symbols for the four Evangelists.[39]

By paying attention to the additions made to the German version for publication in 1964, which appear here in {"French" brackets}, the reader may easily follow what Rosenstock-Huessy chose to make more explicit for the essay's first public appearance. The 1944 original (and its 1954 revision) had been something of a polemic; the 1964 German version is more of a

---

35. Heidegger, *Writings*, 217.

36. Cristaudo, *Religion*, 201.

37. Unpublished letter to Cynthia Harris dated July 16, 1945.

38. There is a table of contents for an early version of *Die Sprache* with that title in the Rosenstock-Huessy Archive in Bielefeld; I am grateful to Gottfried Hofmann for bringing this to my attention.

39. See 117–18, 252–53.

valedictory. Indeed, the later additions come to resemble a running commentary on the original text—almost a conversation the 75-year-old editor was having with his 55- and 65-year-old self.

Some things are clearly more important to the editor than they had been to the author. One of the most profound is his emphasis on "passing on," or re-telling, as a fundamental part of the Christian faith—although he had already written twenty years earlier that a convert's early hearing of the gospel was always meant to be the first step toward passing the faith on in turn.[40] Although some of Rosenstock-Huessy's statements have aroused the ire of feminists over the years, it is striking that in this 1964 *envoi* he twice emphasizes that the spirit moves mankind to a point beyond gender.[41] And, after decades of lambasting his professional colleagues for their "Greek" way of thinking, here he humbly declares his own failure—as a "Greek"—to understand the story of Lazarus![42]

Even in his seventies, he was capable of changing his mind. Few people retain the ability to change their minds over the course of a lifetime without also losing their integrity. We would do well to honor those who do, as other times honored the saints; there are many more men like Lester Maddox than there are like Malcolm X.

The man who had accepted the work of scholarly giants like Adolf von Harnack and Donatien de Bruyne, of kindred spirits like John Chapman and Basil Christopher Butler, and of friends like Franz Rosenzweig and Joseph Wittig, now yielded to the persuasive powers of Jehoshua Grintz and W. H. Cadman.[43] Indeed, the appearance of their articles in *Studia Evangelica*[44] in 1959 (and the defense of the necessary unity of the four gospels in several of the other essays in the volume) may have provided the impetus for his decision to publish "The Fruit of Our Lips" after all. "Jesus the Illiterate," one of the planned codas to "The Fruit of Our Lips," embraces the work of Grintz and Cadman, and the echoes are profound and heartfelt. In that short essay he laid aside all thought of the "Christianity *incognito*" he required of Christians in making common cause with their neighbors, to plead again for an understanding of the true role of the gospels, and of what made Christ the hinge-point of all the eons of human history.

---

40. See 91, 118. The theme is repeated in one of the essays originally intended to follow our title essay in *Die Sprache*, reprinted as Appendix F, 283–93.

41. See 118.

42. See 93–94 and Appendix I, 316–18.

43. Excerpts from their essays appear in Appendix I, 325–27 and 316–21.

44. *Studia Evangelica* published the papers presented to the international congress held at Oxford immediately following the annual gathering of the *Studiorum Novi Testamenti Societas* which had met at Birmingham (U.K.).

III

THAT CHRIST MIGHT BE the hinge-point of history is a claim difficult to make in polite society, let alone in academe. In spite of the honorary theological degree conferred upon him at age 70 by the University of Münster, Rosenstock-Huessy proudly remained a layman all his life (claiming to have an advantage in never having been "a minister nor a theologian by profession").[45] Nevertheless, as a layman who deeply believed in the priesthood of all believers, he consciously and conscientiously accepted "responsibility for God before men."[46] For all the obeisance made to the role of lay people since Vatican II, there is still precious little interest in laypeople's opinions in most theological circles—and there was of course even less interest before our day. Joseph Wittig (like Ernst Michel, Rosenstock-Huessy's collaborator at the Frankfurt Academy of Labor) was considered dangerous in Rome precisely because he championed the role of laypeople in the church.[47] What that dangerous priest (and dangerous Levites like Rosenstock-Huessy and Michel) shared was a belief in faith itself, unconstrained by philosophical or legalistic definitions, a belief that put them at odds both with the established church hierarchies and their watchdogs, the theological faculties.

The strangle-hold of nineteenth-century scholarship still continues, despite Marion Battles' hopeful statements to the contrary.[48] If anything, it has intensified in the intervening decades, as that scholarship has consumed the pastorate as well as the academy, and invaded the "educated" laity of the mainstream churches. I have often had to listen to liberal Protestants declaring that they did not believe in the God of the Old Testament, thus firmly if unwittingly setting the authority of the Gnostic Marcion above that of the four Evangelists. I once confessed to a rightly beloved eminent churchman my belief that all four gospels carried apostolic authority, only to receive the unsettling reply that 99 percent of scholars were against me. The figure may have been a little high, but the difference is one of degree rather than substance.

Elaine Pagels is only the most extreme example of the hegemony of Gnosis in religious studies today, but at least she has the honesty to declare herself a proponent of Gnostic Christianity, and deals with actual, existing Gnostic manuscripts. An entire lineage of "scholars," from Weisse and

---

45. See 69 and Appendix E, 205.

46. See 47.

47. Wolf and Unterburger, *Kirche in Deutschland*, 141–50. I am grateful to Professor Klaus Unterburger for the reference.

48. See her introduction to "The Fruit of Lips" in Appendix D, 179.

Griesbach to Burton Mack, have made careers out of the dissection of "Q," a document no one has ever seen, or even seen mentioned in any document written before 1800, but whose existence is now taken as "gospel." Earnest believers now follow the professors in sifting through the Nag Hammadi manuscripts for "the real story." Any Gnostic manuscript discovered is immediately hailed as offering some new "truth," ignoring the possibility, for which documentary evidence *does* in fact exist, that what they offer is more likely very old untruths.

While Rosenstock-Huessy found the churches full of Gnosis a lifetime ago, today seems to be the hour of its greatest triumph, with the elevation of one generation's priorities over those of all other times. That triumph may be seen most clearly in today's devoutly well-intentioned censorship of the language of centuries of liturgy and hymnody; in the UCC's *New Century Hymnal*, even the work of female poets like Julia Ward Howe and Christina Rosetti (and of the prolific translator Catherine Winkworth) have been altered in the name of gender-neutrality. And scripture itself is not immune to that censorship; a cursory glance at the common lectionary shows what has been conscientiously excised from the public reading of scripture. I understand that many no longer care to believe in the wrath of God, but do they think they can wish it away? or that avoiding the mention of war will do anything to prevent it? Tradition once broken cannot be simply "revived" without distortion, any more than it can be defended with a commitment only to the past. So let us hope that we may live to see its resurrection.

What the years since the composition of "The Fruit of Our Lips" seem to have brought is for the most part a hardening of party lines, a growing identity of any defense of the four gospels as a unified, coherent witness, with a particular (and usually both pre- and anti-critical) interpretation of our tradition. "Conservatives" who see interpretation as open-ended are few and far between; "liberals" who support the apostolicity of the canon are in vanishingly short supply—even Jaroslav Pelikan's *Vindication of Tradition* did not in fact set out to vindicate much of it. In their haste to judge each other, both parties ignore scripture (or at least Matthew 25:31–46). The real questions of our time are whether the conservatives can imagine any *aggiornamento* in interpretation, and whether the liberals can cease sitting in judgment on tradition long enough to remember that it is, in fact, scripture that judges us. Rosenstock-Huessy neither made nor condoned any attempt to retreat to a position held prior to the era of biblical criticism. On the contrary, in consciously rearticulating the truth of Christianity for the post-war period, he proclaims the arrival of a post-critical era.

Just a few years after his death, his stance found a friendly echo in the work of a radical very much surprised to find himself a champion of the canon. I would like to think that, as a conservative expert on revolutions, Rosenstock-Huessy would relish the idea. Does anyone read John A. T. Robinson today? I should hesitate to cite him, as Rosenstock-Huessy passed right over his piece on the "fourth gospel" in *Studia Evangelica* (1959). I suspect he did so because, unlike Rosenstock-Huessy, the Bishop of Woolwich was always careful to hedge his arguments. It has done him little good, for he is just as far out of favor as our author—though in Robinson's case, more as the flavor of last month. But then, anyone who tells uncomfortable truths is best forgotten or, to use a glorious German word, *totgeschwiegen* (ignored to death).

No one who has read either *In the End God* (1950) or *Honest to God* (1963) could call Robinson a conservative—and yet Robinson's 1976 *Dating the New Testament* ends by dating the entire canon within the first century A.D.,[49] thereby allowing the reassignment of almost every canonical entry in the New Testament to the authors credited by tradition. Robinson hedges some on Matthew and the Petrine letters, but clearly accepts tradition on Mark, Luke-Acts, and the gospel and epistles of John, and rails against the presumption of prophecy "after the fact."[50] He admits at the start that his "position will probably seem surprisingly conservative—especially to those who judge [him] radical on other issues."[51]

At the end of the book, while back-pedaling furiously so as not to be seen as buttressing "the fundamentalism of the fearful" or the "conservatism of the committed,"[52] he prints a 1972 letter from C. H. Dodd in which Dodd writes that he agrees that "much of this late dating is quite arbitrary, even wanton, the offspring not of any argument that can be presented, but rather of the critic's prejudice."[53] He also cites A. H. N. Green-Armytage's 1952 statement setting Churchill's prophecy of war in 1935 against the assumptions of the Biblical critics:

> There is a world—I do not say a world in which all scholars live but one at any rate into which all of them sometimes stray, and which some of them seem permanently to inhabit—which is not the world in which I live.... In my world, if I read that Mr. Churchill, in 1935, said that Europe was heading for a disastrous war, I applaud the foresight. In that world no prophecy, however vaguely worded, is ever made except after the event. In my world we say,

---

49. Robinson, *Redating*, 101, 117.
50. Robinson, *Redating*, 337, 13–30.
51. Robinson, *Redating*, 11.
52. Robinson, *Redating*, 356.
53. Robinson, *Redating*, 360.

'The first world-war took place in 1914–1918.' In that world they say, 'The world-war narrative took shape in the third decade of the twentieth century.' In my world men and women live for a considerable time—seventy, eighty, even a hundred years—and they are equipped with a thing called memory. In that world (it would appear) they come into being, write a book, and forthwith perish, all in a flash, and it is noted of them with astonishment that they "preserve traces of primitive tradition" about things which happened well within their own adult lifetime.[54]

This neatly parallels Rosenstock-Huessy's argument in the 1964 version of "The Fruit of Our Lips," based on his own experience with prophecy. In his 1919 essay "Ehrlos–Heimatlos," ERH had prophesied the rise of a *Lügenkaisertum* (an Empire of lies) if Germany did not stop trying to live as though the war had not swept the foundations of the old society away.[55]

At times it is hard to escape Green-Armytage's (and Rosenstock-Huessy's) conviction that the lunatics have taken over the asylum. While Protestantism has been leery of tradition ever since Luther pronounced the Letter of James an "epistle of straw," that incipient doubt has become a skeptical avalanche. (Has the day of the Jesus Seminar come and gone? It would only be fair, as its members seemed to believe that there was no document in the canon without a large admixture of "straw.") Rosenstock-Huessy's own feelings about such pruning of the gospel may be inferred from his judgment on Luther[56] and the fact that his wife's gravestone carries only her name, the dates of her birth and death, and the citation "James 1:25."

To Rosenstock-Huessy, the gospel was an indissoluble unit encompassing the ministry of Christ himself as well as the events that are his four "lips." However unwelcome the fact may be to those who come to Rosenstock-Huessy through an interest in speech and "speech-thinking," he himself believed implicitly in the truth of scripture and its fruits in the two millennia of Christian history, and himself sought to translate the truths of that tradition for the new eon he saw dawning. For him and for Franz Rosenzweig, the root of "speech-thinking" was the creative power of speech proclaimed in Genesis 1:1–2:4. Joseph Wittig, Rosenstock-Huessy's excommunicated Catholic colleague at the University of Breslau, wrote of him: "He did something for me that there was simply no one else to do, because he had something others no longer had, the faith that God's omnipotence

---

54. Robinson, *Redating*, 356.
55. See 121 and Appendix I, 336.
56. See Appendix H, 308.

begins with the impossible."[57] Yet that faith in scripture yielded new and "impossible" fruit like *The Christian Future*. There Buddha, Laotse, and Abraham are lifted up as necessary voices in the universal history of man, but placed in relation to Christ.

> Christian Dogma is not an intellectual formula but a record and promise of life. It does not propose ideas for our minds to master; it tells actual events which can master and transform us as they did the first Christians. It is not a mere topic of thought but the presupposition of sanity.[58]

Similarly, Rosenstock-Huessy's "cross of reality" (which also makes its first appearance in his correspondence with Rosenzweig) is not an intellectual construct imposed on reality. It is a recognition that we are all crucified in every moment: in the tension between the claims of our inner and outer lives; between the claims of our past and the future we seek; and in the conjugation of our life experience from call, to response, to community, and finally to objective reporting of the facts. In the "cross of reality," he assumes with the scholastics that God is the ground of all reality, but sees the cross planted in that ground.[59] Yet Rosenstock-Huessy's life and work also declare that "the ground of all reality" by definition cannot be, and indeed has never been, confined within the Church.

> In their battle against sensuality, [Catholics and Protestants] have both lost . . . the sense for what is rotten and what is ripe . . . [That loss has] seduced them into elevating themselves above God. . . . Where God is headed in any particular time is something we can only hope to scent; and it is our ability to scent [the future] that leads us in every hour, to where God appears in living form. That is why God has turned away from churchly Christianity, in all its permutations. . . . God's ways are not the ways of Christianity: his love seeks to heal all that Christianity has been lacking.[60]

In Germany between 1918 and 1933, he spoke to a generation that had witnessed the end of a world as surely as the first Christians had, and he often quoted Chesterton's line that "the end of the world was long ago."[61] In

---

57. Wittig, *Höregott*, 333. See Luke 1:37.

58. ERH, *Christian Future*, 98.

59. In this he only echoes Augustine and Francis of Assisi. (Augustine and John the Evangelist could be said to provide the bass line to most of ERH's work.)

60. "Die Tochter" in *Hochzeit*, 36–37, also in *Die Tochter* (27–44).

61. From "The Ballad of the White Horse," first published in 1911. ERH claimed to

Das Alter der Kirche, he and Wittig explicitly declare an end to the age of the Church and look forward to Society's inheriting the Church's role as both the marital and the sparring partner of the State. And Rosenstock-Huessy had written Rosenzweig in 1916:

> Do you believe Zionism is a coincidence? Israel's day as the people of the Bible is over. The Church [itself] . . . is the Synagogue of today! . . . Christ has enough people to crucify him in his own Church. . . . The Jews no longer crucify, judge, or sentence any more at all.[62]

This volume is a layman's defense of the unity of the gospel in response to the liberal clergy's *volte-face* to align itself with Voltaire's view of the church in history—perhaps the ultimate *"trahison des clercs."* However, this book also seeks to show truth as having been made anew in the Christian tradition. The scholastics had called their God *"actus purissimus,"* in whom word and deed were one; the subtitle of this book expresses the conviction that the creative act of speech in Genesis also transforms our own lives if our words bear fruit in deeds. Towards the end of his life, Rosenstock-Huessy was explicit about the dimensions of truth:

> A word can be true in its content; it can secondly be true enough to prove the author right; and finally it can be so true that it forces the next speaker to respond and speak in turn. . . . I am concerned with the third aspect of all truth, with its full power to beget a response by changing language. . . . In this process the "four gospels" become a continuation of Jesus' life through the minds that were overpowered by their office as Evangelists. They were re-created as lips of the Word.[63]

Rosenstock-Huessy was convinced that this "third aspect of truth" was the secret spring that drives the endless renewal and innovation that is the history of salvation, anchored in the willingness of people in each succeeding epoch to "live tomorrow's life today":[64]

> [The] gospel . . . necessarily precedes later writings. . . [which] were . . . absolutely still to come. Matthew already anticipated the gospel of John when he wrote his own. That is the real time-revolution of the Christian faith . . . faith in the future's ability

---

know Chesterton *nearly by heart.*

62. FR, *Briefe,* 695–6. The history of the European nations as the new *Old Testament* is the unspoken theme of *Out of Revolution.* See also Appendix H, 307–08.

63. See 110–11.

64. The refrain of Brian Wren's wonderful 1989 hymn, "There's a Spirit in the Air."

> to change the past. ... We are only Christians if we think and speak and act backwards from the end.[65]

So Rosenstock-Huessy is at one and the same time an utterly orthodox believer and an interpreter of scripture and tradition who continually surprises and discomfits the established powers of the churches and the academy—and that is perhaps the best argument for his continuing relevance and the importance of his life and work for the future. As he wrote in his mid-seventies:

> It was the transitory aspect of our laws which had to be achieved and made our own in addition to Adam's mortality, and this is the gift we receive from the Lord and his Apostles: he made possible the death of the law. ... Because the Jews may not change their law, but can at best ignore it, Christ's death remains incomprehensible to them. He was not meant and did not want to become the martyr of a faith; instead he became a blood-witness of our need to shed the garment of any one eon, the need for all our little eternities to die.[66]

IV

AMONG THE PAPERS RECENTLY moved from Four Wells (my grandparents' home in Norwich, VT) to Dartmouth's Rauner Library, I found not only the original typescripts of "The Fruit of Our Lips" and the hand-written manuscript of "Ichthys," but also several draft essays Rosenstock-Huessy had labeled as intended conclusions for *Die Sprache*, to follow directly on the essay "The Fruit of Our Lips." (If I had paid closer attention to the work of Gottfried Hofmann, who arranged and catalogued the manuscripts at Four Wells over the years, and of Lise van der Molen, compiler of the magisterial 1997 bibliography, I might have found them all much sooner.) Both of these intended conclusions resonate in their own way with "The Fruit of Our Lips." Taken in tandem, along with the three main essays in this volume, they provide a unique overview of the mutual dependence and interaction of Rosenstock-Huessy's work on faith and his work on speech.

---

65. See Appendix F, 288.
66. See Appendix G, 299–300.

I am glad to have the opportunity to include these draft essays here, even as appendices. Since so much of the support for Rosenstock-Huessy's argument in "The Fruit of Our Lips" has never appeared in English, and so much of it has been called into question, even by his own editors, I have included excerpts from his sources as well. If the result is that the appendices threaten to overwhelm the "book" itself, so be it.

Appendix A is a translation of Rosenstock-Huessy's hand-written letter to Adele Rosenzweig dated January 1, 1928. Appendix B is a translation of the 1923 presentation copy of "*Ichthys: Leben, Lehre, Wirken.*" Together they make explicit how "*Ichthys*" arose within the intimate sphere that included Franz Rosenzweig and both Margrit and Eugen Rosenstock-Huessy. Appendix C is a 1947 letter of Rosenstock-Huessy's on his and family's history with Judaism and Christianity.

Appendix D is Marion Davis Battles' introduction to her 1978 edition of the title essay. Appendix E is the text of the original 1954 typescript of "The Fruit of Our Lips," with its revisions and hand-written corrections. (Textual details are dealt with in an introduction to the appendix). Appendices F and G contain translations of the two draft essays contemplated as codas to *Die Sprache*, to follow on the heels of "The Fruit of Our Lips."

Appendix H is a reflection of my own on the author's war-time correspondence with Rosenzweig. Appendix I presents excerpts from the sources cited by Rosenstock-Huessy, especially on the gospel prologues. They are followed by a bibliography citing works used by both the author and his editors.

Where I thought Rosenstock-Huessy's idiosyncratic punctuation or style were perfectly clear, I have left them alone. Rosenstock-Huessy rarely capitalized the pronouns for God and Christ; I have followed his lead, except where capitalization is required to make clear a reference which otherwise might not be. I have kept his usage of the word "Man" in the sense beyond gender; it is usually capitalized. I have replaced ERH's underlining for emphasis with *italics*.

The author's footnotes are marked with his initials, as are Mrs. Battles' in Appendices D and E. In the interest of a "foolish consistency," from here on in my own appear in square brackets; in my footnotes, the names of Eugen and Margrit Rosenstock-Huessy, Franz Rosenzweig, Marion Davis Battles, and Georg Mueller, as well as the New Testament, the King James Version, and the following books of the Bible, have been abbreviated as: ERH, MRH, FR, MDB, GM, NT, KJV, Gen[esis], Isa[iah], Dan[iel], Matt[hew], 1–2 Cor[inthians], Eph[esians], Phil[ippians], Heb[rews], 1–2 Pet[er], and Rev[elation].

For what it's worth, I advise skipping *all* the footnotes on a first reading—or, if not the author's, then certainly all of Mrs. Battles' and all of mine. This work was never intended to be read primarily as a learned text.

This book is dedicated to the memory of Freya von Moltke, whose brief introduction to "The Fruit of Our Lips" is the only real addition to the body of the book. The years she spent organizing Rosenstock-Huessy's papers and amassing his correspondence would be sufficient claim on our gratitude, but far more important was her extraordinary generosity to everyone who came to Four Wells to work with those papers—not least to me. Spending day after day with her during the last year of her life is a privilege I will never forget.

During the twelve years she shared my grandfather's life at Four Wells, and in the thirty-seven long years she lived on there alone (making it more her home than anyone's), she was a constant friend to the large and far-flung Huessy family, as well as the beating heart of that wider "family" that is the community of old students and new discoverers of Rosenstock-Huessy's work. She is sorely missed (missed, as the Germans say, "at every edge and corner") and will remain so as long as our memory endures.

It is a great pleasure to be able to present this volume to an English-speaking public at last. No edition is without its errors, and I look forward with equanimity to the day on which some wiser scholar questions the assumptions of this edition in turn.

Raymond Huessy
Pentecost, 2020
Putney, VT

I

In the Cross of Reality
from *Soziologie: Die Vollzahl der Zeiten*
(1958)

Margrit and Eugen Rosenstock-Huessy at his 70th birthday celebration on Bob and Anne O'Brien's farm in Tunbridge, VT, 1958.

THIS FIRST CHAPTER IS taken from the final section of the second volume of Rosenstock-Huessy's *Soziologie, Die Vollzahl der Zeiten* (*The Full Complement of Times*). The first volume of the *Soziologie* has appeared in English as *In the Cross of Reality: The Hegemony of Spaces* (Transaction, 2017). The second volume will appear soon. In adapting the conclusion of the *Soziologie* for *Die Umwandlung*, Rosenstock-Huessy cut two short passages and added three concluding paragraphs.

ALL MEN KILL, BECAUSE to live they must seize upon other living things, and all men die. If there were no antidote for death, however, nothing that happens could become history. The history of mankind is composed on one theme alone: how does love become stronger than death? The scores of this composition—our histories—must be re-issued in as many editions as there are human generations, since the composition is re-scored by the members of each generation whose love manages to overcome murder or death.

Thus history becomes a great song, Augustine's *carmen humanum*; in it every line, perhaps every note, is a human life lived. As soon as—as often as—those lines end in rhyme, love has once more become stronger than death. What may have seemed to be unrhymed coincidences, dreadful accidents, meaningless occurrences, or worthless garbage, become in fact the epoch-making crisis in which the long-tolerated process of decay is finally seen for what it is, sighted in the cross-hairs, and overcome.

It has been this way from the very beginning. This rhyming, this connecting, is man's office on earth; but only since Christ's birth have we actually known that this was our office, rather than some other more limited future or descent. With this retrospective knowledge we can have no trouble retroactively reading the same desire, with its endless attempts to overcome death, into the peoples of pre-history; the same knowledge also condemns us as soon as we neglect our earthly office. That is why so much in our own era stares at us with pre-Christian eyes, and, likewise, why today we must continue to walk many paths first trod in ancient eons. The relationship that rules in biblical history is reversed today. The Bible freed us from the Babel of the nations; it judges the peoples and places salvation in the future. We, however, must now persuade ourselves of the good in our origins and open our eyes to how much we preserve in our own era that runs counter to salvation.

While the Bible no longer sets the standard for our selection of material, we are nevertheless subject to its standard when we make our own value judgments. Thanks to the Bible, our voyage into former times need be no more than a voyage of reflection. Where the Bible weeds the beds of times primeval and proclaims full salvation, I am already at home in its time-reckoning and enjoy the prerogative of contrasting the glory and nobility of primeval times with the stains so clearly visible on our newest developments.

Doctrine always works that way. Amid the current rushing forward, it looks back gratefully to what has already been established. It is the time-sacrifices of the ancients that discovered and established for us the full complement of times.

Neither a world-state as the false heir of the second millennium, nor a world-church as the false heir of the first, may be allowed to usurp these new spaces. In our own midst, while Arnold Toynbee naïvely conjures up that most ghastly of tyrannies, the world-state, I measure the decline and fall of the proudest spirits of our spiritual journey from the visible into the invisible, out of the old eon into the new. Society is the only singular I recognize for the future.

In society's generation-spans in the third millennium, the modern mania of "space and time" will fall, even though it was that very mania which allowed us to explore our world. Our times are plural. Every timely human type is owed its own ways, its own space, and its own ages. The more we recognize their full number, the more we may spread peace. We can only become peaceful, quiet on our own little acre, and full of the resonance of our hour, when we preserve the inheritance we have received: the full complement of times.

And how do we preserve it? Anyone who speaks is moved by the three needs which ensnare us all—on our spaceship earth, it is really death that rules (for all our physicists' attempts to dress it up in the more elegant term "gravity"). As the earth's crew, we dare to challenge that omnipotent rule with: our bodily health, our sexual passion, and our ability to give death meaning in sacrifice and surrender. For ten thousand years, we space-sailors have celebrated these three rites, thanks to which we "take place" as men, which is to say, we take our place as men.

In initiation ceremonies, in orgiastic dance, and in killing the god (or sacrificing the divine)—in these three rites all the peoples in every corner of the earth appear as one in spirit. This threefold epiphany is our religion: flaunting our body's strength, rejoicing in our sexual passion, and triumphing in the power to die are the eternal rites of our planet. We meet these three rites—which correspond to Christmas, Easter, and Pentecost—in all times and places, but since today's "educated" humanists can perceive nothing but concepts, this ABC of ritual is revolting to most of them.[1]

---

1. ERH: Luckily, the educated are beginning to outgrow this limited vision. I can

Here I want only to remind you of that fact before we come to speak of the life, teaching, and influence of our predecessor. That way, the reader will be able to step into the planetary place of the Son of Man from the outset.

---

cite Adolf Jensen's insightful work *Die getötete Gottheit: Weltbild einer frühen Kultur* (*The Slain Deity*). My own *Heilkraft und Wahrheit* (*Healing Power and Truth*) already hit upon this *catholic* foundation of human history and indicates it in the subtitle: *Concordance of Political and Cosmic Time*.

II

Ichthys
Life, Teaching, and Action
as a Reflection of the Trinity

from *Das Alter der Kirche*
(1927)

For the translator, every new undertaking offers opportunities for unfortunate compromises. It is a sad fact, but a fact nonetheless, that some things cannot be translated—or can at best be faithfully, if freely, reinvented in another language. There are words that must be translated now one way, and now another. There are plays on words, and changes in the use of words in one language that can only be approximated in another. This is particularly true of Rosenstock-Huessy's work; he loved nothing better than making use of as many of the variations of a central word as possible within a given essay, and he certainly did so in this one.

The original title of this essay was "ICHTHYS: Leben, Lehre, Wirken"; in it, he rings countless changes on the German verb "wirken." The verb can perhaps best be translated as "achieve" or "effect," and I have translated it in various ways in various places as context seemed to dictate. I have done my best to translate its close relatives as close relatives: the noun "Wirkung" becomes "effect" or "influence"; the noun "Wirksamkeit" becomes "effectiveness"; the adjectival noun, a form of which Germans are particularly fond, "der Wirkende," becomes "the man of action." (German as written, until very recently, made little allowance for the gender-neutral.) "Wirklich" becomes "real" or "actual," but the noun "Verwirklichung," which is ambiguous in English as "realization," becomes "shaping reality" or "actualization," despite the translation's cumbersome nature. (If you prefer the ambiguous to the cumbersome, feel free to think "realization" when you run across those terms.) English does in fact have a complete, if isolated, cognate for the verb "wirken" in that we describe yeast as "working" in bread—and it is that usage with which I close the essay.

A more serious problem arose in translating the German word "Geist," technically "spirit," as in "the Holy Spirit." I was surprised to find that in "The Fruit of Our Lips," Rosenstock-Huessy had himself used "mind" where he used "Geist" in German. So in that essay, I followed his lead, but here I had to find my own way, and did so with some trepidation; after all, "mental" or "intellectual" often means something quite different from "spiritual." (Many such problems facing Anglo-Saxons today can be traced back to the strange sea-change that "spirit" underwent on entering post-Reformation England, just as the confusion of "spirit" and "soul" can be traced to the era of the French revolution.) When the essay was reset in 1964, Rosenstock-Huessy's characteristic emphases and exclamation points were removed; I have restored both to their rightful, if "polemical," place.

Das Alter der Kirche (*The Age of the Church*), in which "Ichthys" was first printed, was the very first book of Rosenstock-Huessy's I tried to read, almost fifty years ago. I had already read and come to love his co-author, Joseph Wittig; I counted on him to see me through confronting my grandfather's work, and he did. "Ichthys" has been my favorite of all my grandfather's many essays ever since, and it gives me great pleasure to see it finally appear in English.

Ever since Albert Schweitzer discovered the vicious circle in which the research into Jesus' life had moved in the previous century and a half, the gulf separating natural, scientific biography of Jesus on the one hand and ecclesiastical, dogmatic Christology on the other, has become inescapably clear. Strong in faith, Schweitzer disarmed both these tendencies of theological research on the question of Jesus Christ, first by publishing his book and then by leaving for the Congo as a simple doctor. Liberal theology has had to abandon all hope of encompassing and comprehending not only the Rabbi Jesus of Nazareth but Christ as well.[1]

On the other hand, the Son of Man, the son of Mary, is in danger of shriveling into a Docetical[2] construct in which something divine occurs, but nothing human can be grasped, nothing comprehensible can be recognized. The vast majority of orthodox church-goers still see actual, completely incomprehensible, miracles in the virgin birth, the resurrection, and the outpouring of the spirit. The "educated" crowd, however its members may have been "educated," sees in Jesus an only-too-comprehensible human being. Either way, our highest spiritual power is no longer aroused, for that power is only ignited by mysteries revealed or by puzzles to be solved.

Today this highest arousal of the spirit befalls the souls of neither the orthodox nor the liberal; neither of them is awestruck at the life and death of Jesus—and so Albert Schweitzer fell silent and went to Africa to heal disease. It seems that we are no longer permitted to investigate that life and death with the tools of our reasoning, but may only follow in his footsteps, overwhelmed and therefore silent. The two parties (more precisely, the two methods) run parallel and unreconciled through the soul of every theologian. Today the contradiction between faith and knowledge creates a yawning gulf not between theology and philosophy, but rather within the theologian himself, who derives his benefice as the vassal of a dogmatic church and his thinking from historical research without assumptions.

The contradiction creates a life-threatening tension, and it is perfectly understandable that the first reaction to it is simply to find a way around it,

---

1 ERH: I refer to Bultmann's *Jesus* [Berlin, 1926].

2 [Docetism, condemned at the first Council of Nicaea, held that Christ's human nature, and hence his human body, was an illusion.]

as Karl Barth did in his *Letter to the Romans* and as the Barthians have done ever ever since. In his concrete biblicism he tried to checkmate both ecclesiastical belief and academic biblical criticism by—moving his pieces to another chessboard altogether. Though a servant of the church, as someone like Barth must be, he is untroubled by the questions surrounding Christ's church; though a scholar, he is untroubled by the research demands of secular scholarship. Instead, all is revealed to him at one moment of world history, in the split second of the crucifixion. He disregards the early history of Jesus (that is, his life) and the later history of Christ (that is, church history) as mere rubble. He imagines himself addressed vertically from heaven, alone beneath the cross, without natural pre-history or an effective history of salvation. This balancing act on the head of a pin stuck neatly between orthodoxy and liberalism, between historical scholarship and church theology, seems to me a completely understandable reaction to the unbearable tension created by our opposite poles.

Our own attempt cannot hope to compare with the demonic force of the Barthians' crucifixion sermon, but it arises from the same situation. This chapter hopes only to open, as quietly as possible, a door already ajar, a door that might lead us out of this unbearable tension and into the open. Hence our tri-partite title, which is neither a mere game with numbers nor a choice made without method. For the time being, the purpose is purely negative in nature: we are attempting to escape the dreadful custom of pairing nouns such as "spirit and nature," or "knowledge and faith"—the beloved fashion of straddling a matched pair of concepts joined in speech by an "and," and usually torn asunder in thought by an "or." This antithesis governs all literature for educated people. All philosophical thought lives by this division of concepts, and due to this constant division in conceptual contradistinction, every single philosophical observation produces opposites. Since theology has been sailing in the wake of philosophy for some time, it has all too often adopted this philosophical attitude itself.

"Jesus and Christ," "the life and teaching of Jesus," "law and love," are paired concepts that schools of thought love to set in opposition. Those pairs are much more than mere vocabulary within a single sentence. Indeed, all scholarly research proceeds in the dialectic of these concepts, and beyond that, the doctrine of the cross and passion of the Lord, on the one hand, and the birth and life of Jesus of Nazareth, on the other, are torn poles apart into separate schools, patterns of thought, and factions in faith and life.

But there is another way for the mind to conceive of reality, and it avoids falling prey to the division generated by conceptual dialectic. It seeks not to paper over reality with an abstract paragraph, as scholarly dialectic does, but rather to discover reality in the first place! This process of discovery is the mind's supreme rational effort, but it has been so long neglected that I must first make its method clear with a far-flung example.

As long as trial-by-combat was the highest spiritual activity in Germanic tribal life, even legal speech remained an act of discovery, constantly re-conceived. Speech had to be open and opening, rather than syllogistic: the formulas of this legal language are fond of joining three points of view, three approaches, in one unified expression. Everyone recognizes these triphonies in the formulas by which the criminal is left to the mercy of the birds of the air, the beasts of the wood, and the fish of the waters. The executioner proclaims the pyre with the formula: Your hair to the smoke, your body to the fire, and your soul to God—a formula that seems particularly instructive in demonstrating the fundamental difference between this manner of speech and our current way of thinking.

How would we formulate it today? Well, we would *think* of something. A modern versifier might perhaps separate the hair and the body "poetically"; the modern writer of prose might set body and soul in opposition. But the old formula does not break down death by fire dialectically as a modern-day poet or prosifier might, but dramatically re-creates the acts of the process in which first smoke ruffles the hair, then fire consumes the body, and finally the soul may return to God. The process rolls by cinematically in a series of scenes. The scenes create the process; the thinker has as yet no "overall concept" of death by fire. No drama can be understood by its title alone, nor do its five constituent acts merely divide the overall concept logically or dialectically. On the contrary, each act must be created and have a life of its own.

Likewise, our three-way formula seeks not to mutilate an existing unity, but to create a paradoxical unity. A blood-curse needs to be "lifted, set aside, and done away with" or "revoked, destroyed, and cast away." "Day, time, and hour" were set. The legal sources—as the abstract jurist might say today—"break down" into continuing regulation, personal command, and customary law. However, the old formula speaks of ancient custom, the law, and the glory of the land (because it is ignorant of the concept of legal sources). It cannot "break the concept down," but rather creates it in these three acts!

One might call the process "associative." The important thing is that each individual association points toward the whole that it also helps to create: the whole rises dramatically out of the movements. Of course there may also be two or four movements. It is not the numbers "2" and "3" in themselves that differentiate this dramatic speaking-in-stages from logic's habit of splitting things into opposites, but the fact that the logical opposites represent only fragments of a whole, mere fractions or subordinate clauses of a sentence. The movements and scenes of creative speech are not fragments, but are complete in themselves, areas with their own color value, whose polyphonic sound uncovers and reveals the law of the movements (or scenes or words). All thought is afterthought, thought about an existing world.

Were any modern-day writer called upon to turn over the body to the executioner and the soul to God, he would derive the ideas of "body" and "soul" from a kind of conceptual file-drawer, where every concept imaginable is stored away. He would stand outside the world, in this case the world of culture, and reset its mosaic with its myriad variations anew, as his own object. The creative speaker on the other hand is the mouth of an unfinished world, one that becomes a world in him; he cannot reach into a cabinet and pull out labeled objects, but is instead seized by the forces of this world, which he attempts to reconcile and name.

All discovering thought proceeds in exactly the same way as the preconceptual speech of law we cited, thanks to which the spiritual world is discovered, and it is only for this reason that we have had to make what may have appeared to be a detour. We turned to the example of the creation of legal precedent only because we could not allow this type of thought to be dismissed as merely "poetic." This is not a question of the mere luxury of art, but of the mind's discovery of the world, so it is not surprising that the creative life of the Christian people had to make use of the same form of expression.

The discovery of a new divine world of the soul cannot be comprehended by the division of words, but only by the act-like arrangement of points of view. At the very threshold of the church the trinitarian formula of Father, Son, and Holy Spirit protects the creative life within; it bars the door against any and all entry by philosophical modes of thought. The three persons of the Godhead mock any effort to understand them as fractions of God. Reason, on the other hand, constantly inclines toward this kind of impoverishment, and thinking *per se* has been only too eager to reconceive the three breaths of the creed as subordinate clauses of the overall concept "God." Unbelief scorns the trinity for just this reason: it is dead to the creative processes of the spirit.

The linguistic secret of the three-persons-in-one is no different from that of ancient German legal language. Here, too, a world is discovered rather than conceptualized; every person of the Godhead must be unveiled—or as the theologians say, revealed—with the full creativity of our soul's spirit, just as the people in legal assembly had to "open up" every legal act of its communal life and unfurl it in imagery. Nevertheless, in every act in which the community experiences itself, at every stage of the legal process, it is aware of its own presence as an undivided whole.

In exactly the same way, the Church knows that God makes himself real with each breath, with every act of faith. On the one hand, the short sessions of a county court, and on the other, the world assizes of the triune God, are woven together out of fully living acts that are not fragments, but complete entities in themselves. If we are not completely off-base in interpreting the trinitarian formula, it seeks to represent the triumph of the grammar of time, of creation by speech, over the logic of purely conceptual thought. If so, this may not just remain a philosophical conclusion but must immediately be turned to treating the partial questions of theology. It must be transmitted by every believer, so to speak.

That is why we set the old formula "Ichthys" (Jesus, Messiah, Son of God, Redeemer) at the head of this chapter and added: "Life, Teaching, and Action." It seems to us that the way we deal with Jesus Christ suffers serious injury as soon as we build it up dialectically on such dualisms as "Jesus and Christ," "life and death," "public ministry and cross." Let us instead try a trinitarian formula that allows us to discover God breathing in and out, and does not merely force us into contradictions.

The sterile dualism of "Jesus" and "Christ" finds its crassest expression in the way this division into opposites has affected our Savior's teaching. No one, from any of the religious parties, seems able to decide whether his teaching belongs to Jesus' life or to Christ's passion and transfiguration. The Sermon on the Mount seems to many the crowning event of the natural spiritual life of the carpenter's son Jesus of Nazareth; the farewell speeches to the disciples appear to just as many as the revelation of the exalted Christ, *Kyrios*. And so the division is made right down the middle, right through what matters most, that is, his spiritual statements.

One of these divisions is made in an attempt to differentiate between what he told his disciples and what he told "the people," but now and then in fact he found true discipleship in the people and encouraged it—and quite often his disciples were neither more open nor more spiritually mature than the people. The mystery of what he had to say cannot be deduced or divined solely on the basis of who was listening. The division of life and teaching—made by the pious and impious alike—arises as a necessary consequence of the unresolved use of the word "life." "Life" can only be set in opposition to teaching because life's conjugation into spirit is not accounted for. Goethe's line "For life is love, and the life of love is spirit" already points toward the conclusion that we must seek some other relation between life and spiritual expression. We are dealing with life-forms and their *metamorphoses* over time, not with contradictions. Goethe's verse is directly connected to the Christian doctrine of the spirit. It belongs to the very essence of "Ichthys" in particular, that in it "life" and "teaching" reveal themselves as transformations of the same puzzle.

Christianity presumes a turning point in every person's life, or rather, it inserts such a turning point into every life. It smashes the generalization "life." The days of life cease to be fractions of a "whole," a life that proceeds uniformly from cradle to grave. A Christian's year is not made up of 365 individual days; a Christian's life is not made up of 70 individual years. The movement of life is separated into several creative acts: before rebirth and after rebirth people live in different worlds. The soul ceases to live an "incremental" life; it progresses in jolting steps, in creative acts.

No one questions the central importance of rebirth. But very often this break is understood as the work of a moment. Conversion is seen as a short momentary event, where in reality it may take as long as five or ten years! What's more the division of life into acts that conversion brings in its wake is not given full weight. Yet conversion presupposes three discrete stages: the time before the turning point, the time of the turning point itself, and the time founded on the completed turn—all three proceed on different levels and have their own internal laws. The stages may be interwoven: certain lines and threads of the old Adam are still bound up in the new; in eddies and vortices the time of confession already rages beneath the surface of the child of nature; and within the time of crisis itself there are occasional glimpses of the golden background of the *vita nuova*. It is precisely because these entanglements and overlappings occur, that it is so important to recognize that these various levels of life are in fact mutually incompatible. They may cross each other, overlap each other, but they can never actually mix. They belong to different divine powers of the soul.

As regards his teaching, we have already indicated that a lot of territory has been left unoccupied between the life of Jesus and the power of Christ, or it has been at most a sort of no-man's-land, occupied now by some forces and now by others. Right in the middle, between life and suffering, there remains Something Else, the spiritual asset spoken by this mouth: the treasure of his insights, his spiritual vision, everything that we know of Jesus' spiritual life only because he shared it with others as teaching. Doctrine speaks of the Savior's teaching and preaching, so we will accept that word for the act of spiritual reflection and vision, but the term "reflection" itself would also be acceptable.[3]

Whose teaching is it, Jesus' or Christ's? The key to reversing the crippling of our speech lies in the relation of his teaching backwards to Jesus' life, on the one hand, and forward to Christ's actions, on the other. Our

---

3. [The published text starts to overlap with the 1923 version here. See Appendix B, 148.]

speech may be healed if Christ refrained from teaching what we must learn anew each day from his actions!

Even after he began teaching in public, Jesus continued his inner life; that alone would be enough to set him apart from all Average Teachers. The average person learns his little verse while young, and once he has acquired subordinates who have no choice but to listen, passes it on. The trained teacher does his research, makes his discovery, and then mounts the podium only to be transfixed there as the type of teacher who no longer goes on living; teaching rules him and squeezes the life out of him. At some point we stop moving and our previous life becomes the roof over our heads. We let the young follow after us and grow up alongside us, but for them to be able to do that we must teach them what we have experienced. This is a law of nature and we cannot simply abolish it because we are afraid we might turn to stone.

How could Jesus abolish this law? Doesn't he want to fulfill, not abolish, that which we must all undergo? Nevertheless we insist that he did not stop at any particular moment but kept on living till the last moment, even though he was already teaching publicly. Another stage follows in the wake of vision and teaching, and the *"perfectus homo"* had to explore all the stages. True, he completely confused his listeners by doing so, for he was always one step ahead of what his listeners were able to perceive in him. While he still seemed to be the carpenter's son, he was already the teacher. While he was considered a rabbi, he was already a prophet. While they took him for a prophet, he was already the Messiah. When they finally took him for the King of the Jews, he was God's servant. And when they recognized him as God's servant, he had already become the crucified Son of God.

He has a head-start that he maintains to the end, and those who live with him can never quite follow along. He never stays put long enough for the others to catch up, and so they run out of breath. The hallmark of the so-called Synoptic Gospels is that they are all still struggling to catch up and so fail to see the previous stages through the lens of the last one. Jesus had galloped away from his physical disciples as well. The first generation of disciples was consumed by the necessity of reconciling the contradictory stages that followed each other in such lightning succession that the world could only see and remember one at a time. Only when they were done could John the Evangelist set his seal on a picture cleansed of all misunderstandings.

Whenever we learn, we are not yet full partners in life. The student of any doctrine remains in its power. John is the only evangelist who is both disciple and more-than-disciple of Him who taught him, and for that reason he can see the spirit of his teacher and the suffering of the one he loved as one, and translate it as one. Please note: Jesus' public actions come after his teaching.

This discovery has a complement in the opposite direction: How does Jesus' earlier life relate to his teaching? We know nothing, or almost nothing, about his life. Shallow novels like *Jesus the Adolescent*,[4] about his childhood or his wanderings, simply prove that we are only too aware of this ignorance. His natural life is passed on to us only in the form of the natural event of his birth and his parents' flight into Egypt for his sake. In other words, we can never know more about the experiences of the natural man Jesus and his path through life than is reflected in his teaching and vision.

We said before that even the mediocre teacher adds to his teaching what he himself has discovered and experienced: the spirit comes after life and proceeds from it. Jesus' teaching must have come to him out of the experience of his earlier life. This earlier life, his "inner life," the development and formation of his life took place "beyond" all the outside world. We have this "beyond" only in the form of the sweet fruit of his teaching; we can only know the heavenly kingdom in his heart to which he bears witness—by that same witness of his. We have no earlier stages that show how it came to him. All that remains "beyond"—and it is this "beyond" that makes immature believers wax so rhapsodic, and metaphysicians pile up lies upon lies.

On the other hand, as soon as Jesus begins his ministry, we know him only through his influence on others, the effectiveness of that influence, how he proved his worth in the outside world. As soon as he becomes *visible*, he is "in this life"; what we know of his life is all a part of his cross. And in showing himself everywhere "in this life," the Christ in him starts and develops everywhere in him. Rabbi Jesus *teaches* us how to cross from the creaturely to the spiritual life, but Jesus the Christ *lives* the other way around, returning from the life of the spirit back into real life! Instead of a "life of Jesus"—which must remain unknown to us—we can only know his actions as Christ, his life as chosen Son, his realization through his messianic office.

All that remains of his earlier life is his teaching. His whole vegetative, natural life is transmuted for us in the fruit of his teaching word, behind which its owner, the office-holder, recedes like any other functionary. Jesus' teaching on the law and the prophets, on the Father and the Heavenly Kingdom, is the purified fruit of inner battles, enlightenment, instruction, and experiences, the results of which were fixed at his baptism in the Jordan, and so themselves lie far behind him. Bud and blossom are no longer visible in the fruit; yet it is their quintessence. The fruit forces us to presume that seed

---

4. [Probably Wilhelm Scharrelmann's 1920 novel, *Jesus der Jüngling*. In 1923, Salesian church in Nazareth was dedicated to *Jesus the Adolescent*]

and blossom went before it—all natural life ripens to insight and wisdom. Jesus does not abolish the law of nature, but fulfills it; he really teaches what he has experienced.

The *perfect tense* of this experience must be taken seriously: it preceded him! Human words come only after an impression is made on us. We may only and can only teach what is already behind us; our formulation in words limps along after events. Human thinking is *after-thought*! We can reflect only on that which has gone before, *quod factum est*. Jesus teaches what he has experienced as Jesus, that is for himself, a being still becoming and not yet binding on others, as a man turned inward. So as a teacher he holds prophetic office; he is the teacher of Israel, the last prophet.

On the other hand, while he is teaching he leads the life of another character altogether, an official personage who lays claim to the power and authority to bind or cast off others: he is a man who decidedly embodies his calling. But his calling is not what one might expect based on his teachings. Because he teaches, he appears to be a professional teacher. But teaching is only the prerequisite of his actions, which are not a rabbi's. His teaching is not the essence of his office; he lives an office that has as yet no line in the budget of mankind's economy; it is an office that he himself forms and invests with dignity.

That is in fact just how the Gospels formulate his public actions. According to them, it is not what he says, but when, where, to whom he says it that betrays the particular character of his function beyond mere teaching. The smallest feature has meaning in the process by which he is revealed. Here we are neither in the private life of a man nor in the intellectual life of a thinker: we are where life no longer has room to play and can no longer change shape out of sight, where it has become rigid, irreversible action, "*praxis*" visible to the world. Actualization[5] is no longer an interior matter, but one of renunciation, one that requires the cooperation of the world. *It is a political existence and is subject to the laws of politics.*

The greatness of this public transformation lies in all the worldly facts, all the hard objective lumps: that John baptizes him, that the disciples react, that Lazarus wakes from the dead, that Judas betrays him, that the Romans crucify him, that Joseph of Arimathea buries him. All these facts are not assignments for the biographer of his soul or the systematizer of his spirit, but for the historian of his creativity and his actions.

His character as the son of God only becomes believable, worthy of belief, because the outer world dovetails with his life. All these dispensations make reality of the picture that Jesus carried within himself of himself

---

5. [*Verwirklichung.*]

and the world. The obedient collaboration of all the worldly powers on his path only confirms him; there is nothing left for him to do but attract those powers to himself. The world grows, falls, rushes toward him, until it has laid him on the cross. He literally attracts and grabs hold of it, merely by awaiting it. There have been and are beautiful lessons in wisdom from every nation. But the inner vision of God becomes believable only when it is shown that the sage had a right to such high thoughts. Not everyone has the right to think high or luminous things, or even to imagine great and daring deeds. Thinking creates obligations.

But no one can anyone simply live out what he has thought through, either. Much as the world demands it, we cannot in fact practice what we preach, at least not as the words are usually understood. Instead, we can only go on living, living out our thoughts each day; our life is changed by our spiritual vision, but life flows on, just as original and surprising as ever. True, it has left the path of mere coincidence and has been molded by the vision granted us in the inner sanctum. Our life is melted down to be recast into action, recast from mere becoming to what is required of the lasting man shaped before God's countenance. The truth granted in vision must be put to the test. And teaching is only a small part, that part we can formulate, of the truth that overwhelmed us in the temple, the inner sanctum where our life is re-created.[6]

This then is the proper place of Jesus' teaching, in between the life of the unbaptized Jesus and the actions of the professing Christ: he teaches what he has experienced, but afterwards the things he taught actually come to pass. On the one hand, his teaching is a result, his success, the fulfillment of his "former life," but his teaching changes from an effect to a cause, from a result to a starting-point, from an end-sum to the initial value of his life's equation. The fruit of the "facts" of his youth becomes the fundamental "factor" of his adult existence, which is based on that factor but at the same time surpasses it. Jesus' teaching smashes the tablets of the law; what else makes a new law possible after this ending other than a fresh start in Christ's actions? Jesus' teaching directs the Christian in life, as Christ's actions directs the church in the political world.

Some may object that Jesus also expressed and interpreted his life as Christ, and that is certainly true: life is not so schematically divided that one period contains nothing of the others. Jesus' experiences as Christ did indeed become words in his sentences as Christ to his disciples—in the farewell speeches, for example. And here lies the sharp division between teaching for those who learn and revelation for the apostles. Jesus' teaching

---

6. [A reference to the last words of FR's *Star of Redemption*. See Appendix B, 145.]

of the people (and of the disciples insofar as they learn) is the fruit of his earlier life, which is why he speaks to his listeners of inner freedom, of the heart's secrets, and of heaven, for instance, hoping as a teacher that they might understand. On the other hand, he has to allow the disciples to share his life although he knows that they do not understand, and that there is one among them who will betray him. He does not need them as hearers of his teaching, but as witnesses of his actions. He lets them take part in the mysteries of those actions, of a man's dying to the world. His words to them on this subject, the increasingly surprising fate of the man of action whom they take for a teacher, are not teaching but evidence, confirmation, proofs, interpretations, and exposition of what they experience in him and in the world: they are not instruction, but drama.

Only with the help of his words to them can they share the experience of his *experimentum crucis*. Christ's words to his disciples bind the collaborators to the "laborator," to the man of action; they bind the limbs to the head. Here the Word has a different mission than when pure doctrine is passed on from person to person, from preacher to flock, in divine commandments. The Word is not teaching, but mortar and bond that creates a field of action. In this field of action all those laws of which "Christian morality" is supposedly ignorant suddenly come into their own: sovereignty and service, office and necessity, division and separation, silence and anger, command and failure, worry and reflection. There is in all this no sin to the man of action.

Jesus constructed Christ's field of action once he had his vision and his teaching behind him. All his powers were concentrated on making this field indestructible, not teaching it. Developing a doctrine of Christ's actions and the way he built his field of action, in addition to Jesus' own teaching, was something only a disciple who had never actually heard Jesus teach could undertake. Of Paul it has rightly been said that he lived what Jesus taught, but taught what Christ lived.[7] That is precisely what we have called Jesus' influence: the effect he had as Christ. And so the enduring prejudice against Paul the "theologian" is part and parcel of the modern excitement over the "life of Jesus," for Paul is the witness to the fact that Jesus' early life has nothing to do with us, but that his teaching, on the one hand, as the end of the law, and his actions, on the other, as the beginning of a new order of things in the Church, have everything to do with us.

A man's early life, his existence as a naïve child of the world, bears fruit in his spiritual yield as a kind of inner "spirit lamp." *Whatever bears fruit is*

7. [It is not clear that anyone other than ERH himself ever said this. He made the same statement in the 1925 essay on adult education, "Andragogik" (see Appendix I, 335–36) and in his American lecture courses.]

without sin. Once we make spiritual atonement for our youthful sins, they are forgiven. The passions of flesh and blood are the indispensable food of insight; no one need be ashamed that he has "a past" as long as he plunged into it with all his heart.

The only relevant aspect of any intellectual or spiritual concern is its ruthlessness toward its human carriers: the purity of their vision, their self-denying truthfulness, and its spiritualizing effect on those who confess it.

The only relevant aspect of actions, however, is the extent to which its powers are consciously engaged, the extent to which they prove their worth in flesh and blood, and the extent to which they fittingly and conformingly master the material they are meant to mold.

The three stages—life, teaching, and actions—belong together. It goes without saying that action without spirit and without the heart's experience is empty; it is the appearance of fruit where there was neither seed nor blossom.

There are sprouts that wither, blossoms that remain unchanged, fruit like empty nuts. The fate of the poor devils who fail to overcome the three infernal princes—of the senses, of thought, and of compelling authority[8]—will meet their destiny in a squandered youth, pointless reflection, and busy-ness without purpose.

The boy awakens to adolescence so that his feelings may "be thought through" to become thoughts; the youth ripens to manhood so that his thoughts may become deeds. If the youth does not eventually overcome his glorious self-squandering, if the student agrees to remain tangled in systems and analyses, the man who inexorably grows out of them, and who must somehow deal with life and its myriad circumstances, will not deal with them well, lamed as he is in soul and spirit. He will fail to find himself carried forward by a fruitful sequence in the electrical circuit of boy-youth-man, and can only work mindlessly, helplessly, senselessly, just keeping busy—with a stunted, curdled view of the world in his head and a squandered heart—and therefore unable to love where he must take action, and unable to work through what was once granted him in visions. Such a man is only outwardly adult and so lacks authority for the freedoms and decisions that every life of action requires. Any work we do that does not flow downhill from the highest life is dead—and goes to the devil.

Here is the sore spot of our existence. Both as individuals and as a people, we have forfeited the natural progression of life's stages. Healing them is the content of all revelation—it seeks not to abolish the law, but to fulfill it. Jesus came to combat the over-wrought enthusiasts in the world,

8. [*Herrschaft*.]

for in him all excess of feeling ripens to clarity in his vision of God. He came to combat the Pharisees in the world, for he relinquishes his clear teaching once it begins to take effect. But he came on behalf of the sinners in the world, for he replaces all worldly activity pursued without thought or feeling with actions based on the vision granted him in the inner sanctum.

The "sinner" seeks life in busy-ness. The man of action knows that busy-ness is only death: he has already lived, and his life has been transfigured in his sight, so that when he looks back at life, it is no longer his life that he rediscovers. He has set sail from his own life, steering back into the world in a vessel not his own, that is to say, back into a new life and into the lives of others, to perfect their lives as well. He obeys his God and his calling. He is drawn onward by that end which he has already experienced once in his life, in self-denial, for a man's true calling is to bend all his powers to effect his end. Young life gushes forth without connections, rising boldly to the very firmament, until at last it finds its own limits. Oriented to the star that rose over it, destined to prove the worth of the vision granted, it descends from the bright space of the spirit down to earthly life and timeliness.

Whether the slope of that path is gentle or steep, it is always a path toward death. On that path our life is forfeit. And this forfeiture of life, the gravitational pull of the goal glimpsed in vision, what Cromwell called "dying by inches," is no "natural" life but indeed its opposite: action as calling. We cannot live "supernaturally" in this life—we are not gods; but we can live out of the supernatural, drawing life from the supernatural which confronted us in our act of vision and illumination, rebirth and change—accepting a call and the action it entails. Theologians' speech often seems so lame because it only mentions the natural and the supernatural and fails to address the healed action[9] of the person touched by the divine as a third act in the drama of life.

This "working in the call" is no simple "humbly walking with your God," but rather *a return* to walking humbly; it is no longer just answering God as an individual, but at the same time taking responsibility for God before men, something that the mere life in us neither knows nor even needs to know. Responsibility for God before men? This is where those laws of real life, about which "Christian morality" seems to know so little, come into their own; this is where the doctrine of authority takes root. Adult humanity and the fields of action that must be founded in human heads and hearts receive their authority from their founders' divine power of attorney. The authority of a man of action is constantly renewed out of his "former life" and its wholeheartedness. Puppets devalue any office they hold; an office

---

9. [*das geheilte Wirken.*]

can only survive as long as the office-holder lets his "former life" flow into his perception and his perception flow into his office, as long as his vocation remains the vessel in which the truth of his life may work itself out and prove its worth.

Authority is really authorship. Nothing important happens without some person laying out a new life along a path from earth to the sun and from the heavens back to earth in such a way that others can follow it after him. Where such paths draw men to them, into them, and after them, there is authority, there is a heightened trail-blazing-and there the *via exaltata* of the trailblazer claims its influence.

Almost no one fails utterly to find his path in life. Almost everyone comes to some degree of influence on some modest life-path. But when the world breaks down completely into enthusiasts, Pharisees, and tax-collectors—when a people seems to consist only of a youth movement's feelings, mere intellectual orthodoxy, and the political organization of labor relations—then a modest path is no longer enough. Then all those who still try to pursue a modest path will find themselves dragged down by its fragmentary nature, and by the equally fragmentary bit of life to which that path is restricted, into a hellish void where they must forfeit all influence. The lack of influence is the constant curse of the intellectual world, for example. Either it fails to force the world of deeds to cooperate, or those who would teach some desperately needed knowledge are deprived of listeners by youth in mutiny. The heart misses the spirit that was its destiny. Then the stream dries up, that stream that once led from the creature in Bethlehem to his vision of God, from his highest vision in the desert to his actions in the midst of creation.

But when it does, God's mercy blazes a new trail for man: new authorities arise, for new people have been privileged to view the trailblazer's path. And in these new people the path with its stations is reestablished, the path that spans from death to birth, and knows three stages between birth and death: life, teaching, and action.

In each of these stages a different order and a different set of connections hold sway. Different things are allowed someone who merely lives than may be allowed to someone who teaches. There are really three different moralities and sets of ethics. The "naïve," those who merely live, obey forces they have not chosen; they are free of all responsibility, free to make mistakes and take detours as necessary. Others act for them, as when Mary and Joseph flee into Egypt for their son's sake. They obey a foreign law.

The teacher, however, sets an example, and "Christian morality" in its narrow sense applies to him most of all. Anyone who wants to draw others along after him must use spiritual means. He may neither strive like Faust, ranging far and wide and always aspiring,[10] nor take arms against a sea of troubles and by opposing, end them.[11] He has come to his own limits, and sets himself apart from truth; so he must teach relatively "selflessly." Vision bears fruit only to those who forget themselves. The teacher is free to pursue any goal of knowledge, but unfree in his means.

The man of action is quite different. Those who act complete and achieve what they undertake. They must resist the seductive lure of new goals and persevere wherever they are stationed, for he "who perseveres in steadfast truth, will make the world conform."[12] They may themselves choose whatever means are required. If profligacy is the pride of youth, a grown man is miserly, husbanding his resources, for he alone knows their proper place. None but he may determine their use nor need answer for it.

In place of "Christian morality," three human laws arise, all three of which we must honor as long as we draw breath. For where we love, we squander. Where we hope, we do not sow like one who teaches and fulfills his duties in faith; where we hope, we plant and nurture our own field of action like a garden, with all a gardener's art. We live in three orders at once, even if each is only revealed in turn, and only completely revealed over a lifetime. The commandments of love are different from those of faith. The hope of the gardener is different from that of the man who plants in faith. The order of action is the manly order of public life, the realm of law. It differs from teaching passed from mouth to mouth in the ivory towers of thought and from the order that applies there. And different again is the circle of the loving community, youthfully bound together, ordered without compulsion.

Time has a different meaning for the natural man, the visionary, and the man of action. We must differentiate three ways of reckoning time. The natural one dates by individual years, epochs, periods of growth and development; rightly so, for we live from the outside in, influenced by the seasons as well as by our environment. Vision, on the other hand, has no knowledge of time. An insight may take eighty years or a second; lost in thought, we know nothing of time's external deadlines. The man of action knows only how much of the work at hand has to be finished on any particular day. Here time-spans of different lengths make no difference, but artful transposition of times makes sense. As a period of action, Jesus' death on the cross "means" the same as half of Goethe's working life. In both there takes place, if in differing perfection, the return to earth of a visionary. The time-span

---

10. [Goethe, *Faust II*, Act 5 (line 11936).]
11. [*Hamlet*, III:1.]
12. [Goethe, *Hermann und Dorothea*, IX:1.]

each man of action needs to see his actions through to completion is different, though the measure of former natural life is almost identical in all cases.

With this point we have our hands on the key to the mystery, newly stirred up by the World War, of the difference between the "political" morality of the statesman as opposed to the morality of the private citizen. It is not that the state and the individual have different codes, but that the creator, the visionary, and the child of nature in us (in each of us, please note) must know what he is doing. As soon as the state and the individual are opposed to each other, you have to make a Leviathan of the state and a lowly Christian soul of the individual. The state is made absolute and set adrift unensouled by divine commandments. However, as soon as the *statesman* rather than the apparatus of state is accorded his rightful place as the carrier of spiritual creation, he becomes none other than the man who must carry out what he is given to do and embody his calling.[13] Then reasons of state and the appeal to mere interest are subordinated to his mission and calling, and may only seek to further that larger mission, that calling, and their own little measure of truth. The mere politician's final hour is come; he forfeits his office as soon as idolatry of the state allows all acts of state to be deemed sacrosanct. Calculation of the ends can only be allowed as much *influence* as *life* and *meaning* are at work in the peoples of the earth, and in their spirits, at the time; the three orders must all be equally powerful.

Only where they mutually spur and challenge each other can humanity's divine trinity be fulfilled. The polemics of both Machiavellian *Realpolitik* and ethical fanaticism are so unappealing because they seek humanity's divine spark in mere dictatorial imposition on the one hand, and in mere bourgeois morality on the other. That is why the full miracle of the trinity had to take on personality in one man, so that the division of man into a diabolical giant and a divine dwarf, into state and individual, could be done away with once and for all. We have always understood, and still understand, only the irreconcilable opposites of "national governmental interest" and private morality, of ethical theory and actual practice. The chattering of the preachers may make the statesman sick to his stomach and the Christians may despair of the world, but God's creation is kept alive because it moves in three mutually determined orders.

That is why the same orderer had to precede us in each of these orders—all have been explored by God, and our own path only follows the luminous tracks he left in all three of them.

Only because God left his traces in all of them can we mortals summon the courage to struggle free of the divine embrace of each separate hour and

---

13. [*verwirklichen, wozu er berufen ist.*]

make the leap from one order to another as the new hour requires. Only those who remain open to the call to change from one of the three personal forms to another—should that be God's will—can still be called living souls. And that was the perfect obedience of the firstborn which He revealed to us.

Does not man collapse beneath this cross? Does not he lose his rigid character and his proud personality? Yes, he loses both these signs of natural age, yet he does not collapse.

What God says stands formed before men's eyes. The words of God are not only the words that his children speak but also the paths they take. The man of action becomes the word that the creator intends to enter into the Book of Life. He receives the name by which mankind will now hear him, call upon him, understand and misunderstand him until Judgment Day.

The only reason we can walk humbly is that God has commanded us to do so not only in a human way, but by name; for everything God has to say, he says in the names that his sons then bear before mankind until their influence is extinguished. From the first day on, our name waits to see whether God will make our life one of name and calling. A name is a gift given at birth, but also an award made when the call comes to us, and an obligation on whatever path that call sheds its light. Names combine life, vision, and actions in our transformation. The trinity in which we stand becomes simplicity through the name we bear, which also bears us up. Jesus' life defies biographical reasoning. His teaching defies the textbooks of morality. His actions entered world history as a foreign body.

His story juts into this world from another. His vision flowed from limitless aspiration; his life bore fruit completely and utterly. But it all happens in the name of God's son, and that is why it happens in divine simplicity. Wherever we may open the book of life without him, wherever life calls out to us, bubbling up anew and unconcerned with us, we soon ask ourselves where the seal of life may be, that name which all human life must bear. When we need a standard and a benchmark for life, he whom we forgot in our love of life itself, the founder of our faith, returns to us again. He is revealed in every form as the fulfiller of our faith, and he returns to us by name.

It takes a long time for languages to unfold, for us to set the events heaven blows our way to their own melody and to sing them. It just takes however long it takes for God's breath to become a living soul. Luther had to write on his wall in the Koburg: *Christus vivit*. We cannot translate the theologian's word *christos* into English if we only transliterate it as "Christ." "*Christus vivit*" can only be translated once the Christian way of life has entered our flesh and blood. Since then, that one man's life draws us on after it in rank and file in the great stations of his life, so that our course too leads us out of our place in life into a "beyond"—where we receive a vision—and back into this life—where we take effective action.

Only then is it possible to express Jesus of Nazareth's path toward death as our Savior in our own language. Instead of *"Christus vivit"* it is: *Jesus works on in us.* And the three breaths of the divine creator, revealer, redeemer is reflected in the image of the threefold God in life, teaching, and actions. Creature of the Father, Brother of the Son, Collaborator in the Kingdom—that is the trinity in us, in mankind.

III

The Fruit of Our Lips
from *Die Sprache des Menschengeschlechts*
(1964)

The wonders of speech, hidden and yet open to all, inspired Eugen Rosenstock-Huessy all his life. He never ceased to approach speech in humility, admiration, and awe. All his new and long-forgotten insights stemmed from this fundamental attitude to which he added profound scholarship and erudition. The outcome is always unexpected and extraordinary—even for people who disagree.

All this applies to "The Fruit of Our Lips," written in English in 1954, and in his own opinion part of the core of his work. This book is neither a commentary on the gospels, nor an analysis of their contents. The gospels, says Rosenstock-Huessy, are the fruit of Jesus' lips, the beginning of an entirely new way of speaking.

Though they are four, they represent one organic whole. They complement each other; where one leaves off, the next one begins, and together they form a roadblock to the past. Together they started a process which has penetrated the ages—a process through which each writer himself is changed, as each addresses himself to one of the great streams of speech which antiquity had created.

Used as we are to taking the New Testament as a religious book, it takes great effort for us to recognize the four gospels as *the* new process of speech, universal and human at once.

—Freya von Moltke

What follows is a translation of the 1964 German version of "The Fruit of Our Lips," including all the material that Marion Davis Battles relegated to endnotes or appendices in *Fruit of Lips*. I have compared my English translation with the hand-corrected English-language typescript of 1954, and in most cases I adopted the wording of the English version; I apologize for any omissions. Passages missing from the German text or which differ significantly from the English version are footnoted; notes and variant text from the English version are prefixed "1954." Passages Rosenstock-Huessy added for the 1964 publication are shown in {"French" brackets}. A few minor additions made to the translated text for the sake of clarity are set in italics in square brackets.

The 1964 German version appeared as the final chapter of Rosenstock-Huessy's great compendium of his essays on speech, *Die Sprache des Menschengeschlechts*. When it was reprinted in 1968, some (but not all) references to the rest of the larger book were changed. As a result, there are occasional citations of "earlier" passages which this book does not contain. Unless a New Testament passage is referenced to a particular printed source, it is safe to assume that it is the author's own translation from the Greek. His translations seldom line up with any published or online translations I have found, but he certainly had occasion to consult Weymouth and Robertson's *New Testament in Modern Speech* and he may have worked with others.

Rosenstock-Huessy always capitalized nouns that refer to God, whether Father, Son, or Holy Spirit, but almost never capitalized the pronouns which substitute for them. I have followed his lead except where not capitalizing the pronoun would result in ambiguity. His notes, and Mrs. Battles's, are marked with their initials; mine appear in square brackets. To combat the resulting proliferation of notes, Mrs. Battles's citations of scripture have been incorporated into the text in square brackets (Rosenstock-Huessy's own citations of scripture have always been in parentheses).

For a discussion of the essay's history and the differences between the English and German versions, see the introduction to Appendix E, 183–88.

Creabo fructum labiorum. [I shall create the fruit of the lips.]
—Isaiah 57: 19

We now leave the first cycle of human speech and enter upon our own era. The ancient cycle began with the prehistoric tribe, among a small group of frantic and frightened, raving and running men who took heart, spoke, and danced, and so progressed from fright, shouting, and running to an inspired way of life. They placed themselves under the power of verbs, pronouns, names, and numbers. Speech made them human by clothing them and investing them with power as the children of Man, as the listeners to the spirits of the dead, as ancestors and descendants. {Their times were engraved on their skins, so they knew to which time they belonged.}

The second stage lifted the heart of Man into a universe. The tattoos on bodies were replaced by the tattoos on the temple walls, when the whole universe spoke to Pharaoh, the Great House of Egypt, or to the Emperor of China, the "son of heaven." {Eternity swung in orbit over his head.} Tell me who speaks to you, and I will know who you are. Pharaoh was anxious to be the sky-world's "thou," the child of the sun and moon and all the stars, the Horus of the horizon of the southern world of noon, and of the northern world of midnight. The listener to the universe, the Son of Heaven, became the heart of a living universe. The hieroglyphs were its tattoos; {they faithfully recorded the cycle of the eon}.

Once ritual had been established in tribe and empire, poetry began. And it led to the green meadow where Nausicäa finds Odysseus on the seashore and where Achilles meets his mother Thetys, the ocean goddess. Since ritual had eliminated panic, poetry could return into "Nature." "Nature" means no more than "the world without panic." Poetry listens to nature without fear; it is a child of peace, the listener of peace and law. {So poetry allows this world's laws or the concluded peace to appear better than they are}. Poetry transfigures nature, as ritual had freed her of panic; but the world remains the same, {divided into many "districts"} where world wars, world riddles, world revolutions, and world chaos lie in wait.

The stream of Homeric poetry ran in one direction, toward the world; Homer took advantage of ritual's attainments. The stream of Israel's psalms ran in the opposite direction; Israel sensed the disadvantages of ritual's multiplicity and imperfection. {They all either laid the spirits of the past or "laid" the gods in an endlessly cycling present.} Israel directed its efforts not toward the "world minus panic," but to {the fact that the rest of creation was still to come}. Israel saw that one rite contradicted another and that neither temples, nor tattoos, nor poems, could ever move beyond their boundaries in time and space. The more rites and temples were built, the more poems were imagined, the greater was the confusion of tongues, the higher the Tower of Babel. Israel retreated from this world of *Tohu* and *Bohu*,[1] [Genesis 1:2] {the world in which, according to the emperor Nero, many eons existed side-by-side.}[2]

It is true that Israel built a temple, but {by the time she did so, she had already arrived at the insight that} God did not live in it: Israel deprived the temple of its power. It is true that Israel circumcised her men, but she did it to the child in the cradle, not to adolescents awaiting initiation. In the clan's fertility rite, the boy was meant to be inspired by the circumcision: Israel deprived this tribal rite of its power {by "pre-poning" it}. It is true that Israel wrote poems, but she never admitted that she herself had "made" them; idols or images made by men could not be worshiped. Israel insisted that she had been spoken to, and had answered, and so Israel disarmed the arts. {She made the genius into a mere respondent.} In these three acts she emptied the three great languages of the heathen—ritual, temple, and art—of their lure and charm as absolutes. The real speech, Israel insisted, was yet to come. It would only be heard by him who could listen to the future, who, as the listener to the revolving eon, as a prophet,{could call from the future into the present.}[3]

When all this had been said, when the Sioux, the Chinese, the Greeks, and the Jews had all spoken, a world came to an end. This was and is the complete cycle of antiquity:

1. The listeners to the dead created rituals {of inspiration}.
2. The listeners to the sky-world and the universe built temples {of eternal return}.
3. The listeners to the law and the peace already achieved became poets and artists {for an audience}.

1. MDB: *formlessness and void.*
2. ERH: Michaelis, *Apokryphen*, 316. [See Appendix I, 334.]
3. ERH: See my "Hitler and Israel," 129-39. [Also in ERH, *Despite*, 178-94.]

4. The listeners to the future {spoke back into the present from the end of time}.

These four stages of speech were united and superseded in Jesus, and for this deed we call him Christ. *Christ is Jesus as the fruit of the lips of antiquity.*

Jesus listened to the spirits of old. The war between the sexes in Adam and Eve and all their offspring was overcome by Mary and her son, superseded all ancient marriage and funeral rites. Jesus had listened the calendar of the sky-world and the government of the universe, for he appeared when Pontius Pilate embodied the worldly unity of the Roman orb in Palestine, and on Good Friday he gave himself up in place of the bloody sacrifices inside the temple gates. Jesus had listened to poetry and the peace already achieved, for his speech certainly transfigures the lilies and the sparrows, the adulteress and the thief; the world outside the city gates held no terrors for him, but he superseded all poems. He wrote no book; when he wrote in the sand, he was himself the true poem,[4] {the *carmen humanum*, in which ever since each of us may resound as one more line}.

Jesus had listened to the future, for the psalms were on his lips and the messianic faith of Israel had formed him, but he was no prophet. That is the first thing reported about him: he is the main event. He didn't await anyone else, he himself was the expected *One*. Because they only knew the types of men who had lived before him, they called him: Joseph's son, carpenter, king, priest, rabbi, prophet, and messiah.

These names clearly denote terminals. They are the final products of the four streams of speech we have uncovered: the last king, the last priest, the last prophet, the Messiah. All these things achieved could only have meant the end of the world, and Jesus was in fact the end of our first world. He took the sins of this first world upon himself. This sentence simply states the fact that in separation, tribal ritual, the temple of the sky-world, poetry in praise of nature, and the messianic psalms, were all dead ends, {in the immutability of their one-sided tendency}. In this sense Jesus' death sentence was the price he paid as the heir of these fatal dead-ends. They slew him because he held all their wealth and riches in his hand, heart, mind, and soul. He was too rich not to share in the catastrophe of the all-too-rich ancient world. {So it was his duty to be the one condemned by the king, the one sacrificed by the priest, the poem of the poet, and the one foretold by the prophet.}

---

4. ERH: See also Ephesians 2:10: *We are God's poem.* [*Poiema* becomes *workmanship* in the KJV].

But the endpoint of the four modes of speech also became the starting point. Jesus founded *the church*, because he was the fruit of all the pure lips of antiquity; he spoke into the four currents created before him. How else could he have spoken? It is true that he quoted Deuteronomy when he formulated the Golden Rule, but we are more than we say. Jesus was not contained in any of the rules and rituals, although he fulfilled and enlivened them all, whenever the poem of his life touched on their themes. He evoked the man who in his every action goes far beyond that action. When they thought he was a carpenter, he was a rabbi. When they called him a rabbi, he was a prophet. When they called him a prophet he was the Messiah. And when they thought he was the Messiah, he revealed himself as the *One* who alone had listened to the free God, the living God only. His real life was always one step ahead of his social role. This excess is "man" in the Christian era. Man is the being that does not adapt. (For John Scotus Eriugena, Bonaventura, and Cusanus, all *excessus mentis*, "excess of mind," is the official expression for the path of a Christian's soul out of her mental prisons.)

We are the children of listening. Because we listen to our parents, we bear their name. Because we listen to the constellations and business cycles of our social world, we are children of our times. Because we listen {to the siren song of poetry}, we are children of nature. And because we listen to the call of our destiny, we are sons and daughters of revolution, {of the future}. Jesus is the son of God. He fulfills and completes the four "listening posts" of the:

> the child of the ancestors,
> the child of the eons,
> the child of nature, and
> the child of prophecy.

He showed, however, that they could only be fulfilled here and now, before our eyes, now in this acceptable year of the Lord which we call "today." One had to become free of all the laws of the four listening posts before one could re-fill them in new life. Jesus was the son of ritual, the son of all spoken words, but by showing himself free of their particular authorities, he became the founder of a new language in which they were all fused for a new start (John 8:25).[5]

And here we come to our dilemma in speaking about him. The nineteenth century cut Jesus' connection with his past. It was an artistic century; it loved life and hated suffering. {It didn't like crosses:} why did he have to die? It concentrated on the life of Christ. Biographies became the fashion,

---

5. [ERH's reading of the verse resembles the Douay-Rheims NT: asked *Who art thou?* Jesus answers *The beginning, who also speak unto you.*]

and so Jesus too acquired a biography. That was new, and quite the opposite of the Christian tradition, which had been "thanatography." A biography ends with the death of the "biographee." Jesus' story only makes sense if his death begins and antecedes our lives. A Christian is a person to whom he already speaks; the body of Christ consists of those who listen to him. But the biographical craze has produced a state of mind according to which it is enough for a Christian to talk *about* Christ and call *himself* a Christian. {And this although the only question he raised is, "Have I sealed the ancient world to you? Do you live after me? Are you free of tribe, profession, audience, and prophecy?"}

To the Rousseau-ites of our days, Jesus is the innocent adolescent, the YMCA hero, the good little boy. The biographers have robbed him of his real name, for he is no longer of any interest to us unless he is the Word. We have shown that true speech means making the fruits of the ends into beginnings. If Jesus' tomb is not the womb of the Christian era, we had better forget his entire story as a fairytale. {The void opens if, when the church speaks of Jesus, he is no longer the vine and we are no longer the branches. He only lived once.}

No criticism of biblical criticism can reverse what has happened. We have written {slightingly} of Jesus, as if he were a speechless child of nature. On the other hand, the history of speech demands that we reconquer Christ's place in its dialectic that is His by right. As the Word that became flesh, Jesus is owed the central position in the history of speech. {But the Nazis, the Jews, the Fascists, the Chinese, and the Marxists deny that the Word is our true ancestor.}

That is our dilemma: for modern men, Jesus is just a man who lived from the year 3 before our era to 28 (or 29 or 33) after its beginning. Neither date is of any concern to us. On the other hand, speech had run its full course with the Red Indians, the Egyptians, the Greeks, and the Jews. Though we no longer speak any of their four languages, and we think none of their thoughts, we can understand them very well indeed. Their meaning lies open to us; we see through them. And for our peace of mind we must discover the reason. How can we make the fruits of the biographical century of Christianity into a seed for our understanding of speech?

Our first steps beyond the critical, analytical, and biographical century should be frankly egotistical. The distress of our time demands the reconquest of the wave continuum of the spirit. We too must speak, and we cannot speak if we are not certain that we stand in the continuum of speech. Speech and love have this in common, that both must be discovered once, for the first time, by each of us, and that they are nevertheless universal. In our first love, we simultaneously discover the time-continuum of all love.

The continuity of history, the order of the universe, the destiny of Man—all are unveiled before the soul who falls in love for the first time. {Because the soul has been seized by love, her eyes are opened and her ears become organs of recognition.} She can solve riddles; she can decipher the flowers and the stars; she can talk, sing, and shout for joy.

To be loved by one other person is to know every phase of time. And the eloquence of love hails from the assuredness that all creatures speak in one tongue. As speakers as well as lovers, we need assurance that we move in a continuum, that our discovery of real life and our words make sense, forever and ever. Otherwise we go mad and all spirit leaves us. It is impossible to assume that when we speak we do anything different from the peoples of all times. Our speech would remain up in the air, a meaningless stammering, unless we have the right to believe that all speech is legitimate and authorized as one and the same life-process from the first day Man spoke to the last. It is, therefore, literally in self-defense that I have to live down the two dogmas of science:

1. that a man's life ends with his death, and
2. that a man's words are only a means of expressing his thoughts.

These two dogmas rob our words of all meaning, and the last fifty years of catastrophe are the logical answer to them.[6] These dogmas are the obvious nonsense of a science that treats man as a part of nature. Against both these dogmas I maintain that we are the fruit of lips and that our lips shall bear fruit. I am satisfied that this makes sense. It restores my right to listen and to speak. But this, like all sense, demands universal application. I have tried to assure the reader that Jesus is the fruit of the four streams of speech that preceded him: he is the fruit of the lips of all antiquity.

My reply to the historical, artistic, literary, biographical, and critical century has been strictly linguistic. God did not just permit an ahistorical little wildflower to blossom somewhere in Palestine. All mankind participated in making this one man, and in as far as we spoke fruitfully, logically, in context, and in a binding manner, and {it only has a future thanks to him}.[7]

We have sketched the four streams of speech that end at the cross in our early chapters.[8] But at the same time the cross also blocks our way back to each of these streams. I may not relapse into tribal ritual or Pharaoh's sky-world; Hitler, who tried to do just that, stands revealed as a madman. And

---

6. [1964 - 50 = 1914.]
7. [1954: The following section was headed "The Heart and the Lips."]
8. [See ERH, *Die Sprache* I, 35–85.]

the other streams are similarly blocked: the modern Greeks, the physicists, and the modern Jews, the Zionists, are certainly not the Greeks or Jews of antiquity. The Greeks glorified the beauty of the universe; our physicists empty it of meaning. The Jews glorified nothing but God; the Zionists raised a university as the first public building in Jerusalem. So the roadblock of the Word is simply a fact; not one of the streams of the speech of ancient men surges through us directly any more.

Since this is so, we must consider Jesus the seed of all speech of our era. As listeners and speakers, as singers and teachers, we are the fruits of his lips. If that is to be more than a play on words, we must inquire boldly into the question of "lips." However wonderful his words may have been, we can no longer listen to the lips of the living Jesus. His lips must reach us nevertheless, but how are we to recognize them?

Answering that question is the task of this chapter: the historically effective lips of Jesus were the four gospels. *The four gospels of Matthew, Mark, Luke, and John are the lips of the risen Christ.* They bespeak the meaning of his death. They are the lips that tell us what it means that his heart broke—and we are expected to be fruits of those lips in turn.

In self-defense a man may take desperate measures, even make bold to acquire a clear conception of fruitful speech. Because Jesus is the road-block that separates us from the fruitful rivers of ancient speech, we must acquire an understanding of his "lips." How were these lips formed? Can it be said that for us, the four gospels are the lips of the Word at his crucifixion? Obviously they cannot suffice unless they avail themselves of all the powers of pre-Christian speech and in doing so, progress beyond anything that had ever been said before.

But can that be true? And why four gospels? Why not one or two? It is our hypothesis that the four gospels are the lips whose fruit we are expected to be, and that they are *his* lips. It follows then that since the four gospels are one organ, his lips, the secret of their unity is *the* secret we must come to understand.

The "naturalistic" century of biblical criticism knew very well that the very existence of the crucified Christ's "lips" would have spoiled their own search for Jesus, the merely natural man. And the biblical critics concentrated their attack in this one argument: that we should not read the four gospels as four. Accordingly, they were traced back to one (this was done by reducing three of them to one and discarding one). Behind the first three "Synoptic" gospels, [Conrad Hermann] Weisse placed a common source, the famous "Q," which we were supposed to believe was the document on which they were all based. The gospel of John however was stripped of its character as a source and relegated to somewhere in the second century, from which remove it could not have much power as witness for the facts. Thus St. John became "legend," while the three synoptic gospels were unified by tracing them to a single written source. Consequently none of them could be considered part of a unified whole, because none could be better than their common "source."

Once the three synoptic gospels were reduced to one source, they became mere material for the reconstruction of the life of Jesus from the remaining material. To "explain" Jesus, Reitzenstein used the oriental mystery cults, Dibelius drew on artistic precursors, Scholem Asch made use of rabbinical traditions. Jesus became in turn the expression of one of the styles or fashions of the life that preceded him. As a roadblock he was simply removed. He now belonged to the same ancient world {from which he was meant to have redeemed us}! He spoke, thought, prayed, and taught like many men of ancient times. There was no reason to make much fuss over this little man from the "Orient." Anatole France summed it all up in Pontius Pilate's remark to a friend: Pilate is sitting on the Riviera, reviewing his interesting career, and says: "Jesus of Nazareth? *Je ne me rapelle pas.*"[9] And indeed there was nothing particularly memorable left behind; according to the critics, Jesus became a souvenir of antiquity. It is no overstatement for me to say that the scholarly reduction of the four gospels to the rubble of mere source-material is the precondition of this result.

But what could convince modern man that the gospels are anything better? In a negative sense, the eagerness to reduce the gospels to practically one has subsided today. What had that eagerness accomplished? The critics had "proven" that a gospel written in Greek, Mark's, was composed first—indeed, there is not much they have not "proven." They had reached the point, for instance, that no one believed the Letter to the Hebrews was written to the Hebrews![10] In other words, every single stone of our tradition was pulled down and turned upside down and made to say the opposite of what it said. But this period of turning things upside down is at an end. It doesn't interest me.

For readers who cannot study the question, I will mention a few facts which put the whole era "from Reimarus to Wrede" in its quest for a historical Jesus in jeopardy. They now form a roadblock against {future} reductionists. We will never locate a historical Jesus "behind" the so-called "material." {Here are the facts:[11]}

9. [France, *Procurateur*, 37.]

10. ERH: Chapman, *MML*, 187n. [Chapman only reports on the consensus in Germany in 1910, which he also finds dubious. See Appendix I, 321.]

11. [These are *facts* to ERH in part because of the complete agreement between De Bruyne and Harnack on dating the gospels. See Appendix I, 337–50.]

1. John writes as an eye-witness who knows the minutest details when he cares to mention them. The apostle is the author of the gospel, and that is why it carries authority.

2. All four gospels are apostolic. Matthew was the converted publican among the apostles {, and he wrote under the eyes of Peter and the sons of Zebedee and Jesus' brother in Jerusalem before the year 42.} Mark obeyed Peter. Luke lived with Paul. John dictated to a Greek secretary.

3. Matthew wrote in Hebrew, not in Aramaic, and he was the first to write.[12]

4. Mark states bluntly that he is quoting Matthew.[13]

These four facts refute in the simplest possible way all the critics who deny the quadrilateral of the four authoritative gospels. I mention these facts for the comfort of those souls who have been intimidated by their awe of this "scholarship." I was brought up among the most outstanding source critics of those days—one of my first books was dedicated to one of them, I. Vahlen,[14] and I myself did a lot of work with sources, with unknown authors, and in reconciling related sources. In 1912, working with a thirteenth-century manuscript in an archive, I read the following sentence on the parchment: "*Multi enim studio contradicendi amiserunt sensum.*" ("In their eagerness to contradict at all costs, many lose the meaning.") {I took fright.} To *contradict* is one thing. Everyone is free to do so, but he may not pretend that his contradiction can ever pull a positive solution out of the mind's magic hat.

Applied to the Bible that means: it is not everyone's business to read the Bible as lips whose fruit the reader is to be. We all have the right to say: "I don't believe that John wrote his gospel," or "we can't know when it was written." We may oppose our "no" to any statement that comes our way from another person, but we may never replace the repudiated statement with a positive statement, solely on the basis of speculation—and that is exactly what the biblical critics have done. They weren't satisfied with merely disbelieving tradition; they had to supply us with a positive statement of who wrote the real story, how it really happened, when the gospels were written, and for what partisan purposes.

---

12. [See note, 76 and Appendix I, 325-27.]

13. [Otto Kroesen suggests that the fourth statement refers to Chapman, *MML*, 5-8. See Appendix I, 319-20.]

14. [Johannes Vahlen, professor of philology with whom ERH studied in Berlin, during Vahlen's last semesters there.]

It is not given to the mind to know reality by negation. Our tradition may be wrong or untrustworthy, but then we just don't have the right tradition; no logical somersaults can produce the "real story." When the mind pretends to act as the creator of actual facts, we have the story of *gnosis* all over again. In education, it is *gnosis* to tell people how education should be and then think: "Now they are educated." In history, it is *gnosis* rules to tell people how history might have been and then think: "Now that's the way it was."

This insight into the negative aspect of a century of criticism shook a great man so deeply that he shelved his fame as an expert in biblical criticism, studied medicine, and went out to Africa {to become a mission doctor.} Before Albert Schweitzer left Europe, he published a book which expressed this insight, his famous *Final Criticism of 150 Years' Search for the Life of Jesus*. In retrospect we may well bestow that title on his book of long ago (1908); its first title was "*From Reimarus to Wrede: A History of the Research on the Life of Jesus*."[15] Schweitzer's departure from Europe for the speechless physical world of the jungle was precipitated by the negative work of the critics. His insight into their failure cured him for quite a while, but in the end his scholarly habits returned and he relapsed: what he had forbidden himself to do for Jesus he now did for Paul. His big volume on the mysticism of the apostle Paul is built along the very lines that he had condemned in research on Jesus.

So Schweitzer became a tragic figure {who broke a magic spell by casting criticism aside and yet never really escaped it}. This may serve as a warning to us all that the work of 150 years can't just be laid aside by a mere act of will. As Schweitzer only negated negation, he failed to establish a new position. When his faith required a positive language again, he fell back into the grooves of received thought. In his preface to his *Mysticism of Paul the Apostle*, Schweitzer is well aware of his own dilemma; he admits that he reads the New Testament as source material and attempts to reconstruct someone's bygone religion from it. The New Testament is definitely not the lips of a voice that created a new dimension of speech, a dimension in which all generations of Man may become brothers and become one. On the contrary, as a son of nature, Schweitzer tries to prove to himself and his readers that every generation has a different spirit.[16]

---

15. [The first edition appeared in 1906, not 1908; a substantially revised edition appeared in 1913. The English translation of the 1906 edition, *The Quest of the Historical Jesus*, appeared in 1910; the revised edition did not appear in English until 2001. Reimarus and Wrede were the scholars Schweitzer set as the end-brackets of the *quest*, because with them, the arguments had come full circle. Bultmann (and others) have since decided to revive the *quest* anyway.]

16. ERH: On this point see Werner Picht, *Albert Schweitzer* (1962). [Picht's *Albert*

III | THE FRUIT OF OUR LIPS

Certainly, every generation has a different spirit, but is it not equally certain that the man who is called the Alpha and Omega, the beginning and end of all times, was just as aware of that fact as Albert Schweitzer, as Paris fashion designers, New York headline-writers, or the German youth movement? It was in fact precisely these spirits of the different times and places that Jesus {summoned}. He decided to do something about the Schweitzers of his day and all days, and he proclaimed that we can apply a power in the world by which these spirits can be laid. Because these ghosts and spirits of the times were uppermost in his mind, he called this new power the "Sane Ghost" or the "healing spirit."

When Schweitzer wrote about Paul, he took on the man who was the first to apply this power on a colossal scale: by Schweitzer's scholarly standard (as opposed to the witness of his practical life-work), both Jesus and Paul fail in their avowed purpose to connect all times to one another, {even though it is loudly stated in the first Letter to the Corinthians and the Letter to the Ephesians}.[17]

In following the vicissitudes of this great and admirable Christian and (to my mind) utterly incomprehensible theologian Albert Schweitzer, I have had to ask myself if I am any better equipped than he was. My great advantage, as I see it, is that I have never been a minister or a theologian by profession. Instead, I was nourished at the very springhead of the art of scrutinizing texts, which when it spread to the theologians made them believe in the mind's gnostic creativity; it made them into history-gnostics. Knowing their premises all too well, I shied away from that vicious circle of first getting a lifetime position that offered a livelihood for dealing with certain authoritative texts, of then spending that lifetime demolishing those texts, and finally, as the result of that demolition, of replacing them with the "real" tradition. We may not wish to be the fruits of his lips, of the gospels; but who is interested in being taught, with great seriousness, as the result of a lifetime of study, that there *never were* any lips?

So I was spared both the temptation that resulted in Schweitzer's book on St. Paul, and the shock that shipped him off to Africa. My approach to the Word that created our era is not confused by {such Scyllas of} theological illusion and {Charybdises of} disillusionment. Instead, I remained convinced that the century of "nature" had simply asked the wrong questions. The critics of both the Bible and Homer were loyal and honest believers in Rousseau, Thomas Aquinas, and Aristotle, and their three authorities all

---

Schweitzer: Leben und Bedeutung appeared in 1960; the English translation (*The Life and Thought of Albert Schweitzer*) appeared in 1964.]

17. [I Cor 3:10–11? Eph 1:4–10? 2:47? Because he read the NT in the original, ERH's references are not always clear unless specified.]

taught that speech was man's natural equipment; the whole house of criticism was raised on the foundation of this dogmatic assumption.

In the face of this naturalistic dogma, how could Jesus be The Word—how could John say "In the beginning was the Word"—how could Matthew cite Jesus' phrase, "I will truly be with you until the end of the world"—and especially, how could the four Evangelists be inspired if man's words were only data for dictionaries and grammar books? They could not. The dogma that speech is as natural to man as it is to the apes compelled four or five generations of professional researchers to produce every imaginable theory of reduction and atomization, just to reduce the gospels to source material. The critics impressed the world and themselves with their own greater honesty and sincerity. Compared to them the fundamentalists often had no brilliance, no wit, and no guts—and in fact the brilliance of this century of analysis was more than fireworks. It was *a genuine outburst of the natural mind.*

And what is the natural mind? The natural mind hopes to know nature, to use and manipulate her. The critics hoped to use the Bible as mere nature, as the source material for a new natural history of humanity, the coming [*natural*] science of evolution. They thought that undertaking such a natural history was possible because their lecture halls and libraries were firmly established in the shadow of the hallowed institutions of church and state. Little did they know that in our era scholarship rests upon both a bond between scholars and laypeople called "church," and a common order of freedom that we call "state."

Before we may criticize at leisure, *we must be at leisure*. No science of Man is truly scientific that remains ignorant of this, its own premise. The premise of a common peace within which the critic may criticize means that the critic himself must maintain the unity and continuity of speech through all ages and with all human groups. For peace is the fruit of speech and is not to be had otherwise, and scholarship presupposes and requires peace. Once this has been understood, speech ceases to be an "object" of the natural sciences. The peace the scholar requires and the speech he would make the object of his studies stand revealed as one and the same process.

In order to remain strictly scholarly, we have divided languages, faiths, and histories into infinite splinters—Aramaic, Spanish, Basque, Masurian—but still counted on the masses' patient faith in scholarship, on their love of truth, on their hope in the coming brotherhood between the scholarly and the untutored. {That was how "Jesus the Adolescent" was fabricated, how Jesus and Judas were psychoanalyzed, how the Jesus myth was written—in short, scholarship sawed away at the faith, hope, and love of the masses whom they still expected to honor them! You may respond to some details in Emmanuel Quint, the weak-minded twin Gerhart Hauptmann dreamed up for Jesus, or in the sentimental little boy to be found in Scholem Asch's work, but never in a million years could those idiots make the individual and the masses of one heart and one mind. We may as well say farewell to free inquiry!} All this might be true, of course, but the road-block to the linguistic past would still be there, Jesus or no Jesus. We live in a different world than Cicero or Gamaliel, Montezuma, or Red Jacket of the Seneca tribe. To define our world is in everyone's interest.

It is not a question of the interests of theologians like Schweitzer or philologists like Bultmann, but of all those who long to live in peace after the two World Wars that nearly threw us back into a truly pre-Christian, pre-Homeric, and pre-Mosaic world. My defense against this assault on my peace, my world, and my era, is based on the *one* dogma that *speech is a continuum*. Now the four Evangelists insist that something happened to this very continuum in their days, and I propose to ask what it was that happened.

The path to my discovery seems obvious in retrospect, and I will try to show the skeleton of my logic. All four Evangelists say unanimously: speaking and writing must be changed, because both have in fact been changed by the Word. If all four are not lying, their own speech and writing must bear evidence of this alleged change. If we can prove that their speech differs, and discover how it differs, from everything that had been said before, the change of which they try to convince us and the change that speech underwent in their gospels will have to be one and the same. "Conversion," "faith," "salvation," "revelation," "speaking in tongues," "outpouring of the Holy Spirit"—all these nearly dead expressions would have to agree with the process that can be observed in the texts of their gospels. That would prove their case.[18]

To sum up: the Evangelists themselves must be the documents of the linguistic change worked by the Word, but the four Evangelists with their new way of speaking need not be the only documents for such a change. Faithful Christians have always been impressed by the change in the nature of Man worked by martyrs and missionaries. To an orthodox Christian, an apostle like Paul, both missionary and martyr, will seem a better witness than Luke's text, and the broad masses will always be attracted by relics, miracles, cathedrals, and monasteries. But for pure reason, for *scholarship*, for the intellect, neither bones nor stones will ever prove that a change of mind occurred. The scholarly conscience in all of us rebels against mere external evidence: monks can be found in India, martyrs and disciples in China, holy shrines in Thailand and Yucatan, cathedrals in Mexico. The mind does not and need not ever admit a historical change in human nature

---

18. [1954: The following section was headed "The 'Speech' of the Four Gospels."]

on such a basis, because it is not the mind's business to trust or believe in external evidence. But the mind cannot help believing in a change of thinking based on a change in style.

The believer has no need of our arguments; in the meantime, however, we shall instruct the unbeliever. We must show him the crucible in which style was chemically transformed, so to speak. In our times it is neither the soul nor the body that is unable to understand Christianity as the precondition of their own truth, but the "mind." Until it succeeds in equating the process by which it *itself* arrives at truth with the process that is conjugated through the four gospels, the mind will never cease to accuse Christianity of being as dead as a dodo and of never having been anything more than a {simultaneously} helpful and scandalous myth.

The "four gospels"—we will use the quotation marks when we refer to them in the singular, as a whole—can prove one thing: the Word changed the world of the mind once and for all. In antiquity, a book was closed to all other books; an ancient school of philosophy was closed to all other schools; a book had a beginning and an end, two covers contained it. That is not true of the four gospels. They respond to a dead-end, to an end of the world. They move through time, and when they end, they have scarcely begun. At the end of all four gospels, John says that the whole universe isn't big enough to contain all the books that could be written about Jesus.[19] That sounds fantastic, but after all, today even this chapter of mine bears witness to the fact that John's cheerful confidence was well-founded. In his youth John must have been just as boyishly merry as his master, for as a very old man John still brags that he could once run faster than Peter (John 20:4).[20] The oldest apostle closed his gospel with a remark of {such} frivolity {that bureaucrats can only furrow their brows at it.} That lack of gravity is a remarkable characteristic of the New Testament or, to put it more carefully, of the whole to which the four gospels are stanzas.[21]

The cheerful exuberance at the end of the "four gospels" contrasts with the tone of the beginning. The "four gospels" open with great circumspection. Matthew is dignified, serious, proceeding cautiously. Through all four gospels we can observe how it becomes easier and easier to speak of the event. There is an acceleration, a growth in articulation and assurance, in all

---

19. ERH: In 1893, Heinrich Julius Holtzman called this *unspeakable hyperbole*, which one would do better to ignore [*Hand-commentar*, 206].

20. ERH: Chesterton closes his glorious essay on Jesus with the gigantic word *mirth* [*Orthodoxy*, 299. See Appendix I, 321].

21. ERH: I am glad that Hubert Cunliffe-Jones poses this question of mine in "The Fourfold Gospel," 14–24. [See Appendix I, 322–23.]

four parts—every one of the gospels displays it—but the growth, although identical in all four cases, finds a very different expression in each case.

The second gospel expresses this growth by its brevity; Mark has 677 verses compared to Matthew's 1,072. Many reasons have been proposed for this abbreviation, as I am well aware, but any stylist knows that a short treatment of a theme usually betrays a greater confidence on the author's part than a long one. {Every succeeding author must abbreviate.} For Peter, who inspired Mark, the issue must have seemed to need less argument. Where Matthew had given complete speeches, Mark was allowed to write that he would make do with a few quotations. {There was much Palestinian local color that was of no interest to the listeners in Rome and in Rome's world.}

Again, Luke peacefully writes two volumes for his deacon, even making references to other writers. We may imagine that he writes neither in the suspense, penury, and danger that Matthew knew; nor in the vestry of the catacombs, both bending before Peter and spurred on by his vehemence, as Mark did; but sitting instead in a room stocked with books and documents, {like Jerome in his study}—at some leisure and with time to reflect on the needs of his pupil Theophilus. What an immense change: from Matthew, the first advocate of Jesus' new world before the great world of the Bible, who speaks to enemies; to the deacon and secretary of Peter, who is eager to do justice to the authority of the prince of apostles; and from him to Luke, who after his master Paul's death has the freedom to teach a faithful young disciple.

And yet there is an even greater growth of articulation to come. For when John dictated to his Greek secretary, he was liberated from all earthly pressure. The pressures brought to bear on Matthew by his enemies, on Mark by his concern for his following, and on Luke by his duty to teach, were all absent. In John the highest degree of artistic, visionary, and rational power is coupled with a childlike exuberance; he takes pains to correct the most intimate details of the tradition in the midst of sublime poignancy. John begins with the superlative: "In the beginning was the Word" and thereby completes the end of Matthew: "I shall be with you until the end of the world, every day." {Together then they enclose end and beginning!} But he ends not with {a fading echo of} a solemn vision of all the times, but with an outburst of youthful enthusiasm {for the glory at the center of them, surrounded by the world's beauty}! "The space of the universe would not suffice to contain all the books about Jesus." Faith, which began with Matthew trembling, with the one undisputable point: "Jesus may rightly be called 'Son of David and Abraham,'" –{by the time John writes, that faith has become an ocean, {on which the believer's ship gains endless time}.

Compared with Peter's virile orders to Mark: "Cut that," "that's enough"; with Luke's broad narrative "as I said before"; with John's "I could go on forever"; Matthew visibly bears the burden of being the loneliest because he is the first. Yet to a superficial eye, John may seem the loneliest for writing in such solitude, while Luke is entrenched in his study like an academic, Mark is at least protected by a faithful congregation, and Matthew confronts a crowd of opponents, trying to get a hearing. But loneliness or solitude in speech is something quite different from isolation for lack of physical contact: we may be lonely in New York and find ourselves very social mentally on a mountaintop. The four gospels show how language, style, or articulation are created by the degree of our moral loneliness {or brotherhood}.

The publican and sinner Matthew had to stand on his careful brief before the entire synagogue and temple of Jerusalem. They are in power; he is an outcast, {or at least a suspect}. Compare him to John, who with perfect assurance labels the holy city Jerusalem both "world" and "darkness" in his first chapter. {That seems natural to us:} she had vanished by the time he wrote. John already lived in the newly ascendant church, which together with him sees the light, perceives the Word, and lurches youthfully forward to greet with joy the Lord's coming into his own. For John, isolation faces Zion, not him.

Matthew wrote while the ramparts of Zion still looked proudly down on him. When he pleaded his case, he could hardly have expected to be allowed to dwell in peace in Jerusalem any longer; he was a wayfarer on a road that led him out of and away from the old order of things. Matthew's gospel is a farewell plea, a last attempt to persuade Jerusalem that it had slain the Just One, because the Jews no longer had the patience to await a radical shift in God's government of the world. Yet it was just this prophetic expectation that had been Israel's only *raison d'etre* in the midst of the world. Obviously then, Matthew's plea had to give Jerusalem its due and its rightful place, and open himself to the new time-reckoning, all in one breath. Everyone knows that Matthew cites a wealth of Biblical passages, but it is no longer enough to know it. Since he was the first author of a gospel, Matthew had no New Testament and no part of a New Testament that would have given him authority to declare the Bible of his day an Old Testament. That someone quotes the Bible need not impress us—even the Devil may quote scripture—but the linguistic significance of the first gospel lies elsewhere. In writing his gospel, Matthew transformed the Bible of his time into the Old Testament. For all readers of Matthew it was already an accomplished fact; for Matthew it was an accomplishment he was quite unaware of before he was done.

In his gospel, Matthew progresses from speaking as a Jew to speaking as a non-Jew—the text is plain. In his first chapter, Matthew begins: "This is the book of the birth of Jesus the Christ, the son of David, the Son of Abraham." In the same first chapter, verse 21, we read: "Jesus shall free his people from their sins." Obviously, we are in Israel, for Matthew seems to see no necessity to explain the "his" in "his people" at all.[22] But by the 28th and final chapter, Matthew's eloquence has carried him beyond the Jewish world. When he comes to reporting the machinations of the priests and elders among the Jews, he writes, "this [has been] common talk among the Jews to this day" [28:15]. Here the Jews are no longer divided into those who believe in Christ and those who do not; the Jews, as Jews, are outside Matthew's family. The fence between them and Matthew is infinitely higher in the 28th chapter than in the first. The outpouring of his experiences, his memories, and his notes changed the writer's own mind.

Every author should become a different person in the course of writing his book. No professor of literature worth his salt would deny the transforming power of writing a great poetic work. A book that is the fruit of lived life separates the man who writes it from the period of his life in which it grew. Fruits always make epoch because their harvest closes the cycle of the seasons: autumn makes the whole preceding year irretrievable.

The wisdom of our tradition consists in the fact that in the first gospel a man writes himself out of Israel by writing up Jesus. Thus, he makes real, makes visible, to his readers that to write "about Jesus" means to reduce the Bible to the Old Testament. That could never have been achieved with argument. A clever lawyer may prove any case by statements, claims, and quotations and yet remain unmoved himself; many people have written essays, perfect logical treatments of Christianity, to prove its claims or refute them—but that doesn't make them into Evangelists. An Evangelist is a man who, by speaking of Jesus, changes his own mind and, because he is in the process himself, leads others into the same process. Matthew's gospel institutes a process {whose power changes the face of the world—and of Israel—for} Christianity is the world as it always was, plus Jesus' death.

Matthew's gospel was the first proof that this *one* addition to the world makes a difference to the world of speech, that everything in the world would have be rewritten in the light of this event. For had Matthew not begun faithfully with purely biblical argument? Had he not begun by writing within "his" people and about them? Modern readers often get bored with the first chapter of Matthew, because the genealogy from Joseph to David and Abraham seems so unimportant, but without it Matthew himself could never have brought himself or his Christian readers to the point where "his people" cease to be his people or theirs!

---

22. ERH: *His* is explicitly stated in the Greek text.

Matthew wrote his gospel standing upright and pleading in danger of his life, and thereby abandoned his Jewish allegiance. He reversed the meaning of the Bible by experiencing that it was no longer the *last* word. The last sentence of his gospel—which the critics have rejected because it does indeed takes us to a new plane—expresses this fact very simply: {"Baptize them in the name of the Father, the Son, and the Holy Spirit."} Instead of the Bible being the last word for the Jews, we are told that Jesus will be with *us* until the end of the world. In this *one* sentence Jesus' short life on earth acquires such momentum that the tiny addition to the world which that life seemed to be at best, suddenly swells to gigantic proportions.

In this one sentence the full power of that addition falls on the reader. This one life rebalances the scales of mankind's history with its own weight; in the other pan lie the times from Adam to Abraham and David and down to the days {of Herod}. In this sentence, which dares to speak of all future history as separate from the Jewish Bible, the gospel becomes gospel in the full meaning of the word, since for the first time the past becomes the past and {the Old Testament} the Old Testament. This is all the more remarkable since Matthew surely had no inkling of the fate of his own book. Since he originally wrote in Hebrew, not in Aramaic,[23] he could hardly expect that it would be preserved in translation as the first book of a Greek canon.[24]

We may now move on and turn our attention to the drama within each gospel, as we have discovered it for Matthew. {Let us start with Luke. Matthew discovered that the Bible was the Testament of a by-gone past.} Together the two books of Luke, the gospel and Acts, form one coherent drama. Paul had not known Jesus in the flesh and does not care to quote his sayings, and yet Paul is able to preach the gospel with the power of a "world heart" as "the right arm of Jesus," as he was later called. Luke's gospel and Acts in combination reveal the identity of Christ. Paul and Jesus, Christ in the flesh and Christ in Paul, are the pillars of the bridge that Luke finds that he has built, much to his own surprise. The "abrupt" ending of Acts has often been criticized. But is it abrupt? Luke's gospel ends: "And they worshipped him and returned to Jerusalem with great joy and were continually in the temple praising and blessing God."[25] His Acts of the Apostles ends: "And Paul dwelt two whole years in his own hired house, and received all that came in unto him, preaching the kingdom of God, and teaching those things which concern the Lord Jesus Christ, with all confidence, no man

---

23. ERH: Grintz, "Hebrew," 32–47. [Grintz changed ERH's mind—in 1944, ERH had written that Matthew wrote in Aramaic. See Appendix I, 325–27.]

24. ERH: I am well aware that some critics assume a Greek original of Matthew's Gospel.

25. [KJV.]

forbidding him."[26] {Hold on to that "great joy" and "all confidence," the way they close the books and identify them.} Now compare the beginning of the two books: the gospel begins with the birth of Jesus, the Acts of the Apostles with the birth of the Church. {Birth is the beginning and joy the ending both times. Where in Matthew a worldly process makes all mankind Jews, in Luke the same process makes Rome into Jerusalem. So here too we miss the sense of the scripture if we treat it as "material." Its purpose is to force us to our own change of mind. No Communist is as thorough a materialist as the biblical critics have been.}

That at the end Paul is in Rome and the temple now stands there, astonishes Luke. {It is true that in today's literature textbooks the first sentence reads: "We write books to make money." Where this sentence is valid, the author sits cynically grinning at the tricks that seduce the customer to buy. A servant of the Word, as Luke understands the expression, *has to* write because otherwise he cannot understand his own heart. In Peter and Paul, the Christ that lived in Jesus lives on for a second generation; Paul's martyrdom doesn't belong in the process and progression we have found in Luke. The thesis that the Acts of the Apostles remained unfinished and ought to have closed with Paul's death is about as profound as the scholarly idea that Homer's *Iliad* "actually" should have ended, or in fact did end, with the death of Achilles. }

{In his duplicate stories, Luke discovered the Holy Spirit's victory over the sequence of the generations, and as he went along he discovered that his report on Jesus in the flesh in Israel and of the Holy Spirit's deeds (Acts 1,2) among the Gentiles (Acts 28, 29) ran *parallel*. But just as Peter managed to keep Mark from including any praise of Peter, so Luke writes not for the glory of Paul, but for the glory of the Lord.} If he had reported Paul's death at the end of Acts—the equivalent of the *Iliad* ending with Achilles' death— he would have destroyed his recognition of the Holy Spirit as "Christ once more." And why did it become Luke's task to unite two generations—Jesus and the apostles—with each other? Why was it necessary to make the parallel between the baptism by fire and the birth of the child in Jerusalem, between Paul's travels through pagan lands with Jesus' proclamation in Israel?

The reason is obvious. Luke himself wrote for a "second-generation" Christian. The problem of "Fathers and Sons" of the spirit existed for Luke and Theophilus as it had between Jesus and the Apostles, also. {There is no inherited Christianity; nevertheless, Christianity appears to approach us in the form of an inheritance.} Luke's Acts of the Apostles parallels his gospel because Theophilus had to be changed from an heir or a Christian by

26. [KJV.]

tradition into a primary and immediate listener to the spirit. Just as Luke's writings reproduce a bridge that spans two generations, his relationship to his reader forced Theophilus to think of his own children. Insofar as Luke succeeded in making the parallel between the gospel and Acts visible, he also succeeded in constructing a bridge for Theophilus into the future church.

A modern reader may hesitate to admit this logic. Why should Theophilus teach his own children and grandchildren differently, just because he read of the parallels between the Gospel and Acts, between Judea and the Empire, between Jerusalem and Rome? What does a book have to do with our own behavior? The modern is right to hesitate: for us, reading is not a phase of action, but for Theophilus reading was something quite different. First of all, the gospel was passed on exclusively by word of mouth. "The Way," as the new life was called, was the way people dealt and spoke with each other. A first-century Christian was introduced to a way of life and, on the way, underway, told of the things necessary to make him a missionary as well—a witness, a confessor, if need be, a martyr. Hearing was nothing but the first step toward telling others. It was not a matter of curiosity, but of salvation. And this was done through the foolish method of oral preaching. The staggering novelty of a written gospel was that anything merely written should rank as gospel truth at all.[27]

Christ had not written,[28] and the whole truth of the cross was founded on his utterly superhuman faith. Who among us would dare to entrust his greatest truth to the silliness of unbelieving neighbors? But since it had once been dared, the example was set and writing was stigmatized as second-rate. It was less good, less desirable, and less trustworthy than preaching. I think that we can still imagine how Matthew wrote with "blood, sweat, and tears," and {at the same time} begged forgiveness for using ink. He needed a valid excuse, for in his day it was taught that it was one of the "fallen angels" who had "taught mankind to write and thereby made many into sinners even unto this very day. For men were not created to give confirmation of their good faith with pen and ink." (Enoch 69:10). I imagine that Matthew took the great liberty of returning to the use of the pen under the devastating impact of the stoning of Stephen: it was the first martyr's blood that permitted the use of ink in the new dispensation. I conclude that from the fact that Stephen's great speech before the priests is reflected in the first chapter of Matthew. (See below, 65–67.)

The glory of the first martyr gave weight to the first Evangelist's written words, where without Stephen they would have been highly suspect. Stephen's

---

27. [1954: The following section was headed "Ink and Blood."]
28. ERH: Vischer, "Rechtfertigung," 320–36 [See Appendix I, 337].

great defense of the spirit's transfer into new forms had to be salvaged, and since Stephen paid for it with his life, the new message would not be defiled by ink. Only with the greatest resistance were written gospels allowed on the new "way," and they were in any case only meant to be read aloud.

We are crazy enough to ask everyone: "Why don't you write?" But with the first disciples of the new spirit it was the other way around: Must we write? May we write? Dare we write? And truth clings to this chastity of mind, which has become even rarer today than the chastity of bodies. *When must we write?* When our lives or those of others are in danger, in self-defense, when it is the only way to maintain our identity in a crisis. We must speak and write and teach and testify when the peace of our soul or our very selves would otherwise disintegrate. A new style is only created under the most extreme pressure.

Matthew won the right to use his pen as a sword when the blood of martyrs reddened the soil of Palestine.[29] Similarly, Mark wrote when the arena and the cross awaited Peter in Rome. Now we maintain that Luke wrote in similar excitement, or under similar pressure, and that is not so obvious. He didn't live in the centers of danger; he lived to the ripe old age of 84—somewhere in Greece, as the canon of the gospels reports. Ernst Renan liked his style so much that he called Luke's gospel the most beautiful book ever written. Now, Renan had a Greek mentality, and his praise may well embarrass us, for Greeks are delighted by the light and playful touch; the emphatic disturbs them because it is less than elegant.

In fact the pressure in Luke is quite different from that which apparent danger arouses in Matthew and Mark. Luke must have lived at leisure when he went over the origins of his faith, and yet Luke also introduces a new and specific pressure into the world of historiography. Chronicles had catalogued the annals of Rome, Paros, and Athens; historians had written of the spirit of Rome that conquered the world in fifty years, and the spirit of the Athenians under Pericles. Similarly, each of the various books of the Old Testament bear witness to the specific mentality of one period. The books that go by Moses' name, the Song of Songs, Jeremiah, Judges, Kings—all bear witness to the transfer of the one spirit into innumerable expressions.

But Luke's first sentence {changes all that}. The inter-temporal character of the spirit becomes his theme: *to be inspired means to translate.* by fixing his attention on the seam between the times, Luke became the first human being who was able to see the spirits of two periods together and put into words the fact that they both serve one spirit, that both are subservient

---

29. [Henry Parry Liddon's famous phrase from *Passiontide Sermons.*]

to the Spirit of all spirits: "ministers of the word," and to "minister" in Greek means no more than to be subservient.

The very meaning of the expression "Holy Spirit" is lost if we fail to hold fast to the idea that it opens the spirits of different times to one another. Any peaceful group of people may have the right spirit in gaiety, harmony, and friendship, without having the Holy Spirit; yet nowadays we treat the right and the wrong spirits as if they moved on the same plane. For Luke that spirit alone is holy which has power over the many fashions of the ages. These fashions of the ages, these spirits of the times, are genuine and real; each generation has its genius. Jesus' genius belonged to his own unique life—{Goethe's genius as the author of *The Sorrows of Werther*, like} Herman Melville's as the author of *Moby Dick*, was "time-conditioned."

But the Holy Spirit is genius to the second power, so to speak. God is the father of all spirits. Jesus' discovery was that genius is not enough, and so he sacrificed his genius, his own spirit, for peace among the spirits of all times. His contribution to history was not his body—how many soldiers have given their bodies for the spirit of their national gods! Jesus gave up his genius because he was determined to break the recurring cycles in the affairs and business of men. He was fed up with the spirits of each individual time, including his own genius, and that is why he didn't write a book. He wanted to turn the hearts of every generation toward one another without considering the mental fashion of their times {or even his own! That is what Luke 23:46 says.[30]}

Luke was privileged to be the first man permitted to show this change in the meaning of the spirit in a book in two parts. In his two volumes, he shows how the one Spirit towers above the spirits. He narrates both the genius of Christ's own walk through Judea and the genius in the "acts" of the apostolic age as facets of one spirit. Ever since, people have asked their historians to communicate more than one period in an evolution. Unless we sense the one spirit at work behind the spirits of different periods, we can never be inspired by history, because then history is dead—and it is dangerous to flirt with the graves of the past. It's absurd to imitate any great man or great deed; it paralyzes us. But history is goods and raises from the dead if we penetrate behind the everyday facts and realize the sum of sacrifices and creative power behind each little well-known fact. The knowledge of historical facts is harmful unless we see through them as either inspired or corrupt.

Every great historian since Luke has admitted a plurality of spirits of the times and undertaken the effort of letting the one spirit shine through

---

30. [KJV: *And when Jesus had cried with a loud voice, he said, 'Father, into thy hands I commend my spirit': and having said thus, he gave up the ghost.*]

all of them. {Thucydides could not do it yet, and Livy even less.} Luke was awarded the first victory over the spirit of one time and the tradition of one country. His books embodied the difference between the one Spirit and the many spirits, in his own language, and between genius and the spirit, in modern terms.

This triumph could not be celebrated by theorizing "about" the spirit. It had to be done in the opposite manner, by openly admitting at every opportunity the manifold diversity of time and place. The Word, which until then had seemed to belong to specific countries and times, now proved itself one and the same in East and West, with Jesus on earth and with Christ risen. The blind fanaticism of any school of thought or national literature, even the zeal of his reader Theophilus, was purified. Theophilus was warned that in every generation the spirit could engender new forms from His loins.

The genius of any one age may never be mistaken for the Spirit of God. For we have just as much of the future as we acknowledge of our past. {Only together may past and future be our articles of faith!} If a man wishes to perish with his own time, nobody can hinder or refute him; we ourselves choose the time limits of our role on earth. In giving Theophilus's church a pre-history of more than one period and with more than one spirit, Luke also gave all Christians a post-history beyond their own period and their own lifetime. History's right to form us depends on the triumph of the power to translate over the "powers that be" in any given age. Of course, this conviction was alive in Stephen, in Matthew, and in their Master, but Luke managed to embody this truth in a literary document. {Greece told of Herakles, but only since Luke do we know of the propagation of the spirit. Saints are not heroes!}

Genius and the spirit of any one time run riot in isolation. Europe's naïve surrender to the spirit of its own *fin de siecle* plunged it into destructive war; people had delivered themselves up to their time, and the spirit of that time became a demon. {As long as we expect every time to have its own spirit, we will abide with the Hitler Youth and the Nazi massacres.} And when we expect the Holy Spirit to exist in a hot-house beyond the reach of the seasons of the human mind, we end in sterility and futility. We should begin to think of each generation as a body of time and of *the* Spirit as the one that connects all these bodies to each other.

It has taken us 1900 years to learn that. Even today, "body of time" is a new-fangled term, but it is the most exact expression and translation we have today for the spirits Luke described and how they were overcome by the Holy Spirit. If and when our times become bodies of time capable of union, we will have achieved what Luke reports in his double book about Jesus and the Apostles. {The dominion of the "one-aged" gods Zeus and

Hera was broken; the divine man is of more than one age! When Jesus said: "You will do greater things than I," he was divine—and he was divine when he resigned the second half of his life to the apostles.}

Theophilus's generation, Luke's readers, saw the fall of Jerusalem and the transition from the apostolic to the episcopal age. The church is distinguished by the rapid progress from one age to another in a breath-taking advance. What Protestantism has often criticized as the rapid corruption of original Christianity is the most excellent proof for Luke's principle of this incessant and constantly changing translation. The martyrs, the bishops, the confessors, the apologists, the Fathers, the monks, the hermits, the missionaries—all these modes of saintliness followed the apostles and Evangelists, the teachers and prophets of the church's first generation, in a rapid succession of scene-changes.

I am inclined to turn Luther's axiom on the value of original Christianity around by saying that I could not believe in the Holy Spirit if he had not relentlessly changed his form of expression. We are continually in the desperate position of having to move from genius to genius and at the same time remain united in One Spirit. It becomes harder with each century, and we must allow our young people a deliberate degree of ignorance lest their own genius be stifled. But we must all proceed out of one spirit, regardless of the multiplicity of times and places.

And that throws light on the progress in *Mark*'s gospel. Like Matthew's and Luke's, Mark's gospel is a victory over the dangers of the time. Peter was in charge of the sheep. (John was quite emphatic about this task [*of Peter's*] at the end of his gospel, and in that he agrees with Matthew.) The true relation between Jesus and the apostles would have been at risk, however, if Peter, the greatest of the apostles, had been considered Jesus' equal. {So it fell to Mark as Peter's amanuensis} to establish once and for all the uniqueness of Christ as the "Son of God." Peter, who had denied the Lord three times, now had to deny that he himself was anything more than a sinful man. If that could be shown for Peter, who was their leader, it would be accomplished for all Christians and forever.

Now Mark does precisely that. He begins simply with the statement that Jesus was the Son of God, and he closes by indicating the endless stream of mission, consisting of "subservients," who obey the {Word} and not Peter or any other carnal authority. It is more difficult to trace this negative process in Mark than the similarly negative process in Matthew. In Matthew, the order that preceded Jesus became the Old Testament; the spirit receded from Israel when Jesus came and {assumed His reign}. In Mark it was shown that Christ alone was the Son of God and would remain so. All future generations were placed under this one and only perfect incarnation because

Peter himself placed himself at an infinite distance below this same Son of God. The process in Mark protects Jesus against the future! The glorification of Peter is triumphantly obstructed and prevented. Mark says that Peter was "afraid" (9:6), while the other Evangelists don't dare to say so; he changes the singular of a word of Peter's in Matthew: "I shall" [17:4] into the more modest "we shall" [9:5]. He cuts his name out whenever an intelligent question is asked. "Peter's house" in Matthew [8:14] becomes in Mark the house to which the four apostles came [1:29]. In Mark, Peter calls himself a "Satan" without the excuse given by the other Evangelists.[31]

We may say too that the climax of Peter's self-denial is that Mark is not allowed to give the name "Peter" to one of the two disciples who see the risen Christ in Emmaus, even though Paul bluntly declares that Peter was the first who saw the risen Lord (1 Cor 15:5). In other words, in Paul's eyes, no higher credentials for an apostolate could be found than the one Mark was ordered not to mention! Luke and John took pains to excuse this silence, in their brotherly concern to mention Peter's primacy (Luke 24:13[-34];[32] John 21 [15–17]).

> In the Marcan gospel Jesus is isolated and wholly misunderstood . . . by his chosen disciples. In Mark this is of vital importance because . . . the salvation . . . is wrought . . . in complete isolation. . . . [Matthew and Luke] are unable to force this through with the staggering brutality of Mark.[33]

The temptation Mark fought is well documented in 13:11 where he reports that Jesus said: "For it is not you who are going to speak, but the Holy Spirit!" Peter, who had denied the Lord during his Passion, now proceeds to protect the Lord from such dependency on frail mortals. He—and he alone—had the right to keep Mark from placing Peter beside the Lord. If you find the result "staggering brutality," you overlook, along with the rest of the critics, the fact that Peter's battle was against his own potential authority: the gospel was to be preached in Jesus' name alone (Mark 16:17). {Peter was hard on himself.}

{And so we come to the fourth gospel.} The process in John is different again, but dramatic progress is made even in this apparently ethereal gospel. John was, like no other apostle, the brother of the Lord by natural sympathy. As a brother he was loved and liked in addition to being called and chosen. Natural congeniality, i.e., creaturely affinity, was John's special source of knowledge.

---

31. ERH: For the details, see Chapman, *MML*, 38–43. [See Appendix I, 320.]
32. [Luke 24:34 certainly implies that Peter was at Emmaus.]
33. ERH: Hoskyns and Davey, *Riddle*, 137–38. [See Appendix I, 329–30.].

The corresponding sources for heightened understanding were Peter's church office, Matthew's experience of having been saved {and of writing for all the disciples}, and Luke's responsibility to the next generation. A teacher like Luke comes to understand better and better because he has immature and unenthusiastic students; a bishop like Peter comes to take greater care because of his responsibility for the salvation of souls; Matthew knows and understands better because he was taken out of a rather opprobrious business life—and experienced deep gratitude for, and joy at, his own salvation.

{As a childlike personality} John understands what no one else could understand at first: the unfolding of a living person. Members of a physical family understand each other's deepest motives; the origins of each of their reactions and gestures is an open book to them. It is no different with kindred spirits, for the spirit precedes the incarnation; the spirit is the Creator's original thought of which {we living humans} are the execution. A kindred spirit, then, understands, by sympathy and "con-geni-ality" in its original sense, where Jesus came from, out of what depth of necessity, out of what pre-legal, pre-national, pre-religious original matrix. As a kindred spirit, John begins with man's real, original place in God's mind, but the path of his gospel leads him from his heavenly home down to earth. The miraculous process in John is the path from the Word in God to the man Jesus in the flesh. John makes Jesus interrupt his most sublime speeches (John 14) with the soberest and most concrete physical movement: "Let us go." Only John passes on this precious testimony to Jesus' realism—and no one else (14:31). Because of his personal and private intimacy, he would never have had to see Jesus from the outside. He lived with him, inside his soul.

But his great victory was his ability to equate his brother Jesus in the little events of everyday life with his cosmic office of Christ. {John saw the Lord as his other self;} his soul was "naturaliter christiana." Therefore he needed no signs or particular happenings to know and understand. He knew him "by heart." In writing his gospel, John learned to recognize that the worldly ways of knowing his Lord's external actions were equally justified. Although he was one with him in eternity, he humbled himself in history as just one of the disciples—that is the beauty of the last chapters in John. Thomas had to see before he believed; such seeing had no persuasive power for John himself, but he faithfully passes on Thomas's story as the type of discipleship furthest from his own. {He honored Thomas's readiness to die (11:16), and} he honored Peter as the one who had authority, even over John—because the Lord had said so [21:15–19]. John progresses from the innermost heart to the outer paraphernalia of social office and position, and thus prevents all naturally Christian hearts from fleeing the world of history and unfolding reality. {John became neither the Pope in Rome nor

III | THE FRUIT OF OUR LIPS   85

a missionary, but acknowledged both as valid. And so both pope and missionary must recognize John's "disturbing presence" in turn.}[34]

All four gospels are processes in which the four Evangelists lay down their human limitations at the foot of the cross and make their individual experience a contribution to the community. Matthew acknowledged that he was no longer a Jew [28:15]. Mark, Peter's disciple, acknowledged that Peter had lost his own name. Luke, Paul's companion, acknowledged that Paul did among the Gentiles what Jesus achieved among the Jews. John acknowledged that although a kindred spirit might encompass the eternal meaning without argument, the faithful soul still had to obey {those who held offices—we must all accept the fact that all processes} in the visible world's division of labor make very slow progress indeed. Our term "acknowledge" is not meant here in the sense of the four gospels, where it means the same as signing a receipt. It took a change of mind in the course of writing for the writer himself to discover the consequences. {He *learns* to recognize—and that learning is his gospel.}

Take Matthew's case. The critics point out his manifold quotations from scripture and tempt us to see him as a legal scholar who writes a marvelous brief for his client. The lawyer, however, always has the last sentence in mind when he writes down the first. Such a brief is planned with *one* purpose and is of *one* mind. (At least that's the theory; I myself don't believe it.) But Matthew begins, "Jesus was King of the Jews," [2:6] and at last recognizes that, "For heaven's sake, I'm no longer a Jew!" [28:15] and leaves Jerusalem.

We turn to Mark. Mark kneels in Peter's service; Peter is his final authority. At the end of his gospel he recognizes that he, Mark, cannot rely on Peter, any more than upon any other sinful man. Mark—however often it may have pained him to hear how Peter struck out a portion of the tradition that redounded to Peter's honor—became courageous enough to transcend his place as Peter's amanuensis. In hearing how Peter downplayed his own value as the prince of the apostles, Mark received a lesson on the unity of the church. The church can be one only if One alone gave it his name—and Mark went to Alexandria in God's spirit, not Peter's.

The change in Luke took place because of Theophilus. Theophilus knew Luke, and though the conversion of the Gentiles may have been all that interested him, Luke's writings changed all that. The original drama was now conspicuous as the eternal matrix of which Paul was only one of many fruits. And so each generation must re-enter this *one* true matrix, {that of the cross!} Since Paul, all generations have had to take their food, their analogy, from the master's gospel before they could go on record as disciples

---

34. ERH: "Die störende Anwesenheit des Johannes," *Die Sprache* I, 259–65. [1954: The following section was headed "Ichthys."]

with their own "Acts" {in competition with the sufferings of the apostles.} Everyone would have to listen to the Evangelists before they could retranslate the gospels as Paul had done. Everyone would have to become teachers of the next generation, so that the young could do still greater things. True, at Pentecost heaven had come to earth (Acts 1) and made a new earth with Rome instead of Jerusalem as the center, but God had chosen One alone to reveal the true heaven. He had to be upheld {as unique, as the immovable quantity.} There was no other way for the same heaven, which is to say God in all human hearts, to renew the earth in every generation.

So Theophilus had to ascend beyond mere baptism. He could now see himself burdened with his own task of translating for his own children, a task as tremendous as the translation of the gospel wrought by Peter and Paul for the Gentiles, in obedience to the Lord. In Luke's two books Jesus' command to baptize the nations grew in geometric progression. They revealed what could and would later be achieved once a Christian was baptized: {he could outgrow his predecessor. This was the only way progress could become possible. "Progress" is only possible thanks to Christ. Vincent of Lerinum has written on this beautifully.}[35]

And John—{the eagle in his soaring flight}—made the journey to a place where he could love the earth as well as heaven, in which he lived, heart to heart, with his master. That is the reason John's last sentence speaks of the space of the universe that wouldn't be able to contain all the books that could be written on Jesus [21:25]. The space of the universe? What was that to John, who had in his vision seen the Word who was with the Father in the beginning, before the universe was created? Yet this same created universe became his last word. He was ready to leave God's heaven and enter His creature "world" for the love for God. He came to see, feel, and taste the material universe, although he himself had no need of it—but God had created it and wished him to love it as well.

There is therefore a remarkable sequence in the writers of the four gospels. Jesus' name in the old church had four parts: Jesus, Christ, Son of God, Savior. The four Greek initials of these four names were read as *Ichthys* (fish).[36] The four gospels proclaim this name. Matthew the sinner knew that the Lord was his personal savior (*Soter*); Mark knew him from the beginning as the Son of God (γιος Θεου, *Hyious Theou*); Luke saw *Christ* who had converted Saul, to whom Jesus had never spoken (for Paul, Jesus could be nothing else but exclusively *Christ*); John, the kindred spirit, knew him as an elder brother, that is, he thought of him as "*Jesus*," personally:

---

35. [*Commonitorium*, Chapter 23: 54–55. See Appendix I, 316, 354.]
36. [See ERH, *Die Sprache* I, 119–42.]

1. Savior,
2. Son of God,
3. Christ, [and]
4. Jesus

were the aspects in whose sign the Evangelists wrote.

And now we see the law of speech set in motion, which always contradicts nature and the mere evolution of time. This law says: *that which is most central or primary in an event is articulated last.* That quality of Jesus' which made him affect his environment most visibly and disturbingly was that he saved sinners. The closest contact with his heart, where he was most purely Jesus, his own truly unique person, was John's. John passes on Jesus' innermost thoughts. Matthew gives all the external proofs for faith in Jesus as the Savior; Matthew was able to relate his experiences first; John could speak last. Why?

The order is strange, but it repeats the experience of Jesus himself, who was visible and valued only toward the end of his walk to his innermost center. That the world at first sees not us, but our surface function, is every living soul's experience. We first become visible through our least essential features; the outer man is known before the inner, the historical facts earlier than their lasting meaning. Only through Pentecost and Paul's experience among the Gentiles did the lasting importance of "Christ" come to be known, while Peter could stick to his own historical experience with the Son of God. *The sequence of the four gospels is necessary, because it reverses the order* that begins with Jesus' natural individuality. *And such a reverse of nature is the necessary sequence of {dawning awareness, of} articulation!*

Ichthys: 1. Jesus, 2. Christ, 3. Son of God, 4. Savior is the correct, "natural" order to describe this individuality. The spoken and written illumination of this individuality became conscious in just the opposite order and sequence: 4. Savior, 3. Son of God, 2. Christ, 1. Jesus. {The two volumes of my *Die Sprache des Menschengeschlechts* deliver many examples of the law of reversed order, as in the chapter on vowels and consonants.}[37]

We now turn to the practical connection between the four gospels and the liberties they take with each other because it is this connection that will deliver the true key to "the four gospels." Before doing so, however, I would like to clarify their interaction with a peripheral example, one which concerns their treatment of *world history*. Every historian who has not specialized in French, English, German, or Russian history, and even an interested layperson, may convince himself that the Russian revolution, including the World Wars, follow the French revolution and the Napoleonic

---

37. ["Die Vokale der Musen," *Die Sprache* II, 773–95.]

wars after four or five generations. A similar time-span separates Cromwell from Robespierre. And it is again four or five generations from Cromwell back to Luther.[38] Why do they erupt after 4 x 30 years? We may not be able to answer that question, but that in no way alters that it is a fact, based on data that are too emphatic to be left unconnected.

This same question irked the early church as well. Obviously, Jesus had come in the nick of time, that is, one generation before the destruction of the Temple. For John in his old age, and the church after 70 A.D., it was clear that Jesus had correctly fathomed the time. He had taken the seed from out of Zion before it could be made sterile there, but this argument could not be made before 70 A.D. Jesus sensed the corruption; he read the signs of the times a generation ahead. Between his crucifixion and the year 70 A.D., the faith of the Christians looked for persuasive arguments which would support this interpretation of history—just as Lenin and Trotsky could foresee world revolutions, while Nietzsche simply smelled the corruption. Stephen in his oral plea (and Matthew in his written plea) to the Judean aristocracy then in power, attempted to prove a logical rhythm for Jesus' appearance.

Before the High Council, Stephen said that since time immemorial, history had repeatedly made such leaps. From Abraham and his family he counted down to Joseph, then to Moses, then to David and Solomon, and finally to the prophets and the Babylonian captivity. "Don't you see," he cried, "that Jesus is a turning point like the captivity, like David, like Moses, like Abraham?" (Acts 7). Stephen's speech was the first Christian "economy of the spirit." In Matthew this plea of Stephen's grows to a law of history. It is fourteen generations from Abraham to David to the captivity, fourteen generations from Babylon to the coming of Christ in the person of a descendant of Abraham and David [1:17]. The so-called "genealogy" in the first chapter of Matthew is no genealogy at all, but a philosophy of revolution and the rhythm of revolution, {and it follows the spirit of Stephen's speech}.

Luke too gave a genealogy of Jesus, but this genealogy was no longer the basis of his {gospel, for in the meantime Jerusalem had been destroyed.}[39] The core of Stephen's great eloquent outburst had been that the spirit changes its expression from age to age. That is simply true—and we must not forget it! Matthew systematized Stephen and said that such an awakening happens in every fourteenth generation. After Paul's apostolate to the Gentiles, Luke no longer needed Matthew's law, which was right for "Israel," but he kept the secret of spiritual transmission in mind, and managed to generalize even

---

38. ERH: On this list, see my *Out of Revolution* [453–82, esp. 462–63].

39. [In 1954, ERH wrote that John was the only one to survive the destruction of the Temple (see Appendix E, 258). It's not clear who or what changed his mind.]

further. He set 3 x 14 generations from Jesus back to the founders of Judaism, but extended the list to 77 generations from God's creation of Adam to the creation of the second Adam, Jesus. And in two cases he replaced the number 14 with 22. We see a principle at work that combines freedom with unity. The common question for all three—Stephen, Matthew, and Luke—is a real question. For those who don't want to recognize it as an eternal question, I can point to a secularized version: {Gibbon asked the question the gospels pose, but for Rome. He didn't ask "Why did Israel fall?" but "Why did Rome fall?"} Well, Rome fell when the spirit left it. {The question has interested people from Gibbon to Spengler, but in the guise of a merely academic question.}

Matthew suggested a regularity. Luke corrected the numbers. The "3 x 14" had proved wrong, so they were changed, but the question itself continued, even if left in suspense, unanswered. This was achieved not by a dialectical process of "yes" and "no," but through the healthy, typical research process of "Yes, but not quite like that." This represents a new *method*: the Greek mind had only moved forward by opposites. A new Christian method was possible because before they began to argue, the different thinkers' hearts and souls had become one. {Modern research is an outgrowth of Christianity because in spite of their different ideas, researchers keep the peace in their hearts and minds.} That is the law of our era. {For Plato, ideas were what should unite his students, but ideas don't do us that favor. Paul had to convert the Greeks, so that there could be progress in the sciences.} Augustine expressed this condition of progress: "*in necessariis unitas, in dubiis libertas, in omnibus caritas*" (in necessary things unity, in questionable things liberty, but in all things charity). Stephen, Matthew and Luke offer the first perfect example I know of {and since then all dialectic is obsolete}.

Stephen cried: "This son of Abraham has himself brought the very sacrifice which Abraham spared his son Isaac. A new eon has dawned ending the history of Abraham's seed." Matthew reflected on this proclamation, and the Son of Abraham becomes the Son of God in his gospel, and for history. Luke comprehended the period from the Son of God Jesus and the Son of God Adam as one time-span and in doing so, Luke created the Christian era. In our schoolbooks this differentiation between a Christian era and antiquity is set at a much later date (533 A.D.).[40] But the actual accomplishment of a new era was the cooperative work of Stephen, Matthew, and Luke,

---

40. ERH: *Christian Future*, 33, 135. In the German version, 209. [The first two passages address the position of the believer (and the church) between a terrible past and the necessary future. The passage cited in *Des Christen Zukunft* (209) proclaims the necessity of multiple witnesses (even over vast periods of time) to understanding real truth.].

and in the third chapter of Luke the new frame of reference, with one era before and another after Christ, is clearly stated.[41]

And now the "four gospels" must be shown to be one. The "four gospels," we insist, are the lips with which the heart of "*Ichthys*" has spoken through the ages, and we must read all of them. We have tried to show why it is that *we* must read *all* of them, by exposing the four levels of nearness to their Master they represent. The Master obviously lived in all of them at *a different degree of distance*. Just as there are near-sighted and far-sighted people, friends and foes, so a man is not fully represented from any of the four vantage points. Jesus claimed to be the savior of sinners, the fulfiller of the law,[42] the redeemer of merely human language, the son of Joseph of Nazareth; we can only hear and understand these four claims on the four wave-lengths of the saved sinner, the converted ritualistic zealot, the emancipated teacher, and the born and yet appointed friend.

Now we must try to prove that the Evangelists too knew of their unity; we know for certain that they read each other, but we cannot separate this fact from the question why one after the other wrote his gospel as a supplement. Did they want to replace one another? If that were the case, why did the church keep all four? Why couldn't the church also admit any of the later gospels?[43]

Let us first clarify the situation with a simile. In his old age, John the Evangelist was asked why his sermon was so short (all he would say was "Children, keep each other at heart"). He gave the famous answer: "For two reasons: it is enough, and the Lord has said so" [1 John 4:7]. The four gospels suffice since each of the four claims made by *Ichthys* had become a "lip" in one man's dramatic change of mind. {The four claims wrested themselves from the Evangelists. Let us hold fast to John's word and} read the four gospels one more time; do they give evidence of mutual dependence beyond the "material" they use? Yes, they do; *they beget each other*.

Every gospel starts at precisely the point to which the previous gospel had progressed on its tortuous path.[44] The last word of one is the overture to, and sets the key for, the next. "The last word" is not meant in a literal or pedantic sense; we understand thereby the last step of thought that was reached in the dramatic progress. If that is so, then the gospels continue one another, each beginning to think and speak where the previous Evangelist had ended, and turning his final word into the opening of a new drama. Matthew's last word [27:54] is that Jesus has become the Son of God in the

---

41. [Luke 3:22–38?]
42. [1954: *of ritual*.]
43. [1954: The following section was headed "End Begets Beginning."]
44. ERH: The two partial writings of Luke are treated as one from here on.

sense of the Trinity. Mark begins with "the Son of God" (not, like Matthew, with "the Son of David"). Mark ends with the "mission of the ministers of the Word" [16:15]. Fittingly, Luke the missionary begins with the "ministers of the Word," and ends Acts with a long statement: the Jews have ears and hear not, eyes and see not, but "the Gentiles will hear" [28:25–28]. John breaks in majestically at this last word of Acts: "Indeed, the darkness has not seen the light, the world has not seen it, but his own have seen the glory and we have seen him" [1:4, 14]. Also, Luke ends with the power of the gospel {and "the one Word" from Isaiah 6}; John begins with the power of the Word. {You can hardly help hearing how they toss the ball to each other.}[45]

This connection between end and beginning is no accident. Each gospel works its way up to its climax. The mantle of the Evangelist falls naturally on the shoulders of the one best prepared {to assume the power of attorney that makes us human: re-telling the story, passing it on. (For God's sake say "proclaim" or "pass on" as Jesus did, instead of "*kerygma*")}.

	Beginning	End
Matthew:	Son of David	Son of God
Mark:	Son of God	Ministers of the Word
Luke:	Ministers of the Word	The Gentiles will hear
John:	The Word can now be heard by all	Jesus, the man, the friend

In overview:

1	Matthew begins:	Son of David and Abraham
2	Matthew ends:	Son of God (Baptize in the name of the Father and the Son and the Spirit)
	Mark begins:	the Son of God
3	Mark ends:	the Ministers of the Word
	Luke begins:	the Ministers of the Word
4a	Luke ends:	gospel: fullness of praise
	John begins:	In the beginning was the Word
4b	Luke ends:	Acts: Jews have neither eyes nor ears; the Gentiles will hear
	John begins:	The world has not seen the light; his own people refused him, we have seen his glory

45. ERH: The *en arche* was already to be found in St. Paul, in the beginning, but with the dreadful balkanization of biblical criticism I don't want to say more here. The interested reader may take a look at the end of the Letter to the Romans [16:25] and the second chapter of First Corinthians [2:7]. In both the Word of God is placed, just as in the beginning of John's Gospel, before time.

5   John ends: This man Jesus in the space of the cosmos
    Matthew begins: Jesus (Christ, Son of David, Son of Abraham)

{The cycle is complete. The "four gospels" are one.}[46] This list, scanty as it is, should be read as the scenario for four dramatic sections of a single act of disclosure.

> Scene 1: Matthew, the tax collector, {tosses his notes and numbers aside} and discovers the full power that human words can acquire when spoken by a man on the way to his death.

> Scene 2: Peter, the boorish fisherman, is called into the center of the last Western "sky world," to Rome with its Man-God Caesar, to Rome with the astrology of her temples and her hieroglyphs. Here he proclaims the true temple, the Word, and the true hieroglyphs of this temple, the ministers of the Word.

> Scene 3: Luke, the Greek physician, versed in the art of healing, is called into the Jewish medium where you say "no" to the physical world and fear contamination by physical idols. He turns this "no" back on the natural law of both the Jews and the Gentiles and proclaims instead the Christian's creative "yes."

> Scene 4: John, the prophet of Revelation, enters the Greek cosmos and frees their art and poetry by making God's poetry his theme. He asks: How does God write a poem?

If we elaborate on *this* scenario, we can untangle the scenes by beginning with John. His case is easiest for us moderns to understand; we understand poetry best, better than science, prayer, or ritual. People have always felt that *John's* gospel was hellenizing or hellenistic, and it was precisely this undeniable fact that made the gospel suspect. Why should Luke the Greek be less hellenistic than John of Galilee? But this is necessary as soon as we treat speech as on advance from somewhere to "somewhither." John was called out of Galilee into the Greek world; Luke out of a medical world into the Jewish spiritual world; Peter was called into the Roman sky-world and later his assistant Mark even went to Egypt, the cradle of all sky-worlds; Matthew, {the modern businessman, takes the path back to the primeval level of ritual and} discovers the price to be paid for all ritual. {All four

---

46. [1954: The following section was headed "The Four Idols: Art, Religion, Science, Manners."]

times, they travel a great distance; the gospel writers do not so much paint as stride.}

Because speech moves, John did not write a hellenistic gospel. Instead, he redeemed the Greek genius for poetry. The Greeks worshipped the *Logos*. They talked and talked to the point of drunkenness: rhetoric, logic, philosophy, and theater were their daily bread. The arts were their vice, their virtue, their life, and their religion. In the realm of poetry, whatever was touched by their magic wand, their art of "making,"[47] was transformed, like the stones that formed the walls of Thebes at the music of Orpheus. We follow Homer's song of Achilles's wrath until at last we weep over Hector, his enemy. And we read the story of "the man," Odysseus, until we believe with Homer that all in all what really matters is the "*Penelopeia*."

Plato was horrified by this genius of his people; he turned against poetry and proposed banning Homer—but Prohibition never works. Their salvation from the obsession with the arts had to come from the Jews. The Jews had dethroned the arts; they had sung their most glorious poetry as mere responses to God {though genius was blazingly alive in them. Inspired by God's spirit,} John received the Apocalypse {as a true genius}—which is to say, lying "as one dead" on the tiny island of Patmos. {Our commentaries don't understand that here all the geniuses of Greece stand as sponsors, to show what happens when genius enters into the Lord's following.} Plato {the son of Apollo} was not allowed to heal the Greek soul {of its intoxication with genius, though he had been scalded by the *morbus poeticus*}. John the Evangelist managed to do it.

How did he do it? His argument was neither man nor wife, Greek nor Trojan, {Eros nor Sophia}; instead he sang of the very power that makes us {love, suffer, speak, and obey}—of Man as God's poem, which is the way the Word became flesh. He reveals the inner poetry of the human being who speaks truth, whether in poetry or prose. John was immune to the poetic disease; {his gospel gloriously dismisses the Greeks as mere reporters. In 12:21 they want to see Jesus; they confuse the photographic image of a body with the insight into a path of life lived out into a fruitful death, with the transfiguration into a child of light. On this path John reports Jesus' most excellent speech; but none of the reporters can understand a single syllable. In spite of the mortal danger of the hour, Jesus and John must have been wildly amused by the ignorance of the press. But honesty demands that I myself be as modest as those reporters, when it comes to the raising of

---

47. [*poesis.*]

Lazarus. Like any Greek I have not yet understood this *pericope* unique to John, but it is obviously at the heart of the gospel.}[48]

As a Greek and a doctor, *Luke* was immune to the *morbus propheticus*, the Jewish negation of all worldly success. In the face of a pluralistic, power-hungry, polytheistic chaos, the Jews maintained that God was the One and Only One. Israel is so right in this respect—just as Greek genius is {largely} right and Plato wrong to {turn away} from it—that Jesus' cross could not overcome their horror at any final {deification}. They crucified him because to them God had to remain "still to come." It took Luke the Greek to make visible the limitations of their "no."

As a doctor of the body Luke knew the healing powers of poison, surgery, and other apparently destructive procedures. Luke could admit that no one is a superman, that no one may claim to be a doctor of social ills—God alone is that. But what if Man were God's drug, his blood plasma, his vitamin, his serum? A human being sent by God may course through society's veins, and be devoured there as Jesus was, but he might have a purifying and healing effect for all that—if he knew what he was doing, as Jesus certainly did. {Despite the rabbis, with that effect the free future of the prophets' God is not jettisoned after all!} This is in fact what Luke proclaims in his gospel and in Acts. Jesus instituted this process {of our becoming divine,} in which a child of God sacrificed himself for his enemies, for a society that reacted violently against him, and he opened men's eyes to this destiny of every child of God, whereby they are "injected into society's bloodstream." So he is "the anointed," the "Christ" whom all others can but follow.

I am only too well aware that the majority of the critics do not regard it as even a remote possibility that Luke's front was the salvation of the Jews. So I think a few technical points may be mentioned that might show that the case is at least undecided. Luke wrote {either in Boeotia or} in Caesarea in Asia Minor; strong Jewish elements in such a church are no wanton premise. He was the first [Evangelist] to write a book in the strict sense that this book could be used for readings in worship parallel to readings from the Old Testament. His constant change of "he says" in Mark into the cultivated style of "he said" has often been noted, and it was necessary if the *pericope* was to have the dignity of being read out loud.

Luke respected the Jewish name for the center of Israel's faith: he uses the name "Jerusalem" 30 times and in 26 of these 30 citations he cites it in the Hebrew form "*Jerusalem*" not in the Greek form "*Hierosolyma*." All the other gospels do just the opposite. Someone who spoke to Jews would be

---

48. ERH: I have come to the first traces of understanding thanks to W.H. Cadman's "Lazarus," 423–34. [See Appendix I, 316–18.]

as considerate as Luke was, to spare the ears of his listeners. It has recently been remarked that his style is full of Hebraicisms and that he quotes the Old Testament not from the Greek, but from the original Hebrew text.[49]

{Clark thinks that this proves that Luke himself was a Jew, but while the evidence is inconclusive, the idea points even more strongly to the care we ascribe to Luke. But let the reader note, Luke avoids the prophetic word "hope" in his Gospel.} The point on which Israel was hardest of hearing—and not by accident, but because of her most profound faith—was that Christians wanted to know that God had finally said "yes" to a man's religious mandate. They knew that God had always kept men back from idolatry, from the temptation of establishing heaven here on earth. The Gentiles deified men with great ease. To show Luke's dilemma, I quote here the terrible hymn to the deified general Demetrios composed by the Greek Hermokles:

> He's the Sun to love you.
> Hail, offspring of Poseidon, powerful god...
> The other [deities]... have no ears, though mighty;
> they are not, or they will not hear us wail:
> Thee our eye beholdeth.
> Not wood, not stone, but living, breathing, real.
> Thee our prayer unfoldeth.
> First give us peace. Give, dearest, for Thou canst:
> Thou art Lord and Master.[50]

Luke must have been thoroughly familiar with this type of blasphemy in politics. The worship of Caesar was strictly in line with this poem, and Luke abhorred it as much as his Jewish friends did. How could he convince them that the delicate line between us mortals and the creator of heaven and earth had not been violated by the new belief in God's son incarnate?

That could only be done in the manner Paul used in his preaching. First, a man must allow God to speak his "NO," in his willingness to suffer. Only after God, as a burning fire, had purged all the dross, all the transient attributes, from a mortal man, can the complete affirmation, the surrender to "YES," be admitted. The naïve mind says: "I should be God, I should be the Messiah, I should be the lawmaker." God breaks this will, but the man who renounces it, who has and does no will of his own, and pays with his life for the unavoidable admixture of self-will in his life—he is "YES." (2 Cor 1: 4-7, 17-20). {Dying we live. Our doing-without makes our deification

---

49. ERH: Clark, *Acts*, xxiii. [See Appendix I, 322.]

50. [1954: *quoted from the translation by J.A. Symonds in the* Oxford Book of Greek Verse [523].

possible. For those whom he loves, God leaves nothing unpunished in this life.}

Following this traverse over the narrow mountain ridge between too much self-confidence and too little, Luke alone has certain reports on Jesus which center around this relation between the naïve first "yes," the divine "NO," and the creative, incarnating, and history-making second "YES." His alone is the great story that Jesus saw a man working on the Sabbath, approached him and said: "Man, if you know what you are doing, you are blessed; if not, you are cursed, and a breaker of the law." (After 6:10 in the *Codex Bezae*). {There the three new levels are created, the first "yes," the "NO," and the "YES" of glory. With that, Jesus advanced beyond Athens and Jerusalem, that is, beyond his own genius and divine law to date and into a new dispensation.}

Only in Luke is Jesus' cross-examination so carefully reported that Jesus himself never says: "I am the Messiah" (14:61–62). Luke knew Mark's book, so Luke's more extensive report may show that he avoided the false appearance which Mark allowed that Jesus declared himself the Son of the Living God. It was of no concern to Mark, for Egyptians, Greeks, and Romans could believe in the apotheosis of a mortal man by self-proclamation; (it did not strike the ear as shrill—Mark could write ambiguously}. But Israel with her awe of the Oneness of God could not admit that anyone could give himself his own rank. {Only the resurrection transforms Jesus into the head of the Son of God—only his blessed death—and} Luke conceded this point. The Jews, not Jesus, speak the decisive words; only that way could a man become the word spoken by God—that is, by not himself elevating any of his own mortal statements to divine truth. {That is the justification used in the "Letter to the Hebrews."}[51]

For Luke the perpetual "concurrence" between the Father's power to make all the world around Jesus act and speak so as to confirm him, on the one hand, and the Son's own deeds, on the other, is the real proof that here God speaks his full "YES" to the Son. In forgoing power for faith, in forgoing the opportunity to cause suffering rather than suffering himself, {he verifies his mission}. In denying himself, he takes over Israel's eternal role {as the seed-people for all mankind}. In accepting defeat, Christianity built this lasting truth of the Old Testament in its very structure. If the prophets had obeyed the command "Say 'no' to the idols," why should it now be blasphemy to say "I obey the command to say 'no' to our will, and 'yes' to the step beyond this 'no'?" From the beginning, it is Luke's concern to

---

51. [1954: *This point, Jesus' own weakness in Gethsemane and upon the cross, was vividly debated in the first century.* Harnack, "Zwei Korrekturen," 62–73.]

prove that with God "nothing shall be impossible" (1:37). And as Jesus dies for his enemies, it is his enemies who must reveal him in his true mission. In this interaction alone can we discern human will from God's will, and only after this can the change of mind occur. By accepting his penalty at the hands of its receivers, the hated bringer of the gospel purifies his will of mere "self"—and this changes the mind of his persecutors. That indeed is Luke's good news.

Since I write as a listener to language, my argument is mainly to those who are not interested first and foremost in "theology" in a narrow sense, and who don't crave all the learned theological arguments on Luke. However, it is only fair to add, for those who are versed in those theological questionings, that Luke did not cover the whole field of Jewish tradition; we will see that when we turn to Matthew. The strictly historical and naturalistic study of the gospels {since 1800 has greatly} oversimplified the battlefronts on which the cross had to be erected. We will see that Greeks and Jews make up only two of the four fronts; in the New Testament, "Gentile" and "Jew" are wrongly considered an exhaustive dichotomy.

The listener to language discovers that Luke attacks a weak point in himself. The greatest piety and the highest type of religion in Jesus' days were found with the righteous of Israel. It was not their inferiority, but their rigor and excellence, that imposed on Jerusalem's priests the duty to condemn Jesus. It was blasphemy for someone to call himself God and claim a seat at the right hand of God.[52] It was no arbitrary resistance the Jews offered, but a highly respectable one, which all men of good will in our own days should again consider praiseworthy.

So Luke's argument is an eternal argument and combats an eternal position of great merit {—devout Jews of today would still have to crucify Jesus}! But Israel rests on a combination of {philosophical} purity and Hebrew {solidarity}; Israel is a chosen people, as much chosen as a people. Luke deals only with Israel's prophetic aspect, and as we will see, the Hebrew side had to be tackled by someone very different.

This must suffice for the third and fourth gospel; in their healing of the *morbus graecus* and the *morbus propheticus*, both gospels became an antidote: John, a Hebrew of the Hebrews, is given the ability to redeem Greek poetry; Luke, the Greek doctor, is able to make Israel's stubborn negation fruitful again. But is there a similar exchange of polarities, a similar transfer

---

52. [Pinchas Lapide points out that the Swedish Grand Rabbi Gottlieb Klein found Matthew 26:64—and the entire gospel of John—full of blasphemous invocations of the *'hidden name of God'* which, according to Jewish tradition, *God was to reveal to all in the messianic age.* (Lapide, *Josephs Sohn*, 126–28). For Klein's argument, see Appendix I, 330–31.]

of energies between Matthew and Mark on the one hand, and their respective audiences on the other? I think there is.

The reader will do well to look back at our earlier chapters, which penetrated to the times before both the Jews and Greeks. We found the human race organized into "engraved times" and "eternity composed in partnership."[53] Now, the two first gospels fulfill for "Egypt" and tribal ritual what John achieved by "unspelling" poetry and Luke achieved by healing the healing "No" of the Psalms. Since today we are infinitely less familiar with either the sky-world and its hieroglyphs or the burial and sacrificial rites of tribal times {than we are with the Bible and Homer}, their cure demands a somewhat more laborious exposition.

We turn to Mark's gospel, the second gospel, and recall the hieroglyphs painted on the walls of the temples that brought heaven to earth. Henry II, Holy Roman Emperor from 1002 to 1024 A.D. and a saint of the Church, still wore as a coronation robe a cloak in which the sun, moon, and stars of the firmament were woven, for the Emperor was the *cosmocrator* (ruler of the universe). He was lifted into the hub of the wheel to unite night and day, to reconcile the north, where the sun never shines, with the south, to which the polar stars of midnight never move. The Emperor, the Son of Heaven as he was called in China, was the prime mover of a world of heaven-and-earth that he reconciled, rescued from chaos, and freed from the threat of panic. His knowledge of the stars and his compliance with them protected the people from the panic unleashed by catastrophes. When the people of our day hold the president of the United States responsible for a world-wide depression, they follow in the footsteps of all ancient nations who believed that a human being raised into the hub of the cosmic wheel could perfect the eternal cycles. The incense burned before the Emperor's statue was means of enlivening his nostrils so that he could smell the harmony and beauty of the universe. Whoever burned no incense, whoever refused to say "Heil Hitler," destroyed the sky-world. He had to die.

Mark's gospel of the true Son of God was written in direct response to this cult. It was written in a world which for safety's sake pretended that the Emperor was the heart {of the eon}, the Son of God, and maintained that pretense with magical formulas, calendars, sacrifices, temples, and hieroglyphs. It was written by men who denied the Emperor's claim, and thereby placed those for whom they wrote at risk of death for high treason against the welfare of the empire.

They preached in the midst of an unchallenged sky-world in which the "abomination of desolation" (that is, Caesar's statue) invaded every corner

---

53. [1954: *rituals and tattoos* and *temples and hieroglyphs*]

as the center of a magically bound universe, even "there where it should not stand" (Mark 13:14), even in the Holy of Holies in Jerusalem. The expression, which I quote from Mark, is first used by Matthew [24:15]. We might have no right to ascribe a particular interest in it to Mark; Matthew, being the first, was catholic in his materials, certainly more catholic than Mark could be in his abridgement. Yet I will quote a few famous sentences from this speech of Jesus' to prove that it had far greater signfiicance for Peter {in Rome} than for any other apostle. This thesis is far from arbitrary, as my two citations should make clear.

The critics have always acknowledged that at least as far as the eschatological images are concerned, Mark is clearer than Luke or Matthew. Weymouth-Robertson remarked, "Certain aspects of the discourse stand out most clearly in Mark's report" and "the clearest outline of this eschatological discourse is in Mark."[54] In other words, Mark took great pains with this speech.

The second and weightier reason is this: this speech on the signs of the sky-world is the only speech that Mark gives in full. Now, if in the whole Book of Mark only one speech out of many to be found in Matthew is reproduced in its entirety, it is thereby placed center stage. {It was particularly necessary in Rome.} This speech, which the reader may look up for himself, describes the astrological sky-world: "the sun shall be darkened and the moon shall not shed her light, and the stars of heaven shall fall, and the powers that are in heaven shall be shaken" [13:24–25]. Until then the main concern of all priestly cults had been to combat such disturbances in heaven; {but, because the gospel destroys the cults,} Jesus' prophecy is meant quite literally. Our modern Nicolais[55] can only shake their heads {at such superstition}. "The details of this description are, of course, not to be taken literally. They are the attempt of poetic imagery to realise what it means that God should intervene in human history."[56]

But the moderns fail to ask how God could intervene as long as the magic of the sky-world was in power! Mark was concerned with curing the *morphus egyptiacus*, not with poetry. What then was his cure? It was simple. It was dangerous. It was: fellowship! {Witnesses, a cloud of witnesses}, were to take the place of the dead stars in the firmament. *Jesus had to take the place of the sun,* {and haven't the saints and Christ done just that?} The

---

54. ERH: Weymouth and Robertson, *The New Testament*, 62 and 118. [118, 62.]

55. [1954: *our modern critics, as true Gilbert Murrays.* See note, 235. Georg Friedrich Nicolai's *Biologie des Krieges* (1918) projected the author's own pacifism back onto the early church. To ERH in 1964, he was no longer *modern.*]

56. ERH: Weymouth and Robertson, 119.

whole gospel of Mark tries to show that Jesus experienced the one complete solar year of a human sun—of a human heart.

None of the people, not one of the disciples, recognized the presence of that perfect life, yet he trusted them all the same. He called them, although they didn't understand him, and from that moment on they were in fellowship with him. (We already know that Peter disclaimed all credit for this.) During "the perfect and agreeable year of the Lord," the disciples were in suspense. In 3:12 he forbids them to say who he is. In 4:11 they are told: "For you the open truth, for the crowds the parables." In 8:31: "They were told for the first time." In 9:9: "He strictly forbade them to tell anyone what they had seen, until the Son of Man had risen from the dead." In 10:38 they are told: "You know not what you are asking." In 10:32: "They were awe-struck, and those who followed him, did it in fear." All along, the only link between them and the Lord is suspense and expectation on their part.

The entire gospel is built around this discrepancy between Jesus' time and theirs. For Jesus is already performing his task; the time is fulfilled. He walks on earth like the sun, but the disciples ask him, "Tell us when these things will be?" (13:4) {They have yet to become stars!}

Why is Mark's gospel so marked by this discrepancy between Jesus, who is openly living the perfect year and his disciples who expect it in some mysterious future? Why is the last chapter of Mark crowded with remarks about the unbelief of the disciples? "Simon, are you asleep?" "They could not believe it." "They were afraid." "They could not believe the signs." "He upbraided them for their unbelief and obstinacy." [16:12,14.]

In fact, the critics have assumed that the gospel of Mark must be mutilated or incomplete because it ends abruptly and on a note of despair. Now, we have already been warned of the rational mind's strange suspicion of the endings and beginnings of creative literature: *Tristram Shandy* with its incredible first page would certainly never pass muster with them. If, however, {the disciples' belated understanding} is the center of Mark's gospel, we may read his ending with complete understanding. This "spurious" ending contains the sentence: "Go the world over and proclaim the gospel to all mankind, and *signs* shall attend those who believe." "So the Lord Jesus having thus spoken . . . sat down at the right hand of God. And they went out and preached everywhere, the Lord working with them and confirming the word by the *signs* which accompanied it" [16:15–20].

The reader may now be well and truly befuddled and only able to shake his head. I trust that a humanistically educated reader might understand that John sang of "the Word" where Homer had sung of "the man," that Luke said "Christ now" where the Jews had only heard "not yet Christ," but that Jesus trumped the hieroglyphs of the sky-world—the astral calendar of the

Son of Heaven or the emperor, the *sol invictus* of the empires—seems too far-fetched.

(Our own world seems so superior to "signs," but if the modern mind needs to draw an analogy, it need only look to the business cycle, to power, and the worship of power. The modern belief in medicine, machines, and hugely endowed institutions is similar to the sun-cult of antiquity. The expressions "influence," "influential," "power," "boom and bust," "cycle," and "depression" are our astrological terms. We use them today not for cosmic processes, but for social ones, but the analogy may serve, just the same, to show that we are quite accustomed to accepting such "constellations" patiently, like rain or sunshine. So even we possess some hieroglyphs that limit us as much as sacred spells. {This much as an aside.})

In any case, the order of the old sky-world is turned into its opposite by Mark's *one* last sentence whereby God confirms the words of the preachers by the signs that accompany them. In the sky-world the word of the Son of Heaven took effect without ever standing the test of the real world. The gods appeared *ex machina*, by means of machinery; the rain or blood was fabricated by priests who acted as Jupiter or Iris. They forced the hieroglyphs to bear witness to truth by black magic, if white magic failed them.

{This astrological front has not been taken seriously for 150 years. In 1958, after its curse had destroyed Germany, Guenther Bornkamm at least dared to mention it—fully 1,900 years after Christ.}[57] *The world as such* {(whether we call it race, fatherland, Europe, nature, development, or revolution)} *has no heart*, but the empires pretended the universe had a heart and ascribed that heart to their ruler. {By his sacrifice Jesus created a worldheart such that every one of his followers can take part in the creation of the world-heart in free, loving answer to him, the Word, in sound and echo, in the beating of his own heart. "Heart of the World" is what the church fathers called him.}

{After the last thousand years of world history, we are more likely to credit and ascribe those healing streams that flow from the cloud of holy witnesses, from all victims of violence, that cause our tiny hearts to beat in sympathy, to God's heart, to the Son's heart. For the dead world and the living God must find common ground in us. God's heart wants to beat through us into the heartless world.}[58]

Jesus became the heart of a living universe through his belief in free response. "The first creation of God's world," as the fisherman Peter called

---

57. [Perhaps a reference to Bornkamm's *Jesus von Nazareth* (1956).]
58. [This section replaces a quite different passage in the original. See 237–38.]

it,[59] was reclaimed from the astrological world by faith in the continuum of all speech. These speakers could hold each others' hands and transmit the new power of one common spirit; they spoke in the name of the Only One who had found this faith in free response, when nobody else had it. His day had gone by, but in the night he left behind him, the limbs of his body could become glowing stars that await the full light of another day. It is the second epistle of Peter that can best prove that we are not amiss in our interpretation: here the heavens—i.e., the sky-world—are all ablaze; they will be destroyed, and a new heaven and a new earth will come, without astrology, "until the day dawn and the *morning star dawns in our hearts.*" (2 Pet 1:19)

This is eloquent: the sky-world of Egypt revolved around the simultaneous appearance of the bright night star Sirius and the sun on the morning of July 19. This was Pharaoh's New Year's day, because day and night, north and south, were reconciled with each other in this one moment. In Peter's words, that had to be replaced by a dawn in the heart of men through Christ, {the new morning star}. But I shrink from making use of this letter, for fear it might harm my thesis: the critics are very severe about this letter and say it could not be Peter's. {Well, I will let the roulette wheel of critical fashions go on spinning.} Here it will have to suffice to bring into focus the front on which the church actually fought: Peter and the papacy, for many the archetype of the power-hungry priest, defeated the temple cults of antiquity {because they humbled themselves to serve as *servi servorum*, as servants of God's servants}.

On the one hand, as a Jewish fisherman Peter was acquainted with the real cosmic processes of weather, water, air, and sky, but on the other, as an Israelite, he was unpolluted by astrology. So here was a man who had been preserved from contamination by the unclean "science" of antiquity, but who was at the same time in excellent command of five {exceptionally sharp} senses. This was the man {whom the Lord over the four diseases chose} to dissolve the old heavens with their local calendars, and to replace the hieroglyphs of Stonehenge or Memphis with the suffering of the martyrs' living bodies. The ministers of the Word became the hieroglyphs of the new temple. {That is why Peter went to Rome, and the cloud of witnesses rose in the litanies.}[60]

On this I may at last quote Peter himself. His first letter is no longer denied him today, and in this letter we see him proclaim victory over the stones of the temple [I Pet 2:4–8]. We can only understand the sentence if

---

59. [1 Peter 1:20?]

60. ERH: Hebrews 12:1. Calling on the saints replaced the horoscope. Every litany is a constellation [*Sternstrasse*].

we remember that these temples were covered with spells and hieroglyphs. Peter explains that he acts not out of "*gnosis*," that is, the predictions of the astrologers, but out of God's "*prognosis*" [1:2]. God called Peter at a time when he could not know what he was expected to do, long before he could respond in "imitation of the one who called" him {or be compared to him} (1:15). And now comes the literal definition: "And you yourselves, you are the living stones and will be set in place in a temple filled with the spirit" (2:5). {Accordingly, the beginning of the "Letter to the Hebrews" must be improved in our translations: "After manifold and changing speech God has at last spoken by a Son, the reflection of God's glory, the hieroglyph for God's being!" It is a question of the only appearance in the New Testament of the word "character" and the word means "hieroglyph."}

{In his "Letter to the Ephesians" the martyr Ignatius physically attacks the stone temples. He is so zealously set on replacing the dead structure of the temple that he calls the Holy Spirit the rope, the cross the new machine, and Christians the stones that this crane lifts high into the divine scaffolding.[61] The once perishable Jesus thus acquires the power to outlive, to outlast, to overcome the stone hieroglyphs of Karnak or on the Rosetta stone. He has God's life.}

So much for Peter in Rome and for Mark, who for just that reason counts as the first bishop of Alexandria and Egypt. The Egyptian disease was cured. {Mark conquered Pharaoh, as Peter did Rome. Whether or not the critics deny Mark his Egyptian office is immaterial.}[62]

Now we are back to Matthew, our first Evangelist. We have little right to expect in him a similarly clear and specific front, because he was the first to write at all, he had to report any- and everything. And we found this to be true in the case of the speech on the sky-world, which Mark only elaborated on {because it was more important in Rome.} And yet, although the first, Matthew is already quite surprisingly specific {as to his particular audience}. The disease he overcomes is with us as much as the others, only this disease is so close to home that it is more difficult—and far more disagreeable—to expose it. We get a glimpse of his character as a specific medicine against a specific disease once we notice that he regards the twelve apostles not as the twelve stars, but as the judges of the twelve tribes of Israel [19:28]. Why does he remind us of them? Could it be, that he was primarily driven to break the taboo of tribal ritual?

We have seen Peter's, Luke's, and John's concerns, and their specific immunities. It might appear that no such specialty was to be found for

---

61. [Chapter 9 of the "Letter to the Ephesians"; see Appendix I, page 316.]
62. [Eusebius and Jerome both claim that Mark became bishop of Alexandria.]

Matthew, which would mean that he equipped himself for his gospel as a bookkeeper and tax-collector. {The prophet Isaiah already retained stenographers—could Matthew have been Jesus' stenographer?} Peter seems to have been an oral person and probably held ink in contempt, but Matthew was only too well-acquainted with paperwork and written records. However, we may expect neither Jesus nor Matthew's fellow apostles to have put him to work in his old field of expertise, where he had used his ability to write {for Caesar's imperial administration}. We must look for him to fight on quite a different front.

Now we read that Matthew was not received in good society, and this is the man who begins his gospel with Jesus' place in Israel's "Almanach de Gotha"![63] He stresses the fact that, {despite external appearances,} his master Jesus belonged to the very best society as the son of kings. And then he goes on to show that Jesus voluntarily abandoned the privileges connected with this social position: "the son of kings should be scot-free" (17:26–27)! He should pay no taxes or customs duties, whether it is a head tax or half a shekel, Jesus said with a smile, but Matthew goes on to say that exactly the opposite happened: he expresses the whole significance of Jesus' life in the style of a financial report. I fear this may grate on my readers' tender sensibilities, but he does actually say: "he came to give his life as a ransom for many" (20:28).

This is no figure of speech for Matthew. Matthew understands Jesus as the rightful heir of the chieftancy, as the heir who instead volunteers to become the sacrifice at the tribe's feast. But by being a voluntary victim, he becomes the first victim {in the history of the world} who can speak. Nobody had ever spoken in that role, for the tribes required their victims to be mute {as our chapter on the tattooed times related}. The association of the ancestors and the living was based on the common meal, at which the dead took part as if alive; the whole funeral and burial rite was founded on this association of the living and the dead. {It was the common superstition of all tribes that} the spirits of the dead demanded food and became bloodthirsty if they went unfed; we continue the custom ourselves our high entrance fees for clubs and fraternities. {The [German] word "*Speise*" ["food"] means "for a lot of money"! It costs us a lot to become members of good society.} Sacrifices were the very core of ritual because they alone incorporated the group and gave it legal status as a public corporation beyond the grave and beyond the accidents of birth and death. Sacrifices were the only means of establishing order and creating legal persons.

---

63. [The German equivalent of Debrett's *Peerage*. 1954: *the social register of Israel.*]

It was essential to speak the proper names and to make the proper movements. They were what we hold to be essential as "table manners." For how many people of our time are table manners the heart of promotion, membership, and career! The table manners of antiquity were {even stricter}. A waiter is not expected to join in the conversation of his own accord; no more do we expect the roast-beef or the fish to start talking. The price of a good dinner party is the complete silence kept by those who serve and by the food which is served. This whole section will be condemned by any reader of taste because I mention the remote possibility that the roast-beef might speak, but that is *Matthew*'s whole point![64] He knew that the verdict "bad taste" could finish off a man more quickly than any crime {—and how often he must have heard that said of him and his companions!} Society expects us to play by the rules.

It is unforgivable to offend against etiquette, and yet I must breach etiquette myself to make sense of Matthew. For that is where his real achievement lies: he is the only Evangelist who tells us about Jesus' flight into Egypt when Herod murdered the children of Bethlehem. The whole point of Matthew is that while Herod could not murder Jesus, decent society murdered him later for his breach of etiquette in insisting on speaking for the victims of that society. *That Jesus spoke as the victim* made him impossible. Matthew scandalized the Jews {by describing Jesus as such}. After all, they had long been so civilized as to make only burnt offerings [of animals and grain]—ever since Abraham had foregone the sacrifice of Isaac. A thousand years later in Sweden, it was still possible for a king to slaughter six of his sons to placate the spirits. When he tried to take the seventh son as well, the people rescued the child, converted to Christianity, and gave up human sacrifice.

Israel, however, the people of Abraham and Moses, {had long since given up human sacrifice} and to this day all Jews believe the gospel offends good taste. We read the word "scandal" in our texts,[65] but "bad taste" would better convey our wincing at an offense against our tastes. The ritual of any society—and I am afraid that we lose sight of this more readily than of anything else—protects itself through a violent recoiling at every offense. It is the same in all times and in all places. The scribes asked, "Why do your disciples offend the traditions of the Elders by not washing their hands before the meal?" and Jesus retorted, "Why do you transgress God's command and deny your parents what they need because it is 'consecrated'? You

---

64. [The crowning absurdity of *Through the Looking Glass* is that at the final banquet, Alice is upbraided by the pudding of which she has just herself cut a slice.]

65. [1954: *The gospel was as much a scandal to the first century as it is to the twentieth.* Hoskyns and Davey, *Riddle*, 261. See also I Cor 1:23.]

have made futile God's word for the sake of your table manners!" (15:2[-6]) "Eating with unwashed hands does not make unclean" [15:20].

As Jesus "sinned," so Matthew also "sins" against the taboo of table manners by presenting Jesus as the speaking victim, as the meat and wine who begin to speak in the middle of the meal. The shock administered by Matthew has been wonderfully formulated by a modern critic:

> The reference to eating Christ's flesh and drinking his blood is impossible in an Aramaic[66] gospel in Jerusalem in the first century; nothing could be more repugnant to Jewish ways and feelings. Words such as these would horrify Jewish residents of Jerusalem, then or now. The Jews were and still are, utterly opposed to the drinking of blood which the Law repeatedly forbade. It would be difficult to imagine a sentence less likely to have been written in a Jewish Christian circle anywhere at any time. No Jewish Evangelist could have recorded it.[67]

This is an eloquent paragraph, and a feeling of nausea may well be aroused in the reader as well. The humor of this passage lies in two facts. The first is that the critic is dealing with John, who in this instance simply affirms Matthew; our critic is trying to deny John's Jewish origin and ignores the precedent of Matthew, who obviously wrote for Hebrews. The second is the modern assumption that every scandal can be avoided. The Jews stoned Stephen, killed James, and imprisoned Peter because they were furious. The lamb, the blood, the bread—all these terms were blasphemies, of course, but the whole history of the Church was built on just this fury. Paul failed in Athens when he tried just once to accommodate.[68] Matthew was abhorred, the gospel was abhorred and—let us be honest—is still abhorred today by men of good taste {as it was by Goethe!}.

The price of all ritual is sacrifice. When we bind ourselves to a ghost of the past, a piece of paper, a house, or a grave, we are apt to spill somebody else's blood, {as we do in war}; so it is to this day. It doesn't matter as long as we are aware what price we pay. Jesus created a brotherhood {of outcasts}, a brotherhood of silent victims by becoming the first of them to speak. Why could he speak? Because he *volunteered*, where up until then the victims had been drafted {against their will}. Even today the Eucharist is a scandal

---

66. ERH: Biblical criticism has made hay with the term *Aramaic* for Matthew. It helped to demote the Evangelist—but Matthew wrote in Hebrew. [See Appendix I, 325-27.]

67. ERH: Goodspeed, "Greek Idiom," 90. [See Appendix I, 324-25.]

68. ERH: Here too it is amusing how biblical critics like Dibelius misunderstand Paul's great mis-step, which Luke reports honestly, hailing it as a rhetorical masterpiece on Luke's part. [See Appendix I, page 323-24.]

to a Jew; it causes a completely literal "dis-gust," as it should to any man of breeding. {The pudenda, that which offends our sensibilities and our shame, are not done away with by denying them.} Matthew knew that all too well. Why was it in worse taste for the victim to call himself bread and wine, than for the high "powers that be" to pass judgment on the Righteous One?

Matthew was immune to the deadly disease of good society. He knew that everything has its price, and that nothing is more expensive than freedom from the taboos of good society. So he stopped calling the first man who spoke for the victims and as a victim by the name that connected him to society, the son of David, the son of Abraham, and the taboo was broken. In his last chapter, Matthew finds himself in the infinitely more exciting society of sinners, and those sinners were bound together not by a club's high initiation fees but by the name of the first victim who had spoken aloud.

That is why, by the way, the legend that Matthew ended his days in Ethiopia is probably true. For to this day the Ethiopians observe both Jewish ceremonial and the liturgy of the New Testament. They circumcise and baptize; they keep the Sabbath as holy as Sunday. It can't be proven, but it would agree with the word of the gospel, if it all went back to Matthew, and for precisely the reason that the disease he fought was the exaggeration of ritual's importance. {Bad taste is not of itself commendable, but woe to those who never outgrow their good manners.}

By illuminating what our breach of good manners means, Matthew hit upon primeval ground within all of us. Indeed, in primeval times, table manners had represented the creative element from which the body politic sprang: the introduction of common meals put an end to our snatching scraps from each other. {Any camp leader can tell you, dear reader, that a group's morality only forms when one person grants another the best morsel.} The introduction of common meals created a new peace of mind, and around the meal for the dead, with the dead, the new incorporation took place. Food was placed between the living and the dead, and both partook of it in *one* spirit and *one* name. Sacrificial meals were the first constitutions of mankind. Here community was enacted because the belly's "unenlightened self-interest" was forgotten when the best morsels were reserved for the dead, and later, for the gods. Something more permanent eclipsed the interests of the living generation; accidents of birth and momentary existence were overshadowed by the eternity of the dead.

In the cooling shadows of this permanent and eternal order, peaceful arrangements were made between friend and foe. Hospitality, the right of the enemy to eat with us, was introduced, was made possible because ritual showed man his place in the succession of endless times. Here people did not eat like animals, but toasted each other by their full names. The toast at meals is primeval also. Men greeted one another {and imagined the dead as companions at table, that is, as continuing to live among them} so that a comrade's life now weighed more heavily in their eyes than their own. Matthew directs our gaze back to these primeval foundations of society.

John spoke to people who knew the arts and sciences; Luke spoke to the greatest high churchmen and Puritans of antiquity; Mark spoke to the civilized inhabitants of the temple states. But thanks to his "bad taste," Matthew penetrated to the most archaic layer of all society, to the tribal layer of ritual, and so Matthew gave us a version of the gospel that was to become the most universal and fundamental characteristic of the new way of life. The Mass and the Eucharist, the inner core of all worship, is identified in Matthew [26:26-29]. Since he made clear that by His sacrifice Christ had purchased the salvation of the sacrificers, the scripture now says: At every meal, the sacrifice that is the bread and wine speaks to the dining community and invites us to join our Master on the other side, so to speak—on the side of the victim.

In the Mass, every listener is invited to sacrifice himself for the salvation and renewal of the world, or to be ready to be sacrificed. In the Mass, the first victim invites the participants to a service in which *they themselves* are the offerings. This fact rarely makes much of a dent in the dullness of the average mind. People have degraded worship to a church parade or a social gathering, but the Church was built on the faith that from now on no worship was allowed unless the participants viewed themselves as the offered sacrifice. The whole expression of a body of Christ whose head is in heaven means just this: we too would crucify our Lord in our rage, our envy, and our indifference—at any time. But our eyes are also opened to what we have done, what we are still doing, and so we solemnly declare: Together with our Head we cross over to the side of the silent victims and offer ourselves to our Maker, so that he may remake us as he pleases. How could a new inspiration ever befall us mortals if we did not offer ourselves as the vessel for the inspiration? Time and again, Man must be torn open by the plowshare of suffering and open himself as the earth does to dew and rain. And ever since one man did this alone and by himself, we no longer have to do it quite alone. In each generation now the size of the group that can be remodeled may grow, until it is possible for all humanity to fall silent, to cleanse itself of the chatter and clatter of the day and listen as one for the spirit.

When the founder of the first Christian university in Japan died, he left a warning to his favorite pupil, Kanamori: "I have reason to believe that you will be my successor. May I caution you against some weaknesses that you will have to combat in the exercise of your new office." He went on to list them. In the excitement of the hour this note was read to the entire grieving assembly along with all the other papers he had left. Mr. Kanamori felt he had been humiliated, left the house, foreswore Christianity, and was a popular lecturer for the next thirty years. But on the death of his wife, with whom he had lived an exemplary life, he could no longer stand his isolation. He returned to his old place and made a public apology. He preached on the text: "We are a living offering."

> A living offering it must be. This is what I did not understand. As the bullocks were brought to the altar formerly, and might break away and hurt the people in the neighborhood, so I did not accept my opportunity, the opportunity of living down this humiliation.[69]

{There has never been a more glorious commentary on Matthew.}

In the Japanese celebration of the Lord's Supper this overwhelming experience of a living sacrifice colors the ritual. The dagger used in the solemn ceremony of ritual suicide so popular among the samurai was brought wrapped in white paper, which had to be folded a certain way, and the whiteness of the paper alluded to the sacrifice of life that is about to take place. From this worldly model, the form of wrapping in white paper was taken over for the bread at communion, which is offered to the communicants in just such a wrapping. In this way the meaning of sacrifice and self-offering is as strikingly translated into Japanese—I dare say—as it is translated in Matthew's gospel from the Old Testament into the New.

Of all the Evangelists, it is Matthew, the most drastic and ill-mannered, who is also writes the most elementary. Through him, we have received the new ritual in writing, and without it, our era would be without dress for its nakedness. It is very nice to lay aside old-fashioned clothes, but our era needs some dress all the same. Now we have received the power of ritual, free of superstition, myth and magic. Anyone can understand Matthew—child and genius, soldier and farmer—unless his heart is closed to the very concept of self-sacrifice. The minds that scorn the sacraments as obsolete or as myth never fail to frighten me by their childishness. What ignorant and uneducated hearts they must have; how the grist-mill of their brains must have crushed all serious experience of life, of their own highest hopes! It is usually these same people who expect to be adored by their families, read by the public, and paid well by their endowed institution. How can they

---

69. [The source of the quote and the detail on the wrapping of the host is not given. The story refers to Niijima Jo and Paul Kanamori of Doshisha University, but is found neither in *Kanamori's Life-Story*, nor in his *Three-Hour Sermon*. ERH may have had the source (or the story) from Samuel Colcord Bartlett, Jr., who spent thirteen years as chaplain at Doshisha before retiring to Norwich, VT.]

expect it unless man's nature is fulfilled by entering the ranks of the offerings? It is our highest nature to be offerings. "Liturgy is only another name for Almighty God's table manners."[70]

These were the four glad tidings: the sacrificial victim made eloquent; the world-heart created by response; God's "no" transformed into a healing medicine for the suffering on the road to a new incarnation; and the human as God's newest poem. The blind alleys of tribal ritual, of temple cult, of Israel, and of Greece were opened up to one another. The four Evangelists succeeded because they were each immune to the specific disease that their tidings swept away.

So please don't call John hellenistic, Mark Egyptian, Matthew Judaizing, or Luke Pauline. The gospel's restoration of free speech proceeded by a matching of opposites! John, the prophetic one, did not write for the Jews, nor did the doctor Luke write for the Greeks {it was the other way around. Fed on the prophets, John overcomes the Greek muses, and the academic doctor, Luke, overcomes the scribes}. The fisherman Peter preaches to overcome the priestly-astrological world, and it is no man of good taste and good standing who surpasses the Old Testament in the first gospel, but the completely unrespectable publican.[71]

Once we keep in mind the specific disease cured by each gospel, its literary style and form immediately appear impeccable. In the eyes of the critics they all have the wrong ending. But if they are read as medicines, their endings are as much to the purpose as their beginnings. As "natural sources" for historical research they are impossible, but as wells of spiritual speech they are sound. Now, we experience something similar with the beginnings and ends of the *Iliad* and the *Odyssey*. How could it be otherwise? What is the beginning and the end of speech? The beginning of a human breath discloses the time and place of a particular act of the spirit. End and beginning bring inspiration down to earth; the end and beginning of any book tell you if it is true or not. This truth is a threefold truth: a word may be true in its content; it may secondly be true enough to prove the author right; *and finally it may be so true that it forces the next speaker to respond and speak in turn.*

Shakespeare compelled Milton to swerve out of the path of earlier poetry because his language was so perfect that Milton complained ("On Shakespeare," 1630). The Church has lived on the truth of the facts told in the "four gospels"; Christians in their own lives have lived on the truth of

---

70. ERH: I am indebted to Father Smith in Bruce Marshall's *The World, the Flesh, and Father Smith* for this saying. [See Appendix I, 333.]

71. [1954: The following section was headed "The Cross of Grammar"]

the men who told them. These two aspects of truth have been effective for a long time. As I said before, I am concerned with the third aspect of all truth, *its forcefulness in begetting a response by changing language.* {In our tradition this third truth is continually proven in new forms,} and I hope I have managed to prove this truth about the four gospels to the satisfaction of the most confirmed skeptic. The gospels were each true enough to force the next speaker to go on speaking above and beyond the last word of the previous speaker.

Each one had to step in where the last speaker had left off. They imparted the concrete time and the scene of their conversation so vividly, that they touch another off to the next move. They sing, over a period of perhaps forty years, the *one* gospel, each in his own key, on his specific wave-length, according to his lights, each passing on the joyous and onerous task to the better man. In this process the "four gospels" become a continuation of Jesus' life through the minds that were overpowered by their office as Evangelists. They were re-created as lips of the Word.

Following his Savior's irresistible call, *Matthew* writes himself out of the City of Man, in which he had been the publican, into the church {of the *oikoumene*}. He was {hurled head over heels} into the new eon with the one command: "Come!"

Mark is inside the church. As Peter's companion, he is not in the front lines but protected from outside pressures. Peter's vehement subjective emotions and his task may absorb his assistant, but Mark has the roof of fellowship over his head {in Peter}. He has no need to change allegiance like Matthew.

Luke narrates. His concern is the documented story of the past {as supported by witnesses}. Having a student before him, he is the cable for transmitting the glorious deeds of the first two generations to those born afterwards, so that no fewer than four generations, from Jesus' parents to the church of Theophilus's children, enter into communion with one another.

John is outside the cycle of command, fellowship, and history. He is at the source, at the eternal *beginning*. With this *one* word "In the beginning"—{and "it will be at the end" in the Apocalypse!}—John renders Jesus the decisive service that removes the event of his death from antiquity. In antiquity, Jesus' death could only have been treated in ritual, in the calendar, in poetry, or in Israel's scriptures. What would have been Jesus' fate in his friend's mouth in Greece? His friend "Iohannis" would have mourned his friend as Homer did Achilles, in an immortal poem, perhaps, or as Plato did, in a "Crito" or an "Apology." In Israel, Jesus' death would have unmasked his experience as a failure; in Israel's eyes God had said "NO" to the crucified Messiah. In Egypt, Jesus would have had the stars against him; a better horoscope, a new cycle with a new Christ, would have to be awaited. In tribal ritual, Jesus would have become the hero of a myth; Christians would have become one more tribe, with his disciples celebrating Easter and his myth enacted annually for his little clan. John's gospel blocks this relapse into ritual, into the cycles of the sky-world, into poetry, and into Jewish negation.

Jesus was not an end and his death was not an ending. Matthew, Mark, and Luke had already reported how *one* free man had broken the unending chains of these cycles and started a new life {outside the old order of things} in One Church all over the world. John seals the event of a new era beyond tribe, temple, poetry, and Israel. The new era would be open rather than cyclical because the four streams of speech had been re-united at the source; they could gush forth for eternity with the same original force as the four rivers of Paradise had on the first day of creation. The endless repetition of cycles is broken, {since or} when the cross, in which these streams of speech met, is held high as the beginning of endless progress. Our era defies cycles.

Of course they still tempt us. At this very moment Western man has nearly been dragged down into eternal recurrence, into Spengler's fatalism: {he speaks of a new Middle Ages, World War III, and other such things}. We must wake up again to the cross of grammar with the help of the grammar of the cross. John placed {the creation of Man by speech} before any of his or our particular historical performances.

"In the beginning was the Word"—the tribe, Egypt, Homer, and Israel were Man's creations because Everlasting Man[72] is the listener, the speaker {and the transmitter}. So every real Man climbs higher than any of his previous rituals of speech. "How can a Christian be subject to Fate?" cried Augustine, "since Fate only means the words that have been said before, and Christ is the Word that is said *now*?"[73] God made man in his image to speak as an eternal beginning, and to the bitter end Jesus remained {as free as his Father}.

Our era can avoid cycles as long as the roadblock of Christianity lies between it and antiquity. {Every father changes his plans when his children have gone astray; God changes his plans out of love for his son, and it is the Son who taught us that.} The three other gospels could still be read by later generations as pre-Christian, that is, as mere history. The whole nineteenth century dispensed with John and concentrated on the first three "Synoptics." Without John, the "gospel" would not exist as more than mere history;

---

72. [A fond allusion to *The Everlasting Man*, the book Chesterton wrote to refute H.G. Wells and which would later have such a profound effect on C.S. Lewis.]

73. [A paraphrase of Augustine, possibly from the *Tractates (or Homilies) on the Gospel of John*, 37:8.]

with John the church overcame the danger she faced of becoming a merely mythological, a merely ritualistic, a merely poetical, a merely fictitious institution. She now sees all her temporal forms in the light of an eternal beginning, because her Founder is always ahead of her and at the head of any of her ways of speech: the Word which is in the beginning, {and sets out on his journey through the times}.

The four Evangelists immunize our era against relapsing into natural inertia and blind cycles. They represent antiquity's cross of grammar in the new era. All speech had long since been poured out into the cross of grammar in drama, lyrics, epics, and theories; but once established, these grammatical forms drove on under their own momentum in spells and endless rituals. Rituals were no longer transparent, but became magic, cycles, routines, intellectual games, the sport of logic and superstition. The Word withered away.

The Evangelists reversed the cross of grammar into a grammar of the cross. One man had lived from "Let it happen" (*fiat*) to "It has happened" (*factum est*), from "Go into the world" to "It is accomplished, my father"—from listening to the call, through poetry and story, to summing up—completing his whole life as one grammatical cycle [Mark 16:15; John 19:30]. The four gospels depicted this circulation, as Hilarius Isaac put it at the end of the fourth century:

> Why were the experiences and sayings of the Lord organized in four volumes and by four authors? Four volumes, four authors, both [*were*] congruous, for we have before us, in the words of Isaiah, the "One Acceptable Year" [Isaiah 58:5, Luke 4:19]. This year is contained in four volumes as in four revolutions [*similar*] to the four seasons through which a year evolves: one season is in need of the other, mutually. Accordingly the acts and sayings of the Lord are circumscribed within the area of four books, each one of which stands in need of the other. Together, they are perfect in conveying the plenitude of time.
>
> Secondly, there was a good reason why it should be organized by four authors. Of the year's seasons, the terms show diversity; of the gospels too the nomenclature is diverse; and if they seem to contradict each other in their words, they do not dissent when they are interpreted in the light of this reason. The seasons of nature, too, are as different as possible in their names, their weather conditions, their astronomical aspect; but in the result of producing the fruits which come to live, they do not dissent.[74]

---

74. ERH: *Corpus Scriptorum*, L 430. [Translation by ERH from the English version

In the context of our whole book[75] we may say that each gospel takes pains to show the entire cycle of life from the imperative by way of the subjunctive and narrative to the indicative. {All four bring eternal matter to articulation.} A particular grammatical figure, however, predominates for each individual Evangelist. Matthew, who had himself experienced the violence of a sudden command, "Follow me!" took the imperative as his guide. Mark who {wrote for and with the prince of the apostles, who wrote the Lord's law journal,} pursued the most "lyrical" motif, that of fellowship.[76] Luke, who had been Paul's companion but no more belonged to the crowd of Apostles than Paul himself had, tells the story from Christmas on as would any story-teller who has no time-span in common with the events that he reports. {He listened to the historical, narrative voice.} But John, who needed no external credentials or events to believe in his friend, {found a starting point for his writing in the eternity of God who gave the Son} his victory over the endless cycles of ritual, eons, and revolutions; over mere novels and mysteries. {The abyss of the times closes with John.} He began with the progress brought on by the Word's power in his eternal indicative "in the beginning was the Word." So Jesus is identified as the freedom {for new beginnings.}

Here, then, *the grammar of the cross* and the phases of all group life became transparent as the cross of grammar. Before a man has been initiated into this cross of grammar—as a faithful follower who hears the call of duty; {as me} the lover whom his soul calls by his name;[77] {as you} the patient who is seized by hope of recovery; and lastly as the thinker who realizes the category of freedom in himself and freely stands against the laws his mind thinks up for nature—before a man has had at least one of these four experiences, he cannot use speech to any reasonable purpose—and speech without experience always {proliferates, like weeds in a garden}. As soon as the gospels were written, this chatter without experience began to dabble in the new facts proposed by the existence of the church.

---

of the essay. On "Hilarius Isaac," see also Appendix I, 327–28.]

75. [*Die Sprache.*]

76. ERH: The fantastic assertion that Mark is older than Matthew, long since disproved by Chapman and Butler, overlooked among other things, the fact that Mark as a war diary had no time for Matthew's speeches. [ERH was a life-long reader of Migne's monumental *Patrologia Latina*; John Chapman is said to have read it in its entirety. After WW I, Chapman was called to Rome to work on the revision of the Vulgate; his *Matthew, Mark, and Luke* was published posthumously in 1937 (see Appendix I, 318–21). Basil Christopher Butler, author of *The Originality of Matthew*, attended the second Vatican Council. Both men were abbots of the English Benedictine abbey of Downside.]

77. [*It is my soul that calls upon my name*: (*Romeo and Juliet*, II:2).]

This dabbling was called *"gnosis."* People tried to think the new life without first having been touched by it in some form of call, as listening, as passion, or as a change of heart. But for the four Evangelists, the whole story in Palestine could not have withstood the onslaught of the Gnostics—from Simon Magus, the fellow who ran around at a time when the blood of martyrs still "reddened the soil of Palestine" proclaiming himself the Savior and his little harlot the Virgin Mary—up to Marcion, the one who acknowledged no other gospel than Luke's and declared that it had fallen directly from heaven.

{So we all have cause, like Harnack, to inspect the "four gospels" on precisely the question of how well they protect us from *gnosis*. Biblical criticism has not taken this seriously enough, and has instead torn the gospels apart, but the four gospels can still protect us as well as they did Christians around 150–180 A.D.}[78] The Gnostic separates the daily life of the writer, teacher, apostle, or speaker from the content of his speech. In other words, the Gnostics have never entered the realm of experience in which the speaker himself has become the fruit of lips and the heart represents the lips of other hearts. *Gnosis* is rampant all over the world today—the churches themselves are full of it. As an attempt to know the world before being transformed by being spoken to, pacifism is also *gnosis*.

For the last century, the love between man and wife has been our last defense against this relapse into *gnosis*. In Juliet's call on Romeo, many a man of the nineteenth century learned to recognize himself, however dimly, as the one who was called into being by the lips of the soul he loved. The generations that followed this past century of great lovers {from Goethe to Selma Lagerlöf} seem to have heard nothing but the call to arms. {Life is redeemed by love; the spirit carries lovers through dangers. But once love is reduced to sex, the spirit seems to take the form of war-fever, and it may be that the war volunteers of 1914 found their time's only antidote to the *gnosis* of the *Magic Mountain*—the volunteers of 1914 loved death!}

{The insight into the structure of the gospels is no luxury.} The teachers of old and young, of girls as well as boys, will corrupt those taught if they go on issuing abstract verdicts in numbers and statistics from their judgment seat. {The much-maligned Heinrich Treitschke was a teacher of genius, for when he described the terrible physical suffering and spiritual self-control of the great French statesman Richelieu, he was not above bursting into tears.} A teacher who is not an initiate in the suffering of one of the four passions of speech is not qualified to teach, for he fails to understand the conditions under which it is meaningful to speak.

---

78. ERH: Harnack, "Evangelien-Prologe," 322–41. [See Appendix I, 346–50.]

The word "freedom" must never replace the experience of liberation, the word "good" must never replace the experience of getting better. {Today it is the particular curse of the educated} that "kindness" so often replaces the passionate need to love, as "adjustment" replaces the experience of personal commitment.

{So it is worth a good man's sweat to lift the meaning of speech into our awareness} and I must invite the reader to bear with me a bit longer. Today it is no longer enough to "understand" the *individual* gospels. {Only taken together can they hold in check the mind of *gnosis*—spinning its wheels, threshing the empty straw of what today we may call biblical criticism, psychology, research into myth, or economic materialism—and only through confession of our own devastation and our own crises of faith. Are there ways in which we can admit the cross of grammar in spite of the arts and sciences of our time?}

New ways do in fact open as soon as thought once more admits that it has no hard and fast position. {Confess to us your real nature as a stream determined by your time and dependent on long time-spans. There "is" no truth outside the long trail of tears from God's eternity into the world; you cannot honestly live out one moment of your reason, or reflect on it, unless you take part in the eternity of the spirit. You must never allow yourself to congeal into a world-view. Your unchanging picture of the world, your oh-so-clever analysis, your educated superiority, your self-reflection, all of Kant and all of Hegel, will only keep you from singing along with the rest of us. God alone is a "mighty fortress" as Luther truthfully sang.}[79]

{Our Adam's inspiration was once fully incarnated in the face of death, that is, in the face of a life-long voluntary sacrificial death; what had been Word became life}. This spirit overflowed into the four gospels through four different channels. Therefore, the text of the "four gospels" is something like a wax model of our mind's circulatory system. If we try to identify the elements of {these four spiritual "bell-metals," to see how they interfere even physically in the lives of the Evangelists as they are transformed, we may approach again the transparent effect that the incarnation had on believers in the old church of the Fathers. The scholastics from Anselm to Schlatter taught that *fides dabit intellectum*, faith will produce understanding. But the faith of the Paris and Heidelberg scholastics is not the faith of the four Evangelists or the church Fathers. They had cried out with Christ, "*Fides creat corpora*," let faith grant face and form. That is the experience of the Evangelists and the nations. Things happen to us, physically and tangibly, according to our faith.}

---

79. [1954: The following section was headed "The Shape of the Four Evangelists."]

As we all know, our body is no mere box or receptacle, but tries to correspond as best it can to our mental processes: {we shiver when a new truth overwhelms us;} we lie dreaming or half-dreaming, and, {defenseless as we are,} we may have our best ideas {or the greatest terrors descend; we sit up and cross our legs} when we wish to think through a variety of versions or impressions; {we go for a walk to converse—and so we change. In other books I have begged the theologians not to lay the yoke of their long-exhausted concepts on us poor believers who still have faith that God is just beginning to create us. For they hinder or deny the process of faith, that physical change that is the only way for the spirit to enter us. They laugh when the believer kneels instead of "thinking it over," the way they do. I could relate a remarkable story of conversion in which a great thinker's superiority collapsed before the stupid kneeling of an even stupider person (not externally or sentimentally, but because the rubble-filled springs of his own soul suddenly dared flow again, perhaps for the first time) and threw him on his knees as well, reforming him physically.} We jump up and pace the floor when we are in a fighting mood.

Obviously, modern man suppresses or misplaces many of these physical reactions to his mental processes. But he uses them in language, even if his body never gets his permission to practice them. We say an artist "conceives" like a woman, that a criminal "breaks down" beneath the weight of the evidence, that a speaker was in a "fighting mood" and that a teacher occupies a "chair." So obviously one bodily response expresses a particular mental attitude better than another.

I imagine Matthew standing and fighting; John lying "as if dead," in the words of Revelation [1:17]; Mark bending down or kneeling beside Peter; and Luke, of course, sitting at his desk. By contrast to these bodily attitudes, the old symbols used used for the four evangelists by the artistic traditions of the last nineteen centuries leave me cold. For all intents and purposes, they have been discarded by all serious artists of the last 150 years, even in ecclesiastical art. Could there be a good reason for breaking with this venerable tradition? May it not be that those well-rooted forms and symbols have become obsolete, antiquated by our very progress, because we have become Christian? We may thank God for this period of formlessness since 1750—because in it a Christian inner symbolism has been maturing {whose fruits are now ripe for harvest}.[80]

80. ERH: The painter Schmidt-Rotluff portrayed the four Evangelists in 1912, just as one spiritual world gave way to another. He did leave out the Old Testament attributes but as a child of the nineteenth century restricted himself to the heads of the four! The Evangelists stare wildly out of the metal which was his material. But God decreed the incarnation, that the Word become flesh, not just a head. See Grohmann, *Schmidt-Rotluff*, 159 and 240.

The old attributes of the Evangelists were the lion for Mark, an angel for Matthew, an ox for Luke, and an eagle for John.[81] These attributes were taken from the four-formed cherubim of the Old Testament, and the cherubim were connected in turn with Egyptian and Babylonian beliefs. These cherubim of the Old Testament were assembled from eagle, bull, lion, and angel, but the Old Testament has long since lost its grip on our symbolic imaginations. The more man becomes a creature of the Word, the more clearly his body performs this office. No animal can be a vessel of speech and sit, stand, kneel, or lie as dead in listening and speaking.[82]

The *Spirit* compels us to take the shape appropriate to listening and speaking man. The Word could not have come into the world if it had not had the power to {carry men and women beyond their gender} in listening and speaking. To stand means to be in action, under orders; to kneel means receive on faith and in peace; to sit means to instruct and narrate; to lie prostrate means to conceive like an artist, the genius of conception and creativity. That no longer seems so far-fetched once we confess the truth that the spirit molds our body and sets our boundaries. The spirit calls our bodies {into its kingdom above the love of the genders; only from the spirit's height can meaning fall on you or me}.[83]

When the "four gospels" became His lips, those lips formed themselves in Matthew {in his stormy departure from the Jews,} motivating Mark to kneel in the innermost sanctum {of Peter's church,} motivating Luke to arrange the reports in two periods, motivating John to advance to the eternal cosmic seat of truth. Thus the four men reached {into the renewed world of re-telling and "passing-on,"} into the innermost sanctum, {into the chain of generations,} and into eternal truth. They reformed the cross of grammar, of which these pages have spoken so often, by forming a grammar of the cross. This cross of grammar unites all mortals {and united, we can speak the truth}. For a moment this cross of grammar had become flesh in a living being, and for this reason he is called the Word. But this earth has no place for absolute truth; it breaks it up into separate times, so the cross is the only place where the full truth of a human heart can be revealed at a glance.

---

81. [1954: *I have collected the archaeological material for many years, and I hasten to say that these attributes are by no means unanimous. When they were first used, the attribution to the individual Evangelists was not as stereotyped as it later became.*]

82. [1954: *Of course, animals also can't embrace or 'grow' in each other's palms by shaking hands.*]

83. [The chapter "The Four Apostles: James, Peter, Paul, and John" was added here in 1954, but not included in the German version. See Appendix E, 255–59. The section that followed it was then headed "The Law of Liberty."]

This great truth is only preserved by the gospels {and they have won themselves a new hearing in every generation,} even in the face of the most ritualistic clergy, the most cynical science, the most legalistic inquisition, and the most superstitious mob. During their own campaigns, in fact, those institutions themselves have had to teach these gospel truths which defied their own natural tendencies, at their own altars, in their own courts, by their own systems, and their own sport palaces. These *four truths* were: first, the freedom of the soul; second, the relativity of every law for the free; third, the cost of freedom; and fourth, the absolute authority of the law for those who are not free.

1. Freedom was not freedom to think, because thought can only think the law. After languishing for four long years as a so-called free-thinker, William James discovered one day that his mind could see only laws. He jumped from his sickbed and declared: "A man must believe that his actions are free; it cannot be proven."[84] This was his gospel truth: he who loves is free. {Love calls us to "pass it on"; the "passer-on" is the liberator.}

2. Freedom makes all laws relative, because he who loves, reads all laws as if they had been established to defend freedom. Marriage is the fruit of love. The Constitution is the fruit of comradeship-in-arms. Science is the fruit of a brotherhood of minds. What freedom is to the founders, the law is for their trusting and grateful heirs. They willingly speak the language of their fathers, as laid down in the laws, because they recognize themselves in the names that are {passed on} to them by the founders.

3. The price of freedom is threefold: time, life, and substance. All three must be given freely to achieve great ends. Where not even one of these three powers is given freely, freedom becomes an empty word. Freedom's way into the world consists of the investment of these three forms of capital in the service of a new love, a new faith, or a new hope. {Without it no soul can reach incarnation.}

4. The relationship between freedom and law is absolute; no one unwilling to pay the price may enjoy freedom. He who is not willing to marry, cannot and can never know what full love between the sexes can be. He who is not willing to suffer for the truth, can never know what the truth is. He who does not defend his country will not and shall never understand what freedom is {though not everything that calls itself a fatherland is one}.

84. [See also "The Soul of William James," in ERH, *Impure Thinker*, 20.]

In these four truths Jesus' four names are re-translated. They are *his* names, in which and under which the gospels were written. Never before had a poem, a law, a prophecy, or a book pointed beyond itself to the price that it cost to compose the poem, to fulfill the law, to receive the prophecy, or to compose the book. The gospels have been abused: they have reduced to mere source material, and every individual word in them has been held sacred.

However, as long as the four gospels are at work, *they protect those who read them from themselves.* This is something quite unknown in antiquity. All the lips of antiquity had {by their very existence} become idols, gods, holy scripture, and authority in and of themselves. {The Greek muse kissed only individual foreheads.} Only those processes that contain gospel qualities, whereby they are done in the heart's name and spoken in His name, can be said to belong to our era. The rest remains pre-Christian, even if it was enacted in 1500 or 1900. Just as the symbols of the four Evangelists were themselves pre-Christian and can only be baptized in His name today, so the Christian era has seen books without number "on" Christianity which {moved to an observing distance from Christ and so} were not themselves Christian. {That went on "from Reimarus to Wrede."} Gradually, in religion, art, science, economics, and education, such make-shift books and theses will have to go. In the light of the four gospels they stand condemned as fruitless words. We are free to live after the era of fruitless words, because we are shoots of the tree of freedom which Isaiah foretold: "I will create the fruit of lips [57:19]."[85]

{Where the church fathers always saw deep meaning in the multiplicity of the gospels, modern biblical criticism has used a particular acid to destroy the meaning of the number four: it dated all the gospels too late. Now finally we can expose the trick by which this late dating was "proven."}

{The approaching destruction of Jerusalem orchestrates the crucifixion. Jesus, Paul, and Peter managed to "pull the church together" as Christian and apostolic at the last possible moment before the fall of the temple. The Evangelists prophesy the fall of Jerusalem in Jesus' words. Aha, say the critics, these are prophecies after the fact, *vaticinia ex eventu*. Once Jerusalem had fallen, these prophecies were invented. And so they make liars of people who wrestled with lions and overcame their fear of death; we never even notice how the Evangelists are turned into Munchhausens, braggarts, and swaggerers—these men who had ruthlessly revealed their own weaknesses as well as those of the other apostles. The most shameless of biblical

---

85. [The following passage replaced the chapter "The Oldest Official Remarks on the Gospels." See Appendix E, 261–67.]

criticism's many impudences is the assumption that the apostles and Evangelists made up the prophecies after the fact—it reduces the foundations of the church to a pack of lies.}

{Any reader who can remain a layman may read my essay "*Ehrlos—Heimatlos*" ("Honorless—Homeless") of 1919,[86] in which I foretold a pseudo-emperor and the destruction of the Jews. From 1918–19 I lived a selfless life, and as Ricarda Huch has said, "Deep within, everyone is prophetic." These gentlemen who have never prophesied because they were never selfless should not dare to lay a finger on the Evangelists—the four would have gone to the cross themselves before inventing a prophecy after the fact. Biblical criticism accuses these heroes of mortal sin. The correct conclusion from the texts at hand is the opposite: the prophecies made an impression because they bore witness to Jesus' gift of prophecy. That is why they were kept alive and written down.}

{This infamous counterfeiting theory has been fully exploited to date the gospels: they all had to come later! Now, I prophesied in 1918, and prophesied correctly; the year is now 1964 and I reprint the prophecies in this book after the fact, some 46 years later. Because Matthew prophesies "after the fact," Mr. Gilpatrick[87] "proves" that the book was written by "someone" in 84 A.D. In 1959 Edgar J. Goodspeed returned the apostle Matthew to his honor as Evangelist in his loving *Matthew: Apostle and Evangelist*. And if we subtract 46 years from 84 A.D. (just as we do from 1964 to 1918), we arrive at a time-span for Matthew of between 38 and 84 A.D.}

{In the year 38 A.D. all twelve apostles lived as a closed corporation in Jerusalem. The Lord had granted them all their powers as one inseparable common hand, and when Matthew picked up his pen, he could only do so as their secretary. Today's criticism arises from the hell of individualism that has ruled since the Enlightenment, so it sees individual Evangelists wandering around like will o' the wisps in the swamp. Oh, each one of them spoke in the name of all the apostles—most of all the latecomers, Matthew and Paul! In the case of the "extra" apostle, Matthew, there is a precious proof. Clement of Alexandria reports (*Stromata* VII, 13):}

> {The apostle Matthew always said: If the neighbor of a chosen one sins, then the chosen one has sinned. If he had behaved as *the Word* called him to, then his neighbor would have been filled with such respect that he would not have sinned.}

---

86. [ERH, reprinted in *Die Sprache* II, 85–115. See also Appendix I, 336.]

87. [David Bade suggests that this may be a reference to George Dunbar Kilpatrick, author of the 1946 *The Origins of the Gospel According to St. Matthew*.]

{This quote is precious because in it the apostles' common hand may be seen. This is not John writing about the *Logos* nor Luke writing of the servants of the Lord. No, the latecomer appeals to the Word, to the Logos, and from this sentence rises the united speech of all the apostles and Evangelists. The so-called late "Johannine" element is well-known even to the first Evangelist.}

{They are all of one mind. The genealogy in Matthew is no more "Mattheine" than the prologue to John is "Johannine." They all believed themselves to be sinners and righteous like everyone else, and only together to be worthy of the healing power of the spirit. This way we can arrive at a sensible dating of the gospels. They are not cheats with prophecies invented after the fact; they are not forgeries with a purpose. The gospels actually accuse the authors or their protectors of the weaknesses to which they fell victim, and they all go back to the most intimate community of the apostles with each other. Matthew wrote for the twelve while they were still together, and I still hope to see the day an honest Bible critic recognizes in these twelve years in Jerusalem, from the crucifixion to Peter's departure, their Lord Jesus' greatest achievement of genius. In this decade the glorious hymn of the Letter to the Phillipians must have resonated and knees have been bent for the first time before the Son.}

{In section A [of the fourth part of *Die Sprache*][88] the language of modern physics is shown to be *trinitarian*—a mixture of national, liturgical, and scientific sources—in contrast to the merely *three-fold* repetition of pagan magic formulas. This language has been emerging since 33 A.D. and appeared for the first time in precisely that decade of waiting in Jerusalem. Just as we find the Lord as the *Logos* in the mouth of all four Evangelists, thanks to Clement of Alexandria's story, and not only in John (fifty years ago John's gospel was dated in the 2nd century for just this "*Logos*-speculation"), so all four Evangelists agree that one word, the word with which our contemporaries replace our faith, is forbidden to them.}

{The word "hope" is missing in all four gospels, despite the fact that the World Council of Churches has proclaimed this same hope to be the heart of faith. Oh, the believing community of the gospels saw the Lord of their faith in the bloody reality of the scars left by his wounds,[89] in the hopeless pain and death of a betrayed, bespittled, and crucified human being! They shared his own faith, that is, they hoped to share the first-born's faith, and so possessed *a hope hitherto impossible*. For Christians, hope only means to be

---

88. [*Die Sprache* II, "In die Zahlensprache der Physik," 221–75.]
89. [*im blutigen Ernst seiner Wundmale.*]

allowed to have their Lord and Master's faith. They have a hope that no one could have had before Jesus himself believed!}

{Instead today's councils (as in Evanston)[90] hammer and drum into us that faith and hope are one and the same thing, citing the Letter to the Hebrews. Take care: for the gospels, the word "hope" is a *forbidden* word. Now the reader may not believe me or, once a word-count proves it, declare it mere coincidence, but the Holy Spirit has done me the favor of cutting off this escape—the four Evangelists wrote more than the four gospels; Luke also wrote Acts. Luke uses "hope" eight times in Acts and not once in his Gospel. That puts an end to coincidence. In his Gospel he denied himself the word "hope"; he forbade himself to use it. Jesus remained the victor through faith, without hope; that is the message of the gospel. Jesus was no "yearning sufferer of starvation for the unattainable."[91] He was no boy, no promising youth, no hopeful theology student. He was the Arnold Winkelried[92] who blazes a trail for us into the kingdom of the dead who end with death, and who leads even death itself back into life. What use would hope have been?}

{Hope radiates from us into the world. It can only be fulfilled by things we deem worthy of hope, which must be things that already exist. I can only hope for something I desire, and I could not desire it if I had not already made its acquaintance; hope is a motion that begins in me. Faith is quite different: in it the Creator approaches his creature to complete our creation. By letting his Father complete his creature and resting entirely in his Father's hand, our Lord stood fast where Adam had run away, and so could be further created by God beyond his own hope. Jesus is not only the second Adam; he is just as much the completely created, final Son, which Adam, and every mere Adam, at first fights off in fear and fright, in the blindness of hope. Jesus did not fight off death, he fulfilled it. The four Evangelists worshipped the final, second Adam and the completely created Son of God in Jesus, and so they did not insult him with the word "hope."}

We are not dealing here with either church history or world history; we are {trying to} lay the foundations for a history of the human spirit. {Our first volume discovered the form of our own present time as "trivial" and "trilemmatic."[93] Physicists speak three languages in their field; doctor and patient must approach each other on a threefold path before they can speak together effectively. The poor bourgeois and the poor Bolsheviks suffered

90. [The second assembly of the World Council of Churches was held in Evanston, Illinois, in August of 1954; its theme was *Christ: the Hope of the World.*]

91. [Goethe, *Faust II*, II:6 (line 8204–5).]

92. [Winkelried, a Swiss soldier who sacrificed his life to open enemy ranks to Swiss attack, is now widely considered a legendary figure.]

93. [*Die Sprache* I, "Die Rasse der Denker," 612–54, especially 638–54.]

hunger and thirst in their dialectic until even Stalin raised the three-fold character of speech in 1950.[94] The innovation of the third millennium will be the recognition that the sacral form of the trinity must now be translated into a secular *trivium* and a social trilemmatic. The "fruit of lips" goes on bearing fruit without cease. The whole first volume of our book[95] is like a gigantic charade that is solved in the second.}

The spirit moved the chieftains and the priests, the poets and the prophets. They were all driven by this power without being able to account for the power that drove them. For this reason, men were driven by spirits to cross-purposes; the confusion of tongues and the incessant war between tongues became the rule.

This was all changed by the Son, who paused. He halted the mere flow of talkative, news-mongering, mystical, or practical humanity. He discovered that these tendencies were evil and poisonous in separation, although each was complete and highly efficient in and of itself. Jesus did not say that poetry or magic, ritual or prophecy were not excellent. He knew they were, and he proved how well he knew them with his creative invention of a new ritual, his poetic gift for parable, his easy superiority to the possessed and demons, and his prophetic insight into the future of the world'- history. Yet, though filled to the brim with all four streams of speech, he emptied himself of all of them [Phil 2:7–8].

The {heir}, the harvest of all times, decided to change into the seed of a future completely protected against mere times. The old dividedness of the human soul, those canyons that the flooding streams of speech had caused in us, was to cease. {Since Christ's birth all times are contemporaries!} Jesus placed himself between the era of the canyons and our own lives lest we too be swayed too much by the avalanche blasts, the obsessions that drives all unbelievers forward by the mere inertia of their intellectual jargon. {The more religious it is, the more pompous it becomes; the more artistic it is, the lewder it becomes; the more learned it is, the more perverse it becomes. . .}[96]

To this day, we have nothing to bear us up but name-giving speech, cosmic writing, natural poetry, and prophetic vision. We may call them mores, science, art, and politics. But that is only a slight difference in terms compared with antiquity, in which the mores were tattoos enounced at the tribe's gatherings, the "science" carved as runes in the temple's cosmic body,

---

94. [Perhaps a reference to Stalin, *Sprachwissenschaft*. Berlin: Dietz, 1951.]

95. [*Die Sprache*: this version of "The Fruit of Our Lips" was the final chapter of the second volume.]

96. [Ellipsis in the original.]

the art consecrated by one of the muses, and political change was the proclamation of wars "to the death."

The "time-cups" {or "time-bowls"} formed on these wavelengths—through "Oyez, harken, listen, be silent!" in all law-making assemblies; in the "Contemplate! measure! enter! ascend!" of all the cosmic temples; the "Sing, tell, say, adorn, glorif!" of all nine muses; the "Thou shalt tell them, thou shalt warn, flee, expect, fall prostrate, emerge, promise, hope!" of all prophecies—these times Jesus wove together into one strand. {In him the time-cups overflowed into each other. For this very reason, during the past century of Greek sectarianism,} liberals could take him for an artistic genius, psychoanalysts for a tribal chieftain, emancipated Jews for one of their many prophets, and fundamentalists for a cosmic power. An anatomy of his soul would doubtless find all these elements.

As he had to atone for the division of these four "offices" of human speech, he had to master them all himself, but they were only the resisting objects against which he pressed out the new life. He cast off his four primeval offices insofar as they were the dead-ends of ancient ritual, cult, prophecy, and poetry; after showing that he could heal, rule, teach, and sing, he dismissed them all as not good enough.[97] And by giving up his own role as heir, as harvest, he made the end into a beginning. His whole life is like an insurmountable wall on which is written: "Never again!" The blind avalanche of one-track reasoning lost its momentum when he intervened.

The humanity of the final man is in our offices as judge, scientist, artist, and prophet. Our divinity is in renouncing eevery one of these offices when they separate mankind. Jesus yielded his own spirit so that nothing pre-Christian, nothing that preceded him, could enter the new creation. He placed himself between the past and future, and nothing of the man Jesus was allowed to enter the new order of his second body, the church. People who speak of his sacrifice often fail to understand this: he interposed his whole life from its beginning, and not just his last days, between the past and our era. His own life was used up in this housecleaning; he volunteered that even his own flesh belonged to the old eon. That is why it makes sense to speak of the risen Christ as the first cell of the new body of our own humanity.

Jesus Christ is the first name in a {universal} language of mankind. The sacrifice of our own private, professional, and accidental nomenclature is our contribution to the new common, universal, unanimous tongue we

---

97. [1954: *a biography of Jesus cannot be provided. . . He was bringing into being a new order and working out a purpose—in complete isolation. The future order which it was the purpose of Jesus to bring into being, depended upon what he said and did, and finally upon his death.* Hoskyns and Davey, 248–50.]

have in common, founded in and on his name. The Letter to the Hebrews expresses it quite simply: "Your sacrifice consists of being satisfied that his Name precedes all other words of your vocabulary" (13:15).[98]

Now this is what matters today. The Word cannot come into the world unless we usher it in, in every age, into our own language, our own home, and our own neighborhood. In every age, the acceptance of that name is considered a scandal and ridiculous. All natural {temperaments}, the Greeks and the Romans, the Hebrews and the Goths, hate the idea that a new language could come into being here and now, a new language that robs their great literature and codices, their handbooks of science, and their "Knigges" of their ultimate value.[99]

Since that is exactly what the name "Christ" on our letterhead means, all four "anti-gospel" parties, {all the "dysangelists"—Darwin, Marx, Gobineau, Nietzsche—} all declare that the very mention of Jesus Christ's name to be bad taste, and as we have seen, it really is in bad taste.[100] They declare him unscientific; as we have seen, he is unscientific. They declare him blasphemous; as we have seen, he is blasphemous. And they declare him inconsistent; as we have seen, he is inconsistent. {Because the same name has to be proclaimed anew every day, in every year, and in every century, in a new language, it can never sound proper, scientific, pious, or logical. If it did, it would become powerless!}

The name of the Word is our sacrifice. When we are {too ashamed, or} too timid to mention His name, whether for reasons of taste, for scholarly objectivity, for good feeling, or systematic consistency, we exclude ourselves from the new eon and from the crucial language of free men. {Generally we prefer to vegetate *before* Christ's birth, like those who psychologize Paul, and} we will soon boast that there is no "after Christ's birth," no "A.D." The times roll on happily without Christ, roll right on past him.}

The present crisis, then, is between the deep longing in all of us to move beyond the denominations, and the high necessity to confess the scandal and ridicule of the cross. The Word of Mankind will remain a helpless stammering, a vile repetition of dead words, if—whether for reasons of taste, custom, science, or system—we decline to respond to our sponsor,

---

98. ERH: Reginald Heber's glorious anthem "Holy, Holy, Holy" demands that the saints cast *down their golden crowns around the glassy sea.*

99. [*Knigge* refers to Adolph Franz Freiherr von Knigge's 1788 treatise *Über den Umgang mit Menschen* (*On Human Relations*), a philosophical approach to etiquette, in contrast to the utilitarian approach exemplified by Emily Post.]

100. [In ERH's speech at Union Theological Seminary in 1954, the *dysangelists* were Darwin, Marx, Freud, and Nietzsche.]

to understand his stand, and to dare the world with the disreputable words "Christ" and "Christian."

If Jesus is the Logos, the Word, we must become what the Greeks called "*homologoi*," which means "of the same Word." We must revamp our words by explicitly making him the key to all of our own words, and we must each do it in our own way. We can now state the simple reason for this iron law of speech in our era: when we speak or act, the fruits of our words and actions are hidden from us. In weak moments we all think we can get away with empty, lying, or conventional phrases. And like to imagine that such words or deeds have no consequences. We say: "I was driven to say it, it was fear, self-interest, or pity speaking." And this explanation seems to excuse us. But what do we really mean by such remarks? We claim that we are only cogs in the wheels of blind fate; for all these usual explanations for the way we speak connect our remarks with a reason, cause, or motive, which hails from the past. All our excuses look backward.

Jesus' sayings all look forward. Every one of them only makes sense in light of the future. Not one of them was "caused" by any precedent, convention, excuse, reason, or motive. On the contrary, all his antecedents advised against every one of his actions and sayings. He said what he said and did what he did because he could not help bringing about a future that was different from the past. As Ambrose Vernon put it: "Jesus went to the cross because he couldn't help it."[101] "By their fruits shall ye know them" is not, alas, true of us, but it is of the Lord. In his crucifixion the conflict between the "backward" justification—by precedent, motive, environment, or piety—and the justification by "forward" love becomes perfectly clear.

Anyone who lives under His cross knows that he is not excused by any rational, social, natural, or physical propensities. He knows of course that man is by nature a coward, by nature a conformist, that man is defined by labels and held in bondage. But after Christ he also knows that this is only one side of the ledger. The heavier the pressure of conditions, prejudices, tradition, and nature exerted on man, the more necessary it becomes that "*this*" man feel provoked to break these chains of mere causation. Now people had made their Spartacus rebellions, their nasty doggerel, and their psalms of repentance before Christ. The new law that he proclaimed was this: {thanks to the blood of the Word,} one's own words were the *starting places* for a new incarnation. Facing forward, every one of his acts was a seed that bore

---

101. [Ambrose White Vernon (1870–1951), professor of theology at Yale, founded departments of biography at both Carleton College and Dartmouth College He was one of the three men to whom ERH dedicated *The Christian Future*. MDB cites Vernon's *Some Turning Points in Church History* as the source of ERH's quote, but the statement does not appear there. It was perhaps a famous classroom remark.]

fruit in unending times to come. Not one of his acts could be understood by his contemporaries—but we can, because we see all the implications. The implications become explicit with the passage of time. {They were invisible in 33 A.D., but impossible to overlook in 1933 A.D. No one knew in 33 that he was crucifying God—in 1933 Hitler knew it perfectly well, yet Nazi clerics called Hitler Christ.}

So Jesus was the first man who proved {the power of the "not-yet-created"} by not giving in to any temptation to reap the harvests of the past, as Satan urged him to do. In our time, we can all skim the milk for the cream; we can all make big salaries if we take the "little jobs" that are already organized and therefore well-paid. But my life as God's poem, as society's scapegoat, or an earnest of the spirit, as Paul called it [1:14], has no place in the budget or any going concern in society. Anyone who is nothing more than a child of God is superfluous. There is no place for him in the surveys, questionnaires, or statistics because he counts for as little as the child in the manger for whom the innkeeper had no room. How could he? Jesus was unforeseen, unpredictable. And yet, get this well, he was foretold and visible. In going to the quacks of the soul, the average citizen wishes to be taught that he is predictable, and yet he doesn't want his neighbor to see through him—he is secretive and superstitious at the same time. {Jesus, on the other hand, was an open secret.}

Although unaccustomed to doing so in our world of speechless thinking, the reader may now be equipped to analyze the four terms of this way of the cross, in which we predicate the core truth of speech and the power of speech over our lives. In the Christian life between past and future, one tension is between "foretold" and "unpredictable." The other tension is between "predictable" and "unpromised." To tackle the latter tension first, the dead soul can easily be understood: he takes the line of least resistance. The psychologist he consults comforts him by saying: "Well, your behavior is normal. You are afraid, you are sexually restless," and so forth. The client is glad to hear that anyone in his circumstances would act the same way. This man is predictable. If you know his needs and urges, you know what he will do next. He is so repetitive that he can never expect to be promised or heralded, because there is no hope of his making a new contribution. He has always existed—we have known this type of man since Adam's day. So he is very careful not to be seen through in his private religion, in his private opinions and private affairs. People like to call this "privacy," or lisp the formula "on a personal level." This is certainly one way to divorce the potential powers for doing unpredictable deeds and saying unpredictable words, from our highly predictable actual behavior..

This phrase "on a personal level" is a wonderful way of cheating ourselves. A "person" is a man who, insofar as he is truly "personal," clearly lets truth shine right through him, makes it his own. The expression "person" means to let something shine through, to become transparent, to stand revealed and to be representative. From 1942 to 1945, Eisenhower had no "private life," because he represented the American G.I.'s. Here is a person: here he stands, here he lives, and he is realized here and nowhere else.

The constant abuse of the expression "personal" for unused freedom, for concealed opinions, for private affairs, forces us to avoid the word today. It is sick.[102] To most people it only means that they keep some secrets to themselves. That is their balm and comfort, for it means "although we are predictable, although we follow the law of averages, yet you don't know everything about me. Hence, you are not totally my master and boss" A man who was both, completely known as well as completely predictable, would obviously be in the hands of psychologists {and a living corpse.} The explicable man must make at least the weak attempt to play hide-and-seek.

There is another way, however. You may be one hundred percent known, for all your handicaps and disadvantages as Jesus was, and still remain free and unpredictable. He could clearly be seen to be without office, without beauty, without power, and without family. And they were deceived in him, not because they knew him and his personal life, but because they didn't believe that he, of all people, was the Promised One, the one man whom the sages had foretold as the one truly free man, who could be nothing else than a seed of the future, the first word of a second creation, {the fulfillment of the fourteen "creations" in Isaiah 40:57}. Jesus was not invisible, but he was also foretold, promised as the harvest of all the sighs of all men of all ages in their caves of predetermination, fate, and scientific predictions. He was a person in that he let the spirit become transparent; and on his face, the reflection of God's freedom to create the world outshone all the blood, sweat, and tears with which the mortal man in fact expired [2 Cor 4:6].

We speak of the three persons of the Trinity, because they are the three ways in which God's full power is reflected and leaves its mark on us. The "three persons" are not three disconnected individuals—none of the three persons of the Trinity can be found "on a personal level." They are the three faces on which God goes on shining forth: they are the Father, the Son, and the Spirit. In the Son, God conquers the death of our soul, through which we would have to live predictably and concealed. In the Son, God stands revealed {and heralding and creating}.

102. ERH: See "Liturgical Thinking" in volume I [of *Die Sprache*, 465–92] and the five glorious chapters [on Sonnet LIX] "Vom Weltbuch der Person" in Florens Christian Rang's *Shakespeare der Christ* (*Shakespeare the Christian*), 55–73.

So the Son restores the true order between words spoken and lives lived. Words are meant to be orders given and promises made. Lives should be orders carried out and promises fulfilled! This, as we saw, has been the essential aim of all speech and ritual, since man first spoke. The purely indicative use our "thinkers" and our schoolbooks make of speech is mere grave-digging or afterthought, following along after the events that speech makes possible. Jesus showed that all words spoken before him called him forth, ordered him into existence insofar as they were real prayer, real longing, real prophecy, and fruitful imagination. And he fulfilled them all.

And so he revealed what we do when we speak: speaking we believe in seed and harvest, promise and fulfillment, command and report. We believe that in the beginning the Word was, and that at the end the incarnation will be {because the gift given us in the Word's further birth through Christ in each generation is added to our naked birth. Man the Re-teller, the Passer-on, began as the Son of Man and as the Word he perfects us to God's own kind.}

APPENDICES

Appendix A
A Letter to Adele Rosenzweig
(1928)

THIS IS ONE OF 133 letters that Eugen and Margrit Rosenstock-Huessy wrote Franz Rosenzweig's mother, Adele, between 1916 and her death in 1933. At times, the couple seem to have passed the responsibility of corresponding with her back and forth between them. "Tante Dele" was an difficult and unhappy woman who threatened and attempted suicide several times, but forbearance was necessary on both sides.

The other people referred to in the letter are: "Fräulein [Julie] von Kästner," Mrs. Rosenzweig's live-in companion; "Rafael," Franz and Edith Rosenzweig's son, then five years old; "Lotti," Margrit's younger sister, who remained close to "Gritli" and "Eugen" for the rest of their lives and close to Freya von Moltke after their deaths; "Hansli," the couple's only child; and "Anna," Anna Beinert Henke, the Rosenstock-Huessy's housekeeper, cook, and sometime nurse-maid, baby-sitter, and governess), recently married at the time of this letter.

Anna did not leave the Rosenstock-Huessy house in the Wardeinstrasse after all; the basement rooms, which the Rosenstock-Huessys had finished after they bought the house in 1923 as a place for students and professors to meet socially, were rebuilt into an apartment for Anna and her husband, Traugott. When the house was sold to the Eitner family in 1933, it was with the condition that the Henkes be allowed to stay on. In 1935, Anna smuggled Margrit's jewelry into Switzerland, convincing the German border guards that it was worthless by wearing all of it at once, making herself up heavily, and acting the floozy. (And if Anna had not put Franz Rosenzweig's "Gritli letters" into the grandfather clock being shipped to the Rosenstock-Huessys in the U.S., the true story of *The Star of Redemption* would never have been told.) She later provided life-saving counsel to many people buckling under Nazi rule, including Professor Eitner. When the Soviet army advanced on Breslau, she fled to the West with her two sons, Heinz and Hellmuth, and was "resettled" in Göttingen, where she died in 1977. Anna was a woman of remarkable courage and wisdom, and she deserves to be long remembered.

Adele (Arlsberg) Rosenzweig, around 1928.

LENZERHEIDE BEI CHUR   JANUARY 1, 1928

Dear Tante Dele,
I just wrote the number 1928 for the first time, up top. Every new year arrives, is lived out, and is written away more quickly than the last. But the way you end and begin them is important, so I begin this year with a letter to you—around noon, after Gritli, Lotti, Hansli, and I all had breakfast together. We all wish you and Fräulein von Kästner[1] a good new year. A good year—what we probably mean is: all the individual good things in life worth wishing for, but should we shout them out one at a time like some obstreporous child? I don't think so, since "only the true mix makes it happen."[2] Whatever life is like, it's good[3]—if we are only capable of living it. That's just what makes Rudolf Binding's "Life Experienced" such a refreshing book.

My next appearance in Cassel is already set. The religious eminences of Wuppertal have been so bold as to book me now for a lecture on September 28th. I accepted, so as to be sure of what we in Breslau call a "trip West." And that reminds me that I recently met Dr. Prager again after many years, in Breslau, and we were both glad. He stood by me in a hopeless environment (school reform), where I came to unpleasant notice with a lecture on adult education. Right away, I talked him into taking part in the Buber gift. This is another really original idea, and I look forward eagerly to seeing what comes of it. I was so proud of my own contribution that Franz's mere toleration of it rankled. Oddly enough, that's just the way things seems to be between him and me, for ever and always: I never know how something will strike him or how he will judge it. As a reverend in Galsworthy says of the Rabbi Jesus, so uncongenial to Franz: "He is incalculable."[4]

By the way, when I woke up this morning I found myself thinking: isn't it funny, that the Jews have been—as Rafael would say—"middit" their

1. [*Julie von Kästner . . . of Russian nobility, had escaped from the Bolsheviks and was considered a pioneer in education. She lived as a companion with my aunt Adele Rosenzweig.* (Alsberg, Witness, 24).]
2. [Goethe, *Faust II*, line 6850.]
3. [Last line of Goethe's "Der Bräutigam" (The Bridegroom).]
4. [Galsworthy, *Escape*, 635.]

fellow-citizen Jesus for 1,927 years. I conclude that certain "offices and guild-memberships" will not be offered me as quickly as I have sometimes naïvely expected—it's confoundedly difficult to get really "middit" someone, but once you've managed it, there's no swaying or soothing it away. Life knows of no release for these tangled knots—they just stay tangled. I always used to count on the drama ending in harmony, reconciliation, and cries of joy. But no, people just remain "middit" each other. That was what occurred to me when Below[5] died—that old matador of vitriol has now passed on: well-rewarded, still un-assaulted and un-refuted.

Lotti gave us Shakespeare's *Sonnets*. And they contain another improbable statement, which one can probably only judge correctly after a long life. After many years of acrimony with his beloved, Shakespeare writes this:

> O benefit of ill! now I find true
> That better is by evil still made better.
> And ruin'd love, when it is first built new
> Grows fairer than at first, more strong, far greater.[6]

This verse continues to trouble me. My experience refutes it—on the other hand, I am inclined to search for truth among the poets, "until his ink were tempered with love's sighs" as it is in the Sonnets. And there's something else: Shakespeare's statement that the benefit of "ill" consists in its tearing up the better, and that renewed loves grows in greater beauty, power, and scope, touches on a thought in my *Alter der Kirche*, in "Life, Teaching, and Influence," where I polemicize against Franz. I say there that the adult is not capable of walking humbly with his God. He can at most walk humbly again. Just the way an adult can not be a child, but only become like a child (which is not the same thing as "being" one).

Behind this sonnet and my dissent from the Franzian thesis that life after the vision of the star of redemption (the last word of the "Star") could be simply the same life as before the vision—the essay *ICHTHYS* came to me five years ago as a commentary on the last sentence of the "Star"—behind these uses then stands the great theological thesis of the "*felix culpa*" of mankind, which is to be found in Augustine and in the Easter liturgy ever since: "Happy the guilt of mankind that required such a solution!" and requires it anew every day!

This word of the *felix culpa* has always been a stumbling block for strict church people. Beyond that, its formulation in the liturgy has its precedent

---

5. [Georg Anton Hugo von Below (1858– 1927) was a conservative constitutional historian who considered the nation-state the end-point of all history.]

6. [Sonnet 119.]

in a love song of Ovid's, which may be found on the same level as Shakepeare's sonnet.

So many contradictions and curiosities converge here: The claim that shattered love can be whole again goes against all experience. Experience teaches us that knots stay tangled—and that the Jews have stayed "middit" Jesus for 1,928 years. So my theological insight runs contrary to my practical insight. Eugen against Franz, Augustine, Ovid, and Shakespeare—they all stand together against orthodoxy. The personal and the general are so confused that I am sorry not be able to portray the *"felix culpa"* and in some form get it across. It would have been a better contribution to last year's *Festschrift* for Franz. That is why I am telling you this somewhat complicated, but only apparently merely philological, story. I believe that love does in fact become greater and better, just not always between the same two people.

Lotti is leaving Thursday; I leave Sunday. Gritli and Hansli are staying on and will, I hope, have the snow that we have missed so far. But it is beautiful here for all that. Of course Anna, as a newly-married woman, feels drawn to her husband. She is finally going to leave us in the course of this coming year—a real revolution in the state of both our house and our lives. What does the next act look like? That question mark brings to a convenient end the New Year's letter of

    Your old
    Eugen

Appendix B

Life, Teaching, and Action
an interpretation of the last two words of
"The Star of Redemption"
(1923)

Rosenstock-Huessy completely rewrote the opening of the essay for publication in 1927. The 1923 original and the 1927 text begin to run parallel at a point four or five pages in, as footnoted. After that point, additions made for publication are shown in bracketed italics. Passages which were altered rather than added are footnoted with the prefix "1927."

Leben, Lehre und Wirken.

Eine Auslegung der letzten
beiden Worte
des „Kreuz der Erlösung"

Wer Wahrheit schaut, des Leben reift
zur Lehre;
Wer Wahrheit lehrt, des Lehre wirkt
die Tat.

Zum 10. März 1923.

Who views the truth, sees life mature to teaching;
Who teaches truth makes teaching lead to deeds.
for the 10th of March, 1923[1]

✡ 531

GOD, WHO IS THE last and the first, unlocked for me the gates of the sanctum that is in the innermost center. He allowed himself to be viewed. . . .

The vision on the height of the redeemed world above shows me nothing different from what the word of revelation commanded me in the midst of life: and walking in the light of the divine countenance is allowed only to him, who follows the words of the divine mouth. If—he has told you, O Man, what is good, and what does the Eternal One your God require of you but to do justice and be good with all your heart, and walk humbly with your God. . . .

To walk humbly with your God—in that nothing further is required than an utterly present trust. But trust is a big word. It is the seed from which faith, hope, and love grow, and the fruit that ripens from them. . . .

> To walk humbly with your God—the words are written over the gate,
> the gate which leads out of the mysterious-wondrous
> glow of the divine sanctum, in which
> no man can remain and live.
> But whither do the doors
> of the gate open?
> You don't know?
> INTO LIFE.

> You fear the theologian's outer dress,
> Which seem to you far Eastern foreign-ness?
> In spite of that you dwell with "word and vita
> And action" here on Santa Margherita!

1. [March 10, 1923 was MRH's 30th birthday.]

Biographies, diaries, and letters have been our favorite food all our lives. What we want from reading is life itself, the way it runs first one way and then another, the way it brings people together and tears them apart, the way a heart finds its inner self and grows into it. We are children of a biographical century. Even the Beginner and Fulfiller of our faith has been given a biography—more than enough of them, in fact. The "historical Jesus" has been the great experiment of modern theology; in its myriad versions it has quietly transformed Christ into our brother and the first-born among many. In its effort to find new ways to tell and describe the natural life of our Lord and master, it has awakened in us the same biographical sympathy with the subject to which we are otherwise glad, and irresistibly drawn, to succumb.

But Jesus left us no diaries and letters. Basically he has no biography— the very thing we find "interesting," that ensnares us unawares, is missing. No wonder then that the "quest for the historical Jesus" could receive the *coup de grace* from Albert Schweitzer. It had such an effect on him that he turned his back on the natural life and experience of Jesus and entered the mystery of Christ. Christ's power and justice drove him to the Congo. He broke abruptly with all natural life, and his interest in the merely natural life of Jesus broke off as well.

This powerful leap explodes the usual division among the church parties, since it sets Christ's power against the orthodox watchers of Zion, who have hammered Christ's words and the values of the church into dogma and law. It also sets Christ's power against liberal piety, which believes it already possesses the divine secret in the "purely human" and which therefore revolves around the life of Jesus.

But was everything the liberals have built up to anchor Jesus in our souls in vain? Was it all just an idle game? The deed in response to Christ, which Schweitzer lives out as one example, is a mystery. Every aspect of our lives flows from such secret springs, which we neither know nor can explain to others; every decision I follow through on, large or small, breaks through a known barrier in an unknown way, and lets life send up surprising shoots.

But mysteries are made to be unfolded—the hidden power of life is meant to be brought into the light. The secret Christ is to be elevated above all the world and to connect all people: child and chattel, prince and serving-girl. Jesus Christ has to be known among the people, and then he must abandon his rule so that the sick and the suffering may be served, the divine commandment obeyed—for his sake but without a sideward glance in his direction.

We commit ourselves to a teaching we have been taught, whereas we do the work that is given us to do today. There is no way to avoid this dichotomy of the old word and our new work. The mute deed out of Christ's power is not enough. The Schweitzer who researched the life of Jesus and the doctor in the Congo form an indissoluble unit. It is the theologian who authenticates the doctor here; the one on whom truth dawned who authenticates the one who carries it out. For the spiritual past bears witness for the mute action—that it does not happen on a whim, but out of that power which is our very being. Mystery too requires its proclamation: the Good Samaritan did not precede the preacher Schweitzer in vain.

And here we have arrived at the dividing line within Christianity, at the question whether we are Christians or not. We do indeed live with the natural man, but break through to overcome ourselves thanks to the supernatural. But in this rise and fall, how does Christian proclamation, the word of doctrine, fare? Does proclamation still have the power to seize us?

II.

Today Christianity is no longer a power, a strength, or a force in the life of the nations. In one man's breast, things may roar and shake tremendously from time to time, yet he remains alone. When it comes to action in the real world, there is nothing for him but the mute and wordless deed. No bond of spiritual community connects the living actors.

What we do share again today is that we are shaken our core; we share the "crisis" in the sense of the *Barthiani*, the "act of faith" and the decision, or whatever else the moment of conversion to God is called. That is something people will talk to each other about.

But everything that happens after our conversion happens in isolation again, loses its voice, and can only be kept alive with effort and violence out of the breast of the individual. *The effect of conversion has become a private affair.* And now each one of us has to deal with this private affair on his own, for the rest of his life. For shaping reality[2] means having the rest of life ahead of you, so maybe twenty, thirty years, or more.

Thirty years are nothing to sneeze at. It is a burden to go on living for a full thirty years after the "act of faith" purely on the basis of a spiritual turning-point and out of its fulfillment—on your own, *privatim*—and can easily end in exhaustion. How can anyone endure it?

Yet mainstream Christianity has no prescriptions to offer. How the gold of our vision of truth might have a uniform effect throughout a long life remains unspoken. None of what does get prescribed for our real life, our life after conversion, our "Christian," our "believing," period, whether short or long—none of it has any staying power or context. It is the bathwater of

---

2. [*Verwirklichung.*]

"Christian morality," watered down, without any juice or power, and therefore useless for our daily undertakings at home, in politics, in our careers and the economy—the things we must thoughtfully plan and build. In this venture the melancholy stanzas of pseudo-Christian ethics sputter out.

Reality has long since moved on from Christian morality to the business of the day; the person who has not once admitted the validity of the saying that the ends justify the means, no longer counts. People are tired of lies. But does this state of emergency in which we have no common language for our real lives as Christians, for our actions, have to continue?

And with that we are back to the starting-point of our reflection. For "Christian morality" is nothing more than the attempt to weigh us down with a complete version of Christ's teaching, a divine law, a rigid doctrine that can only bore us, instead of giving us a common language as a people bound together in action.

But "Christ's teaching" does not exist. Between the "life of Jesus" of the liberals and the "power of Christ'" of the orthodox there is a piece of territory left unoccupied or at most left as no-man's land, occupied now by the former and now by the latter. Right in the middle between his life and his influence stands his teaching. Whose teaching is it, Jesus' or Christ's?[3]

The key that might unlock the crippling of our speech today lies in this teaching's relation backwards to Jesus' life and forwards toward Christ's actions. Our speech can be liberated if it turns out that Christ did not teach[4] the things we must learn anew each day from his deeds!

Even after he began teaching in public, Jesus continued his inner life; that alone would be enough to set him apart from all Average Teachers. The usual person learns his little verse while young, and once he has acquired subordinates who have no choice but to listen, passes it on. The educated person[5] does his research, makes his discovery, and then mounts his podium only to be transfixed as the type of teacher who no longer goes on living; teaching rules him and squeezes the life out of him. At some point we stop moving and our life becomes the roof over our heads. We let the young follow after us and grow up alongside us, but for them to be able to do that, we must teach them what we have experienced. This is a law of nature and we cannot simply abolish it because we [*are afraid we*] might turn to stone.

How could Jesus abolish this law? Doesn't he want to fulfill, not abolish, all that we must undergo? Nevertheless we insist that he did not stop at any particular moment, but went on living till the last moment, even though

---

3. [The published text begins to run parallel with the 1923 version here; see 40.]
4. [1927: *refrained from teaching.*]
5. [1927: *the trained teacher.*]

he was already teaching publicly. [*Another stage follows in the wake of our vision and teaching, and the* "perfectus homo" *had to explore all the stages. True,*] He completely confused his listeners by doing so, for he was always one step ahead of what they were able to perceive in him. While he still seemed to be the carpenter's son, he was already the teacher. While he was considered a rabbi, he was already a prophet. While they took him for a prophet, he was already the Messiah. When they finally took him for the King of the Jews, he was God's servant. And when they recognized him as God's servant, he had already become the crucified Son of God.

He has a head-start, which he maintains to the end, and those who live with him can never quite keep pace. He never stays put long enough for the others to catch up, and so they run out of breath. The hallmark of the so-called Synoptic Gospels is that they are all still struggling to catch up and so fail to see the next-to-last stages through the lens of the last one. Jesus had galloped away from his physical disciples as well; the first generation of disciples was consumed by the necessity of reconciling the contradictory stages that followed each other in such lightning succession that the world could only see and remember one at a time. Only when they were done could John the Evangelist set his seal on a picture cleansed of all misunderstandings.

[*Whenever we learn, we are not yet full partners in life. The student of any doctrine remains in its power. John is the only evangelist who is both disciple and more-than-disciple of Him who taught him, and for that reason he can see the spirit of his teacher and the suffering of the one who loved him as one, and translate it as one. Please note: Jesus' public actions come after his teaching.*]

This discovery has a complement in the opposite direction. [*How does Jesus' earlier life relate to his teaching?*] We know nothing, or next to nothing, about that early life. The shallow novels about "Jesus the Adolescent," about his childhood or his wanderings, simply prove that we are only too aware of this ignorance. His natural life is passed on to us only in the form of the natural event of his birth [*and his parents' flight into Egypt for his sake. In other words,*] We can never know more about the experiences of the natural man Jesus and his path through life than what is reflected in his teaching [*and vision.*]

We saw[6] that even the mediocre teacher adds to his teaching what he himself has discovered and experienced. [*The spirit comes after life and proceeds from it.*] Jesus' teaching must have come to him out of the experience of his earlier life. This earlier life, his "inner life," the development and formation of his life took place "beyond" all the outside world. We can sense this

---

6. [1927: *We said before.*]

"beyond" only in the form of the sweet fruit of his teaching.[7] We can only know the heavenly kingdom in his heart to which he bears witness by that same witness of his. We have no earlier stages that show how it came to him. All that remains "beyond," and it is that "beyond" which makes immature believers wax so rhapsodic [*and the metaphysicians pile up lies upon lies*].

On the other hand, as soon as Jesus begins his ministry, we know him only through his influence on others, the effectiveness of that influence, how he proved his worth in the outside world. As soon as he becomes *visible*, he is "in this life"; what we know of his life is all a part of his cross. And as he shows himself everywhere "in this life," the Christ in him starts and develops everywhere in him. Rabbi Jesus *teaches* us how to cross from the creaturely to spiritual life, but Jesus the Christ *lives* the other way around, returning from the life of the spirit into real life! Instead of a "life of Jesus" [*—which must remain unknown to us—*] we can only know his life as Christ, his life as divinely chosen child,[8] his actualization through his messianic *office*.

All that remains of his earlier life is his teaching. His life is transmuted into the fruit of his teaching word, behind which its owner, the office-holder and the functionary, must recede.[9] Jesus' teaching on the law and the prophets, on the Father and the Heavenly Kingdom, is the purified fruit of inner battles, enlightenment, instruction, and experiences, the results of which were fixed at the time of his baptism in the Jordan, and so themselves lie far behind him. [*Bud and blossom are no longer visible in the fruit; yet it is their quintessence. The fruit forces us to presume that seed and blossom went before it—all natural life ripens to insight and wisdom.*] Jesus does not abolish the law of nature, but fulfills it. He really teaches what he has experienced.

The *perfect tense* of this experience must be taken seriously: it preceded him! Human words come only after the impression has been made on us. We can only, may only, teach what is already behind us; our formulation in words limps along after events. Human thinking is *after*-thought! We can reflect only on that which has gone before, *quod factum est*. Jesus teaches what he has experienced as Jesus, that is for himself, a being still becoming and not yet binding on others, as a man turned inward. So as a teacher he holds prophetic office; he is the teacher of Israel, the last prophet.

On the other hand, while he is teaching he leads the life of another character altogether, that of an official personage who has[10] the power and

---

7. [1927: *We have this „beyond" only in the form of the sweet fruit of his teaching.*]

8. [1927: *his actions as Christ, his life as the called Son.*]

9. [1927: *His whole vegetative, natural life has passed into the fruit of the teaching Word, behind which its carrier, the office-holder, must recede like any other functionary.*]

10. [1927: *lays claim to.*]

authority to bind or cast off others: he is a man who decidedly embodies his calling. But his calling is not what one might expect based on his teachings. Because he teaches, he appears to be a professional teacher. But teaching is only the prerequisite of his actions [*which are not a rabbi's. His teaching is not the essence of his office; he lives an office that has as yet no line in the budget of mankind's economy, but one that he himself forms and invests with dignity.*]

That is in fact just how the Gospels formulate it.[11] [*According to them, it is not what he says, but when, where, to whom he says it that betrays the particular character of his function beyond mere teaching.*] The smallest feature has meaning in the process by which he is revealed. [*Here we are neither in the private life of a man nor in the intellectual life of a thinker:*] Where life no longer has room to play, can no longer develop unobserved, it becomes rigid, irreversible action, "*praxis*" visible to the world. Shaping reality[12] is no longer an interior matter, but one of outwardness, of renunciation, one which requires the cooperation of the world. [*It is a political existence and is subject to the laws of politics.*]

The greatness of this public transformation lies in all the worldly facts [*all the hard objective lumps:*] that John baptizes him, that the disciples react, that Lazarus wakes from the dead, that Judas betrays him, that the Romans crucify him, that Joseph of Arimathea buries him. All these facts are not assignments for biographers [*of his soul or systematizers of his spirit*], but for historians [*of his creativity and his actions*].

His character as the son of God only becomes believable, worthy of belief, because the outer world dovetails with his life. All these dispensations make reality of the picture that Jesus carried within himself of himself and the world. The obedient collaboration of all the worldly powers on his path only confirms him; there is nothing left for him to do himself but attract those powers to himself. The world grows, falls, rushes toward him, until it has laid him on the cross. He literally attracts and grabs hold of it merely by awaiting it.

There have been and are beautiful lessons in wisdom from every nation. But the inner vision of God becomes believable only when it is shown that the sage had a right to such high thoughts. Not every one has the right to think high or luminous things, or even to imagine great and daring deeds. Thinking creates obligations.

But no one can simply live out what he has thought about, either. Much as the world demands it, we cannot in fact practice what we preach [*at least not as the words are commonly understood*]. Instead, we can only

---

11. [1927: *his public actions.*]
12. [*Verwirklichung.*]

go on living, living out our thoughts as befits the day; our life is changed by our spiritual vision, but life flows on [*just as original and surprising as ever*]. [*True,*] It has left the path of mere coincidence and has been molded by the vision granted us in the inner sanctum.¹³ It has been melted down to be recast into action—from becoming to tackling what is required of the lasting man shaped before God's countenance. [*The truth granted in vision must be put to the test. And teaching is only a small part, only that part which we are able to formulate, of the truth that overwhelmed us in the temple, in the Holy of Holies where our life is re-created.*]

This then is the proper place of Jesus' teaching—in between the life of the unbaptized Jesus and the action of the professing Christ. He teaches what he has experienced, but afterwards the things he taught actually come to pass. On the one hand, his teaching is a result, his success, the fulfillment of his "former life," but his teaching changes from an effect to a cause, from a result to a starting-point, from a sum¹⁴ to the initial value of his life's equation. The fruit of the "facts" of his youth becomes the fundamental "factor" of his adult existence, which is based on this factor but at the same time surpasses it. Jesus' teaching smashes the tablets of the law; what else makes a new law possible after this end other than [*a fresh start in*] Christ's action? Jesus' teaching calls the Christian into life,¹⁵ and Christ's action directs the church in the [*political*] world.

Some may object that Jesus also expressed and interpreted his life as Christ, and that is certainly true: life is not so schematically divided that one period contains nothing of the others. Jesus' experiences as Christ did indeed become words in his sentences [*as Christ*] to his disciples [*—in the farewell speeches, for example*]. But here lies the sharp division between the disciples and the world.¹⁶ Jesus' teaching of the people [*and the disciples, insofar as they learn*] is the fruit of his [*earlier*] life, which is why he speaks to his listeners of inner freedom, of the heart's secrets, and of heaven, for instance [*hoping as a teacher that they might understand*]. On the other hand, he allows¹⁷ the disciples to share his life although he knows that they do not understand, and that there is one among them who will betray him. He does not need them as hearers of his teaching,]but as witnesses of his life.¹⁸ He lets them take part in the mysteries of his action, of a man's dying into

---

13. [See the opening quote from *The Star,* 145.]
14. [1927: *the end-sum.*]
15. [1927: *directs the Christian in life.*]
16. [1927: *teaching for those who learn and revelation for the apostles.*]
17. [1927: *has to allow.*]
18. [1927: *of his actions.*]

the world. His words to them on this subject, the increasingly surprising fate of the man of action whom they take for a teacher, are not teaching but evidence, confirmation, proofs, interpretations, and exposition of what they experience in him and in the world [*they are not instruction but drama*].

Only with the help of his words to them can they share the experience of his *experimentum crucis*. Christ's words to his disciples bind the collaborators to the "laborator," to the man of action; they bind the limbs to the head. Here the Word has a different mission than it does where pure doctrine is passed on from person to person, or from preacher to flock, in divine commandments. The Word is not teaching, but mortar and bond that creates a field of action. In this field of action all those laws of which "Christian morality" is supposedly ignorant suddenly come into their own: sovereignty and service, office and necessity, division and separation, silence and anger, command and failure, worry and reflection. There is in all this no sin to the man of action.

Jesus constructed Christ's field of action [*once he had his vision and his teaching behind him*]. All his powers were concentrated on creating that field,[19] not teaching it. Developing a doctrine of Christ's life[20] was something only a disciple who had not physically heard Jesus teach could undertake. Of Paul it has rightly been said that he lived what Jesus taught, but taught what Christ lived.[21] That is precisely what we have called Jesus' action: the effect he had as Christ. And so the enduring prejudice against Paul the "theologian" is part and parcel of the modern excitement over the "life of Jesus," for Paul is the witness to the fact that Jesus' early life has nothing to do with us, but that his teaching [*on the one hand, as the end of the law,*] and his actions [*on the other, as the beginning of a new order of things in the Church,*] have everything to do with us.

III.

A man's early life, his "inwardness,"[22] bears fruit in his spiritual yield [*as a kind of inner "spirit lamp"*]. Whatever bears fruit is without sin. Once we make spiritual atonement for our youthful sins, they are forgiven. The passions of flesh and blood are the [*indispensable*] food of insight [*no one need be ashamed that he has "a past" as long as he plunged into it with all his heart*].

19. 1927: *making that field indestructible*
20. 1927: *action and the way he built his field of action, in addition to Jesus' own teaching*
21. [It is not clear that anyone said this, other than ERH. The statement is repeated in the 1925 essay on adult education, "Andragogik." See Appendix I, 335-36.]
22. [1927: *his existence as a naïve child of the world.*]

The only important aspect of any spiritual/intellectual content is its preservation for the world and its practical effect upon the world:

its ability to be accepted, disproved, or renewed. Only a thought's effectiveness redeems it from the curse of mere thinking.[23]

The only important thing about action, however, is the measure of flesh and blood, of spirit and truth, dissolved in it and invested by it.[24] Action without spirit and without the heart's experience is empty; it is the appearance of fruit where there was neither seed nor blossom.

To hell with inwardness, if it remains emotion instead of ripening to reflection. To hell with intellectuality if it fails to give way to action.[25]

The boy awakens to adolescence so that his feelings may "be thought through"; the youth ripens to manhood so that his thoughts may become deeds. If youth does not one day eventually overcome its "big noise," if the academics [*consent to*] remain tangled in systems and analyses, the man who is [*inexorably*] produced from them, who must somehow deal with life and its myriad circumstances, will not deal with them well, [*lamed as he is in soul and spirit*]. He will fail to find himself carried forward by a fruitful sequence in the electrical circuit of boy-youth-man, and can only work mindlessly, helplessly, senselessly, just keeping busy[26]—without knowing, that is without a vision of, what he does, and so lacking all authority for the freedoms and decisions that every life of action requires.

Any work we do that does not flow downhill from the highest life is dead—and goes to the devil.

23. [1927: *The only relevant aspect of any intellectual/spiritual truth is its ruthlessness toward its human carriers, the purity of their vision, the self-denying truthfulness and its spiritualizing effect on its adherents.*]

24. [1927: *The only relevant aspect of actions, however, is the extent to which its powers are consciously engaged, the extent to which they prove their worth in flesh and blood, and the extent to which they fittingly and conformingly master the material they are meant to mould.*]

25. [1927: *The three stages—life, teaching, and actions—belong together. It goes without saying that action without spirit and without the heart's experience is empty; it is the appearance of fruit where there was neither seed nor blossom. There are sprouts that wither, blossoms that remain unchanged, fruit like empty nuts. The fate of the poor devils who fail to overcome the three infernal princes—of the senses, of thought, and of compelling authority—will meet their destiny in a squandered youth, pointless reflection, and busy-ness without purpose. The boy . . .*]

26. [1927: *with a stunted, curdled view of the world in his head and a squandered heart—and therefore unable to love where he must take action, and unable to work through what was once granted him in visions. Such a man is only outwardly adult and so lacks authority for the freedoms and decisions . . .*]

LIFE, TEACHING, AND ACTION   155

Here is the sore spot of our existence. Both as individuals and as a people, we have forfeited the natural progression of life's stages. Healing them is the content of all revelation—it seeks not to abolish the law, but to fulfill it.

Jesus came to combat the over-wrought enthusiasts of the world, for in him all excess of feeling ripens to clarity in his vision of God. He came to combat the Pharisees of the world, for he relinquishes his clear teaching as soon as it yields to action. But he came on behalf of the sinners of the world, for he replaces all worldly activity pursued without thought or feeling with actions rooted in the vision granted him in the inner sanctum.

The "sinner" seeks life in busy-ness; the man of action knows that busy-ness is only death: he has lived, and his life has been transfigured in his sight, so that when he looks back at life, it is no longer his life that he rediscovers. He has set sail from his own life, he steers back into the world in a vessel not his own, that is to say: back into a new life and the life of others, to perfect their lives as well. [*He obeys his God and his calling.*] He is drawn onward by that end which he has already experienced once in his life, in self-denial, for a man's true calling is to bend all his powers to effect his end. Young life gushes forth without restraints [*rising boldly to the very firmament, until at last it finds its own limits*]. Oriented to the star that rose over it, destined to prove the worth of the vision granted, it descends from the bright space of the spirit down to earthly life and timeliness.

Whether the slope of that path is gentle or steep, it is always a path that ends in death. On this path our life is forfeit. And this forfeiture of life, the gravitational pull of the goal seen in visions, what Cromwell called "dying by inches," is no "natural" life but indeed its opposite: [*action as*] a calling! [*We cannot live "supernaturally" in this life, we are not gods; but we can live out of the supernatural, drawing life from that supernatural which confronted us in our act of vision and illumination, rebirth and change—accepting a call and the action it entails. Theologians' speech is often so lame, as it only mentions the natural and the supernatural and fails to address the healed action of the person touched by the divine as the third act in life's drama.*]

This [*"working in the call"*] is no simple "walking humbly with your God," but rather a return to walking humbly; it is no longer just answering God as an individual, but at the same time taking responsibility for God before men, something that the mere life in us neither knows nor even needs to know. Responsibility for God before men? This is where those laws of real life, about which "Christian morality" seems to know so little, come into their own [*—this is where the doctrine of authority takes root*]. [*Adult humanity,*] The fields of action that must be founded in human heads and hearts, after all, receive their authority from their founders' divine power of attorney. The authority of a man of action is constantly renewed out of his "prior life" and its wholeheartedness. Puppets devalue any office they hold. An office can only survive as long as the office-holder lets his "former life" flow [*into his perception and his perception flow*] into his office, as long as his vocation remains the vessel in which the truth of his life may work itself out and prove its worth.

Authority is really authorship. Nothing important happens without some person laying out a new life along a path from earth to the sun and back to earth in such a way that others can follow it after him. Where such paths draw men to them, into them, onto them, and after them, there authority, a heightened trail-blazing, [*and the* via exaltata *of the trailblazer,*] takes effect.

Almost no one fails utterly to find his path in life. Almost everyone comes to some degree of influence on some modest life path. But when the world breaks down completely into fanatics, Pharisees, and tax-collectors, when a people seems to consist only of a youth movement's feelings, intellectual orthodoxy, and the politics of the workers' struggle,[27] then a modest path is no longer enough. Then all those who still succumb to modest paths find themselves dragged down by the partial life through which it leads and achieve no influence at all.[28] The lack of influence is the constant curse of the intellectual world, for example. [*Either*] it fails to force the world of deeds to cooperate [*or those who would teach some desperately needed knowledge are deprived of listeners by youth in mutiny. The heart misses the spirit that was its destiny.*] Then the stream dries up, that stream which once led from the creature in Bethlehem to his vision of God, from his highest vision [*in the desert*] to his action in the world.[29]

But when it does, God's mercy blazes a new trail for man; new authorities arise, for new people have been privileged to view the trailblazer's path. And in these new people the trail with its way-stations is reestablished, the trail that is strung between death and birth, and knows three stages between birth and death: life, teaching, and action.

---

27. [1927: *and the political organization of labor relations.*]

28. [1927: *Then all those who still try to pursue a modest path will find themselves dragged down by its fragmentary nature, and by the equally fragmentary bit of life to which that path is restricted, into a hellish void where they must forfeit all influence.*]

29. [1927: *in the midst of creation.*]

IV.

In each of these stages a different order and a different set of connections hold sway. Different things are allowed someone who merely lives than may be permitted to someone who teaches. The former obeys powers he has not chosen; he is free of responsibility—free to make mistakes or take detours as necessary.[30]

The teacher, however, sets an example, and "Christian morality" in [*its narrower sense*] applies to him most of all. Anyone who wants to draw others along after him must use spiritual means. He may neither strive like Faust, ranging far and wide and always aspiring,[31] nor take arms against a sea of troubles and by opposing, end them.[32] [*He has come to his own limits, and sets himself apart from truth; so he must teach relatively "selflessly." Vision bears fruit only to those who forget themselves. The teacher is free to any end of knowledge, but unfree in his means.*

The man of action is quite different.] Those who act complete and achieve what they undertake. They must resist the seductive lure of new goals and persevere wherever they find themselves,[33] for he "who perseveres in steadfast truth, will make the world conform."[34] They may themselves choose whatever means are required. If profligacy is the pride of youth, a grown man is miserly, husbanding his resources, for he alone knows their proper place [*none but he may determine their use nor need answer for it*].

In place of "Christian morality," three human laws arise, all three of which we must honor as long as we draw breath. For where we love, we squander. Where we hope, we do not just sow like one who teaches and devoutly fulfills his duties; where we hope, we plant and tend our own field of action like a garden, with all a gardener's art. We live in three orders at once, even if each is only revealed in turn, and only [*completely*] revealed [*over a lifetime*]....[35]

The commandments of love are different from those of faith. The hope of the gardener is different from that of the man who plants in faith. The order of action is the manly order of public life, the realm of law. It differs

---

30. [1927: *There are really three different moralities and sets of ethics. The "naïve," those who merely live, obey forces they have not chosen; they are free of all responsibility, free to make mistakes and take detours as necessary. Others act for them, as when Mary and Joseph flee into Egypt for their son's sake. They obey a foreign law.*]
31. [*Faust II*, Act 5: line 11,936.]
32. [*Hamlet*, III:1.]
33. [1927: *where they are stationed.*]
34. [Goethe, *Hermann und Dorothea*, IX,1.]
35. [A section of the original is cut here, and after the cut, the text continues.]

from teaching passed from mouth to mouth in the ivory towers of thought, and from the order that applies there. Different again is the circle of the loving community, youthfully intimate, ordered without compulsion.

[*Time has a different meaning for the natural man, the visionary, and the man of action ... but God's creation is kept alive because it moves in three mutually determined orders. (See 25–26.)*]

That is why the same orderer had to precede us in each of these three orders—all have been explored by God, and our own path only follows the luminous tracks he left in all three of them.

Only because God left his traces in all of them can we mortals summon the courage to struggle free of the divine embrace of each separate hour and make the leap from one order to another as the new hour requires.

[*Only those who remain open to the call to change from one of the three personal forms to another—should that be God's will—can still be called living souls. And that was the perfect obedience of the firstborn which He revealed to us.*

Does Man not collapse beneath this cross? Does he not lose his rigid character and his proud personality? Yes, he loses both these signs of natural age, yet he does not collapse.]

What God says, stands formed before men's eyes. The words of God are not just the words that his children speak, but the paths they follow. The man of action becomes the word that the creator intends to enter into the Book of Life. He receives the name by which mankind will now hear him, call upon him, understand and misunderstand him until Judgment Day.

The only reason we can walk humbly is that God has commanded us to do so not only in a human way, but by name; for everything God has to say, he says in the names that his sons then bear before mankind until their influence is extinguished. From the first day on, our name waits to see whether God will make our life one of name and calling. A name is a gift given at birth, an award made when the call comes to us, and an obligation on whatever path the call illumines. Names combine life, vision, and action in our transformation. The trinity in which we stand becomes simplicity through the name we bear, which also bears us up. Jesus' life defies biographical reasoning. His teaching defies the textbooks of morality. His actions are foreign to world history.[36]

His story juts into this world from another. His vision flowed from limitless aspiration; his life bore fruit completely and utterly. [*But it all happens in the name of God's son, and that is why it happens in divine simplicity.*]

---

36. [1927: *His action entered the world as a foreign body.*]

Wherever we may open the book of life without him, wherever life calls out to us, bubbling up anew and unashamed, we soon ask ourselves where the seal of life may be, that name that all human life must bear.

When we need a standard and a benchmark for life, he whom we forgot while on the path we trod, the initiator of our faith, emerges as the perfector of our faith, emerges from all other forms, and he returns to us [*by name*].

It takes a long time for languages to unfold, for them to set the events heaven blows into them to their own melody and to sing them. It just takes however long it takes for God's breath to become a living soul. Luther had to write on his wall in the Koburg: *Christus vivit*. We cannot translate the theologian's word *Christus* [into English] if we only transliterate it as "Christ." "*Christus vivit*" can only be translated once the Christian way of life has entered our flesh and blood.

Since we now see and know how human life is laid out in its great stations,[37] that its course leads out of life into a "beyond" [*—where we receive a vision—*] and back into this life [*—where we take effective action*]. Only then can we express Jesus of Nazareth's path toward death as our Savior in our own language. Instead of "*Christus vivit*" it is:

Jesus works on in us.

[*And the three breaths of the divine Creator, Revealer, Redeemer are reflected in the image of the threefold God in life, teaching, and action. Creature of the Father, Brother of the Son, Collaborator in the Kingdom—that is the trinity in us.*]

Whither do the doors of the gate open?

You know whither.

. . . .

---

37. [*1927: Since then, that one man's life draws us on after it in rank and file in the great stations of his life, so that our course too leads us . . .*]

Appendix C
"A Letter to an American Friend"
(1947)

IN 1918, ROSENSTOCK-HUESSY WROTE his wife that "the world considers me a Christian who used to be a Jew; even if what I had been was in fact a pagan, I am still considered to have been a Jewish pagan."[1] This letter provides the background for that claim—as well as for Paul Mendes-Flohr's statement that "both Rosenzweig and Rosenstock-Huessy were converts" from the secular faith of their time "to their respective faiths."[2] In *I Am an Impure Thinker*, Rosenstock-Huessy published a letter he had written to the Rev. William MacNair in 1946, on the topic of "conversion," in which he used the word on the condition that MacNair understand it in the sense of *metanoia*, as used in the Letter to the Hebrews, a turning away from dead works.[3] The following letter, printed verbatim, may have been written to MacNair also. (A later copy is in Collection MS-522 at Dartmouth's Rauner Library.) Even if it was not, it should certainly be read in context with that letter, as together they show how Rosenstock-Huessy himself looked at the question of conversion. In 1957 he would write his friend Georg Müller that he never converted at all.[4]

1. Unpublished letter dated June 21, 1918.
2. ERH, *Despite*, x.
3. ERH, *Impure Thinker*, 182–90, perhaps a nod to Rudolf Ehrenberg's commentary on the Letter.
4. Unpublished letter dated January 21, 1957.

{WRITTEN IN 1947 TO another American friend}[5]

The story of my being covered with the name of Christ today seems the story of exactly one century: 1848 to 1947.

In 1848, the event happened in Berlin (which corresponded to the Bastille, the 14 of Juillet in 1789). The Liberals made a revolution. My grandfather was eighteen years old, a Jewish student. He demonstrated, fought, received a scar. And the brother of my grandmother, the only man of this generation of my family whom I ever knew and who exercised considerable influence on my development Dr. Paul Waldstein, was then a boy of 12, who woke up to life by this revolution. My grandfather, by the way, was Moritz Rosenstock but *my mother's* father. My mother and my father were cousins and had the same name. (My father's father was a *Fuhrmann*[6] in a tiny hamlet halfway between Breslau and Posen. He died in 1870.)[7] Moritz Rosenstock and Paul Waldstein were typical representatives of Jewish German assimilation.

Moritz Rosenstock taught school in Posen (which was then German). He was an energetic man who at the age of 42 took his Ph.D. at the University of Berlin on the remarkable theme "*Juden und Germanen auf dem Boden des Römerreichs.*"[8] This booklet I discovered at Harvard in 1933.[9] I had never seen it nor heard of it before, but it illuminates quite well his concern and that of his descendants. He was called to one of the two Jewish establishments of the educational Enlightenment of 1800, as its head in 1870.[10] This was in Lessing's town, Wolfenbüttel, and this Jewish founda-

---

5. [The "American friend" addressed apparently read German, as no translations were provided in the letter. Rosenstock-Huessy's 1946 letter to the Rev. Francis McNair (a friend of his friends Henry and Rosamund Greene) refers to an earlier letter which, despite the dating of the surviving copy, may be this one.]

6. [A carter.]

7. [Almost 20 years before ERH was born.]

8. [*Jews and Germanic Tribes in the Territory of the Roman Empire.*]

9. [In 1974, I took ERH's *Das Alter der Kirche* out of that same library; I was the first person to borrow it since the year I was born. Such long-term holdings are the defining function and the glory of research libraries.]

10. [The *Samsonschule*, founded by the Braunschweig court Jew Philipp Samson

tion, in an old castle, ranked with a corresponding Protestant girls' academy, the so-called "*Schloss*,"[11] which was a pedagogical seminary which produced women teachers. My grandfather threw open the school open to Christians, and his daughter went to the—then strictly denominational—evangelical[12] seminary and became a schoolteacher. In these two actions of grandfather and mother, my die was cast.

In the meantime, Paul Waldstein was sent by Bismarck to Budapest, where he became an influential journalist and made friends with the great men of the Magyar nobility. He later retired to Vienna, and he always was an active member of the Lutheran church there, in protest against the Roman-Catholic clergy which was so over-powerful in Austria-Hungary.

I was born in 1888. My father, in 1870, had been prevented from studying history or from going to America by the death of his father, in as much as he had to support his stepmother and his stepsister. He had great political ambition, was president of the young businessmen's association. Gibbon, Ranke, Thiers, Mommsen were his daily reading to the last days of his life, and he prepared himself for a parliamentary career. He led the battle against corruption in corporations, but all this bogged down completely with the rise of anti-Semitism after 1878 and the victory of the 14th amendment, or its parallel in Germany about the same time. That is, the corporations at that time used to make young bankers on their boards to silence their criticism. My father's friends accepted these bribes on the whole and got rich with the growth of industry.

My father made two decisions which decided his life. One: to withdraw wholly from politics because of anti-Semitism. Second: to have nothing to do with Big Business. He remained independent, a small banker. Sought as an expert in court for some great financial scandals, as an honorary judge in the courts of commerce, and elected to represent the small independent banking firms on the board of the Berlin Stock Exchange, he, however, never did have real recognition or outlet of his powers. Historian and statesman he had wished to be; both were denied him. In proud independence he lived a more and more isolated life, *vir justus* but absolutely reticent; a free thinker, for sheer pride he would not deny his Judaism, which on the other hand meant nothing to him. The slow spiritual starvation of this powerful character, his growing "*müet*,"[13] must have set in as early as the eighties.

---

in 1786. The school was radically overhauled in 1807 by Franz Rosenzweig's great-grandfather, Samuel Meyer Ehrenberg.]

11. [*the castle.*]
12. [Protestant.]
13. [The French word for a usually silent letter.]

When I was born in 1888, my mother was strong enough to prevent my being circumcised as a Jew. A purely negative situation now was created. Her own flight of thought, at the same time, found expression in a book on Shakespeare's *Tempest*, which was printed under the pseudonym of Paul Rohden, in 1890. So, she must have carried it with her while I was on my way. She viewed *The Tempest* as the High Song of Religious Toleration and Humanism. And in this interpretation, she expressed her own vision. Ever since, not only was she wide awake intellectually, but with every year that my father became less articulate, she became more profoundly restless in her religious center. She had borne eight children. By 1900 she was more and more given to religious inspirations. There were equally hostile to Judaism and to Christianity. Her symbol became the globe, the ball. In its rotundity, she found some strange satisfaction and peace, as the symbol of some glorious future. She wrote a very powerful prose. But her complete liberal isolation from any tradition frustrated every one of her ambitious attempts. Her liberal voltairian traditions made her despise all Revelation as superstitious. Yet, her deeper forces of telepathy, intuition, etc., were all on the side of this life. She was destroyed by this irrevocable clash of her ideology and her deeper structure. She wanted always to convert me to her free thought and yet new religion. As late as 1938 I wrote her, "Mother, we will try to live with you if you can leave our faith alone and not spit at it in our own house." This she was not willing to concede! She had to prosetylize for her private—and "ball"-circumscribed, her purely secular and unorientated philosophy. As faith is the decisive sword that defines new loyalties, we could not take her in, as suicide of the spirit is forbidden. But the inevitable catastrophe happened. Staying in Leipzig, she was a witness of the pogroms in November, 1938; at the age of 80, she showed her heroic spirit. She wrote me a letter blessing us, all and sundry, saying: *Ich fühle, dass meine Kräfte dieser entsetzlichen Zeit nicht gewachsen sind.*[14] And took poison.

My father had died in great peace in 1927, at 74, with full consciousness, taking his leave from us all, and glad to go, at the right hour. He specially blessed me in the strange wonderful worlds: "My son, *ich denke, dass Du alle Deine Dummheiten zur rechten Zeit gemacht hast.*"[15] This has always seemed to me the most subtle of praises. His paternal right to call my acts folly was not abandoned. Yet they were reinstated as meaningful. He had seen us in our congregation in Frankfurt and understood that it was a truly brotherly fellowship and said so in so many words. He never had seen any Christianity in action before but believed in ours. He also had the great

14. [*I feel that I lack the strength this terrible time requires.*]
15. [*I think you managed to get all your tomfoolery out of the way at the right time.*]

satisfaction to sit in one of my lectures. I had a good day of eloquence. And he was vindicated in his son. As he had been a magnificent speaker without any opportunity to speak or for using this gift, he was gratified that I was not the ordinary bore.

I first was sent to the ordinary school of the sons of courtiers and bankers. The school was in the Tiergarten and the boys probably 2/3 Gentiles and 1/3 Jewish. When I was first in my class, and the youngest, at 13, some incident happened—a conflict with another school, not *Gymnasium*, but *Volksschule*. I have forgotten all the details, except that I marched, smallest brat that I was, proudly in front of our crowd and a boy who led the "people" dumped his books with great ease on my head. I was ascribed a slight concussion, but it was nothing serious. However, the upshot of it all seems to have been that my mother, as well as myself, built this up into a case of anti-Semitism; and in a completely illogical turn, [I] took advantage of the incident to get out of the rich man's school, where I had flourished too easily, in my *own* judgment. I had delivered there a Latin oration on Caesar's March 15, spontaneously, to everybody's great surprise. With this action, I walked out and transferred to the *Joachimthalsches Gymnasium*.

This was a 300-year-old public school,[16] founded by the Hohenzollerns in 1605, and now located in Berlin, 35 minutes from our home, but still a boarding school for 3/4 of the pupils who usually were ministers' and manufacturers' sons from little places in Brandenburg Province. Boys from Berlin were at a handicap as we were only day students. But as it was considered the best school for Greek and Latin, Wilamowitz, Planck, Harnack, Mackensen, etc., had their boys go there.

Now, I should perhaps explain that at home we had three holidays: Christmas, Easter, Pentecost. All were celebrated with every Christian ceremony, singing, tree, eggs, etc., except church-going. As there was much making of music at home, chorals were our daily bread. Christmas was *the* center of the whole year. [Many of my early *opuscula* were written for my parents as Christmas presents. The earliest one which I can remember was on Notker of St. Gall (10th century) and his translations into Old German from the Latin, and was written on beautiful quarto sheets of genuine parchment.]

This will explain why in the Joachimsthal, where I was the only boy registered as Jewish, I took the "Christian Religion" course (which, with our established church, was *de rigueur* for Christians right down the twelve years of *Gymnasium*!). At fifteen, I decided to become a Protestant minister and to write a great book, *The Organization of Mankind*. I was treated very

---

16. [In the British sense—what Americans call a "private school."]

badly because I was Jewish, because I was a day student, and because I was irritatingly young, two years younger than the average. When I was 14, we went to Switzerland for the first time. I fell in love with a Swiss girl of 18 who was very good to me and who received my first poetry. I think that the new school and this love forever decided on my Christian-Gentile future. Action, however, was not taken before I was 18.

I had gone to study in Zürich at 17. I was terribly lonely, and the summer term, in 1906, ended with an appendectomy in the Zürich Hospital. A Christian aunt (my mother's sister)[17] and old Dr. Waldstein, from Vienna, came to Zürich to look after me. We spent a month near the Vierwaldstätter See. They told me that I should regularize the facts of my situation and confess my faith. Because of the operation, I returned to Berlin in the fall and did just this. I joined the Church, with one of my classmates and his mother as my godparents.[18] This classmate during the next few years—he was a poor boy, wholly supporting himself by tutoring—provided me with many tutorships in rich people's houses, thereby throwing me out of the rut of my class situation as well. This already had been the lucky result of the new, frugal school. It carried over now. I did not realize at the time that it was the most definite and permanent implementation of my Joachimstal school and of my baptism, as it changed my social situation. As a banker's son, one usually at that time in Germany, did not go as a tutor into other people's families. I mention this, because baptism did not have other startling external results. It regularized my past. And my parents recognized, by their acquiescence to my step, that they had educated me as a Christian in every way except by name.

I have always felt that my entrance into the Christian Church was terribly unromantic, matter of fact, because it came *so late*. My own positive action with regard to the faith was a perpetual approach to Catholicism for the next ten years. I visited leading Catholics, devoured Chesterton, studied medieval liturgy, and later was very orthodox in my own theology. (You have seen the three articles on this in the *Journal of Religion*??)[19] But this altogether is a different story and should not be mixed up with my finding myself a Christian, or at least the conscious citizen of a Christian world.

17. [Probably Agnes (Rosenstock) Wurzmann of Frankfurt, his mother's sister.]

18. [*Heinrich Kluge* is written on the surviving carbon copy in Freya von Moltke's hand. Fritz Herrenbrück recently found the church registry of the baptism with the Kluge's signatures. ERH may have joined the church in the fall of 1906, when he was 18, but the baptism did not take place until December 1909.]

19. [Presumably Dorothy Emmet's and Alexander Altmann's articles on ERH's correspondence with Rosenzweig, and ERH's coda to it, "Hitler and Israel, or On Prayer." All were published in the *Journal* in 1945.]

If you don't understand this complete lack of *action* on my part in becoming a Christian, you cannot understand my *conversion* in 1918/19, which consisted in my not becoming a Roman Catholic fanatic, in obedience to the living voice of God. *This* was my own and personal Christian experience, as a singled-out, unique soul! Baptism was what it was meant to be, a basic not a crowning fact! I was not a person, but it enabled me to become a person by entering the church.

Two generations who were not at home in Israel had preceded me. As their [*child and*] grandchild, I became a Christian. My friend Rosenzweig always got furious if I dared to mention my Jewish ancestry. "I have been in your parents' home," he would say. "You are a Gentile."

Appendix D
Introduction to " Fruit of Lips" (1977)
by Marion Davis Battles

By using the word 'plan' we are compelled to call into every occult counsel of God the comforting presence of the Name who is above all names... My own lifework has centered around the parallel task to overcome the Toynbees, the van Loons, the Spenglers and the Gibbons by a true economy of salvation, a "full count of the times."[1]

IN HIS OWN WORDS Eugen Rosenstock-Huessy has succinctly stated the meaning of his vast literary effort which extended from 1912 to his death in 1973, both in Europe and in the United States. To list his works would be tedious. A bibliography was compiled some years ago which shows the range of his knowledge and interest.[2] Such accumulations of information were meaningless to him, however, unless they went far beyond "systems of the Aristotelians and Platonists and the logical positivists who would like to have us feed exclusively on the dead hindquarter of God's full Logos."[3]

Rosenstock's own words are quoted verbatim here in an attempt to identify the force that drove his pen day after day, year after year across countless pages of manuscript. To use the word "drove" probably most closely describes the way the man wrote. He wrote, quite literally, in a white heat of passion, burning up page after page of paper as his large handwriting filled the lines.

He was the despair of editors and publishers, for he usually refused to revise anything he had written.[4] And anyone so innocent as to accept an invitation to revise his manuscripts—the invitation was never offered by

1. MDB: ERH, "Generations of Faith," *Hartford Quarterly*, 1:3 (1961), 15.
2. MDB: Included in ERH, *Geheimnis*, 307–315, and in *Bibliography*, 1–9. [Since surpassed by Lise van der Molen's exhaustive 1997 *Guide to the Works of ERH*, now available online at the Eugen Rosenstock-Huessy Fund's website, www.erhfund.org.]
3. MDB: "Generations of Faith," 16.
4. [ERH was indeed the despair of his publishers, but for quite the opposite reason: he continued to revise and add material, even after books were in galley proofs.]

the author himself—suddenly finds himself confronted by a portrait or a painting. It is like trying to revise a work of art which, though it has faults, speaks eloquently to the viewer. Moving a phrase here, altering a word there, changing the order of sentences, brings about swift and complete disaster. The "painting," the work of his mind, lies in shambles under the editor's pen. The page no longer speaks but stares back at the reader noiselessly. The editor retreats before the presence of a burning spirit, a gigantic intellect, a truly creative genius.[5]

Though the style may leave one in despair, the leaps of the mind cause chagrin, the occasional error of fact provoke a momentary feeling of "Aha! he is not infallible"—the pages are alive with a message, a life-and-death message, which like the hounds of heaven, tracks the reader "down the nights and down the days." The hierarchy of meaning readily apparent in a carefully articulated style replete with connectives is absent in Rosenstock.

To understand to any extent the manner of his mind, one must look at his life. Eugen Rosenstock was born in 1888 into an educated, prosperous family of Jewish background in Berlin. His prodigious intellect manifested itself at an early age and, in the style of a German scholar-schoolboy, he wrote learned articles on various subjects. He completed university and became a *Privatdozent* at Leipzig in 1912 in jurisprudence. His classical education was thorough in the way nineteenth-century German scholarship was thorough. He was in active military service between 1914 and 1918. These years were truly seminal for his later career. He had met Franz Rosenzweig, a student of his at Leipzig in 1913, who had turned from his study of medicine to philosophy and history. Rosenzweig, a nominal Jew who had in 1909 declared himself Christian in every respect, met Rosenstock one night in 1913 and a searing discussion took place when the two men opposed each other, not as Jew and Christian but as faith in philosophy against faith based on revelation. Rosenstock was a confirmed Christian who confronted the unformed Judaism of Rosenzweig. The results of their confrontation lasted a lifetime for both men. The long struggle in which they engaged is chronicled in the correspondence of the two men, published in 1935.[6]

Rosenstock's intimate understanding of the Jew, of the Old Testament, of the role of the Chosen People, set him apart for the task he had undertaken. His grasp of the effect of the divine "No" on Israel through the ages allowed him to cast aside the preoccupation of biblical scholars with the quest for the historical Jesus. In fact, he pointed to Adolf von Harnack, the idol

---

5. [Two of his best-known works in English were heavily edited by others: *Out of Revolution* by Henry and Rosalind Greene, and *The Christian Future* by their son-in-law, George Morgan. MDB means well, but this myth does a disservice to all concerned.]

6. [FR, *Briefe*. MDB reverses the sequence of events. See Appendix H, 303–11.]

of the scholarly world, as the symbol of the paganizing of Christianity. Furthermore, his knowledge of classical antiquity, of the Greek as over against the Jew, showed him the difference between the poetry of Homer and the Psalms of David. For the Jew, the only poetry is a response to God. Such insight allowed him to pierce the veil which enshrouds the Greek mind, the very Greek mind which, in God's economy, permitted the birth of the doctrine of the Trinity, while remaining anathema to the mind of the Jew.[7]

For Rosenstock, "Egyptian darkness" is a term which appears and re-appears in his works.[8] His understanding of the cyclical nature of the Egyptian calendar was that the alternation between Isis and Osiris, between time of flood and time of harvest, regulated the Egyptian people's behavior for a year at a time.[9] "The calendar was the spell cast by the cosmos upon the human will."[10] The Jews replaced this calendar and "unspelled" it by their own calendar of God's acts with his people. Passover was not a "spring" festival; Sukkot was not a "harvest" festival. The struggle of the Jews with the forces of the sky-world, as the author calls them, was ended by the birth of Jesus, which served as a barrier, a dam forever preventing the tides of history from flowing back behind this event. "The last day of Israel was created when, to speak in a figure, Mary, inside the Promised Land, was told to flee into Egypt, and when the son of Abraham offered himself as a sacrifice."[11]

Rosenstock grew up in a Europe alive with the quest for the historical Jesus, as exemplified by Albert Schweitzer's own life on the one hand and the demolition of the historical Jesus by Ernest Renan.[12] Both men represented the triumph of Gnosis, the mind as the creator of real fact, the triumph of re-creating history as it might have been, and believing it was that way. The nineteenth century preoccupation with biography cut Jesus off from his

---

7. [This is more MDB than ERH, for whom the Trinity is impermeable to *the Greek mind* (see 38)—and was even to be found in Israel; see ERH, "The Jewish and the Christian Trinity," at www.erhfund.org. MBD refers to *the Jew* where ERH was always careful to speak of *Israel*.]

8. [ERH is not alone. The phrase has long been used by Bible-literate authors as diverse as Heine, Bulgakov, and Ingeborg Bachmann, to illustrate a moral condition to which liberation is the answer. The New York *Times* used the phrase, if more literally, as long ago as 1879.]

9. [To ERH, the calendar in which Egypt gloried was the vast revolving cycle of solar and sidereal time, in which Pharaoh was a star in a constellation brought down to earth. This is the calendar which the Jews scorned, replacing Egypt's temples of "tattooed" stone with a tent, and the great "Sothic" cycles of 1,460 years with the seven-day cycle of the Sabbath.]

10. MDB: "Hitler and Israel," *JOR* 25 (1945) 136.

11. MDB: "Hitler and Israel," 130.

12. [This precis confuses and garbles the arguments in "Ichthys" and "Fruit."]

past, for biography ends with the death of the individual. Christian tradition has always been concerned with "thanatography." The empty tomb, and the events which followed, sealed antiquity, for as the Word became flesh, Jesus became the center in the history of Speech. Thus we must make the fruit of biographical Christianity of the last century into a seed for our understanding of speech.

Indeed, the passionate message of "Fruit of Lips," exemplifying as it does Rosenstock's "speech philosophy," is permeated by the *Logos*. Our author sees in human language, divinely given, and its grammatical categories, a primordial fundament to all subsequent philosophical and scientific efforts to categorize reality. The moods of grammar he correlates with the interlocking modes of the Four Gospels. Together they embody the "grammar of the cross"; the four cannot be separated from each other.

Rosenstock views the streams of human speech from a combined vertical and horizontal perspective. Horizontally, or historically, he sees speech streaming across five millennia "from plain chant to radio broadcast." Vertically, he sees the totality of speech in two basic levels of primary and secondary intonation, each subdivided further into the various uses to which language is put.[13] Here, our concern is not with the details of this "Table of Levels of Intonation," but with the fundamental distinction between the memorable eloquence of prayer, military command, and the derivative, ephemeral talk of everyday business and living. For our author, the wellspring of all human discourse, whether spoken or sung or played, is plain chant, as latterly preserved in Hebrew Prayer and the Roman Catholic Mass: all else is "a mere shadow of the light that flooded the old language when man first cried to God."[14]

It is this deepest level of speech, "halfway between the song of an artist and everyday speech," that Rosenstock endeavors to show forth in the Gospels. No "secondary intonation"—exemplified in the ephemeral jottings of the Biblical critics—is to stand in the way. To tell and to tell on calls for a full-throated language that breaks through the pale periods of mere prose, generation-bound as they are.

Rosenstock's own words too, forged in the crucible of his mind, cannot be set within the rectangular limits of a printed page. They demand their own "lining out," their own shape on the page. In this respect, Rosenstock is better heard than read: even in the extant tapes of his discourse the absent speaker seems more present than in the deceptive quiet of a sea of print.

---

13. MDB: ERH (with F.L. Battles), *Magna Carta*, 154, 168–77. [This passage confuses statements made in a school grammar with the conjugation of reality through the grammar of the cross. See ERH, *The Origin of Speech*, 38–72.]

14. MDB: *Magna Carta*, 154.

The chant of his message defies any scheme of musical or typographical notation. This fact, so obvious to one attuned to Rosenstock's message and manner, was quite unconscious to the author himself. He would have denied that what he said and wrote was at the level of plain chant. Advised to 'line out' the most passionate portions of his Tippett Lectures, rather than to set them within the aleatory margins of typography—as letters and spaces mechanically dictated to the printer—he repudiated the idea.[15]

Yet for the prose-jaded late twentieth century reader's eye, the editor has chosen to single out several passages whose strophes sing above the murmur of their context. These passages, set in the conventional typography our author demanded on one page, are lined out on the facing page. The reader will thus sense the flights which his prose takes. In deference, however, to the author's deeply felt belief, already noted, that the only true poetry, the opposite of the *morbus poeticus*, is psalm in response to God, the author's typography has not been altered in the text. Such rearrangement of the printed page is done only to bring to the reader some of the intensity of the author's prose and to hint to those who never heard him speak the passionate speech which transfigured his whole being into a vehicle of the Spirit. By this device, the voice of Eugen will more distinctly reach the reader's inner ear, when his outward eye fails to comprehend.

One motif in the thought of Eugen Rosenstock-Huessy which occupies a central place in *Fruit of Lips*, as it does in infinitely varied ways in his other writings, is that of the ring.[16] We must view the ring not as a wheel, eternally turning through eternally repeated cycles, as exemplified by what our author calls "Egyptian darkness," but as a line, bent back upon itself where, in the closing of the ring, end and beginning, first day and last day of Israel, meet: "End begets beginning." The progression of the Four Evangelists, beginning with Matthew and ending with John is as a ring closed. This unitary way of viewing the Gospels, in all their variety, contrasts greatly with the fragmenting approach of Biblical critics who see in the contrasts and contradictions of the Evangelists a justification to shatter their concerted witness. Here Rosenstock stands with the Fathers of the Church: like them he has grasped the fact that unity, dynamic unity, glorying in the infinite nuances of the Four Evangelists, is to be chosen over against a Gnostic or Marcionite, Mani or Tatian who endeavors to construct one gospel of static sameness out of a heap of disassembled fragments. The disjointing of the

---

15. [See the first sentence of the next paragraph.]

16. [The *motif* of the *ring* occupies no particular place in "The Fruit of Our Lips," nor does it appear in any of ERH's other works.]

Gospels, fruit of the labors of two hundred years of criticism, has planted a seed. In this book that seed is beginning to sprout.

"The ring of the Gospels is closed."[17] The ring, also, of Rosenstock's literary labors is closed. In *Fruit of Lips*, which our author regarded as the crown and center of his career, we have his last and most important word. The love of his life was the Word Incarnate. In his autobiographical "Biblionomics"[18] he states,

> Ever since my conversion to the full life of the spirit in World War One, I have been very suspicious of my right to give too much weight to books. For instance, without Wittig's sufferings, the *Alter der Kirche* never would have occurred to me. Without the *sauve qui peut* of Hitler's rise in 1931, I would not have felt free to write my favorite book, *Die Revolutionen*.

His books then were written in response to definite occurrences in his life. World War I was most certainly the watershed between the world of *cogito ergo sum* (I think therefore I am), the philosophical outlook which he maintained led to the munition dumps of World War I, and the new epoch, the time of *respondeo etsi mutabor* (I answer, even though I am changed),[19] which the author used as his motto. The frustrations with Cartesianism, the refusal to regard himself as a mere observer outside the Cross of Reality, the toneless quality of scientific language which marked the German university at that time, the absence of its polarity, prayer, in the life of the nation led him further and further away from his fellow academics. He devoted himself while teaching at the University of Breslau to the founding of work camps and establishing of centers for adult education as a means of healing the wounds of the war.

When it finally came time for him and his family to emigrate to the United States in 1933, he had already experienced a much more important inner immigration of the spirit. This came during the period of renewal and overhauling in concert with the group of friends who "as though living on Patmos" founded a small publishing house in 1919, the *Patmos Verlag*. Now the "secret" of the university became manifest.[20] How far it had strayed from

17. [The phrase *the ring is closed* is quite common in 19th and 20th century German prose, appearing in the works of Berthold Auerbach, Gustav Freytag, and even Rudolf Bultmann. One early source is an 1855 work by Ferdinand Kürberger, whose work ERH probably knew, as it provided mottoes for both Theodor Adorno and Ludwig Wittgenstein.]

18. MDB: "Biblionomics," 21.

19. [ERH himself translated his motto as *I respond although I will be changed*.]

20. [MDB here fuses conflicting elements: ERH's 1950 speech on the *secret of the university* (*Geheimnis*, 17–34), the history of the German university in *Out*, and the

its origins of God of the Lutheran Reformation as the informer through the grace of God of *Wissen und Gewissen* of the minds of the councillors to the princes![21] The self-righteousness of the modern university, her "Greek" mind, as the author calls it, had rendered the university a tool of Hitler, the spell-binder, the man who took the German nation back to pre-Christian times.

In the United States, the ring was forged and reforged many times. We know that *Fruit of Lips* is his ultimate ring. In its first and English form, completed in 1954, it could not be published in his own lifetime. He was adamantly against it, holding that the grip of liberal critics upon the Gospels was then so intense in the Anglo-Saxon theological world, that his solitary voice would go unheard. But by 1964, he sensed a turning of the tide; hence, in that year, the book was published as "Die Frucht der Lippen" as part of *Die Sprache des Menschengeschlechts* (vol. 2, 796–903); then in 1968 it was reissued in a smaller book, *Die Umwandlung des Wortes Gottes*.

The time has come, four years after his death, to publish the original English version, for the tides of Biblical criticism have even in our land begun to turn. Yet, between 1954 and 1964, between the English of "Fruit" and the German of "Frucht," Rosenstock's thought matured and deepened. By means of selected notes and a few brief appendices, the present editor has attempted for English readers to show something of that growth of the author's thought. Otherwise, the editor has used a light hand, confining her annotations to brief references or explanations.

This is a book to be read and re-read, not a candidate for a speed-reading enthusiast. Reader, if at first you do not understand, ponder, read again, read aloud. There are deep thoughts here that will elude the hurried, hasty reader.

MARION DAVIS BATTLES
"Marford"
Norwich, Vermont
August 1977

Patmos group's criticism of the complicity of Germany's institutions in the disastrous war. The faults of the German university and their criticism long predated Hitler's rise to power.]

21. MDB: *Geheimnis*, 20. Also found in *Out*, 395, 398, 412–17.

Appendix E
*The Fruit of Our Lips,
or Why Four Gospels?*
(1954)

Top: Margrit and Eugen Rosenstock-Huessy at Four Wells in 1952.
Below: detail of the title page of the 1954 typescript.

```
THE FRUIT OF OUR LIPS

              or

WHY    FOUR    GOSPELS ?


         " I shall create Fruit of Lips".
                              Isaiah.
```

WHILE WORKING WITH THE archive at Four Wells, I discovered several typescripts of the English-language original of "The Fruit of Our Lips." The oldest was a 99-page typescript, probably from 1944. The longest was a hand-corrected typescript dated 1954 with three interpolated chapters (the "Presentation," "The Four Apostles," and the "Epilogue"). As almost everything in the 1954 typescript also appears in the 1978 *Fruit of Lips*, I believe that it is the text that Freya von Moltke gave Marion Davis Battles after Rosenstock-Huessy's death.

If the chapters interpolated and the handwritten corrections made to the typescript late in 1954 are removed, what remains is the intermediate clean typescript which, Rosenstock-Huessy wrote his friend Georg Müller, had found its final form in 1946.[1] (Just for the next few pages, I'll refer to it as "Q.") It consists of the earlier 99-page text with a substantial addition to the final section, (then called "Revelation," though it appears in the 1954 revision as "The Word Himself"), as well as a few other scattered paragraphs.

"Q" is clearly the basis for the 1964 German version, as the German version contains almost none of the changes made to the typescript late in 1954. The chapter "The Oldest Official Gospel Prologues" was replaced in the German version, but probably not for fear of the critics, as Mrs. Battles surmised. The remaining text makes just as clear that Rosenstock-Huessy accepts tradition on the apostolicity of the gospels, while the suppression deprived him of the corroborating testimony of both De Bruyne and von Harnack.[2] It is more likely that he wanted to add new material to his two-volume *Sprache des Menschengeschlechts* and had to sacrifice something to maintain an equivalent number of signatures. (Rosenstock-Huessy's improvements to a manuscript at every stage of production were a constant source of conflict between the author and his post-war publishers.) What replaced the missing chapter are passionate arguments against the evangelists' having "prophesied after the fact" (supported by Rosenstock-Huessy's own experience of prophecy in 1919) and against the post-war conflation of faith and hope.

1. [Letter dated July 8, 1954. This unpublished correspondence is now held at the archive of the Lutheran Church of Westphalia. See the bibliography, 355.]

2. [See Appendix I, 337–46 and 346–50.]

In the summer of 1954, Rosenstock-Huessy sent "Q" to Müller. At some point after sending it to Müller, but before Christmas of that year, Rosenstock-Huessy returned to the typescript, adding the hand-written corrections and the three "chapters" mentioned above. In a letter dated December 9, 1954, he told Müller that he had written a chapter on James, Peter, Paul, and John, so "The Four Apostles" was likely the first of the three "new" chapters to be written. The other two were probably added over the next two weeks. (From the jumble of typos and typed and hand-written corrections in the interpolated pages, it is clear that Rosenstock-Huessy typed them himself.) By November 1955, Müller had translated "Q" into German and was still "eagerly looking forward" to "The Four Apostles," but he may never have received the chapter; there is no reference to it in their subsequent correspondence, and it does not appear in the German version.[3] At some time between 1960 and the publication of the German version in *Die Sprache des Menschengeschlechts* in 1964, Rosenstock-Huessy edited Müller's translation of "Q" and added a good deal of new material. All the new citations in the 1964 German version are from sources published well after 1954: there are several citations from the 1959 *Studia Evangelica,* and the cited works by Werner Picht and Jehoshuah Grintz were both published in 1960.

The hand-corrected 1954 typescript offers its own puzzles. Mrs. Battles acknowledged Clint Gardner's note to the effect that the text of the epilogue did not come to him as part of the essay.[4] But interestingly enough, the additions to "Q" (the "Presentation of This Book," the chapter "The Four Apostles," and the "Epilogue" with Gardner's note) all fit neatly into that text's pagination. The "Presentation" is numbered 1–6 "of the presentation," setting it before the numbering of the text itself; "The Four Apostles" is hand-marked as pages 95a–95f and lies between pages 95 and 96 of the text; the "Epilogue" is paginated to pick up precisely where the hand-corrected text leaves off; and all three pieces are listed in the table of contents prepared for the essay in 1954. So we may safely assume that the "Epilogue" was meant to be as much a part of the text as the other pieces added in 1954. The table of contents and the "Presentation" certainly point to a planned publication of the English-language version. The "Presentation" is dated "Advent, 1954," which sets an end-date for the manuscript's completion.

It is not as clear when the essay was written or the first 99-page typescript made, but there is one clue. Rosenstock-Huessy kept careful count of the passage of time since the outbreak of the Great War. In the

---

3. [GM letters to ERH dated November 10, 1955, and April 2, 1956.]

4. [The note on the first page of the "Epilogue" typescript, dated 11/15/65 and signed CCG, says *this section not in basic set when handed to me, but in a separate folder. Also not in the German text.* See 184, 275–79.]

THE FRUIT OF OUR LIPS, OR WHY FOUR GOSPELS? 185

hand-corrected typescript he mentions the "last thirty years of catastrophe," which makes no sense for the span from 1924 to 1954, but rhymes perfectly with the span from 1914 to 1944; in the 1964 German version, the reference is to "*fifty* years of catastrophe." In the original text, he writes of General Eisenhower as the living representative of the GI's in the present tense; in the German version he uses the past tense and adds "from 1942 to 1945." No books published after 1944 are cited in the original text or in "Q." So I think we may safely date the original text to 1944.

Based on Rosenstock-Huessy's delight in the quote from *The World, the Flesh, and Father Smith* (a Book of the Month Club selection in June of 1945), I first thought the hand-written corrections might date from that year or soon after. With the exception of that quote, however, none of those corrections appear in the German text, so they were probably all made later in 1954. It is possible that Rosenstock-Huessy only read *Father Smith* in the summer of 1954 and so made note of it in the manuscript he sent to Müller; incorporating that note may even have been what set off the Advent revision of "Q."

Oddly enough, Mrs. Battles' 1978 edition contains passages that do not appear in the 1954 typescript. I briefly considered the possibility that Mrs. Battles might have worked from a later version, since lost, but her text otherwise follows the typescript too closely—so closely that it even reproduces its typos: "*Korrekturen* ins *Hebräerbrief*" for "*im Hebräerbrief*" in the (now reformatted) footnote on page 232, for instance. It was only on returning to re-check my translation of the German version that I discovered the solution to the puzzle. Despite all her careful footnoting, Mrs. Battles had not in fact sequestered all the variant German text in the chapter endnotes and appendices. Where she considered the later version more eloquent, more congenial, or merely more "politically correct," she had imported whole sentences from the German version into the original, in her own sometimes puzzling translations.

The basic mystery of the 1978 edition, however, is the way Mrs. Battles's editorial hand wavered from one page to the next. Sometimes she replaced Rosenstock-Huessy's awkward compound verb forms (such as "does point") with simpler forms ("points") and sometimes she did not. Sometimes she replaced his eighteenth-century use of capitals for Important Subjects and sometimes she did not (in at least one case, she even added capitals where he had not used them himself). Some of her changes are what the Germans call a *Verschlimmbesserung*, an improvement in name only; others, such as replacing the generally accepted phrase "Biblical criticism" throughout the text with "criticism of the biblical texts," remain inscrutable.

While I was glad that the text was available in English in any form, I had long thought the 1978 edition inferior to its German cousin, first and foremost because the Battles edition let the title essay travel alone. But Mrs. Battles also indiscriminately mixed her own notes with the author's, sometimes even neglecting to credit him for his, and she relegated most of the material he had added for the 1964 German edition to the chapter endnotes or appendices. I also disliked her habit of setting passages she found particularly beautiful opposite the actual text, lined as poetry—in spite of reporting in her introduction that Rosenstock-Huessy had himself absolutely rejected the idea.[5] However, all of that paled beside what I could not help feeling was her occasional, and occasionally complete, misunderstanding of Rosenstock-Huessy's work. (Why she built up a common proverbial German saying into a "concept" of "the ring," for instance, is a mystery.) For better or worse, I have included her introduction as Appendix D, where it may speak for itself.

Pride famously comes before a fall. In assembling this book I have had to learn the hard way that it is more difficult to assemble an edition true to an author's intentions than I had thought, especially if those intentions alter over time. I have come to see that the work Mrs. Battles did to elucidate the text and its many references deserves as much respect as her efforts to bring the work to light in English in the first place. While it is hard to imagine Rosenstock-Huessy letting anyone get away with writing that his "style may leave one in despair, the leaps of the mind cause chagrin, the occasional error of fact provoke a momentary feeling of 'Aha! he is not infallible,'"[6] I know it is a feeling many have shared.

For all my quibbles with Mrs. Battles's thought, her style, and her translations (which sometimes left me in despair in turn), I must acknowledge that I followed in her footsteps. I began in the conviction that this Appendix should restore the text of the 1954 typescript, and began to retype it verbatim. The more I typed, however, the more I began to feel that I was not serving Rosenstock-Huessy's stated intention "to keep the text readable." Much of the essay was composed in eloquent English and it certainly displayed a dazzling vocabulary, but it was also true that occasionally the word order was, if not entirely German, certainly foreign. Paragraphs ran on for pages, consisted of a single sentence, or were broken in odd, not to say willful, ways. Commas came either singly or in battalions. With clarity as my only goal, I began to edit.

---

5 [See Appendix D, 177.]
6 [See Appendix D, 174.]

I replaced words or phrases clearly mistranslated from German ("when" ["*wenn*"] written for "if"; "look through" for "see through"; the confusion of "by," "from," and "of," as translations of the single German word "*von*," or verbs in the perfect tense where English uses other tenses). Then there were the confusions as to English usage ("like" for "as," "in" for "into," and vice versa). Soon, as Mrs. Battles had before me, I found myself changing punctuation, adding or changing paragraph breaks (not always in the same places Mrs. Battles chose), moving clauses within sentences (as Mrs. Battles had before me), replacing *all* of the compound verbs and removing almost all of the unusual capitalization. Many if not most of these changes had also been made in the 1978 edition, but had gone unnoted, so I scrupulously marked all the changes. I footnoted the significant changes from the 1954 typescript and the 1978 edition and set *all* the words I added or substituted in *italics* within brackets. So the end result was that my "finished" text no more resembled the unadulterated English text of the hand-corrected 1954 typescript than the 1978 edition had. But I considered it an improvement.

So did the board of the Eugen Rosenstock-Huessy Fund, initially; but when I presented a second version a year later, incorporating some of the board's comments on the first, I found that considerable resistance had arisen. One former student of Rosenstock-Huessy's called my edited text a parody of the original, saying that anything other than a scholarly edition preserving the historical document intact would be of no value whatsoever. As a result, much as I had wanted to offer the "readable text" promised in the "Presentation," I had no choice but to withdraw mine. (Perhaps it will find another home one of these days.)

So, this Appendix offers something even truer to the original than I had originally intended: a nearly exact copy of the hand-corrected 1954 typescript, with all the original capitalizations, the oddball footnotes, idiosyncratic spelling and sentence structure, and the rampant Teutonicisms, including the verb tense and preposition variants. (I am profoundly grateful to Frances Bracken Huessy for her careful comparison of my electronic file with the original typescript, when I had worked on the piece so long that could no longer see the trees for the forest. Any omissions or mistakes are mine.)

The hand-written corrections and additions Rosenstock-Huessy made to the body of the typescript in Advent 1954 appear in {"French" brackets}. One or two additions [*in italics in brackets*] remain where that seemed the simplest way to aid understanding. Rosenstock-Huessy's own notes are marked with his initials; his citations of scripture appear in parentheses. A number of Mrs. Battles's notes are included, though edited for length; they and her citations of scripture are also marked with her initials. Places where Mrs. Battles diverged from the typescript are footnoted with the prefix "1978," as references to the German version carry the prefix "1964." My own notes appear in square brackets. I have dropped Mrs. Battles's references to Eusebius's *Church History* and her identification of names—anyone unfamiliar with the names of Oswald Spengler, Gilbert Murray, or Dionysus Exiguus may now turn to Wikipedia.

For what it's worth, I advise skipping *all* the footnotes on a first reading—or, if not the author's, then certainly all of Mrs. Battles' and all of mine. This essay was never intended to be read primarily as a learned text. The original manuscript may now be found in the Eugen Rosenstock-Huessy Archive at Dartmouth's Rauner Library, as part of Collection MS-522 (Box 101, folder 19).

The PRESENTATION: Is there a Christian Era?

1. The Speech of Antiquity
2. The Heart and the Lips
3. The "Speech" of the Four Gospels
4. Ink and Blood
5. I c h t h y s
6. End Begets Beginning
7. The Four Idols: Art, Religion, Science, Manners
8. The Cross of Grammar
9. The Shape of the Four Evangelists
10. The Four Apostles: James, Peter, Paul, John
11. The Law of Liberty
12. The Oldest Official Remarks on the Gospels
13. The Word Himself
14. Revelation
15. Epilogue: Faith and Time

1 Y   of the Presentation

The Presentation of this book.

La Presentacion de este Libro, the Spaniards call the presentation of their book to the reader. I shall try to present the intent of this book as precisely as I can, in this introduction.

Blasphemers are more helpful than the lukewarm. The Blasphemer at least makes a noise when he points out / what seems to him the weakest link in the chain which links God and men.

Adolf Hitler— during the "thousand years" of his World Domination —set off his own epoch by stating: "the solar constellation of Christianity has ended." In this hissing remark, the existence of a Christian Era was relegated to the limbo of the past: "There no longer is a Christian Era." Accordingly, the term Christ in B. C. and Anno Domini were dropped from German terminology.

But the lukewarm men have pushed in this direction for a very long time. A glance into Toynbee, Spengler, Nehru, Berr's Histoire Universelle, the Cambridge History, the American Textbooks of History and— especially — the curricula of our History Departments— all do point into the same direction as Friedrich Nietzsche and his theologian-friend Franz Overbeck had pointed with regard to the Christian Era. The counting of the years after the Birth of Christ belongs — this is the majority opinion already — with the Jewish Era from the Creation of the World, with the Hedschrah of Muhammed, or with the years ab urbe condita, after the founding of Rome (753 B. C.). It is an arbitrary single era, one among many. Hence, the Christian Era is no longer recognized as making epoch among all previous eras. And the year Zero is not treated as the turning point and the gateway into a new, the final, and, last not least, our own Era. Few people doubt th We are free to start a new Era like Hitler; any time we wish to do so. From Nietzsche to Hitler, active destruction of the era has

The Presentation of this book

La presentación da este Libro, the Spaniards call the presentation of their book to the reader. I shall try to present the intent of this book as precisely as I can, in this introduction.

Blasphemers are more helpful than the lukewarm. The Blasphemer at least makes a noise when he points out what seems to him the weakest link in the chain which links God and men.

Adolf Hitler—during the "thousand years" of his World Domination—set off his own epoch by stating: 'the solar constellation of Christianity has ended.' In this hissing remark, the existence of a Christian Era was relegated to the limbo of the past: "There no longer is a Christian Era."[7] Accordingly, the term 'Christ' in B.C. and Anno Domini were dropped from German terminology.

But lukewarm {men} have pushed in this direction for a very long time. A glance into Toynbee, Spengler, Nehru, Berr's *Histoire Universelle*, the Cambridge *History*,[8] the American Textbooks of History and—especially—the curricula of our History Departments—all do point into the same direction as Friedrich Nietzsche and his theologian-friend Franz Overbeck had pointed with regard to the Christian Era.[9] The counting of the years after the Birth of Christ belongs—this is the majority opinion already—with the Jewish Era from the Creation of the World, with the *Hedschrah* of Muhammed, or with the years *ab urbe condita*, after the founding of Rome (753 B.C.). It is an arbitrary single era, one among many. Hence, the Christian Era is no longer recognized as making epoch among all previous eras. And the year Zero is not treated as the turning point and the gateway into a new, the final, and, last not least, our own Era. Few people doubt that we are free to start a new era like Hitler, {any time we wish to do so.} From Nietzsche to Hitler, active destruction of the era has proceeded. But looking back we can see two more definite stepping stones which have given this last attack its opportunity.

---

7. [In 1941, Rom Landau also claimed that *we have it from the Führer's own lips that 'today the Christian era is replaced by the National Socialist Era'* and cited a speech Hitler gave in Nürnberg in 1936 (*Hitler's Paradise*, 47). An excerpt from the only speech I have found with a similar text from Nürnberg that year may be found in Appendix I, 328–29.]

8. [MDB labeled ERH's citation of Nehru "falso" and suggested that he had meant "Nietzsche." She was apparently unaware of Jawaharlal Nehru's *Glimpses of World History*—either the 1,000-page 1942 original or the 1960 abridgment. The full title of Berr's book is *En Marge de l'Histoire Universelle*. It is unclear which of the Cambridge *Histories* ERH refers to here.]

9. [In *The Christian Future*, ERH says that Overbeck's abandonment of the Christian era *has penetrated the masses. It signifies the capitulation of theology before 'science' and is part of the suicide of Europe*. (73, n5).]

For 150 years people have concentrated their eforts on the Life and Times of Jesus. Innumerable books have tried to change him, the Lord of the Eons of Eons, the Second Adam, the Son of Man, the Judge of this World, into a contemporary of Kaiphas, Judas, Tiberius, and Pilate. They have searched his vocabulary for colloquialisms of his own place and time. Now, as a child of his time he lost all power over the times. As children of our own time, we disappear with that time. Of most people, after the obituary, no trace remains; of Lincoln Stanton could say: 'Now he belongs to the ages.' We have not heard this said for a long time.

This zeal for the transient environment of Palestine in Jesus' days, then, is one step away from {understanding} his right to give our era his name. But their is an older {slip during} the last centuries with their immersion in world conquest and world knowledge. Strangely enough, Roman Catholics, Reformed and Lutheran thinkers have equally {committed} this {slip}. It is their constant mistranslation of the {Biblical} terms for era, {for the} ending and closing of eras, and for Christ's relation to the epochs of History. The centre of this confusion is known to {every} reader who has ever heard the formula of the prayer, 'World without End.' When the King James' Version used this wording {in 1611}, the phrase was already wrong. But today, it is fatal and antireligious.

Why? The term 'World' in Shakespeare's days still had some ring of the Whirling tides of time in it, but today, 'World' means the universe expanded in space. And so {The phrase of our prayer states} that this world never comes to an end. But the Greek text means the very opposite. It runs: 'and into the eons of eons,' thereby stating that the world comes to one end after another, {only God remains}. Just as we jokingly exclaim: "... period!," {so} the Bible knew that man had to live in the perpetual expectation of an end of his little world. Each "eon" was such one *aion* of man's orientation, computation and organisation. And now in this fantastic caleidoscop of human eras, and worldly {catastrophical} endings, the Breath of a new Spirit was {breathed} and {it} enthroned the Master who would initial[10] as well as subscribe eras and out of whose mouth the beginnings and the ends of all the eras would be interpreted and understood.

Our {rapidly spreading} Pentecostal sects are, of course, filled by the tremor of this specific meaning of Christinaity. But already 150 years ago, the Universalists harped on the same sore point of Thomistic, Lutheran, and Calvinistic Doctrine: Nothing, according to the Bible, is eternal except God. Eons may punish souls during their times. But the punishment in hell {is} of one eon only (Aionios) and this {can} not mean 'eternal'. This wrong

---

10. 1978: *who would initiate.*

translation of *aionios* = eternal,[11] "for ever and for ever," still fills our theological dictionaries. It is palpably wrong. It has poisoned theology. But it has prepared people to think that we either live for the moment or for eternity. But if so, there is no Christian place for an era, an epoch, an age. Then one second and the complete absence of the time flow are the two extremes between {which poor me} is suspended. This is crude nonsense.

I do not live by or for the latest news. And I do not {care for} the very notion of any timeless eternity.

Poor mortal, I am stung with a constant sense of time. But I can cover time-spans from one day to a year to a generation to a century, with my intent and my understanding. And I am asked to believe that neither my creator nor the man who revealed him to us do enter upon the measures of time which alone I can understand? I know, they do. For, I have lived through epoch making events which have changed the lives of all men on this globe. And in the light of the Lord of the Eons, I have found my path through these ends of my world and the beginnings of the next aion. To tell me, 'Oh, the Christian era has been a helpful myth in the past, but now we don't need it any longer,' is like telling me: 'the raft on which you passed the abyss must be condemned'. I have found that there is a way of living through the end and the beginning of an era in perfect freedom, neither as the slave of capitalism nor as the slave of communism, neither as merely a German nor as merely an American, neither as a soldier nor as a scholar. And I should now go and destroy the raft, my raft, simply because people who never passed an abyss, say: "There is no abyss; therefore the Lord of Continuity through all the abysses between eras, can be put up at our rummage sale of old wear."[12]

And nowhere are we less instructed for our polonaising[13] through epochs as God gives them and takes them, than in our theological literature or instruction.

In this situation, I have had to learn anew in what the Christian Era consists. I have tried to distinguish it from the times in which Spengler, Toynbee, Nietzsche, Darwin, Sartre prefer to live. I have had to understand that ever since ZERO, the Christian Era is rivalled by all the preceding pagan eras in our midst. The positive value of the last century's eclipse of the Christian Era has become quite clear to me. {Its} total omission of Christ's universal chronology[14] and {its} concentration on the "times of Jesus," is of great help to you and me and to all of us who wake up after the Great Flood.

11. 1978: aionios *as eternal*.
12. [Probably the German phrase *alte Ware*—extra inventory or *old rubbish*.]
13. [*Polonaise*: in German, a chain of dancers, like a conga line.]
14. 1978: *of Christian universal chronology*.

APPENDIX E

We now see how much paganism and how much balking at the Christian Era from inhabitants of pagan eras or eons, is still with us. A.D. and B.C. indeed cannot be understood by the academic professionals. As a student in our leading Theological "Cemetery" Wrote to me in despair: 'Here, the veil of the Temple has not {yet been torn asunder}.'

The reader, I do hope, finds here in simple language what constitutes the Christian Era; I have said it by {symphonizing the Four Gospels}. They, more than anything else, have been mangled by Biblical criticism.[15] The rascal Robert Graves, a corrupt Genius, is the last jester about the gospel and the gospel writers.[16] I have tried to get myself and my readers out of the bottomless pit of Biblical criticism and its dividing the four gospels into three versus one, the Synoptics and John. I have accepted the first statement of the New Testament, that a New Era has started, and I have thought that obviously, the gospels themselves might be stepping stones in the formation of this new Aion. {Instead of a mere harmony of the gospels, I have asked: Are they movements of a symphony?} Of course, they are. And he who climbs this stair of the wondrous four events, called the gospels, according to Matthew, Marc, Luke, John, understands again the wondrous 'Anno Domini' by which we count the stepping stones of the incarnation, {of the Christian Era}.

Technically, this book presupposes that you can if you wish, read the four gospels yourself. The only stress laid on you is this that I do treat you as of age and as capable of listening to an argument on all four gospels in unity. I would have considered any other treatment an insult to your own literacy and maturity.

I had to mention some errata of scholarship as any reader may have run into one or the other of them. But I have tried to keep the text readable as one sustained argument and therefore have not cluttered it with proofs of erudition. Anybody who cares to look for such credentials, may find them in my THE CHRISTIAN FUTURE (New York 1946), and THE DRIVING POWER OF CIVILIZATION (Boston 1950) {and in many other places. Erudition is presupposed as a natural.}

But what are credentials when we ask ourselves: Is there a Christian Era?

> Advent 1954
> Four Wells, Norwich, Vermont

15. [Throughout the essay, MDB replaced this generally accepted phrase with *criticism of the Biblical texts*.]

16. [Perhaps a reference to Graves' *King Jesus* (1946). There have been many more *jesters* since.]

{1. The Speech of Antiquity}

We leave the first cycle of human speech {when we} enter upon our own era. The {ancient} cycle began in the primitive tribe, among a little group of frantic and frightened, yelling and bouncing men, who took heart, spoke and danced, and proceeded from fright, yelling and bouncing to an inspired way of life.

They placed themselves under verbs, pronouns, nouns, and numbers. Speech made them human by dressing and investing them with power, as the children of Man, as listeners to the spirits of their dead.

The second phase lifted the heart of man into the universe. The tatoos on the body were replaced by the tatoos on the temple, as the whole universe spoke to the Great House of Egypt, to Pharao, and to the Emperor of China, the Son of the Skyworld.

Tell me who speaks to you and I shall know who you are. Pharao was anxious to be the Ka[17] of the skyworld, the child of sun and moon and all the stars, of Horus of the Horizon, of the Southern World of Noon, of the Northern World of Midnight, as the listener of the universe. The Son of Heaven became the heart, the hieroglyphs became the tatoo, of a living universe.

Once ritual was established in tribe and empire, Poetry, {the third flower of antiquity,} began. And it led us into the Green Pastures where Nausikaa meets Odysseus on the sea shore and where Achilleus meets his mother, the ocean's goddess Thetys; since panic was eliminated by ritual, poetry could return into "Nature." "Nature" equals: "the World minus panic." Poetry listens unafraid to nature because it is the child of peace, the listener of peace and law.

Poetry, however, can {not} make the world's laws or peaces better than they are. Poetry transfigures that nature which ritual has freed from panic. But the world still is the world, in many districts where world wars, world riddles, world revolutions, world chaos looms.

The Homeric stream of poetry ran in one direction, towards the world. Homer took advantage of ritual's attainments. Israel's stream of psalms ran in the opposite direction. Israel felt the disadvantage of ritual's multiplicity and incompleteness.

Israel directed its efforts not towards "the World minus panic," but towards the fact that it still was full of panic. Israel saw that ritual contradicted ritual, and that neither temples nor tatoos nor poems ever would get outside their own local and temporal boundaries. So the more rituals or temples were built, or the more poems imagined, the greater became the confusion

---

17. MDB: ERH, *Impure Thinker*, 37–40. [*ka* = *thou*. See 59.]

of tongues, the higher the tower of Bable. Israel withdrew from this world of Tohu and Bohu,[18] {of locally restricted myths}.

Israel built a temple, it is true, but they added that God did not live in it; Israel voided the temple. Israel circumcised her young men, it is true; but they did it to the child in the cradle, not to the initiate adolescent; in the clan's fertility rites the boy was meant to become inspired as a bisexual being, by circumcision. Israel voided this rite. Israel wrote poems but she denied that she "made" them; no idols or pictures made by men could be worshiped. She insisted that she was told {by the living voice of God} and that she replied. Israel voided the arts. In these three acts, she emptied the three great "speeches" of the heathen, the tribal, the templar, the artistic, of their lure and charm as absolutes. The real speech, Israel insisted, was yet to come. It only was heard by him who could hear the future, who could live as the listener to the revolving Eon, as the prophet of the future.

When all this had been said, when the Sioux had spoken and the Chinese, the Greek and the Jew, one world came to an end. This was and is the complete cycle of antiquity:

1. Listeners to the spirits of the dead, created Ritual.
2. Listeners to the skyworld and the {cosmic} universe, built the temples.
3. Listeners to laws and {cities} already achieved, became poets and artists.[19]
4. Listeners to the future, became prophets.

These four phases of speech were unified and superseded in Jesus. And because of this action, he is called the Christ. Christ is the fruit of the lips of antiquity. Jesus had listened to the spirits of old. The sex war in Adam and Eve and all their offspring was overcome by Mary and her son who superseded the {ancient} marriage {as well as} the burial ritual. Jesus had listened to the 'skyworld' calendar and the government of the universe for he came when Pontius Pilate represented the mundane[20] unity of Rome's orb, in Palestine. And on the day of Easter, he himself replaced the bloody sacrifices inside the gates of the temple. Jesus had listened to law and peace already achieved, for his speech certainly transfigures the lillies and the sparrows,

18. MDB: *formlessness* and *void*. [Gen 1:2.]

19. [ERH replaced *law and peace* with *laws and cities* here, but not in the following paragraph.]

20. [Probably *earthly*.]

the adulteress and the thief; outside the gates of the cities of men, the world held no terrors for him. But he superseded all poems. He wrote no book; when he wrote in the sand, the real poem was he himself.[21]

Jesus had listened to the future. For the psalms were on his lips, and the Messianic faith of Israel formed him. But he was no prophet. This is the first thing we are told of him. It is central. He was not expecting somebody else, he was the expected one. They called him, because all they knew were the men who had lived before him: Joseph's son, carpenter, King, priest, rabbi, prophet, messiah.

These names clearly signify terminals. They are the terminals of the four streams of speech sketched by us. The last king, the last priest, the last prophet, the messiah—all this {achieved} would simply mean the end of the world. And Jesus was the end of our first world indeed. He took the sins of this first world upon himself. This sentence simply states the fact that tribal ritual, skyworld temples, nature-praising poetry, messianic psalms, in separation, end{ed} as dead ends {unless they were renewed}.

In this sense, Jesus paid the penalty of death for being the heir of these dead ends. They slew him because he held all their riches and wealth in his hands and heart, his mind and soul. He was too rich not to share the catastrophe of this all too rich ancient world.

But the terminal of the four modes of speech also became the starting point. Jesus founded the Church since he was the fruit of all the pure lips of antiquity. He spoke in the four currents created before him. How else could he speak? He did quote Deuteronomy when he formulated the golden rule. But we are more than we say. Jesus was not contained in any of the rules and rituals although he filled and enlivened them all, when the poem of his life touched on their themes. He {evoked by his prayer} the man who, in every act, exceeds this act noticeably. When they thought that he was the carpenter, he was the rabbi. When they called him rabbi, he was the prophet. When they called him prophet he was the Messiah. And when they called him {Israel's} Messiah, he stood revealed as the One {Son of Man} who had listened to the free God, to the living God only. His real life always exceeded his social role. This excess is "man," in the Christian era. That which will not adjust, is man.[22]

We are the children of listening. Because we listen to our parents, we bear their name. Because we listen to the constellations and conjunctures of our social sky, we are children of our times. Because we listen to the lure of

---

21. ERH: Compare: "We are God's poem" Ephesians II,10. [*Poiema* becomes *workmanship* in the KJV].

22. ERH: "Excessus mentis" is an official term with John Eriugena, Bonaventura, and Cusanus, for the Christian soul's life.

law,²³ we are children of nature. And because we listen to the call from our destiny, we are sons and daughters of the Revolution.

Jesus is the {heir of antiquity}.²⁴ He filled and fulfilled the four "listening posts" of:

> Child of the ancestors {in tribes,}
> Child of the times {in empires,}
> Child of nature {in Greece,}
> Child of revolution {in Israel.}

However, he showed that they could only be fulfilled here and now before our eyes in this acceptable year of the Lord called Today. One had to be free from any one of the laws of the four listening posts, before one could refill them with life.

Jesus was the son of ritual, the son of all the words spoken. But by showing that he was free from their separate authority, he became the founder of a new language in which they all could be fused for a new start.

Now, here we come upon our dilemma when speaking about him. The 19th century cut Jesus' connection with his past. It was an artistic century. It loved life and hated suffering. It disliked the question, Why did he have to die? It concentrated on the life of Jesus. Biographies became the great fashion. So Jesus too received his biography. This was new. It was the opposite of the Christian tradition. This had been 'thanatography'. A biography ends with the death of the "biographee." The story of Jesus makes sense only when his death begins and antecedes our lives. A Christian is a man to whom He speaks. The Body of Christ are those who listen to him. But the biographical craze has produced a state of mind according to which it is enough for a Christian to speak *of* Christ and to call *himself* a Christian.²⁵

To the Rousseauites of our days, Jesus is the adolescent of innocence, the Y.M.C.A. hero, the good boy. The biographies have deprived him of his real name. For to us he is uninteresting, unless he is the Word. We have shown that to speak means to make beginnings the fruits of ends. If the tomb of Jesus is not the womb of the Christian era, we had better forget his whole story as a fairy tale.

The voiding of the ecclesiastical manner of speech about Christ has happened. No criticism of Biblical criticism can unmake it. They have written down Jesus into a speechless child of nature. On the other hand, the history of speech requires a reconquest of Christ's place in its dialectics {and

---

23. [Probably *rule*.]

24. [Before ERH's handwritten correction, *son of God*.]

25. [MDB imported *Yet, the only question which he raises, runs: 'Have I sealed antiquity for you? Do you live after me?'* from the German version; see 63.]

THE FRUIT OF OUR LIPS, OR WHY FOUR GOSPELS? 199

antiphons}. As the Word, which has become flesh, Jesus occupies the center in the history of speech.

This, then, is our dilemma: To the modern man, Jesus is just a man who lived from 3 B.C. to 27 or 29 A.D. This is of no concern to us. On the other hand, speech had gone full cycle through Red Indian, Egyptian, Greek and Jew, and we speak neither of their four languages nor think their thoughts any more. Yet we can understand all four of them very well. We look them through.[26] Their meaning is opened to us. And for our peace of mind, we must know the reason.

How can we make the fruits of the last century of biographical Christianity into a seed for our understanding of speech?

{2. The Fruit of Lips}[27]

Our first steps beyond the critical, analytical, biographical century should be frankly egotistical. Our times' need is a reconquest of the wave continuum of the spirit. We, too, must speak. And we cannot speak unless we are sure that we continue to speak {and that we may reach into posterity}. Speech has this in common with love that although both are discovered by the individual, once for the first time, they also are {far-reaching}.[28] In a man's first love, he also discovers the {time-continuum} of all love; the continuity of history, the order of the universe, the destiny of man, all stand disclosed to the soul who falls in love for the first time. By his falling in love, his eyes are opened and his ears are sensitive to identities {through all generations}. He can read the riddles, he can decipher the flowers and the stars, he can speak and shout and sing. To {be} love{d by}[29] one other person, means to know every {phase of time}. And the eloquence of love hails from the assuredness that all creatures speak in one tongue. As speakers as well as lovers, we need assurance that we move in a continuum, that our discovery of real life and our words make sense {forever and forever}. Otherwise we go mad and all spirit leaves us. It is impossible to assume that we do something different when we speak, from the peoples of all times. Our speech would be up in the air, a meaningless stammering unless we have the right to believe that all speech is legitimate and authorized as one and the same life process from the first day on which man has spoken to the last.

It is, therefore, literally in self-defense that I have to live down the two dogmas of science: 1. a man's life ends with his death; 2. a man's words are

26. [Probably: *see through them.*]

27. [This section heading does not appear in the table of contents, and is superseded by another. See below.]

28. [ERH replaced *universal* with *far-reaching*. MDB used both, another clue that she worked from this typescript. See 63.]

29. [ERH's handwritten correction evokes a deeper truth and a greater mystery.]

merely means of expressing his {vapid} thoughts. These two dogmas void our words of all meaning, and the last thirty years of catastrophe are the logical answer to them.[30] These dogmas are the obvious nonsense of a science which treats man as nature {and does not see its own claim of being valid and true}.[31]

Against these two dogmas, I hold that we are the fruit of lips, and that our lips shall bear fruit.

I am satisfied that this makes sense. It restores my right to listen and to speak. But this sense as any sense demands universal application. I have tried to satisfy the reader that Jesus is the fruit of the four streams of speech preceding him. He is the fruit of the lips of all antiquity.

My answer to the historical and artistic and literary and biographical and critical century has been strictly linguistic. God did not make a nice unhistorical wildflower somewhere in Palestine. All mankind participated in making this man, in as far as they had spoken fruitfully, consequentially, commitally, continually.

{2. The Heart and the Lips}

The streams of speech which came to an end on the cross, {we have sketched}. But at the same time the Cross blocks the road backwards towards any of these streams. I cannot relapse into tribal ritual or Pharaonic 'skyworlds.' Hitler who tried precisely this, stands revealed as a madman. And the two other streams are blocked, too: The modern Greeks, {i.e.} the physicists{,} and the modern Jews, {i.e.} the Zionists{,} certainly are not {the} Greeks or Jews of antiquity. The Greeks glorified in[32] the beauties of the cosmos; our physicists empty it of meaning. The Jews glorified nothing but God. The Zionists have built a university in Jerusalem, as their first communal building. This road-block of the Word, then, is a fact. Not one of the streams of speech of ancient man surges through us, directly.

Since this is so, we must consider him the seed of all speech of our era. As listeners and speaker, as singers and teachers, we are the fruit of his lips.

If this shall be more than a pun, then, we must inquire boldly into the question of "lips." The lips of the living Jesus, wonderful as his words must have been, cannot be listened to by us.

30. [1914 plus the *last thirty years* dates the original version to 1944. 1964: *fifty years of catastrophe*.]

31. [The added clause is ambiguous. Perhaps: *and does not see how its own claim of being valid and true roots in the continuum of speech.*]

32. [Perhaps: *gloried in the beauties*, or *glorified the beauties*, as in *the Jews glorified nothing but God.*]

His lips must reach us. But how to recognize them? By this question the task of this {book} is determined.³³ The lips of the historically effective Jesus have been the four gospels. The four gospels of Mathew, Marc, L{u}ke, John are the lips of the risen Christ. They bespeak the meaning of his death. They are the lips which tell us what it meant that this heart broke. We have been expected to be the fruits of these lips.

In self-defense man may do desperate things. In self-defense we may make bold to acquire a clear conception of fruitful speech. Since Jesus is the road-block which separates us from the fruitful rivers of speech of the ancients, we must acquire a knowledge of his "lips." How were these lips formed? Can it be said that the four gospels to us are the lips of the "Word" at its crucifixion? Obviously, they cannot suffice unless they avail themselves of all the powers of pre-Christian speech and by doing so, progress beyond anything ever said before.

But, then, can this be true? And why four gospels? Why not one or two?

It is our hypothesis that the four gospels are the lips whose fruits we are expected to be, and that they are His lips. It follows that since the four gospels are One organ, his lips, the secret of their unity is the secret we have to understand.

The "naturalistic" century of Biblical criticism knew very well that the very existence of "lips" of the crucified Christ would block their own study of Jesus, the natural man. The attack of Biblical criticism was concentrated on this one argument: That we should not read the four gospels as four. Accordingly, they were reduced to one: This was done, by keeping three and rejecting one. Behind the three first, the synoptic gospels, one common source, the famous "P," was placed by Baur; this, we had to believe was the document from which the three all came.³⁴ The gospel of John was stripped of its source character and relegated somewhere to the second century from which distance it could not bear much testimony on the facts. Thus St. John became "legend," while the three synoptic gospels were made one by reducing them to a written source. Consequently they could not be called unified, as they could not be better than their "source."

Indeed one source by itself is as good as another. One source is not sacred. Once the three synoptic gospels were reduced to one source, they became simply material for our reconstruction of the life of Jesus from all

33. [*Book* replaced *chapter* here. The essay was clearly once intended to be part of a larger book, perhaps the English-language equivalent of *Die Sprache* which ERH was told was *impossible to publish* (*Christian Future*, 128, n2).]

34. [Perhaps a typo for Q, or perhaps a confusion with Graf and Wellhausen's "priestly" Old Testament author. 1964: *Behind the first three "Synoptic" gospels*, [Conrad Hermann] *Weisse placed a common source, the famous 'Q.'* (See 65.)]

the material. Reitzenstein used Oriental mystery religions, Dibelius used artistic models, Scholem Asch used Jewish Rabbinic traditions to explain "Jesus." Jesus became alternatingly the expression of one of the styles or modes of life preceding him. He was dissolved as the road-block. He belonged with antiquity. He was speaking, thinking, praying, teaching like many men of ancient times. There was no reason to fuss about this man, the little man from the "Orient." Anatole France summed it all up in the remark of Pontius Pilate to a friend. Sitting on the Riviera and reviewing his interesting career, Pilate said to his interviewer: "Jesus of Nazareth? *Je ne me souviens pas*."[35] Indeed, there was left nothing memorable about him; according to the critics Jesus became a souvenir of antiquity.

It is not an overstatement to say that the scientific reduction of the four gospels to the rubble heap of source-material is the condition for this result.

But what can convince modern man that the gospels are anything better? Negatively, the eagerness of reducing the gospels to practically one, has vanished nowadays. What had this eagerness achieved? The critics had "proven" that a Greek gospel, Marc, was the gospel which originated first. There was nothing indeed, which they had not proven. For instance they had succeeded to a point where nobody believed that the Letter to the Hebrews was written to the Hebrews.[36] In other words, every one stone of our tradition had been turned upside down and was made to say the opposite from what it said. But this period of turning upside down is at an end. It has no interest to me. For readers who cannot study the question I may mention some facts which put the whole era "from Reimarus to Wrede" in its quest for an historical Jesus "behind" our source material, in jeopardy. They form a road-block now against the reductionists. We shall never know an "historical" Jesus "behind" so-called "material."

1. John writes as an eye witness who knows the minutest details when he cares to mention them. The apostle is the author of the gospel. Therefore it carries authority.

2. All four gospels are apostolic. Matthew was the converted publican among the apostles.[37] Marc obeyed Peter, Luke lived with Paul. John dictated to a Greek secretary.

---

35. ["*Jésus, de Nazareth ? Je ne me rappelle pas.*" France, *Procurateur*, 37.]

36. ERH: Chapman, Matthew, Mark and Luke, 1937 p. 187, note 2. [Chapman only reports on the consensus in Germany, which he also finds dubious. See Appendix I, 321.]

37. [After dropping *Peter and the Zebedees* and correcting *Jesus' brother*" to "*James (John's brother)*, MDB imported *he wrote under James (John's brother's) eyes in Jerusalem before the year 42* from the German version. See 67.]

3. Matthew wrote in Aramaic[38] and he wrote first.
4. Marc states bluntly that he is quoting from Matthew.[39]

These four facts simply refute the critics who attacked the quadrilateral of four authoritative gospels. I mention these facts for the comfort of souls who are intimidated by the awe before this "science." I was brought up among the outstanding source-critics of those days. One of my first books was dedicated to one of them, I. Vahlen,[40] though it was written in another field. I did a lot of work with sources and unknown authors and relations between sources myself. In 1912, working in an archive over a 13th century manuscript, I read this sentence on the parchment: "*multi enim studio contradicendi amiserunt sensum.*" Many, in their eagerness to contradict at all costs lost the understanding. I was impressed.

To contradict is one thing. Everybody is free to do so. But he is not free to pretend that his contradiction ever can pull a positive solution out of the mind's magic hat.

Applied to the Bible, this means: It is not everybody's business to read the Bible as the lips of which the reader is to be the fruit. It is anybody's privilege to say: I don't believe that John wrote his gospel or we cannot know when it was written. Man can affix his No to any statement coming to him from any other man as much as he may attach his Yes to it. Never, on the other hand, can he replace the repudiated statement by speculation. This, however, is exactly what the Biblical critics have done. They have not acquiesced in disbelieving tradition. They have positively told us who wrote the real story, and how it looked and when our gospels were written and for which partisan purposes.

It is not given to the mind to know reality by negation. Our tradition may be wrong and untrustworthy. But then we simply do not have the right tradition. No logical somersaults can produce the positive story. When the mind tries to act as the creator of real facts, we have the story of Gnosis all over again. Gnosis in education is when you tell people how education should be and then think: "Now they are educated"—Gnosis in history is when you tell people how history might have been and then think, "Now, it has been this way."

---

38. [1964: *Matthew wrote in Hebrew, not in Aramaic.* See 67 and Appendix I, 325–27.]

39. [Otto Kroesen suggests that the evidence is found in Chapman, *MML*, 5–8. See Appendix I, 318–21.]

40. [Johannes Vahlen, professor of philology with whom ERH studied in Berlin, during Vahlen's last semesters there.]

This insight into the negative aspect of a century of criticism, impressed a great man so deeply that he shelved his fame as an expert of Biblical criticism, studied medicine and moved out to Africa to treat Negroes.[41] Albert Schweitzer before leaving Europe, published his book which expressed this insight, his famous "Final Criticism of 150 Years of Research on the Life of Jesus." This title, we may bestow on his book, now, in retrospect. Its first title was "Von Reimarus bis Wrede, Geschichte der Leben Jesu Forschung". ("The Quest of the Historical Jesus," is the English title.) Schweitzer's leaving of Europe for the speechless physical world of the Jungles was precipitated by the negative work of the critics. His insight in their failure cured him for quite a while. In the end, however, his scholarly habits returned and he relapsed. That which he had forbidden himself for Jesus he now did for Paul. His big volume on the mysticism of Paul was written on the very lines he had condemned in research of Jesus.

Hence Schweitzer has become a tragic figure, straddling a fence, rejecting criticism and unable to stay away from it. This may warn us that the work of 150 years is not readily dismissed by sheer violence. Schweitzer by negating negation, did not establish a new position. When his faith required positive speech once more, he lapsed into the grooves which were in existence. In his preface to the Mysticism of the Apostle Paul, Schweitzer is aware of his own dilemma. He admits that he reads the New Testament as a source. He wishes to reconstruct out of its material somebody else's far distant religion. It definitely is not the lips of a voice which created a new dimension of speech, the dimension in which all the generations of men may become brothers and one. To the contrary, as a son of nature, Schweitzer wishes to prove to himself and to his readers that every generation has a different spirit.

Certainly every generation has a different spirit. But is it not equally certain that the man who was called the A and the O,[42] the beginning and the end of all times, knew this one fact as well as Albert Schweitzer or a Parisian fashion-maker or a New York headlines-writer, or the German Youth Movement? In fact it was precisely these Ghosts of the different times and places which aroused Jesus. He decided to do something about the Schweitzers {and Bultmanns}[43] of his own days and of all days. And he said that we could introduce in the world a power by which these ghosts could be laid. Because

---

41. 1978: *to treat Africans*. [*Negroes* would have been a polite term for ERH in 1954, as *colored people* was for the founders of the NAACP.]

42. [The "Alpha" and "Omega" in our gospels are simply "A" and "O" in German.]

43. [Though MDB included every other handwritten correction in the typescript, she deleted this reference to Bultmann.]

these ghosts and spirits of the times were uppermost in his mind, he called the new power the Sane Ghost and the Healing Spirit.

When Schweitzer wrote on Paul, he dealt with the one man who had first applied this new power on a colossal scale. By Schweitzer's scientific standards—not his practical—both men, Jesus and Paul had failed in their own avowed purpose of connecting all times.

Following the vicissitudes of {Schweitzer, of} this great and admirable Christian and—to me—completely ununderstandable theologian, I had to ask myself if I was better equipped. My great advantage as I see it, is that I never was a minister nor a theologian, by profession. Instead, I was nourished at the very springhead of the art which when it spread to the theologians made them believe in the mind's gnostic creativity, made them into history-gnostics. Knowing their premises too well, I shied away from the vicious circle of first getting a position for a lifetime, a livelihood for dealing with certain authoritative texts, of then spending this lifetime by demolishing these texts, and finally replacing them by the "real" tradition as the result of this contradicting. We may not wish to be the fruits of His lips, of the gospels; but who is interested in being taught, with great seriousness, as a life study, that there were *no lips*?

By staying away, I was spared the temptation as well as the shock of Schweitzer, the temptation which produced his Paul, the shock which shipped him to Africa. My approach to the Word which made our era has not been marked by this kind of theological illusion and disillusionment. Instead, I remained convinced that the century of "Nature" simply had asked the wrong questions: the Biblical and Homeric critics were loyal and honest believers in Rousseau, Thomas Aquinas, Aristotle. These, their three authorities, taught that language was man's natural equipment. On the basis of this dogma, the whole house of criticism was raised. How could Jesus be the Word, how could John say: "In the Beginning was the Word," how could Matthew quote Jesus as saying: "I shall be with you verily to the end of the World" in the face of this naturalistic dogma? And especially, how could the four gospels be called inspired, if the words of men were data of the dictionary and the grammar book? They could not. The dogma that speech is as natural with man as it is with the apes, compelled four or five generations of professional workers to produce every thinkable theory of reduction and atomization which would reduce the gospels to material. The critics impressed the world and themselves with their own greater honesty and sincerity; compared with them, the fundamentalists often had no brilliancy, no brains, no guts. And indeed, the brilliancy of this century of analysis was more than a firework. It was the genuine outburst of the natural mind. What is the natural mind? The natural mind hopes to know and to

206   APPENDIX E

employ and to manipulate nature. The critics hoped to employ the Bible as mere nature, as source material for the new natural history of mankind, for the coming natural science of evolution. This undertaking of a natural history, they thought possible because their college halls and libraries seemed firmly established in the shadow of revered institutions like Church and State. Little did they know that scholarship is based on a common bond between laity and scholars called the Church, and on a common law of freedom called the State, in our era. Before we can criticize at leisure, *we must be at leisure*. No science of man is truly scientific which remains ignorant of this, its own, premise. The premise of a common peace within which the critic may criticize, means that he, the critic himself must uphold the unity and continuity of speech through all ages and between all groups of men. For peace is the fruit of speech, and is not to be had otherwise. And science needs, presupposes, requires peace.

Once this is understood, speech ceases to be an "object" of natural science: The peace needed by the scientist and the speech which he makes the object of his studies, stand revealed—as one and the same process. To study man, in sociology, piece-mea{l}, individual by individual, class by class, nation by nation, one man here, one man there, Spanish, Greek, English, history or grammar, as separate individuals, or bodies of knowledge, and at the same time to live by a peace created in the name of one hope in science, one faith in the laity, one love for the Truth, is too much of a contradiction.[44] This, the 19th century undertook and it exploded speechlessly! If the natural method is applied to Jesus, he becomes a glowing boy scout (Spemann and many others; consider a book title like "Jesus the Adolescent"), or the psychoanalytical twin of Judas (Rank and others) or a powerless idiot (Gerhard Hauptmann) or just sentimental (Scholem Asch).

Now all this may, of course, be true. But the roadblock into the linguistic past would still be there, Jesus or no Jesus. We live in another world than Cicero and Gamaliel, Montezuma of Mexico and Red Jacket of the Seneca tribe. To define this our world, is everybody's concern.

It {does not have to be} the concern[45] of theologians like Schweitzer{,} or {of} philologists, but {of} everybody who wishes to live in peace because two world wars have nearly plunged us back into a truly pre-Christian,

---

44. [This sentence may be what drove MDB to say *his style may leave one in despair* though there are others like it. Perhaps: *To study man piece-meal (individual by individual, class by class, nation by nation—one man here, one man there, Spanish, Greek, or English) in sociology, history, or grammar (as separate bodies of knowledge) and at the same time to live by a peace created in the name of one hope in science, one faith of the laity, one love for the truth, is too much of a contradiction.*]

45. [Perhaps: *It must be the concern not only of theologians.* .]

pre-Homeric, pre-Mosaic world. My defense against this onslaught on my peace, my world, my era, is based on one dogma: Speech is a continuum.

Now the four Evangelists insist that something happened to this very continuum in their days. Hence I propose to ask: What did happen? My way of finding this out, seems rather obvious to me in retrospect. And I now shall try to state the skeleton of my logic:

All the four Evangelists say unanimously: Speech and writing must be changed, in fact they *are* changed, by the Word. If they do not lie, their own speech and writings must bear evidence of this alleged change.

If we can find out {that} their speech differs and in what respect it differs from anything said before, the change of which they try to convince us and the change which speech underwent in their gospel writing, will have to be one and the same change. "Conversion," "faith," "redemption," "revelation," "speaking in tongues," "pouring out of the Holy Ghost," all these quite dead terms, could be identified with the process to be observed in the texts of their gospels. This would prove their case.

{3. The Speech of the Gospels}[46]

To sum it all up, the gospel writers themselves must be the documents of the linguistic change by the Word.

The four Evangelists in their new way of speaking, would not be the only documents of such a change. Faithful Christians will continue to be impressed by the change in the nature of man by martyrs and missionaries. An apostle like Paul who was both martyr and missionary will seem a better witness to an orthodox Christian than Luke's text. And greater masses will always be attracted by relics, miracles, Cathedrals and monasteries.

But for the pure mind, for *science*, for the intellect, neither bones nor stones will ever prove that a change of mind occurred. The scientific conscience in all of us rebels against such external evidence. Monks are found in India, martyrs and disciples in China, shrines in Thailand and Yukatan, cathedrals in Mexico. The mind does not and need not trust in a historical change of man's nature ever on such a basis, because it is not the mind's business to trust, to believe in external evidence.

But the mind cannot help believing in a change of mind from a change of style.

The believer, then, will not have to wait for our arguments. The unbeliever, however, has to be shown. The crucible in which a style is chemically so to speak, transformed, must be shown. And it is "the Mind," in our times,

46. [The table of contents lists this section as "The Speech of the Four Gospels."]

not the soul or the body, who is unable to understand Christianity as the medium of his own mental and scientific truth. Only when the intellect is able to identify the process by which it arrives at truth, as the process which proceeds in the four gospels, will the mind go back on its accusation that Christianity is as dead {as} a dodo and never was anything but a salubrious or opprobrious myth.

The "four gospels"—we shall use quotation marks when we treat them as a Singular, a Whole—can prove this one thing: The Word did change the world of mind for good.

A book of antiquity is closed to all other books. A school of thought in antiquity is closed to all other schools. One book: It begins and it ends. Two covers contain it.

This is not true of the four gospels. They respond to a dead end. They continue through a change of mind. They progress through time, and, at the end, *they barely begin*. At the end of all four gospels, John says that the whole cosmos was not big enough to contain all the books which it would be possible to produce on Christianity. This sounds fantastic. But after all, this, my own book,[47] is proof that John's mirth had cause. John must have been as boyishly cheerful as his master. As a very old man, he still boasted that he once ran faster than Peter (John 19:4).[48] The oldest apostle ended the last gospel with a remark of not very strict seriousness; this is a notable feature of the New Testament, or, more cautiously, of this Whole of which the four gospels are stanzas.

The exuberance of the end of "the four gospels" contrasts with the tone of the beginning. "The Four Gospels" opens on a tone of circumspection. Matthew is dignified, serious, and moving cautiously. All through the four gospels, we may observe that it becomes gradually easier to speak of the event. There is an acceleration and a growth in assurance in the four parts. This growth in articulatedness and assurance may be shown in every one gospel. But this growth though identical finds a very different expression, in each case. The second gospel expresses the growth by being brief. Marc has 677 verses compared to Matthew's 1,072. There are many reasons for this as I well know. But when everything is said, it remains true, that *ceteris paribus* the brief treatment of a theme usually betrays greater confidence of the author than a lengthy one. To Peter, the inspirer of Marc, the task must have seemed to need less argument. Where Matthew had given the complete speeches, Marc was allowed to write that he would only give some quotations.[49]

---

47. [Again, *book* replaces *chapter*.]
48. [The reference is to John 20:4.]
49. [Otto Kroesen suggests that the source is Chapman, *MML*, 5–8. See Appendix I,

THE FRUIT OF OUR LIPS, OR WHY FOUR GOSPELS? 209

Luke, again, is comfortably writing two volumes, at his desk, with references to other writers. We may figure him writing neither in the suspense, penury, danger of Matthew, nor in the vestry of the catacombs and bending before Peter, spurred by the Apostle's vehemence, as Marc, but sitting in a room equipped with books and documents, in some leisure and with time for reflection, and writing for his student Theophilus. What an immense change from Matthew the first advocate of the new world of Jesus before the great world of the Bible who speaks to enemies, to the deacon or secretary of Peter, who tries to satisfy the authority of this prince of the apostles{,} to Luke, who, after his master's Paul death, is free to instruct a faithful young disciple. And yet, there is an even greater growth in articulatedness to come. When John dictated to his Greek secretary, he was removed from any earthly pressure. The weights which loaded down Matthew, from enmity, Marc from obedience, Luke from his duty to teach, were absent. The highest degree of artistic and visionary and rational power is coupled with a childlike exuberance and hurry. He takes pains to correct intimate details of the tradition in the midst of sublime poignancy. John begins with the superlative: "In the *beginning* was the Word"—and by the way therein supplements Matthew's ending: "I shall be with you to the *end* of the world, every day."

But he ends not with this solemn vision through time, but on the tone of a youthful outburst: "The space of the universe would not be able to contain all the books on Jesus"—Faith which began tremblingly with the one indisputable point that Jesus could be called legally "the Son of David and of Abraham," has become an ocean when John writes.

Compared to Peter's virile orders to Marc: "Cut this out; this will do. Enough has been said," to Luke's broad narrative "as I said before," to John's "I could go on forever," Matthew carries the burden of being the loneliest because the first, very visibly. And yet, for a superficial eye, John may appear to be the most lonely one, writing in great solitude, while Luke is academically entrenched in a study, and Marc lives protected at least by a faithful congregation, and Matthew stands in a crowd of opponents trying to get a hearing. But, solitude, or loneliness, in speech differs widely from solitude by lack of physical contact. We may be lonely in New York and very social mentally on a mountain peak. The four gospels show how speech or style or articulation is created by our degree of moral loneliness.

Against the whole synagogue and temple of Jerusalem, the publican and sinner Matthew must stand on his careful brief. They are in power; he is an outcast.

319–20.]

Compare John: Jerusalem, the Holy City, is labelled with perfect assurance "The World" and "Darkness" in John's first chapter. Well, of course, she had vanished when he wrote. Already, John lives in a new rising world who together with him sees the light, perceives the Word and runs boyishly and joyously forward to greet the Lord's coming into his own. For John, the solitude is with Zion, not with John.

Matthew wrote with the echelons of Zion standing proudly. While he delivered his speech, he could scarcely hope to dwell in peace in Jerusalem any longer. He was a wayfaring man, on the way out and away from the old order of things. Matthew's gospel is a farewell plea, a last attempt to convince Jerusalem that they had slain the Just because they had not expected any longer a radical change in the methods of God's government of the world.

This very expectation, however, had been the only *raison d'etre* of Israel in the midst of the world. Obviously, then, Matthew's plea had to do justice to Israel's righteous[50] place and to the new dispensation, in one breath. Everybody knows that Matthew is filled with allegations[51] from the Bible. But to know this, will not suffice. Being the first writer of a gospel, Matthew had no New Testament and no part of the New Testament which could have given him the right or the power to treat the Bible of his day as the Old Testament. That a man quotes the Bible, is not impressive to us; even the Devil may quote Scripture. But the linguistic significance of the first gospel lies in something else. By writing his gospel, he transformed the Bible of his day into the Old Testament. The Bible of Israel became the Old Testament in the process of his writing. For all readers of Matthew this was an accomplished fact. For Matthew, it was the accomplishment of which he did not become conscious before it was done.

Matthew marches and progresses in his gospel writing from speaking as a Jew to speaking as a non-Jew. The text is plain. In his first chapter, Matthew begins: This is the book of the birth of Jesus the Christ, who is a son of David, a son of Abraham. In the same first chapter, verse 21: "Jesus shall free his people from their sins." Obviously, we are in Israel. For, it does not seem necessary to Matthew to explain the pronoun "his" in his people at all. But in chapter 28, the last, Matthew's own eloquence carried him beyond the Jewish world. When he came to describe the machinations of the priests and elders of the Jews, he wrote: "This became common talk among the Jews to this day. . . " The Jews no longer are divided into believers and unbelievers in Christ. The Jews as Jews are outside Matthew's family. The fence between them and Matthew is infinitely higher in chapter 28 than in chapter 1. The

---

50. [Perhaps: *rightful.*]
51. [Perhaps: *quotations.*]

outpouring of his experience, his memories, his notes, changed the writer's own mind. Everybody should become a different person by writing a book. No professor of literature will deny this eventually in writing a great book in poetry. A book which is the fruit of lived life, separates the man who writes, it from the period of his life in which it grew. Fruits always make epoch because their season follows a cycle of seasons: Harvest time makes the whole previous year irretrievable. The wisdom of our tradition consists in the fact that in the first gospel a man writes himself out of Israel by writing up Jesus. Thus, he realized[52] for his readers the fact that to write up Jesus meant to write down the Bible as the Old Testament. This could not have been achieved by argument. A clever lawyer may prove any case by affirmations, claims, quotations and yet remain unmoved himself. Many people have written exercises, perfect logical treatises, on Christianity, to prove or to refute its case. This did not make them into evangelists. An evangelist is a man who by speaking of Jesus, changes his own mind; by being in process, he leads others into the same process. The gospel of Matthew instituted the process of seeing the world and Israel in a new light because it was this very process itself. Christianity is the world as it always has been plus the death of Jesus. Matthew's gospel was the first proof that this one addition to the world would make a difference to the world of speech, that everything in the world would have to be rewritten in the light of this event. For, had not Matthew faithfully started with purely Biblical argument? Had he not begun to write inside or within "his" people. Modern readers quite often are bored with Matthew's first chapter because the genealogy through Joseph through David to Abraham seems so impertinent.[53] But without it, Matthew could never have driven himself and his Christian readers to the point where "his people" have ceased to be his or their people.

Standing upright and pleading in danger of his own life, and then abandoning his Jewish allegiance, Matthew wrote his gospel. He reversed the meaning of the Bible by experiencing that it was no longer the *last word*. The last sentence of the gospel—critics have rejected it because it takes us, indeed, on a new plane—expresses this fact very simply.[54] Instead of the Bible being the last word, for Jews, they are told that Jesus will be with them daily until the end of the world. In this one sentence, the short life of Jesus on earth suddenly acquires such momentum that the little addition to the world which this life seemed to be at best, suddenly grows to gigantic proportions. In this sentence, the full power of the addition breaks upon the

---

52. [In the sense of *made real*.]
53. [Perhaps: *seems of so little pertinence.*]
54. ERH: "Baptize in the name of the Father and the Son and the Holy Spirit."

reader. This one life balances in the scales as heavily as the whole history of mankind from Abraham and David down to the days in which Matthew lives. In this sentence, which dares to speak of all the future history as separated from the Jewish Bible, the gospel has become gospel in the full sense; because only now, has the past become the past and the Bible the Old Testament. This is all the more remarkable as Matthew certainly had no inkling of the fate of his own book. Writing in Aramaic,[55] he hardly could expect it to be saved as the first book of a Greek Canon, by a translation.

We now might go on immediately and draw attention to the drama inside each gospel, as we have tried to show for Matthew. We might show how Peter succeeded to force Marc that Peter's honorable mentioning was to disappear from the gospel and his weaknesses to be put in. The human drama between Marc and Peter was as real, and as much a change of mind as Matthew's discovery of the Bible as the Testament of a bygone Past. And in Luke, the two books, Gospel and Acts, are one drama. Paul has not known Jesus in the flesh, and does not care to quote his sayings. And yet Paul is able to preach the gospel with the power of a "world heart," as "the right arm of Jesus," as he later was called. Gospel and Acts reveal the identity of Christ. Paul and Jesus, Christ in the flesh and Christ in Paul, are the pillars of the bridge which Luke built to his own surprise. The "abrupt" ending of Acts has often been criticized. But {is it abrupt}? Luke's Gospel ends: "But they worshiped and returned to Jerusalem with great joy and were in the temple all the time, praised and lauded God." His Acts end: "Paul stayed in his rooms for two years, receiving all visitors, preached the kingdom of God and taught the Lord Jesus with all joy unrestrictedly." {Now} compare the beginnings {of Gospel and Acts}: "Jesus is born"; "the Church is born." In Peter and Paul, the Christ who lived in Jesus, lived for another generation. Paul, at the end, is in Rome.

Where Paul is, there now is the temple, this to Luke's own amazement. Paul's martyrdom did not belong into Luke's process and progress. The thesis that Acts remained unfinished is as {valuable} as the {modern} proposition that Homer's Iliad should have ended or {once} did end, with the death of Achilleus![56] Luke discovered the duplication, the victory over the sequence of generations, by the Spirit, and he discovered, as he went along, that his histories of Jesus in the flesh in Israel and of the acts of the

---

55. [1964: *he wrote first in Hebrew, not in Aramaic*. See Grintz reference, 76, and Appendix I, 325–27.]

56. [The typescript carries a footnote here *See above, p.* without a number. Since the *Iliad* is not mentioned earlier in this essay, ERH must have intended to include an essay which did in the larger work he planned. He discusses the ending of the *Iliad* in "Die Vokale der Musen," *Die Sprache* II, 773–95.]

Holy Spirit (Acts 1, 2) with the Gentiles (end of Acts 28, 29) ran *parallel*. But as Peter had prevailed so that Marc had to omit all praise of Peter, so did Luke not write for the glorification of Paul but of the Lord. The death of Paul told at the end of Acts—just as the death of Achilleus at the end of the Iliad,—would have *destroyed* the recognition of the Holy Ghost as "Christ once more." And why became it Luke's task to identify two generations, Jesus and the apostles, by one work in two parts? Why had the baptism of fire at Pentecost to be the parallel to the birth of the child in Bethlehem, and the journeys of Paul through the gentiles the parallel to Jesus' teaching in Israel? The reason is obvious. Luke himself wrote to a "second-generation Christian." Between him and Theophilus, the question of "Fathers and Sons" of the Spirit existed as between Jesus and the apostles. The crux of Christianity is the law of nature that nothing which we inherit comes to us in the {attractive} form of newness. Luke's Acts parallel the Gospel because Theophilus had to be changed from a hereditary or traditional Christian into a primary and immediate listener of the Spirit. As Luke's writings reproduced a bridge over two generations, so Luke's relation to his reader forced Theophilus to think of his own children. In as far as he succeeded in building the parallel between Gospel and Acts, in so far he also succeeded in building the bridge from Theophilus into the future Church. {He wrote for four generations: Jesus, Paul, Theophilus, Theophilus' heirs.}

The modern reader may be hesitant before admitting this logic. Why should Theophilus treat his own children and grandchildren differently because he read of the parallel between Gospel and Acts, Judea and the Empire, Jerusalem and Rome? What has a book to do with our own behavior? The modern is right to hesitate. To read, for us, is not a phase of acting. But to read, for Theophilus, was something quite different. First of all, the gospel in general was spread exclusively by word of mouth. THE WAY as the new life was called, was the WAY in which people lived and spoke, to the exclusion of books. A Christian of the first century was introduced into a way of life and under way, on the way, was told the things necessary for his becoming a missionary himself, a witness, a confessor, possibly a martyr. To hear was nothing but the first step for telling others. Curiosity was not served but salvation. And {its continuous flow} was achieved by the foolishness of oral preaching. The tremendous novelty of the written gospels therefore, was that anything written should be admitted to the rank of gospel truth at all.

{4. Ink and Blood}

Christ had not written. And the whole truth of the cross was based on this, his sheer incredible and certainly super-human faith. Who among us dares entrust his greatest truth to the silliness of unbelieving neighbors? But since this had been dared, the example was set. And writing was stigmatized as second-rate. It was less good, less desirable, and less trustworthy, than preaching. I think that we still can realize that Matthew wrote with blood, sweat, and tears, asking forgiveness for the use of ink. He needed a valid excuse. For, "one of the fallen angels" was considered, in his days, "the one who instructed mankind in writing and thereby made many men sin until this day. But men were not created to aver their faith with pen and ink."[57] I think that Matthew took the great liberty of returning to the use of the pen (defiled though it was then as it is today by the makers of books without end) under the impact of the stoning of Stephen. This would mean that the first blood spilled cleansed the first ink employed in the new dispensation. I conclude this from the fact that Stephen's great speech before the priests is reflected in the first chapter of Matthew.[58]

The glory of the first martyr gave weight to the otherwise highly suspect {ink-}written words of the first gospel writer. Stephen's great defense of the transfer of the Spirit into new forms had to be salvaged. After Stephen had paid for it with his life, the sacred new message would not be defiled by ink. The gospels were {the} reluctant admission of writing into the new WAY. By the way, even then they were meant to be read out loud.

We are so crazy as to ask anybody: Why don't you write? But with the first disciples of the new spirit it was the other way round: Must we write? May we write? Dare we write? And the truth rests on this chastity of our minds which has become more rare than chastity of bodies. *When must we write?* In danger of life, our own or others, in self-defense, if it is the only way of saving our identity in a crisis. We must speak and write and think and teach and testify when we and our mind would disintegrate without. We speak lest we go mad. It all amounts to the rule that a new style will not be created except under supreme pressure. Matthew gained the right to use the pen as his sword when the blood of martyrs reddened the soil of Palestine. Similarly, Marc wrote with the arena and the Cross waiting for Peter in Rome.

---

57. ERH: Book of Henoch, 69, 10. [The quoted sentences do not appear in the 1944 text. Goodspeed's article cited later (106, 214) is probably the source of ERH's reference. See also Appendix I, 324–25.]

58. ERH: Below [78–89, 214–25].

Now, our contention is that Luke wrote with a similar excitement or pressure. And this is not so obvious. He was not in the centers of danger. He lived to a ripe old age—84—in Greece somewhere as the Canon of the Gospels tell us. And his style pleased Ernest Renan so well that he called Luke's Gospel the most beautiful book ever written. Now, Renan had a Greek mentality. And we may feel embarrassed by his compliment; for the Greek {mentality} is apt to praise the playful and the light touch. The emphatic hurts him as less elegant.

Indeed, the pressure in Luke is very different from the excitement created by the obvious dangers which surrounded Matthew and Marc. Luke must have been at leisure when he went over the origins of his faith.

Nevertheless, a new and specific pressure was introduced into the world of history writing by Luke. Chronicles had listed the annals of Rome and Paros and Athens. Historians had written up the spirit of Rome by which it conquered the orb in fifty years, or the spirit of the Athenians under Pericles. Similarly, the various books of the Old Testament all testify to the specific mentality of one period. The books under the name of Moses, and the song of songs, and Jeremiah, and Judges, and Kings, {are translations} [*of*] One Spirit into innumerable expressions. Therefore, the first sentence of Luke also gives us the clue to his theme.[59] The Intertemporal character of the spirit became his theme. *To be inspired means to translate*; by fixing his attention on this seam between the times, Luke became the first human being who was able to telescope the spirits of two periods and to envisage them as subservient ("Ministers of the Word," to minister means to be subservient, in Greek) to one spirit, the Spirit of all spirits.

The very meaning of the term Holy Ghost is lost if we cease to make him include the spirits of the times. Any peaceful group, in gaiety, harmony, friendship, goodness may have the right spirit without having the inclusiveness of the Holy Spirit. But today, we usually compare the right and the wrong spirit often as though they moved on one plane. For Luke, this alone is Holy which has power over many fashions of the ages. These fashions of every age, these spirits of the times are genuine and real. Each generation has its genius. Jesus' genius belonged to his own unique life. Herman Melville's genius as the author of Moby Dick and Pierre was "time-conditioned." But the Spirit is genius to the second power so to speak. God is the father of all spirits. The discovery of Jesus was that genius was not enough. And so he yielded his genius, his own spirit for the peace between the spirits of all times. Not his body was his contribution to history—how many soldiers

---

59. [MDB imported *the first sentence of Luke changes this* from the German version. See 79.]

have given their bodies for the spirit of their national gods—Jesus gave up his genius because he decided to break the endless recurrence of the cycles in the affairs and businesses of man.[60] He was fed up with the spirits of each time, including his own genius. For this reason, he wrote no book. For, he wanted to turn the hearts of all the generations to each other regardless of their mental fashions.

Luke was the first man who was privileged to put this change in the meaning of spirit into a two-phase book. In his two volumes, the Spirit was made to tower over the spirits. The genius of Christ's own walk through Judea and the genius in the actions of the {apo}stolic age were both narrated as facets of one spirit. Ever since, the people have asked from their historians to give them more than one period in an evolution. America would have no history which inspires unless its history {can} be divided clearly into great periods. Unless we may sense One spirit to be at work behind the spirits of several periods, we cannot get excited over history.[61] History is dead and it is dangerous to flirt with the graves of the past. To imitate any great man or deed, is absurd and always paralyzes. But history is good and rises us from the dead when we penetrate behind the facts and realize the amount of sacrifice and creation behind every little fact which surrounds us. The knowledge of historical facts is *harmful* unless we look them through[62] as either inspired or corrupt.

Any great historian after Luke has admitted a plurality of spirits of the times and has tried to let One spirit shine through them all.

The first triumph over the spirit of one time and the fashion of one country was given to Luke. In his books was embodied the difference between genius and Spirit, in modern terms, or between THE spirit and the many spirits, in his terms.

This triumph could not be celebrated by theorizing "about" the Spirit. It had to be done in the opposite manner, by making the fullest allowance for the diversity of time and place, at each occasion. THE WORD, which before {had seemed to} belong to specific countries and specific times, now proved to be one in East and West, with Jesus on earth and with Christ risen. The blind fanaticism of any school of thought or national literature, the zeal of the reader Theophilus, were purified. Theophilus was warned that the Spirit would {emit} new forms out of his loins in every generation. The genius of one age could not be mistaken for the spirit of God. For, we

---

60. [Luke 23:46. KJV: *And when Jesus had cried with a loud voice, he said, 'Father, into thy hands I commend my spirit: and having said thus, he gave up the ghost.*]

61. [MDB imported *we cannot be inspired by history* from the German version. See 80.]

62. [Probably: *see through them.*]

have exactly as much future as we recognize as our past. Future and history are our articles of faith.[63] If a man wishes to perish with his own time, nobody can hinder or refute him. The time limits of our role on earth are our own choice. By giving the Church in which Theophilus found himself a prehistory of more than one period and more than one genius, Luke gave all Christians also a posthistory, beyond their own period and age. The right of history to mould us at all, depends on the triumph of the Power to Translate over the powers that be at any one age. This conviction, of course, lived in Stephen, in Matthew, and in their master. But in Luke, a literary document was allowed to embody this truth.

The genius and the spirit of any one time runs riot in isolation. A naïve surrender to the spirit of the times plunged Europe into two destructive wars. Man had given time the reigns[64] over {himself}. And the spirits of the times became demons. If we expect each time to have its own spirit, we shall {abide} with the Hitler Youth in Massacria.[65]

{However,} if we expect the Holy Ghost to exist in a hothouse outside the seasons of the human mind,[66] we end in sterilization and futility. We should begin to think of each generation as One Body of Time, and of the Spirit as one, connecting all these bodies. It took 1900 years to learn this. A Body of Time, to this day, is a new-fangled term. But it is today's most correct expression and translation of Luke's spirits which were superseded[67] by the Holy Ghost. If and when our times become bodies of time, we will have done that which Luke described as the acts of Jesus and of the apostles.

The generation of Theophilus which read Luke, saw the fall of Jerusalem, and the transition from the apostolic age to the episcopal. The Church is distinguished by the rapid progress from one age to another, in a breath{-}taking advance. That which Protestantism has often criticized as the rapid corruption of Source Christianity is the most excellent proof of Luke's principle of incessant translation. The martyrs, the bishops, the confessors, the apologists, the Fathers, the monks and hermits, the missionaries, all these

63. [MDB imported *only together may future and history be our articles of faith* from the German version. See 81.]

64. [Probably: *reins.*]

65. [MDB imported *with the Hitler Youth and Nazi massacres* from the German version (81). "Massacria" is a stronger condemnation, writing off all Germany as guilty of the deaths of its own best citizens, Jews and "Aryans" alike, along with the millions of foreign Jews.]

66. [MDB imported *the human soul* from the German version. I also consider it an improvement, but I followed ERH here and used *mind* in translating the 1964 version. See 81.]

67. [MDB imported *mastered by the Holy Ghost* from the German version. See *overcome*, 81.]

modes of saintliness followed upon the apostles and the evangelists and the teachers and prophets of the first generation of the Church, in a swift change of scene. I would turn round Luther's axiom of the value of Source Christianity and would say that I could not believe in the Holy Ghost unless he had changed his forms of expression relentlessly, {even as in Luther and his prince}. How to proceed from genius to genius and yet to proceed in One spirit is our trouble again. It becomes harder in every century and we must allow our young people a deliberate amount of ignorance lest their genius be stifled. But proceed out of One spirit we all must, despite the variety of times and places.

This throws light on the progress in Marc's Gospel. As in Matthew and in Luke, Marc's Gospel is a victory over the dangers of time. Peter was in charge of the sheep. (John is very emphatic on this topic, at the end of his Gospel, and he agrees with Matthew.) The true relation between Jesus and the apostles was at stake if Peter, the greatest of the apostles, could be considered too much of an equal to Jesus. Peter's Gospel then, had to establish once and forever, Christ's uniqueness as "the Son of God." Peter who had denied the Lord, now had to deny that he, Peter, was more than a sinful man. If this could be done for Peter, who was the leader, it would be accomplished for all Christians forever. Now, Marc does exactly this. He begins simply with the statement that Jesus was the Son of God, and he ends with the endless stream of mission to be carried out by "subservients," who obey the Lord and do not obey Peter or any carnal authority. It is more difficult to trace this negative process in Marc than the similar negative process in Matthew. In Matthew, the order preceding Jesus became the Old Testament; the spirit receded from Israel when Jesus came and took over. In Marc, it was shown that Christ alone was and would remain the Son of God. All future generations were put under this one and only perfect incarnation, because Peter placed himself at an infinite distance under this same Son of God. The process of Marc protects Jesus against the future. The glorification of Peter is victoriously obstructed and prevented. Marc says that Peter was "afraid" (9,5)[68] when the other Evangelists do not dare to say so; he changes the singular of a word of Peter in Matthew: "I shall," into the more modest "we shall."[69] He cut out his name when an intelligent question was asked. "Peter's house," of Matthew, in Marc becomes the house to which four of the apostles came.[70] Peter has himself called "Satan" in Marc without {the}

---

68. [The reference is to Mark 9:6.]
69. MDB: Matt 17:4, Mark 9:5.
70. MDB: Matt 8:14, Mark 1:29.

THE FRUIT OF OUR LIPS, OR WHY FOUR GOSPELS?   219

exculpating explanation given by the other Gospels.[71] And it may be called the climax of Peter's self-denial that Marc is not allowed to give the name Peter to one of the two disciples who saw the risen Christ at Emmaus.[72] Yet, Paul bluntly says that Peter was the first man to see the risen Lord. In other words, no higher credentials could be found, in the eyes of Paul himself, for an apostolate than the one on which Marc was ordered to be silent! Luke and John took pains to make up for this silence in their brotherly care to mention Peter's primacy.[73]

> In the Marcan gospel Jesus is isolated and wholly misunderstood . . . by his chosen disciples. In Marc this is of vital importance because . . . the salvation . . . is wrought. . . in complete isolation. . . . Matthew and Luke are unable to force this through with the staggering brutality of Marc.[74]

The temptation fought by Marc is well stated in 13:11 when Jesus is reported to have said: "For it is not you who are going to speak but the Spirit." Peter who had denied the Lord at his Passion, now proceeds to protect the Lord against such dependancy on frail men. He had the right, and he alone, to prevent Marc from placing Peter near the Lord. If the result was found to be of "staggering brutality"; the critics overlooked the fact that Peter's battle was against his own potential authority. In Jesus' name only shall the gospel be preached (Marc 16.17).

The process in John is different again, but dramatic progress is made nevertheless in this apparently ethereal gospel. John was the {friend} of the Lord, by natural sympathy, as no other apostle. As a brother, he was loved and liked in addition to being called and chosen.[75] Natural congeniality, creature-like affinity, was John's special source of knowledge; {similar sources of enhanced understanding were} Peter's office in the church, Matthew's experience of being saved, Luke's responsibility to the next generation. A teacher like Luke comes to understand better and better because of his having immature and unenthused students. A bishop like Peter comes to take great care because of his responsibility for the salvation of souls, Matthew knows and understands {better be}cause he has been taken out of a rather opprobrious business life and feels deep gratitude and joy for his own

---

71. ERH: Chapman, p. 38 ff. [–53. MDB "corrected" this to *18ff*, but the reference is to Chapman's fourth chapter. See Appendix I, 320–21.]

72. MDB: Mark 16:12.

73. ERH: Luke 24,13ff. John, 21. chapter, Paul, I Cor.,15,5.

74. ERH: Hoskyns and Davey, the Riddle of the New Testament, p. 137 f. [MDB questioned ERH's use of ellipses here, but see Appendix I, 329–330.]

75. MDB: John 19:26, 21:7.

salvation. John as a kindred spirit, understands that which nobody else will understand at first: The origin of a living person.[76] Members of one physical family understand each other's backgrounds, the origin of each other's reactions and gestures lies open to them. It is not different with kindred spirits. For, the spirit precedes the incarnation, a spirit is the original thought of the creator of which the living man is the execution. A kindred spirit, then, understands by sympathy and "congeniality," in its genuine sense, where Jesus came from, out of which depth of necessity, out of which pre-legal, pre-national, pre-religious, original matrix. John begins, as a kindred spirit, with the real, the original place of {his divine friend} in God's mind. But the progress of his gospel leads him from this heaven to earth. The miraculous process in John is the road from the Word in God to the man in the flesh Jesus. John makes him interrupt his most sublime speeches with the sober and concrete physical movement: "Let us go," and it is John who keeps this precious testimony of Jesus' realism, and nobody else (14:31). His personal and private intimacy would not have had to look at Jesus from the outside ever. He lived with him on the inside of his soul. But that he should identify his brother Jesus {in} the small events of everyday life, {together with the Word's} cosmic office {as Christ}—this is John's victory. {The valet de chambre cannot see the hero. John saw the Lord as his alter ego.} John's soul was "naturaliter Christiana."[77] Therefore, he did not need signs or happenings to know and understand. {He knew him by heart, "mente cordis."} In writing the gospel, John learned to recognize the worldly ways of {knowing} his Lord as equally justified; being one with him in eternity, he humbled himself to be only one of his disciples, in history! This is the beauty of John's last chapters: Thomas had to see before he believed; {such Missourianism}[78] was quite inconceivable to John himself: but John transmitted {the story of Thomas} faithfully, as the approach to Christ most opposite to his own. And he glorified Peter, as the one who was in authority even over John because the Lord had said so.[79] From the innermost heart to the outer paraphernalia of social office and position, John proceeds and thereby forbids all hearts who are Christian by nature to flee the world of history and realization.[80]

76. [MDB imported *the genesis of a living person* from the German version, see *unfolding*, 84]

77. [ERH uses the term in quite a different sense than Tertullian in his "Apology" (*Patrologia Latina*, 1:377).]

78. [Missouri is the *Show Me* state. The breadth of ERH's knowledge was peculiar in every sense of the word.]

79. MDB: John 21:15–19.

80. [In the sense of actualization or the shaping of reality (*Verwirklichung*). See *unfolding reality*, 84.]

{5. ICHTHYS}

All four gospels, then, are processes by which four apostles could deposit their human limitation at the foot of the cross and make their individual experience into a contribution: Matthew acknowledged that he was no longer a Jew, Marc, Peter's disciple, acknowledged that Peter had lost his own name, Luke the companion of Paul acknowledged that Paul did among the Gentiles that which Jesus had done among the Jews; John acknowledged that although a kindred spirit may understand the eternal meaning without argument, it is equally necessary {that} the faithful soul obeys in the division of labor in this visible world with its very slow progress.

Our term to acknowledge, {used of the Evangelists} here is not meant to be the same as signing a receipt. It took a change of mind during the writing, to discover the consequences for the writer himself!

Take Matthew's case. We are tempted, by the critics who point to his many quotations from Scripture, to see in him a lawyer who writes a marvelous brief for his client. The lawyer has the last sentence in mind when he writes the first. Such a brief, {we are told,} is planned on one plane, and is of one mind (at least this is the theory; I do not believe in it). But Matthew begins: "Jesus was the king of the Jews" and at the end, he knows of himself: "For heaven's sake, I no longer am a Jew," and leaves.

We turn to Marc. Marc kneels at Peter's service. Peter to him is the last authority. At the end of his gospel, he knows that he, Marc, cannot rely on Peter, as little as on any other sinful man. Marc—how often may it have pained him to {obey} Peter {in deleting} a piece {redounding to Peter's honor}—became courageous enough to transcend his place as Peter's amanuensis. In hearing from Peter, how the prince of the apostles {disowned} his own worth, Marc received a lesson {on} the unity of the Church. The Church can be one only if only One gives the name to her body. And Marc went to Alexandria in God's spirit, not in Peter's. The change through Luke was wrought on Theophilus. Theophilus knew Luke. And the conversion of the Gentiles easily was for him the only thing in which he was interested. But the writings of Luke changed this. The original drama now was conspicuous as the eternal matrix out of which Paul was only one single fruit. And so, every generation must re-enter this one genuine matrix; after Paul, all generations would have to take their food, their analogy, from the gospel of the master before they could go on record as disciples with their own "acts." All would have to listen to the Evangelist before they could translate the gospel as Paul had done. All would have to be teachers of the next generation so that the younger might do greater things still. True enough, heaven had come to earth on Pentecost (Acts 1) and made a new earth, with Rome, instead of Jerusalem, in the center. But one man alone had been placed in the position to reveal the true heaven. He had to be upheld if the same heaven, that is God in human hearts, should come and renovate the earth in every generation. Theophilus, then, had to ascend beyond mere baptism. He now could see himself burdened with a task of translation for his children as tremendous as the translation of the gospel wrought by Paul and Peter, for the Gentiles, in obedience to the Lord. In Luke's two books, Jesus' command to baptize the nations grew in geometrical progression. For, it revealed what would and could be achieved afterwards: Christians once baptized, could stand on each other's shoulders and grow to ever new heights. And John—John, the hermit on Patmos, came to see the earth besides the heaven in which he lived, heart to heart, with his master. For this reason, the last sentence of John speaks of the space of the universe which could not contain all the books on Jesus. The space of the universe? What was this to John who {in his vision} had seen the Word which was with the father in the beginning before the universe was created. Yet this same created universe became his last word. He was ready to leave God's heaven and to enter His creature "world," for the love of God. He came to see and feel and taste this material universe of which he had no need. But God had created it and wished him to love it, too.

There is, therefore, a remarkable sequence in the writers of the four Gospels. The name of Jesus in the ancient church consisted of four parts— Jesus, Christus, God's Son, Saviour. The four Greek initials of his four names were read as ICHTHYS, (ichthys: fish).[81] The four gospels reproduced this name. Matthew the sinner knew the Lord to be his personal saviour (*soter*), Marc knew him from the first as the Son of God (γιος Θεον),[82] Luke saw in him the "Christ" who converted Paul, to whom Jesus never had spoken: to Paul, Jesus could not be Jesus but Christ exclusively, and John, the kindred spirit, understood him as an older brother, and that is, he thought of him as "Jesus," personally.

4. Jesus
3. Christus
2. Son of God
1. Savior

were the aspects under which the four Evangelists wrote.

And now enters the law of speech into action which contradicts nature and the mere evolution of time always.[83] This law says: That which is most

---

81. ERH: The cryptogram ingeniously concealed and yet told the claims of the House built on the fish in a persecuting world.

82. [(*h*)*yos theou*.]

83. [Perhaps: *And now the law of speech which always contradicts nature and the*

THE FRUIT OF OUR LIPS, OR WHY FOUR GOSPELS?   223

central or primary in an event shall become articulated last.[84] The quality of Jesus by which he reached farthest and most visibly and perturbingly into his environment was that he saved sinners. The closest touch with his heart, where he was most Jesus, his own real unique person, was for John. John gives the innermost thoughts of Jesus; Matthew gives all the {external} credentials of Jesus as the Savior. Matthew could tell his experience first; John could say it last. Why? The order is strange, but it repeats the experience of Jesus himself, who was visible {and "worthed"}[85] only {towards} the end {of his walk} as to his innermost {center, which just the same had moved him from the start}. That the world sees not us but our {"surface"} function first is the experience of any living soul.[86] We first are visible by our least central features. The outer man is known before the inner; the historical acts are known before their perpetual meaning.[87] Only through Pentecost and Paul's experiences among the Gentiles the perpetual meaning of the "Christ" became known, while Peter could stick to his own historical experience with the living Son of God. *The sequence of the four gospels is necessary because this sequence reverses the order* which begins with the natural individuality of Jesus. *And such a reverse of nature is the necessary sequence in human articulation!* Ichthys, (1. Jesus, 2. Christus, 3. God's Son, 4. Savior) is the correct natural order for describing this individuality. The linguistic, spoken, written evidence of this had to become conscious in the opposite order and sequence (4. Savior, 3. God's Son, 2. Christ, 1. Jesus).

We shall now turn to the practical connection between the four gospels, the liberties they took with each other as in this connection the real key to "the Four Gospels" will be found. Before doing so, however, I wish to give a peripheral example of their interaction.

The example concerns the treatment of World History by them. History is rhythmical. Any historian who has not been specialized in French or English or German or Russian history, and any interested layman can see for himself that the Russian Revolution and our present World Wars follow

---

mere evolution of time enters into action.]

84. ERH: Any book on logic or psychology of education mentions the fact that the first in experience is the last in mental deduction and vice versa. It seems strange that our historians never have made use of this law, in their treatment of our sources. The structure of the Three Men in the Fiery Furnace song [Dan 3:6] is the most explicit example of this. These men sing because they are in mortal danger; hence they speak of everybody else before they speak of themselves.

85. [Probably: *valued*.]

86. [MDB has *not us but our worldly function*, which is not to be found here or in the German text.]

87. [MDB imported *long-term* from the German version, see *lasting*, 87.]

the French Revolution and the Napoleonic Wars after four to five generations. A similar timespan separates Cromwell from Robespierre. And again, it is four to five generations from Cromwell back to Luther.[88] Why did they break out after 4 x 30 years? We may not be able to answer the question. That does not alter the fact that it is one,[89] based on data which are too impressive to be left unconnected.

This same question irked the early church. Obviously, Jesus had come in the nick of time, that is one generation before the destruction of the Temple. For John in his old age, and the Church, after 70 A.D. Jesus' correct timing was obvious. He had taken the seed out of Zion before it was made sterile there. But before 70, this argument could not be used. Jesus scented the corruption. He interpreted the signs of the time one generation ahead. Between his crucifixion and the year 70, {the} faith {of the Christians} looked for scientific argument {which would support his interpretation}. Lenin or Trotzki could foresee the World Revolution from a logical study of Revolutions, long before 1914, while Nietzsche simply smelled the corruption. Stephen in his oral and Matthew, in his written plea to a Judean aristocracy in power tried to prove a logical rhythm for the arrival of Jesus. History had taken leaps, ever so often, Stephen said before the Council. Abraham he listed and his family down to Joseph, i n the first place. Then Moses. Then David and Solomon, finally the prophets and the Babylonian captivity. Don't you see, he exclaimed, that Jesus is a turning point like the captivity, like David, like Moses, like Abraham?[90] Stephen's speech was the first Christian Economy of the Spirit. In Matthew, this plea of Stephen grew into a law of history. Every 14 generations, he wrote, a transfer of the spirit is recorded: There are 14 generations from Abraham to David, 14 generations from David to the captivity, 14 generations from Babylon to the coming of Christ in the person of a descendant of Abraham and David.[91] The so-called genealogy in the first chapter of Matthew is a philosophy of revolution and of the rhythm of revolutions.

Luke, too, gave a genealogy of Jesus. {Only,} this genealogy was no longer intended as the basis of his argument. The core of Stephen's great eloquent outburst had been that the spirit changes his expressions time after time. This—and we must not forget it—simply is true. Matthew systematized it and said that it had happened in every fourteenth generation. Luke who after Paul's apostolate to the Gentiles, did not need {Matthew's}

---

88. ERH: On this list (1517, 1649, 1789, 1917), see my *Out of Revolution* [453–82, especially 462–63. 1978: 492ff.]

89. 1978: *that does not alter the fact that the question does exist.*

90. ERH: Acts 7.

91. MDB: Matt 1:17.

"law," kept the riddle of spiritual transfer in mind. But he could afford to generalize further. He gave 3 x 14 generations from Jesus to the founder of Judaism; and he extended the list to 77 generations from God's creation of Adam to Jesus. On the other hand, he replaced the number of 14 by 22 in two instances. We see a principle of freedom in unity at work. The common question is a real question to all three, Stephen, Matthew, Luke. For those who do not recognize it as an eternal question, I may point to its secular version on which we come in a rather isolated manner when we go on asking why the Roman Empire fell when it fell. Well, it fell when the spirit had left it. Then, kingdoms fall. So our classroom question about the Roman Empire simply singles out one instance of the whole riddle of "duration" in which people always must be interested. {How long will our own order last?}[92]

Now Matthew suggested a regularity. Luke corrected the figures. The 3 x 14 had proved wrong. So, they were changed. But the question itself though unanswered, was left in suspense. This was achieved not by a dialectical process of Yes and No, but by the typical research process of "Yes, perhaps, but certainly in a different manner." This was a new method; the Greek mind had always moved by opposites. The new method was possible because heart and soul of the various thinkers had become one before the argument started. If conducted in a modern scientific manner, research depends on unity of mind on essentials. This is an attainment of our era. Augustine expressed this condition of scientific progress by his famous "in necessariis unitas, in dubiis libertas, in omnibus caritas."[93] Of this, Stephen, Matthew, Luke, have given the first perfect example of which I know.

Stephen exclaimed: The Son of Abraham has made the very sacrifice which Abraham spared his son Isaac. A new eon has come ending the history of Abraham's seed. Matthew reflected on this exclamation and the Son of Abraham became the Son of God, in his gospel, and for history. Luke comprehended the period between Jesus the son of God to Adam the son of God as one time span. {He levelled the break made by Abraham.} Luke created the Christian era. In our textbooks this distinction between Christianity and antiquity is ascribed to a much later date (533 A.D.)[94] But the

92. ERH: {When Carthage fell, her conqueror Scipio turned to his friend Polybius: "Polybius, a glorious moment, but I have a dread foreboding that some day the same doom will be pronounced upon my own country." Was it not perhaps for this wisdom of the Romans that their empire lasted as long as it did?}

93. [MDB's claim that the quotation derives from Peter Meiderlin rather than Augustine has since been superseded by the claim made for the Reformation turncoat Marco Antonio de Dominis. In time, Augustine may receive the credit again. See Luke 3:22–38 for a possible parallel to Stephen and Matthew.]

94. ERH: See *The Christian Future*. [The typescript contains no page number; the German version cites 33 and 135–37, which address the position of the believer (and

actual accomplishment of a new era was the cooperative effort of Stephen, Matthew, and Luke. And in Luke's third chapter the new frame of reference, one era before, one after Christ, is clearly stated.[95]

And now "the four Gospels" have to be shown to be one, even in a literary sense. The "four gospels," we insist, are the lips through which the heart of "Ichthys" has spoken through the ages. We must read them all. Why *we* must read them *all*, we have tried to evince by recognizing the four layers of nearness to their Master which they represent. The Master obviously lives in all of them *at a different degree of distance*. As there are shortsighted and farsighted people, friend and foe, so a man is not represented fully at any one of the four distances. Jesus claimed to be the Savior of sinners, the fulfiller of ritual, the Redeemer of merely human language, the son of Joseph of Nazareth; we can hear and understand these claims only on the four different wave lengths of the saved sinner, the converted ritualistic zealot, the emancipated teacher, the born and yet appointed friend.

Now we must try to show that the Evangelists knew of their unity, too. We know, of course, that they read each other. But we cannot separate from this fact the question why, then, one after another wrote his gospel in addition. Did they wish to replace one by the other? If so, why did the Church keep all four? Why could the Church not admit any of the later gospels?

{6. End Begets Beginning}

Let us first use a simile to explain the situation. John the Evangelist was asked in dotage why his sermon was so short that he would only say: "Children, keep each other at heart." He gave the famous answer: "For two reasons: it is enough and the Lord has said so."[96] The four gospels suffice since every one of the four claims made by Ichthys has become "lips" in one man's dramatic change of mind. The Lord had made these four claims, no more. And he has said so. Let us read the gospels once more: Do they give evidence of mutual dependence beyond the "material" used? Yes, they do. *They beget each other*. Every gospel begins exactly at the point to which the previous gospel has progressed on its tortuous path. The last word of the one is the overture,

---

the church) between a terrible past and the necessary future.]

95. [The preceding paragraph and its statement are not in the 1944 typescript. The "clear statement" may be Luke's juxtaposition of the naming of the year (in 3:1–2) and Jesus' ministry (3:2–3) on the one hand with the prophecy of Isaiah (3:4–6) and all of history up to Jesus (3:22–38) on the other.]

96. MDB:1 John 4:7.

and sets the tone, for the next.[97] "The last word" is not meant in a literal or pedantic sense; by it, we understand the last step of thought, reached in the dramatic progress.

If this is so, then the gospels continue each other, beginning to think and to speak where the previous evangelist had ended, and turning his final word into an opening of a new drama. Matthew's last word is that Jesus has become the Son of God, in the sense of the Trinity. Marc begins: The Son of God (not; "the Son of David," as Matthew). Marc ends with the {"}Mission of the ministers of the word{"}.[98] Fittingly, the missionary Luke begins with "the ministers of the word."[99] Luke, {furthermore,} ends Acts with a long statement: That the Jews have ears and do not hear and have eyes but do not see, but "the Gentiles shall hear."

Majestically, John breaks in at exactly this last word of Acts: "Indeed, the darkness has not seen the light, the world has not seen it, but his own have beheld his glory and we have seen him."[100] Also{,} Luke ends with the power of the gospel; John begins with the Word's Power.

This is not an accident, this connection of end{s} and beginning{s}. Laboriously every gospel works itself up to its climax. Easily, the mantle of the gospel writer then falls on the man who is prepared best to take over at this very point:

	Beginning	End
Matthew	Son of David	Son of God
Marc	Son of God	Ministers of the Word
Luke	*Beginning {of his gospel}* Ministers of his Word	*End of Acts* The Jews have no ears and no eyes; the Gentiles shall hear
John	The world, the darkness has not seen; His own have beheld his glory	

---

97. ERH: Luke's two books are treated here as one work. For this, the reasons have been given in the text before.

98. MBD: Mark 16:15.

99. MBD: Luke 1:2.

100. MBD: John 1:4, 14.

Survey

1	Matthew	Beginning		Son of David and Abraham
2	Matthew	End		The Son of God (baptize in the name of the Father and the Son and the Spirit)
	Marc	Beginning		The Son of God
3	Marc	End		The Ministers of the Word
	Luke	Beginning		The Ministers of the Word
4a	Luke	End:	Gospel	Fullness of praise
			Acts	Fullness of speech
	John	Beginning		In the Beginning was the Word
4b	Luke Acts	End		The Jews have no ears. The Gentiles shall hear.
	John	Beginning		The World has not seen the light. His own people gave him no welcome. We have beheld his glory
5	John	End		This man Jesus in the space of the universe, {now redeemed as God's World.}
	Matthew	Beginning		Jesus (Christ, Son of David, son of Abraham)

{7. The Idols: Art, Religion, Science, Manners}[101]

This list scanty as it is should be read as the scenario of four dramatic actions.

> Scene One: Matthew, the tax collector, digs beneath the figures and concepts of his accounts and discovers the full power which human words may acquire when they are spoken on a man's way to his death{, as his seed.}
>
> Scene Two: Peter, the boorish fisherman is placed in the center of the last Western sky-world, in Rome with The God-Man Caesar, the astrology of her temples, the hieroglyphs; {here he} proclaims the true temple, the Word, and the true hieroglyphs of this temple, the ministers of the Word.
>
> Scene Three: Luke the Greek physician, versed in the art of healing, is placed in the Jewish medium of No to the physical world and of fear of contamination with physical idols, and places this

---

101. [In the table of contents, *The Four Idols* . . .]

No between the natural law of Jews as well as Gentiles, on the one side, and the new creative Yes of the Christian.

Scene Four: John, the prophet of Revelation, comes into the Greek cosmos, and frees their art and poetry by making God's poetry his theme. He asks how does God write a poem?

When we now implement this scenario, we shall unravel the scenes by beginning with John. For, his case is the easiest for us moderns to understand. The reason is that we understand poetry best, better than science or prayer or ritual. {We have idolized art; hence we know its law.}

4.[102] John's Gospel has always been described as Hellenizing, or hellenistic. However, this very fact made the gospel suspect. Why should Luke, the Greek be less hellenistic than John of Galilee? But this is necessary as soon as we treat speech as a pro-ceeding from {'}somewhere{'} to {'}somewhither{'}. John was called into the Greek and Luke into the Jewish world of mind; Peter was called into the Roman sky-world and later his amanuensis, Marc, even went to the cradle of all sky-worlds, to Egypt. Matthew the ill-mannered, discovered the price to be paid for ritual.

Because speech moves, John did not write a hellenistic gospel. Instead, he redeemed the Greek genius of poetry. The Greeks worshiped the Logos. They talked and talked to a degree of drunkenness. Rhetoric, logic, philosophy, theatres, were their daily bread; the arts were their vice, their virtue, their life, their religion.

Whatever their poetry, their art of making, touched with its magic wand, was transformed, like the stones which formed the walls of Thebes under the music of Orpheus. We followed Homer's song of Achilleus' wrath until we wept over Hektor, his enemy. And we read the story of "The Man," Odysseus, until we believed Homer, that it was, after all, and really, a "Penelopeia."

Plato had been frightened by this genius of his people. He had turned against poetry and proposed to abolish Homer. But Prohibition never works. The salvation of the Greek {errand,}[103] "plane" as the greatest Greek orator, John Goldenmouth,[104] called this Odyssey of genius, the salvation had to come from the Jews. The Jews had voided the arts, and had sung their psalms and prophecies not as poetry but as responses. Accordingly, John, in

---

102. [ERH begins to number the gospels to match the *scenes* at the beginning of the chapter, heading his discussion of John as 4. But then he reversed himself and numbered his discussion of Luke as 2. Mark was not numbered 3, but Matthew begins with a hand-written 4.]

103. [Probably: *errancy*.]

104. [Goldenmouth = Chrysostom.]

the first and last Christian prophecy, in Revelation, had received his vision on Patmos, lying on the ground as one dead. And for this very reason, John the Evangelist, not Plato, was in a position to emancipate the Greek mind.

How was it done? Not man or wife, not Greek or Trojan became his great argument. Instead he sang that very power which makes man able to write poetry, man as God's poem. This is the meaning of The Word which became flesh. In the fourth gospel the inner poetry of the man himself who writes or speaks, albeit poetry what he says, was revealed.[105] John could do it because he was immune against the morbus poeticus which had seared Plato.

2. Luke, as a Greek and as a physician, was immune against the morbus propheticus, the Jewish negation of the world's successes. God was One, One only, the Jews maintained in the face of a pluralistic, power seeking, polytheistic chaos. Israel is so right in this respect—just as Greek genius is right, and Plato wrong to forbid it,—that even Jesus could not overcome their horror of any final realization. They crucified him because God had to remain in the future. It took the Greek Luke to make evident the limitations of their "No." As a doctor of the body, Luke knew of the healing powers of poison, of surgery, of many seemingly negative processes. Luke could admit that no man is superior; {or outside the body politic. Nobody} therefore, can claim to be a doctor of society's ills. God alone "i s."[106] But if man were God's drug, blood plasma, vitamin, serum, to be injected into the system? A man of God enters the arteries of society and may be devoured there, as Jesus was. Yet, will he purify and cure it, as the Christ if he knew what he did. In this case, God's Oneness as upheld by the prophets is not jettisoned. And this, indeed is Luke's gospel in the gospel and in acts. Jesus has instituted this process by which men sacrifice themselves for their enemies, for a society which reacts violently against them. And he who opened men's eyes to this destiny of any child or man, of being "injected into the bloodstream of society," is the anointed, the "Christ" whom all others can but follow.

Very well do I know that the front of Luke towards a salvation of the Jews is not even considered a remote possibility by the majority of the critics. Therefore, some technical points may be mentioned which should suffice to make his case at least a *non liquet*,[107] from the purely external evidence. Luke probably wrote in Caesarea in Asia Minor. Strong Jewish elements in such a church are no wanton premise. He was the first to write

---

105. [Perhaps: *the inner poetry of the man himself who writes or speaks, whether or not what he says is poetry, was revealed.*]

106. [Spacing a word out is a common form of emphasis in German.]

107. [Literally: *it is not clear.*]

a book in the strict sense that this book could be used for readings at the services in church as parallel readings to the Old Testament. His constant change of the "he says" in Mark, to a cultivated style of "he said," has often been noted. This was needed when the perikope was to have the dignity of being read out loud.

Luke respected the Jewish name of their religious center. For, he uses the name "Jerusalem" thirty times, and in 26 of these 30 places, the form is the Hebrew form Jerusalem, not the Greek form Hierosolyma. All the other gospels do the opposite. Somebody who spoke to Jews, would be as considerate as Luke and spare the ears of his listeners. Quite recently, it has been held that his style is filled with Hebraisms, and that he quotes the Old Testament not from the Greek but from the Hebrew *original* text.[108]

The point on which Israel was hardest of hearing, and not by accident but because of her most profound faith, was that God could be known to have said "Yes" to a man's religious mandate. God was always keeping man away from idolatry, away from the temptation to erect heaven on earth already. We have mentioned, in the letter on Hitler and Israel,[109] the fact that the Gentiles deified a man with great ease. To show Luke's dilemma, I now quote the terrible hymn to the deified Demetrios which a Greek, Hermokles, had composed for the general Demetrios:

> He's the Sun to love you.
> Hail, offspring of Poseidon, powerful God . . . !
> The other gods . . . have no ears, though mighty;
> they are not, or they will not hear us wail:
> Thee our eye beholdeth.
> Not wood, not stone, but living, breathing, real.
> Thee our prayer unfoldeth.
> First give us peace. Give, dearest, for thou canst;
> Thou art Lord and Master.[110]

Luke must have been thoroughly familiar with this kind of blasphemy in politics. Caesar's worship was strictly in line with this poem. Luke

---

108. ERH: Albert C. Clark, Acts of the Apostles, Oxford 1933 p. XXIII. Clark thinks that this proves Luke to have been a Jew himself. To me, this is not conclusive. But of course, it would prove the significance which we ascribe to Luke even better. The old 2d-century preface to the gospel contradicts it, however. [1978: 33. MDB added that *Clark is quite discreet in his statement*, but see Appendix I, 322.]

109. 1964: See my "Hitler and Israel" in the *Journal of Religion*, Chicago 1945, 129ff. [Also in ERH, *Despite*, 178–94.]

110. ERH: Quoted from the translation in the Oxford book of Greek verse, by J. A. Symonds [523. ERH substituted *gods* for *deities* and changed Symonds' capitalization and punctuation.]

abhorred it as much as his Jewish friends. How could he convince them that the delicate line between mortal men and the Creator of Heaven and Earth, was not destroyed by the new belief in God's Son Incarnate?

It could only be done in the manner in which Paul did it in his preaching. First, man must allow God to speak his "NO," by his willingness to suffer. Only after God, as a burning fire, has taken from man, as mortal man, all the dross and the transient attributes, can the complete affirmation, the unconditional surrender to "Yes" be admitted. The naïve mind says: "I should be God"; "I should be the messiah"; "I should be the lawgiver." God breaks this will. But the man who has not his own will, and does not his own will, and pays the penalties for the unavoidable admixture of self will in his life, he is "Yes."[111]

Following this traverse over the narrow mountain ridge between too much self-confidence and too little, Luke alone has certain reports on Jesus which center around this relation between the naïve first Yes, the divine No, and the creative and incarnating and history making second Yes. His alone is the story that Jesus saw a man working on the Sabbath. He approached him and said: "Man, if you know what you are doing, you are blessed. If not, you are cursed and a breaker of the law" (After VI, 10).[112]

Solely, in Luke, is the cross-examination of Jesus so carefully stated that Jesus himself never says: "I am the Messiah." Marc allowed Jesus to say (14:61)[113] "I am the Messiah." Luke knew Marc's book. Therefore, his more extensive report may indicate that he respected the scandal given by Marc's rather indifferent admission that Jesus had called himself the son of the living God. Egyptians or Greeks or Romans could believe in the apotheosis of mortal men by their own proclamation. But Israel with her awe of the Oneness of God, could not admit that any man could give himself his own rank. Luke conceded this point: They, the Jews, not Jesus, speak the decisive words. A man can become the Word said by God only if he himself does not exalt any of his own mortal statements into divine truth.[114] For Luke, the perpetual *concurrence* between the Father's power to make all the world around Jesus act and speak as they did, and the Son's own acts and saying, is the real proof that here God said a full "Yes" to the Son. Since the Son forwent power for faith, forewent the opportunity of making suffer for

111. ERH: II. Corinthians, 1, chapter 4 ff., 17 ff.

112. [1964: *in the Codex Bezae, one of the earliest surviving MSs of the N.T.*]

113. [Mark 14: 61-62.]

114. ERH: This is the argument also used by the Letter to the Hebrews. {This point, Jesus' own weakness in Gethsemane and upon the cross, was vividly debated in the first century; see von Harnack, "Zwei dogmatische Korreturen im Hebräerbrief," Berliner Akademie der Wissenschaften, 1929, 62–73.}

suffering himself, he exhibited his proper credentials. He who denies himself, thereby plays Israel's eternal role of the admonisher, himself to himself. In this manner, by accepting defeat, Christianity built the truth of the Old Testament into itself. If the prophets had heard the command: "say No to the idols," why should it be blasphemy now to say: "I hear the command to say No to our will and Yes to the step beyond this No?" And so Luke's point from the beginning is that with God nothing is impossible (I, 37). And as Jesus dies for his enemies so his enemies must reveal him in his true mission. By this *interaction* alone does the human will become discernible from God's will. And only after this can the *change of mind* occur; in the fact that the hated bringer of the gospel accepts the penalty from the hands of the receiver{s}, the bringer's will is purified from his mere self. This changes the mind of the persecutors. This, then, is Luke's gospel.

Since I write as the listener to language, my argument is mainly to those who are not at all interested in theology properly speaking and who, therefore, do not first wish to hear about all the highly learned arguments inside theology about Luke. However, it is only fair to add for those who are versed in these critical investigations, that Luke did not cover the whole field of Jewish tradition. We shall see this when we turn to Matthew. The strictly historical or naturalistic study of the gospels has oversimplified the battlefronts on which the cross was erected. We shall see that Greek and Jew were two out of four fronts while "Gentile" and "Jew," in the New Testament often are considered to be an exhaustive dichotomy.

The listener to language finds that Luke attacks a weak point in himself. The greatest piety, the highest type of religion, in Jesus days, was found with the righteous of Israel. Not their inferiority but their rigor and excellency, imposed on the priests of Jerusalem the duty to condemn Jesus. It was blasphemy to call oneself God and to proclaim one's seat at the right hand of God. It is not an arbitrary resistance offered by the Jews, but a highly respectable one which all the good people of our own days consider to be praiseworthy again.[115] Luke's argument, then, is an *eternal* argument and fights an eternal position of great merits. But Israel was a combination of prophetic purity and of Hebrew solidarity. Israel is a chosen race, chosen as well as race. Luke dealt with the prophetic aspect of Israel only. We shall see that the Hebrew side had to be dealt with by someone very different.

---

115. [This argument lines up with ERH's and FR's statements in their wartime letters. See Appendix I, 307.]

This must suffice for gospel four and gospel three: morbus graecus and morbus Propheticus found their antidote.

John the Hebrew prophet is able to redeem Greek poetry, and Luke the Greek doctor, can re-fertilize Israel's stubborn Negations: But is there a similar exchange of polarities, a similar transfer of energy between Matthew and Marc, on the one side, and their respective public, on the other? I think it is. The reader will do well to look back upon our former chapters which penetrated before Jews and Greeks likewise. We found temples and hieroglyphs, and rituals and tattoos organizing the human race. Now, the first two gospels achieve for Egypt and for tribal ritual the same emancipation which John achieves by "unspelling" poetry and Luke by healing the healing "No" of psalms. Since we today are infinitely less familiar with the sky-world and its hieroglyphs or the ritual of burial and sacrifice in the tribes, their cure demands a somewhat more laborious exposition.

[3.] We turn to Marc's gospel, Number two, and we remember the hieroglyphs painted on the walls of the temples which brought heaven to earth. The Emperor Henry II, a saint of the Church (1002–1024 A.D.),[116] wore as his mantle of coronation a cloth on which the sun, the moon, the stars of the firmament were woven. Because the emperor was the *cosmocrator*, he was lifted into the hub of the wheel to unite night and day, to reconcile the North where the sun never shines, to the south to which the polar stars of midnight never move. The emperor, the Son of Heaven as he was called in China, was the prime mover of a reconciled, a non-panicky, non-chaotic heaven and earth. His knowledge and compliance with the stars shielded the people from the panic of catastrophes. When the people of our days hold a President of the United States responsible for a world-wide depression, they follow in the foot-steps of all ancient nations who believed that the eternal cycles could be perfected by a human lifted into the hub of the wheel. The incense burned before the emperor's statue was a means to enliven his nostrils so that he might smell the harmony and beauty of the universe. He who did not burn incense, did not say "Heil Hitler," destroyed the Skyworld. He must die.

Against this daily situation, the gospel of Marc on the true Son of God {was} written. It {was} written in a world which for the sake of security pretended that the emperor was the heart of its world, was the Son of God, and which upheld this with spells, calendars, sacrifices, symbols, temples, hieroglyphs. It {was} written by men who denied the emperor's claim, and who, therefore, plunged those for whom they wrote the gospel, in imminent danger of death for high treason against the welfare of the empire.

---

116. [Henry II was Holy Roman Emperor from 1002–1024.]

They preached in the midst of an unchallenged Sky-world, with "the abomination of Desolation,"[117] a king's statue, standing in the center of a spellbound universe, "standing where it ought not," in the center of the Holy of Holies in Jerusalem. This speech which I am quoting here from Marc, is given in Matthew first.[118] And we would have no right to ascribe to Marc any special interest in it. Matthew, being the first, was very catholic in his materials, certainly more catholic than the shorter Marc. And yet, I am going to quote some famous sentences from this speech of Jesus and I am going to affirm that for Peter, this speech had greater significance than for any other apostle. Two reasons can I give for justifying this {thesis} which otherwise would be arbitrary. First, the critics always have acknowledged that Marc is clearer as to the eschatological picture than Luke or Matthew. Weymouth-Robertson remark: "Certain features of the discourse stand out most clearly in Marc's record of it." And, "the clearest outline of this eschatological discourse is in Marc."[119]

Marc, in other words, has taken great pains with this speech. The second and weightier reason is this: this speech on the signs of the sky-world is the only speech which Marc gives in full. All other speeches were curtailed by him or omitted. Now {if} one speech out of many {in Matthew is} given completely, within the whole book of Marc, {it} thereby is placed in the center of attention.

In this speech which the reader may look up for himself, the astrological sky world is described: "The Sun will be darkened and the moon will not shed the light, the stars will be seen falling from heaven and the forces which are in the heavens will be disordered." As these disorders were prevented to happen by the imperial {or Pharaonic} spells of the sky-world, Jesus' prophecy of the end of their power, is meant literally.

Our modern commentators as true Gilbert Murrays, however, shake their heads sadly:[120] "The details of this description are of course not to be taken literally. They are the attempt of poetic imagery to realize what it means that God should intervene in human history." But, the modern fails to ask, how could God intervene as long as the sky-world was in power? Marc was concerned with the cure from the morbus egyptiacus, not with poetry. What, then, was his cure{?} It was simple. It was dangerous. It was: fellowship. Men had to take the place of the dead stars in the firmament.

117. ERH: Marc 13, 14.
118. MBD: Matt 24:15.
119. ERH: Weymouth and Robertson, *New Testament*, 62 and 118. [118, 62.]
120. ERH: Weymouth Robertson, p. 119. [ERH accuses the commentators of following Murray, Regius Professor of Greek at Oxford, in seeing everything as mythic rather than real. 1964: *our modern Nicolais*. See note, 99.]

Jesus had to take the place of the Sun. Marc's whole gospel tries to show that Jesus has lived the one perfect solar year of a human sun, a human heart.[121] But the people, nobody, not even one of his disciples, have recognized the presence of the good life.[122] But he has trusted them nevertheless. He has called them when they did not understand, and they have been in fellowship with him. We know already that Peter declines all merits in the case. The disciples during the perfect and acceptable year of the Lord, were in suspense. In III, 12, he forbade them to say who he was. In IV, 1, they are told: for you the open truth, for the crowds the parables. In 8, 31 "They were told for the first Time. . ." In 9, 9 "He strictly forbade them to tell anyone what they had seen until after the son of Man had risen from the dead." In 10, 38, they are told: "You know not what you are asking." In 10, 32, "they were awe-struck and those who followed him did so in fear." All the time, the only link between them and the Lord is suspense and expectation on their part.

Around this discrepancy of Jesus' time and their time the whole gospel is built. For, Jesus is already performing. The time is fulfilled. He walks on earth as the sun. But the disciples ask him: "Tell us when these things will be (XIII, 4) ".

Why is Marc filled with this discrepancy between Jesus who lives the perfect year and the fellowship who expect it in some mysterious future? Why does the very last chapter of Marc abound in statements of the disbelief of the disciples such as "Simon, are you asleep?" "They could not believe it," "They were afraid." "They did not believe them either." "He upbraided them for their unbelief and obstinacy?"[123]

In fact the critics have thought that Marc's gospel must be mutilated or incomplete because it ends so abruptly and on a note of despair. Now, we are already warned against this strange suspiciousness of reason against the ends and the beginnings of creative literature. Tristram Shandy certainly would not pass muster with them, for its incredible first page. If a belated fellowship, however, is the center of Marc's gospel, we may read its end with perfect understanding. This "spurious" ending says: "Go the world over and proclaim the gospel to all mankind. And *signs* shall attend those who believe." "So the Lord Jesus having thus spoken . . . sat down at the right hand of God. And they went out and preached everywhere the Lord working with them and confirming the word by the *signs* which accompanied it."[124]

---

121. [Mark 4:11.]

122. [Perhaps: *Nobody, not the people, not even one of his disciples, recognized the presence of the good life.*]

123. MDB: Mark 16: 12, 14.

124. MDB: Mark 16:15–20.

The reader now will be thoroughly befuddled and shake his head. That John sings "the Word" where Homer had sung "the Man," that Luke says "Christ now" where the Jews only had heard "Not Yet Christ," a humanistically educated reader, I trust will have no trouble to relate. But that Jesus destroyed the hieroglyphs of the sky-world and the astral calendars of the Sun-God Emperor, the Sol Invictus, of the empires, seems so far fetched because our own world seems so superior to "signs." If the modern mind wishes to have an analogy, it is the social cycle of business, the power and the worship of power which may be used as analogy. The modern belief in medicine, machines, in a hugely endowed institution, is of a nature similar as the sun cult of antiquity. The terms "influence," "influential," "power," "conjuncture,"[125] "cycle" and "depression," are our astrological terms. They are now used for social conditions, not for cosmic occurrences. The analogy may be valuable, just the same, to show that we too are accustomed to accept such "constellations" patiently, like rain and sunshine. This means that we, too, have some hieroglyphs which confine us as sacred spells. However this may be with us; {in any case} the order of the ancient sky-world was reversed by the one last sentence of Marc, that God confirmed the words of the preachers by the signs which accompanied them. In the sky-world, the word of the Son of the Sky took effect without standing the test of the real world. The Gods appeared ex machina, by machine; the rain or the blood was produced by priests who acted the Jupiter or the Isis. The hieroglyphs were bound to come true by black magic if the white magic forsook them.[126]

The Christian ministers of the word replaced this riskless magic by the highly risky belief in the continuum of a word spoken from the bottom of the heart because it would provoke all the good spirits in the hearers in an inpredictable degree and manner. Had not Jesus himself "yielded the spirit" (15, 37) throwing himself into a heartless world full of faith that a free response would answer his call, that a fruit would come out of the seed of his life? *The world {as such, the cosmos}, has no heart!* {Precisely this, the pagans had tried to believe. He who} does not recognize the fields of force created by the spell of sacred names, who does not recognize that chaos and panic are exercised[127] by venerable names, will be reluctant to acknowledge the process by which these fields of force collapsed under the shock of the new faith. The catholic church replaced the sorcery and spell of the temples not by ignoring them but by replacing astrology through faith in the spirit of fellowship. The difference between a son of heaven, placed in the center

---

125. [Conjuncture = *Konjunktur* = economic situation, boom or bust.]
126. [The following passage was replaced in the 1964 German version. See 101.]
127. [Probably: *exorcised*.]

of the universe commanding the stars and winds as the emperor of China did till 1911, and the Son of God, lies in this one difference. The emperor of China does not risk his own life in proclaiming the New Year. Is this the whole difference? It is indeed. We who buy patent medicines, big names, psychologically sold to us, have difficulties in distinguishing between white and black magic. We either fall victim to advertising or we do not believe in any power of the Word. Peter believed that Jesus had created a new aeon by his faith in fellowship. The twelve stars which bowed to Joseph in his dream, Jesus had replaced by the twelve apostles whose feet he washed and who did not respond before fifty days after his death. But he called them, in his unlimited faith in a future free response on their part. And as soon as the first response came in complete freedom when they were alone, a new heart burst upon the dead world. The real heaven and the real earth now became visible, "the whole world over," that is wherever a man was willing to risk his life for those who resisted him.[128]

Jesus became the heart of a living universe by his faith in a free response. "This first creation of God's World" as Peter calls it[129] was reclaimed from the sky world by faith in the continuum of all speech. These speakers could hold each other by their hands and transmit the new power of one common spirit. They spoke in the name of the only one who had started this faith in free response when nobody had it. His day had gone by. But in the night which he left behind him, the people could become bright stars, waiting for the full light of another day. That we are not amiss in our interpretation, could be proved most directly from the second letter of Peter. Here, the heavens—id est the sky world—are all ablaze. They will be dissolved. A new heaven and a new earth will come, without astrology, "until day dawns and the morning star rises in your hearts" (Peter, second letter II, 19). This is eloquent. For the sky world of Egypt had as its center the simultaneous appearance of the brightest star of the night and of the sun, on July 19. This was New Year's Day as night and day, north and south, seemed to be reconciled at this one moment. In Peter's words, this was to be replaced by the dawn in the hearts of men, the new heaven. But, alas, I shrink from making use of this letter because this may do harm to my thesis since the critics are very severe about this letter and say that it cannot be Peter's.

It, therefore, must suffice to bring into focus the actual front on which the Church fought. Peter and the papacy, archetypes of the power-lusting priest for many, came into existence as victors over the temple cults of antiquity.

---

128. [The 1964 German version runs in parallel again from here on.]
129. MDB: I Pet 1:20.

THE FRUIT OF OUR LIPS, OR WHY FOUR GOSPELS?   239

A Jewish fisherman, Peter was on the one hand conversant with the real cosmic processes of weather, water, air and sky. On the other hand, as an Israelite, he was not polluted by astrology. Here, then, was a man preserved from contamination with ancient science but in excellent command of his five senses. This was the man picked out to dissolve the old heavens with their local calendars, to replace the hieroglyphs of Stonehenge or Memphis by the suffering of the living bodies of the martyrs. The ministers of the word became the hieroglyphs of the new temple.

For this, at least, I am allowed to quote Peter himself. His first letter no longer is denied him today. In this letter, we find him proclaiming the victory over the stones of the ancient temples.[130] And we only will understand the sentence if we remember that these temples were covered with spells and hieroglyphs.[131] Peter exclaims that he acts not by "gnosis," the prediction of the astrologers, but by the "prognosis" of God.[132] {God} called {Peter} at a time when he did not know at all what he was expected to do, {and} before he could respond in "*imitation of the One who has called*" him (I, 15). And now comes the literal definition: "And yourselves, you like living stones and be built up into a spirit-filled temple" (II, 5).[133][134]

So much for Peter and Marc, the later bishop of Alexandria in Egypt. The Morbus Egyptiacus was cured.

{4.} Now we are back to our first evangelist, to Matthew. We have little right to expect from him a similarly clear and specific front. Since he was the first to write at all, he had to report all and everything. And we found this to be true, in the case of the speech on the sky-world {on} which Marc elaborated. And yet, Matthew though the first is surprisingly specific. And the disease which he overcomes, is with us like the other diseases, only, this disease is so close and so near ourselves that it is more difficult and more disagreeable to discover. We get a glimpse of his character as a specific

---

130. MDB: I Pet 2:4–8.

131. [The typescript once contained a note here: *See the [. . .] of the Temple*, but it was obliterated in ink.]

132. MDB: I Pet 1:2.

133. ERH: Correspondingly, the beginning of the letter to the Hebrews [1:37] has to be corrected in our translations: "After partial and varied speech God has spoken through the Son, the {reflection} of God's splendor, the Hieroglyph of God's core!" It is the only occurrence of the word "character," hieroglyph, in the New Testament.

134. ERH: Ignatius, writing to the Ephesians, vividly combats the temples of stone. He is so keen to replace the dead structures of the Temple that he calls the Holy Ghost the rope the Cross the new {crane or derrick,} and the Christians the stones which by this crane are lifted to the altitude of the divine building. [For an online source of Ignatius' letter, see Appendix I, 316.]

medicine against a specific disease when we read (XIX)[135] that he expects[136] the twelve apostles not as the twelve stars but as the judges over the twelve tribes of Israel. Why did he remember this? Could it be that he felt the necessity of breaking the taboos of tribal ritual peculiarly strong?

We have seen Peter's employment, and Luke's, and John's {because of their specific immunities.} It would appear that {Matthew} could not and would not be employed for {curing} anything which had to do with literature or writing. For as oral as Peter the fisherman must have been and as much as he probably detested ink, Matthew certainly was familiar with paper work and written records, only too well. Since we do not expect him to be used inside his old activities where he had used writing for superficial purposes to say the least, we may expect him to fight elsewhere.

Now, we read that he was not received in good society. And on the other hand, he begins with Jesus' place in the social register of Israel. He stresses this fact that his master belonged in the very best society, as the son of kings. And goes on to show that there were privileges connected with this social place which Jesus abandoned. "The son of kings should be scot-free" (17, 27)[137] He should not pay customs duty nor any tax, be it capitation tax or the half-shekel tax as Jesus smilingly says (17, 27). But, Matthew goes on to say, the reverse happens. He expresses the whole meaning of Jesus' life in terms of an account: and I am sorry to grate the refined feelings of the {suburban} reader, but he does say: He gave his life as the price for buying back many. (20, 28). This is not a figure of speech with Matthew. Matthew understands Jesus to be the right[138] heir of the chieftaincy who instead volunteers to become the victim at the tribe's feast. But by being the voluntary victim, he becomes the first victim in the world who can speak. Nobody had ever spoken in this role, but victims {though mute} were essential. The association between the ancestors and the living was based on the common meal at which the dead partook as though alive, and the whole burial and funeral rite was based on this association between the dead and the living. The spirits of the dead asked for food, and these ghosts were bloodthirsty if they were not fed, according to the faith or superstition of all tribes. We accomplish the same by high entrance fees into clubs or fraternities. We become members, in this manner. Sacrifices were the core of ritual since they alone incorporated the group and gave it a legal status as a public

---

135. MDB: Matt 19:28.
136. [1964: *regards*. See 103.]
137. [The reference is to Matt 17:26.]
138. [Probably: *rightful*.]

corporation, beyond the grave, beyond the accidents of birth and death. Sacrifice, then, was the only means of establishing order and of creating legal persons.

And to speak the proper names, to make the proper movements at these sacrifices was essential. They were that which we hold essential as *table manners*. To how many people of our own time, table manners are the yardstick of promotion, membership, fellowship? The table manners of antiquity were equally strict. With us, a waiter at table is not expected to join the conversation of his own accord. Even less do we expect the roast-beef and the fish to talk. The price of a good dinner party is the complete silence kept by those who serve and by the food which is served. And my whole paragraph will be condemned by any reader of good taste because I mention the remote possibility that the roast beef might speak. And this is Matthew's whole point. The verdict "bad taste"—how often had he heard it turned against himself and his bad company—he knew to be more murderous for a man than any other crime. Society expects us to play the rules of the game. It is inexorable if we break these etiquettes. And yet, I had to commit this break of etiquette myself if I wished to introduce Matthew at all. For herein lies his real achievement. He is the only Evangelist who tells of Jesus' escape to Egypt when Herod murdered the children of Bethlehem. The whole point of Matthew is that though Herod could not murder him, he was murdered by good society for his breach of etiquette, because he insisted to give or lend speech to the victims of society. That *Jesus spoke as the victim* made him impossible. Matthew scandalized the Jews. After all, they had nothing but burned offerings since Abraham did not slaughter Isaac. They were highly civilized. In Sweden it could still happen a thousand years later that a king butchered six of his sons to placate the spirits. When he turned to his seventh son, the people saved the child, became Christians and gave up human sacrifices. But {Israel} after all, was the nation of Abraham and Moses. To this day, all Jews think that the gospel is in bad taste. We read the word "scandal" in our texts,[139] but "bad taste" would really convey better the whincing under an outrage against our taste{s}.[140] The ritual of any society—and I am afraid, we lose sight of this more readily than of anything else—protects itself by this violent recoiling. It does so at all times and in all places. Matthew: "Why do your disciples transgress the tradition of the Elders by not washing their hands before meals?" The Scribes asked. "Why do you," Jesus retorted, "transgress God's command and deny your own

---

139. ERH: {The Gospel was as much a scandal to the first century as it is to the twentieth." Hoskyns and David, p. 261}.

140. [Probably: *the wincing at an outrage against our tastes*.1978: *the whining under the Gospel.*]

parents something they need because it is 'consecrated'?" "You have made futile God's words for the sake of your table manners" (15, 2).[141] "Eating with unwashed hands does not make unclean."

Against the taboo of table manners, Matthew "sins" and Jesus "sins." For, Matthew shows Jesus as the speaking victim, the meat and wine who begin to speak, in the midst of dinner. The shock administered by Matthew is wonderfully formulated by a modern critic:

> "The reference to eating Christ's flesh and drinking his blood is impossible in an Aramaic gospel in Jerusalem in the first century; nothing could be more repugnant to Jewish ways and feelings. Words such as these would horrify Jewish residents of Jerusalem, then or now. The Jews were and still are, utterly opposed to the drinking of blood which the Law repeatedly forbade. It would be difficult to imagine a sentence less likely to have been written in a Jewish Christian circle anywhere at any time. No Jewish evangelist could have recorded it.[142]

This is an eloquent paragraph and the feeling of vomiting is probably well nigh aroused in many a reader. The humor of this passage lies in two facts: first, that the critic deals with John[143] who in this matter simply affirms Matthew. The critic tries to refute the Jewish origin of John. And he ignores the case of Matthew, who obviously wrote for Hebrews. The second humorous fact is the modern assumption that every scandal can be avoided. The Jews stoned Stephen, killed James, jailed Peter because they were furious. The lamb, the blood, the bread, all these terms, of course, were blasphemies. But the whole history of the Church was based on this fury. Paul in Athens when he for once tried to be adaptable, was a complete failure. Matthew was abhorred and the gospel was abhorred, and, be honest, is abhorred by all men of good taste, today.[144]

The price of all ritual is sacrifice. When we bind ourselves to a ghost of the past, to a piece of paper, to a house, to a grave, we are apt to spill somebody else's blood for the purpose. And so it is to this day. This is all right if it is in our consciousness which price we pay. But Jesus created a brotherhood, the brotherhood of the silent victims, by becoming the first speaker among them. Why could he speak? Because he *volunteered* where

---

141. MDB: Matt 15:2-6.

142. ERH: Edgar J. Goodspeed, ["Greek Idiom,"] *Journal of Biblical Literature*, 1944, p. 90 is the author of the paragraph quoted in the text. [See Appendix I, 324-25.]

143. MDB: John 3: 54-56.

144. [In the typescript, a footnote is indicated here but not given. 1964: Goethe is named among *the men of good taste*. See 106.]

before the victims had been drafted. But the Eucharist is still a scandal to a Jew. It makes him vomit, quite literally, as it would any man of etiquette. Matthew knew that the pudenda of life were real. That it was less bad taste to speak as the victim, as bread and wine, than to do the act of condemning the Just. He was immune against the mortal disease of good society. He knew that everything has its price. And that nothing is more expensive than freedom from the taboos of good society. And so he ceased to call the first man who had spoken for the victims and as a victim, by his name in society, son of David, Son of Abraham, as he had begun in Chapter One. This taboo was broken. Matthew, in his last chapter found himself in the infinitely more exciting society of sinners who no longer were bound together by high entrance fees, but by the name of the first victim who had spoken out loud. It is not impossible, by the way, that Matthew went to Ethiopia. Now, the point of this mission would be that the Ethiopians, to this day, observe the whole Jewish ceremonial as well as the New Testament liturgy. They circumcise and baptize; they observe the Sabbath as well as the Sunday. One cannot tell; but it would be in accordance with the Word of the gospel if this duplication happened because of Matthew. Because only the superstition of ritual was the disease which he fought. Manners must be; but manners are not more than manners.

Matthew by illuminating the breaking of table manners, went over primeval ground. In primeval days, the table manners had been the creative elements from which the body politic sprang. Instead of snatching food from each other—in our {CCC}[145] camps of the unemployed, this beastly snatching was not rare and always indicated {the loss} of camp morale— like the animals, the introduction of common meals created a new peace of mind. Around the meal for the dead or perhaps more exactly with their dead, the new incorporation took place. Food was placed between the living and the dead and both partook of it, in one spirit and in one name. Hence, the sacrificial meals were the first constitutions of mankind. Here it was that the community was enacted because the stomach's enlightened "self"-interest was forgotten when the best pieces were reserved for the dead and later, the gods. Permanency eclipsed the interests of the living generation. The accidents of birth and of being alive, were overshadowed by the eternity of the dead. In the cooling shadow of this permanency and eternal order, peaceful arrangements were made between friend and foe; hospitality, the right of the enemy to eat with us, was introduced and became possible because ritual showed man his place in the succession of endless times. Here, people did not eat like the animals but they toasted each other by their full name.

145. [Civilian Conservation Corps. See Preiss, *Camp William James.*]

The salutation at meals is primeval. Man greeted each other and thought of each other at meals as {"}convivials{"}, {id est} as co-livers, as the other fellow's life counted more in one's own eyes than the "self," now.

To these primeval foundations of society Matthew takes us back. John spoke to peoples who knew the arts and sciences. Luke spoke to the greatest religionists and puritans of the ancient world. Mark spoke to the civilized inhabitants of the temple state. But Matthew penetrated, by his "bad taste," to the most archaic layer of all society, to the tribal layer of ritual. Hence, Matthew gave a version of the gospel which had to become the most universal and the most fundamental feature of the new Way of Life. The Mass and the Eucharist, the inner core of all divine services, is written up in Matthew.[146]

Since he made it clear, that Christ bought, by his sacrifice, the salvation of the sacrificers, it was now written that the victim of every meal, that bread and wine, spoke to the dining communion[147] and invited them to shift with their master to the other side of the counter, so to speak, to the side of the victim. In Mass, every member is invited to be sacrificed or to be ready to be sacrificed, for the salvation and the renovation of the world. In Mass, the first victim, invites the others, the partakers, to a service *in which they themselves* are the offerings. In the dullness of the average mind, this fact rarely makes a dent. People have degraded the divine service to a church parade or a social gathering. But the church was built on the faith that from now on, no divine service was permitted unless the people considered themselves as the sacrifice offered. The whole expression of a Body of Christ, with the head in Heaven, meant exactly this, that we who would crucify the Lord every day, in our rage and envy and indifference, now, with our eyes opened once for what we have done and are doing, declare solemnly: We now, together with our head, step on the side of the silent victims and offer us to our Maker so that he can remake it[148] as he pleases. How else could ever a new inspiration befall us as a people unless we offer ourselves as the body for this inspiration? Time and again, man has to be ripped open by the ploughshare of suffering and open himself like dry and desiccated earth to dew and rain. And ever since one man did this manifestly all alone and by himself, his congregations relieve the members of the total pressure of absolute loneliness. In every generation, the group which may be remodeled, may increase, until the whole of mankind will be allowed to fall silent and to cleanse themselves from the chatter and clatter of the day, and to listen to the spirit simultaneously.

---

146. MDB: Matt 26: 26–29.

147. [Perhaps: *dining community*.]

148. [it: *us, the sacrifice*.]

When the founder of the first Christian University in Japan died, he left a note to his favorite pupil: "I have reason to believe that you will be my successor. May I caution you against some weaknesses which you will have to combat in the exercise of your new office." And he went on to list them. In the excitement of the hour, this note was read by all the people present at his death as all other papers he left. Feeling humiliated, Mr. Kanamori fled the house, denied the Christian faith, and became a popular lecturer for the next thirty years. But when his wife with whom he led a model life, died, he could not stand his loneliness. He returned to the old place, made a public apology, and preached over the text that we shall be a living offering.

> A living offering it must be. This is what I did not understand. As the bullocks were brought to the altar formerly, and might break away and hurt the people in the neighborhood, so I did not accept my opportunity, my opportunity of living down this humiliation.[149]

And in the Japanese celebration of the Lord's Supper, this overwhelming experience of a living sacrifice colored the ritual. The dagger used in the solemn ceremony of formal suicide so popular among Samurai was brought in wrapped in a white sheet of paper which had to be folded in a certain manner. The whiteness of the paper alluded to the sacrifice of life that was to take place. From this worldly model, the form of wrapping in white paper was taken over and the bread at communion was offered to the communicants in such a wrapping. The meaning of the sacrifice and of offering is thereby translated into Japanese in as striking a manner, I dare say, as it is in Matthew's gospel translated from the Old into the New Testament.

Matthew, the most drastic, the least mannered,[150] also is the most elementary evangelist. Through him, we have received the ritual in writing. Our era would otherwise have been without any dress for its nakedness. It is very nice to leave obsolete cloth[151] behind you, but our era needed dress, some dress, just the same. Now we received the power of ritual free from superstition or myth or magic. Everybody can understand Matthew, child and genius, warrior and farmer, unless his heart is alien to self-sacrifice. The minds which scorn the sacraments as myth or obsolete, never fail to frighten me by their childishness. What an ignorant and uneducated heart they must have; how the grist-mill of their brain must have crushed all serious experience of life and of their own deepest hopes. Usually, these same

---

149. [The sermon was by Paul Kanamori, acting president of Doshisha University after Niijima Jo's death. See note, 109.]

150. [Probably: *the most ill-mannered.*]

151. [Probably: *clothing.*]

people expect to be adored by their family, read by the public, paid by their endowed institution. How can they expect it unless man's nature is fulfilled by his entering the ranks of the offerings? It is our highest nature that we should be offerings. {"Liturgy is only another name for almighty God's table manners."}[152]

The victim made eloquent, the world-heart created by responses, the No of God turned into an intermediary medicine of suffering on the road to a new incarnation, the human soul God's newest poem, these were the four glad tidings. The blind alleys of ritual, temple cult, Israel, Greece opened up to each other. And these four men succeeded because they were immune {to} the specific disease of speech which their tidings deluged. This is the reason why it is faulty to call John hellenistic, Marc Egyptian, Matthew Judaizing, Luke Paulinian. The restoration of free speech by the gospels proceeded by a matching of opposites. {Neither does the} prophetical John write {for} the Jews, {nor does the} learned Luke {write for} the Greeks. The fisherman Peter writes for the scientific world. And not a man of good taste and good standing matches the Old Testament, by his first gospel, but the in no way venerable publican.

{8. The Cross of Grammar}

Once we keep in mind the specific disease cured by each gospel, their literary form and style immediately appear to be impeccable. In the eyes of the critics, {not one of the Evangelists} has the right ending. All, when read as medicine, prove as right at the end as in their beginnings. They are impossible as sources for natural history. They are sound as wells of speech. Now, we experience something similar with the ends and beginnings of the Odyssey and Iliad. {The critics destroyed the ends as we read them now.} And how else could it be? What is {the} end and {the} beginning of speech? The beginnings of a human breath disclose the time and place of this particular act of the spirit. End and beginning bring an inspiration down to earth. End and beginning of any book declare whether it is true or not. But this truth is a threefold truth. A word may be true as to content; it may be true enough to be verified in its own author{'s actions}; *finally, it may be so true that it compels the next speaker to respond and to go on speaking.* Shakespeare compelled Milton to swerve out of the path of poetry since his

---

152. ERH: This statement is made by Father Smith in Bruce Marshall's "The World, The Flesh and Father Smith," Boston, Houghton, Mifflin 1945. [See Appendix I, 333.]

speech was so perfect that Milton complained.[153] Of the truth of the facts told in the gospel, the Church has lived. On the truth of the men who said it, in their own lives, the Christian world has lived. These two aspects of the truth have been effective for a long time. My mind as I have explained before (p. {20})[154] is concerned with the third aspect of all truth, *its forcefulness in begetting response, {in changing language.}* This third truth is a question of the power of style. And this truth about the four gospels, I have proved to my own mind's satisfaction and I hope to the greatest skeptics satisfaction: The gospels were true enough to compel the next speaker to go on speaking above and beyond the last word of the last speaker. Each one had to step in where the last speaker left off. They were imparting the concrete time and scene of their speech so vividly to each other that they touched each other off, to the next move. They sing, over forty years perhaps, one gospel, each in his own key, on his specific wave-length, according to his lights, in handing the joyful and arduous task over to the better man, one after another. In this act, then, the "four gospels" become a continuation of Jesus' life through the minds which were made over by their office of Evangelists. They were created in the lips of the Word.

Matthew, by the irresistible call of his Savior, writes himself out of the City of Man within which he had been the publican, into the Church. He is precipitated or projected into a new Eon, by the one word: Come!

Marc is inside this church and by his relation to Peter, he is protected from outside pressure. Peter's vehement subjective emotions, Peter's task absorb his helper, but Marc has a roof over his head, the roof of fellowship; he does not have to change allegiance.

Luke narrates. His is the documented story of the past. Having a student before him, he is the cable {for transmitting} the glories of the first two generations, {to} the later born so that {not less than} four generations now are in communion, from Jesus to the Church of Theophilus' children.

John is outside this cycle of command, fellowship, history. He is at the source, in the eternal *beginning*. By this one word: "In the Beginning," John renders Jesus the decisive service, which takes the event of his death out of antiquity. In antiquity, Jesus' death could only have met the treatment by ritual, by calendar, by poetry, by Israel. In the eyes of a friend, in Greece, to take the poetical world first, what would have been Jesus' fate, at best? The friend John would have mourned the friend, as Homer mourned Achilleus, in an immortal poem, in a "Kriton" or "Apologia" by a Plato, perhaps. In Israel, death would have refuted Jesus' enterprise as a failure. God, in

153. ERH: "On Shakespeare," 1630 [the poem by John Milton].
154. [See 110.]

Israel's eyes had said No to the crucified Messiah. In Egypt, Jesus would have had the stars against him; a better Horo-scop{e}, a new cycle with another Christ would have to be waited for. In tribal ritual, Jesus would have become the hero of a myth. Christianity would have become one more tribe, with his disciples celebrating Easter, and with his myth enacted annually, for his little clan. John's gospel blocked this relapse into ritual, skyworld's cycles, poetry, and Jewish Negation. Jesus was not an end, his death was not an end. Matthew, Marc, Luke had told already how one free man had mastered the unending chains of these cycles and had started a new life outside the ancient city of man, in One Church all over the world. John sealed the event of a new era, beyond tribe, temple, poetry, Israel; the new era would be open instead of cyclical, because the four streams of speech were now reunited and could gush forth in eternal originality as on creation's first day; the unending repetition of cycles was broken if the cross in which these streams of speech met, was held forth as the beginning of progress. Our era defies cycles. Of course, it is tempted by them; at this very moment, Western Man has been nearly dragged down to eternal recurrence, to Spengler's fatalism. It must wake up again to the cross of grammar with the help of the grammar of the cross. John placed Man's power to create speech before any of his particular historical performances: "In the beginning was the Word—Tribe, Egypt, Homer, Israel, were man's creations. Because everlasting man[155] is the listener and the speaker. Hence, man is superior to any one of his previous rituals of speech. "How can Christ be under fate!" Augustine exclaimed, "since fatum means the words which have been said before, and Christ is the Word which is said Now."[156] God has made man in his image to speak as an eternal beginning and Jesus had remained free to the bitter end.

Our era is not cyclical as long as the road-block of Christianity lies between it and antiquity.

The three other gospels could still be read as mere history, by later generations. The whole 19th Century dispensed with John and concentrated on the first three gospels, the "synoptics." Without John, the "gospel" would not have existed as more than mere history. In John, the church conquers her danger of becoming a purely ritualistic, a purely mythological, a purely poetical, a purely fictitious institution. She now sees all her temporal forms in the light of an eternal beginning, because her Founder always is ahead of her and of any of her ways of speech: The Word which is in the Beginning.

The four Evangelists immunize our era against the relapse in mere natural inertia and blind cycles. They represent the cross of grammar of

---

155. [A fond allusion to Chesterton's *Everlasting Man*.]
156. [This is probably ERH's own translation or a paraphrase.]

antiquity in the new era. In the cross of drama, lyrics, narrative, and judgment all speech was moulded. But once established, these grammatical forms drove on under their own momentum in endless rituals. The rituals could not be looked through[157] and became magic, spell, cycle, routine, play of the intellect, sport of logic, superstitions. The Word languished.

The Evangelists reversed the cross of grammar into a grammar of the cross. One man had lived from fiat to factum est, from "Go out into my world" to "It has been done, my father," from listening to the call through poetry to story, to summing up, completing his whole life as one grammatical cycle. The gospels depicted this cycle.[158]

As Hilarius Isaac put it, at the end of the Fourth Century:[159]

> Why were the experiences and sayings of the Lord organized in four volumes and by four authors?
>
> Four volumes, four authors, both was congruous. For we have before us, in the words of Isaia, the One Acceptable Year.[160] This year is contained in four volumes as in four revolutions similar to the four seasons through which a year evolves: one season is in need of the other mutually. Accordingly the acts and sayings of the Lord are circumscribed within the area of four books of which one stands in need of the other. Together, they are perfect in conveying the plenitude of time.
>
> Secondly, there was a good reason why it should be organized by four authors. Of the year's seasons, the terms show diversity; of the gospels too the nomenclature is diverse; and if they seem to contradict each other in their words, they do not dissent when they are interpreted in the light of this reason. The seasons of nature, too, are as different as possible in their names, their weather conditions, their astronomical aspect; but in the result of producing the fruits which come to live, they do not dissent.[161]

In our modern terms, we may say that each gospel is aware of the perfect cycle of this life from Imperativus personalis to Subjunctivus Lyricus to Narrativus Historicus to Indicativus Abstractus. But each gospel writer was

157. [Probably: *seen through.*]

158. MDB: Mark 16:15, John 19:30.

159. MBD: *Obviously the author here rests his attribution of the authorship upon his friend and colleague. Joseph Wittig, who in 1905 published at Bresau a work entitled* Der Ambrosiaster Hilarius. [See Appendix I, 327–28.]

160. MDB: Isa 58:5, Luke 4:19.

161. ERH: Corpus Scriptorum Ecclesiasticorum Latinorum L, 430 [ERH's translation from the Latin].

stirred up by one especially; Matthew who had experienced the violence of a sudden order: Follow me, took his clue from the Imperativus personalis; Marc wrote for and with the prince of the apostles, took his clue from the fellowship of the twelve, a strongly lyrical note; Luke who was Paul's companion and had not lived in this fellowship as little as Paul, wrote from Christmas on, as any narrator who has no particular time span in common with the events he narrates. And John, who did not need any outer credentials or events to believe in his friend, took his clue from Jesus' victory over the endless cycles of ritual, of eons, of revolutions which engulfed the ancient world. He began with the progress brought on by the power of the Word, in his Indicativus Abstractus: In the Beginning was the Word. And there{by} defined Jesus as {God's} Freedom {to come out of his silence and to speak his final Word. Jesus now revealed the last silence of his father.}[162]

Here, then, was *the grammar of the cross*. And now, after all the gropings of the ages, the phases of all group life became transparent, as the cross of grammar.

Before a man is not initiated into this cross of grammar as a citizen who listens to the call of duty, as a lover who hears the soul of his life call upon his name, as the patient who sees his chance to get well, as the thinker who realizes[163] the category of freedom for himself despite the laws which his mind thinks up for nature—before a man has not {made} at least one of these four experiences, he uses speech to no reasonable purpose. {However, this profitless type of speech without experience is with us.} As soon as the gospels were written, this speech without experience began to dabble with the new facts proposed by the existence of the church. This dabbling was called *gnosis*. People tried to think the new life without being touched by it first in some form of call, listening, passion, or change of heart. Therefore, except for the four gospels, the whole story in Palestine would not have withstood[164] the onslaught of the Gnostics from Simon Magus who ran around at a time when the blood of the martyrs still reddened the soil of Palestine, and proclaimed a little harlot to be Mary, and himself the Savior, to Marcion who admitted no other gospel but the one written by Luke and declared that

162. ERH: {Ignatius, Letter to the Magnesians ch. 9: Jesus is God's Word, coming forth out of God's silence.}

163. [realizes = *makes real*.]

164. ERH: This is proved by the discovery, made by Harnack: that the Gnostics forced the Church to {rally around the four evangelists in sheer} self-defense. {She} issued a statement with regard to the origin of the four gospels between 150 and 180 A.D. Harnack, Berlin Akademie S.B. 1928, 330ff. This statement is precise and authentic and irrefutable. {See p. [261–67, "The Oldest Official Remarks on the Gospels." See also Appendix I, 337–50.]. I rally around the four evangelists in sheer. . .} [*self-defense, myself?* The sentence remains unfinished in the typescript.]

this had fallen down from heaven directly. The Gnostics separate the life of the writer or teacher or apostle or speaker from the content of his speech. In other words, the gnostics have not entered the realm of experience in which the man himself is the fruit of lips, and the heart of somebody else' lips. Gnosis is all over the world today. The Churches themselves are filled with it. Pacifism is gnosis, an attempt to know the world before having been spoken to. During the last century, our last ramparts against the relapse into gnosis, have been the earthly love between man and wife. In Juliet's call on Romeo, many a man of the 19th Century even so dimly, learned to know himself as called forth to be the lips of the soul whom he loved. The next generations who follow this last century of the Great Lovers seem to hear nothing but the call to arms. And it may be that in the experience of this call, they for the time being, find their only antidote against Gnosis. For this reason, the insight into the structure of the gospels is no luxury. The teachers of the old and of the young, of girls as well as of boys, will corrupt those taught if they go on with their innumerable numbers and facts in the abstract[165] of the judgment seat. A teacher who is not an initiate in one of the four ways described above is not qualified to teach. He does not understand the conditions under which it is alone meaningful to speak.

Because the word "freedom" has replaced the experience of freedom, "goodness," the experience of getting better, "kindness" the experience of falling in love, adjustment the experience of a personal commitment, every effort should be made to make the mind conscious of the grammar of meaningful speech.

It is for this reason that I invite the reader to bear with me a little bit longer in this chapter. It will not suffice to "understand" the four gospels. We also need means to bring their insight to fruition. This can be done if means and ways exist to make the cross of grammar visible, in the arts and symbols of our society's imagination. I do think that new ways open up from our discovery into the grammar of the cross at a time when we seem to be paralyzed by fictions, myth, repetition, suspicion {and when words have lost their meaning. We move in a vacuum.}

{9. The Shape of the Four Evangelists}

The Spirit of Man was fully incarnated once, and it was impressed on the four gospel writers in four different manners. Hence, the four gospels are so to speak four wax models of the {typical melodies} of the human mind. Let us tentatively extend the lines of these mental profiles far enough to the

165. [Probably: *in the abstraction.*]

point where their impact on the body of each evangelist becomes transparent. Our body, as we all know, is not a kind of wooden box or receptacle, but it tries to correspond as best it can to our mental processes. {Our bodies are expressive of the whole man.} We lie dreaming or half-dreaming and we have our best ideas. We sit down when we wish to think through a variety of versions or impressions. We kneel or "we break down," as we graphically say, when we are overcome by a desire to recognize some higher power than ours. We jump up and pace the floor when we are in a fighting mood. Obviously, modern man suppresses or misplaces many of these physical reactions to mental processes. But in his language he uses them even though his body may have never been skilled[166] to express them. We say that an artist "conceives" like a woman, that a criminal "broke down" under the weight of the evidence, that the speaker was in a "fighting" mood, that a teacher occupies a "Chair."

Obviously, then, one bodily response expresses one mental attitude in preference to another.

I think of Matthew as standing and fighting, of John as the visionary in the words of "Revelation," lying on the ground as one dead of Marc as bending over or kneeling next to Peter, and of Luke, of course, as sitting at his desk.

In contrast, the old symbols used for the four evangelists by the artistic traditions of the last 1800 centuries[167] leave us cold, or at least, they leave me cold, and they have been discarded practically for the last 150 years by all artists of rank, even in ecclesiastical art. Could it be that there was a good reason for this discountenance[168] of a venerable tradition? May it not be that these inveterate forms and symbols were obsolete, antiquated by our very progress, and that we may be grateful for the interval of formlessness after 1789 because now, a simpler form of symbol nearer to our understanding, has been maturing?

The old attributes of the gospelmakers were the lion, for Marc, an angel for Matthew, an ox for Luke, and the eagle for John.[169]

These attributes were taken from the complex Cherubim of the Old Testament, the forms of which in turn were connected with Egyptian and Babylonian beliefs. These Old Testament Cherubims were composed of

166. [Probably: *trained*.]
167. [1,800 years, or 18 centuries.]
168. [Perhaps: *discontinuance* or *discounting*.]
169. ERH: For many years, I have collected the {archeological} material for many years, and I hasten to say that these attributes are by no means unanimous; when they first were used, the attribution to the *individual* evangelists was not as stereotype as later.

eagle, bull, lion, angel. The Old Testament lost its grip over our symbolic imagination long ago.

But could it not be, that man is in his very body, moulded into the carrier of the Word, in distinction from the animal world? No animal can sit or stand or kneel or lie perfectly prostrate as one dead, as a vessel of speech, in listening and expressing.[170] The Spirit compels us to take shape in a way appropriate to listening and speaking man. The Word could not have come into the world if it had not the power to mark out the man who speaks, and the ways in which he speaks. To stand means to be under orders, in action. To kneel means to receive on faith and in peace, to sit means to instruct and to narrate, to lie prostrate means to conceive like the artist, the genius of receptivity and creativity.

It does not seem arbitrary to proclaim the truth that the spirit does mould the body, and does prescribe us our shape. The Spirit does call upon our bodies and we conform to him.

---

170. ERH: {Also, of course, animals also can't embrace or "grow" in each other's palms by shaking hands.}

95a

10. THE FOUR APOSTLES

Religions create faces. An agnostic student of anthropolog[ist] went to Iraq and reported that he found the same physical stock divided by religions to such an extent that by now, this stock looked like four different races: "Le Sette religiose hanno una tendenza a sviluppare un tipo anthopologico proprio"(Giuseppe Furlani). But this takes us too far afield. However, it had to be stated that with the four gospels, new peoples and new races , new nations actually are set into motion. My "Autobiography of Western Man", called "Out of Revolution" has described the creation of these new branches over the last one thousand years . And the secular historians have not even reported tha[t] this book is a book on The biological history of the species Man. For the power of the gospel to create FRUIT of LIPS, is denied except at Mass when the gospel of St. John cannot help reminding people of this incarnating force of God's word.
But although I cannot enlarge here on the ever increasing power of recreating races ever since the times of the apostles, I think the reader may be helped if he can see some model case

of such rebirth in the ranks of the evangelists themselves. The four evangelists themselves had experienced the new life and as little as their texts are accidental but square and fundamental and indispensable, so are they themselves not a motley crowd,but a wonderfully influenced quadrilateral. A few words must suffice.
The four evangelists represent four phases of the Church. And the four phases are represented by James (the brother of John)whom the Highpriest had executed in 42 A D, of Peter who went to Antioch and to Rome, of Paul who did not live to see the destruction of Jerusalem as little as Peter or James and of John who as the only apostle survived the end of the Temple . First of all, the whole synoptic problem boils down to the fact that three evangelists wrote under the guidan[ce] of apostles who did not see the fall of the old Israel, and therefore had to write quite differently from John.

Second , not however second in importance, is the help which

{10.} The Four Apostles[171]

Religions create faces. An agnostic student of anthropology went to Iraq and reported that he found the same physical stock divided by religions to such an extent that by now this stock looked like four different races: "*Le Sette religiose hanno una tendenza a sviluppare un tipo antropologico proprio*" (Giuseppe Furlani).[172] But this takes us too far afield. However, it had to be stated that with the four gospels, new peoples and new races, new nations actually are set into motion. My "Autobiography of Western Man," called "Out of Revolution," has {described} the creation of these new branches over the last one thousand years. And the secular historians have not even reported that this book is a book on {the} biological history of the species Man. For the power of the gospel to create the FRUIT of LIPS, is denied except at Mass when the gospel of St. John cannot help reminding people of this incarnating force of God's word. But {although} I cannot enlarge here on the ever increasing power of recreating races ever since the times of the apostles, I think the reader may be helped if he can see some model case of such rebirth in the ranks of the evangelists themselves. The four evangelists themselves had experienced the new life and as little as their texts are accidental but square and fundamental and indispensable, so are they themselves not a motley crowd, but a wonderfully influenced quadrilateral. A few words must suffice.

The four evangelists represent four phases of the Church. And the four phases are represented by James (the brother of John) whom the Highpriest {had executed} in 42 A.D. of Peter, who went to Antioch and to Rome, of Paul who did not live to see the destruction of Jerusalem as little as Peter or James and of John who as the only apostle survived the end of the Temple. First of all, the whole synoptic problem boil down to the fact that three evangelists wrote under the guidance of apostles who did not see the fall of the old Israel, and therefore had to write quite differently from John. Second, not however second in importance, is the help which we receive when we see each gospel in its full temporal function under one specific mighty plenipotentiary of the Lord. Let us survey the four gospels as sources for the rule of the inspiring apostles.

Who ever thinks of James as great or important? However, he was the brother of John; this alone should make us pause. He was a martyr. He it

---

171. [The table of contents adds: *James, Peter, Paul, John*. See 189. This chapter, added in 1954, was not included in the 1964 German version.]

172. MDB: *religious sects have a tendency to develop their own anthropological types.* [MDB cites a 1957 *Festschrift* for Furlani, but the quote is from Furlani's entry on *Iraq* in the 1933 edition of the *Enciclopedia Italiana*.]

was who held the first Church in Jerusalem together; he it was who seems to have been respected highly by the learned and lawful Jews. He seems to have had a religious experience not just as the Lord's disciple, but on his own as a zealot in the days of the Baptist. From all this, his authority over Matthew's gospel may be divined. Certainly, Matthew wrote under this great Bishop's eyes. Certainly, the beginning of the Christian {era} of world history which is proclaimed in the 25th chapter of Matthew, verses 30 to 45,[173] of a history composed of the alliance between the Church and the underdog at any time and in any place, is an announcement of such public significance, of such revolutionizing scope that Matthew's Bishop must have approved of it. The Liberal critics have submerged this new chronology, this new era in which kings, emperors, Priests cease to count and in which the underdog shall make epoch, as though here was just a new parable or a sentimental moralism. But Matthew has placed this announcement of a new {Eon} in which every single step would be the healing of the wound of one sin, one disease of the body {of the cosmos} after another, he has placed it between the life and the Passion, that is at the most central spot in his gospel. These incredible fifteen verses {became} James' and every Bishop's guiding light ever since. The reader should reread it to convince himself that here we have the lasting program of {World History in the new Aion. That is why the 19th century did not read it.} To conceive that it was written under the eyes and with the consent of Jesus' first successor and at a time when the Jews were still the first addressee of the good news, underscores once more the majesty of Matthew's plea. "Do not count the kings of Israel, do not count the prophets, do not count the series of high priests"—all these genealogies were undertaken at that time and played a tremendous role in the imagination of the Jews—no, do count every tear dried, every pain alleviated, every abuse reformed, as the hours of the new aion. This {truly is World History} though {proclaimed} in the narrow confines of Jerusalem. No wonder that such a new constitution was unacceptable. James lost his life; Matthew lost his people.

That Peter, step by step, was led out of this narrow precinct of the Holy City into the world of Juppiter and Isis, that he was very much against his will, made to dine with Roman officers and speak to people who did not know who Moses or Abraham or David were, this miraculous purge has allowed Marc's gospel to be written and probably has {finally} brought Marc into the one land {of Egypt} that had to be gospelized[174] as though the Jews

---

173. [Probably: *verses 31 to 46*.]
174. [Probably: *evangelized*.]

had never existed. The strange renunciation of anything Jewish in Marc is the result of this slow emancipation of Peter himself.

Luke learned from Paul how the curious individual mind of the common Greek mediterranean world, had to be spoken to. Not like Peter who found strong emperor worship and Egyptian or Roman religion in his way, Paul had to deal with the pluralism of esoteric and personal piety. No Roman would doubt that Gods had to be worshipped in public liturgy. But the inner man of the Greek KOINE had grown fastidious. Inner piety seemed enough. Why go to the bloody spectacle of crucifixion, of political rowdiness, of public disturbance? Why incarnate when a pure heart was all that God wanted? Why change the world? Why proselytize? Why replace anything spiritual because it was not good enough, as long as it was refined compared with the mob's superstitions? Again, this apostle had been hewn out gradually from a Jewish fanatic into a man who had to remember every word from his Greek College days in Tharsus. Who had to dig deep into those layers of his training which his father had given him and for which he never had cared too much? Greek schooling, Greek Poetry, the Roman citizenship, the knowledge of a trade, all these things {to Paul} became of vital importance the more his Jewish puritanic zeal for the Law had to be revised by the new Law of Liberty based on the voluntary sacrifice of one's own will. Peter, the native of Palestine, was directed Romeward. We would misread Paul if {we} overlooked his deliberate {first} course from Tarsus for Jerusalem. He was not directed from Palestine towards Rome; he was turned around {from his fanatic longing for Jerusalem to} rediscover his own Gentile background of Asia Minor, of the Roman Empire, of Greek craftsmanship, of the world wide Greek spirit.[175] {Not every Jew from Tarsus returned to Jerusalem. But Saul did. And now he was Paul.}

{This "Gentilized"} Paul writes to the Romans; he simply includes Rome into this reappropriated non-Jewish World of the whole Mediterranean and he treats Rome as he might have treated Spain, if he really went there. That the most spirited of men was asked to rediscover or to unearth the Spirit in the secular places which had contributed to his formation, made Paul the model of the Jew who had to readmit his Gentile heritage.[176] {The non-Jewish elements of his background were no longer repressed. Therefore} he could become the teacher of the Gentiles on the highest plane of Jewish spirituality and therefore the Purity of the "One God through Christ in the Spirit could replace the 'Harken Israel, the Lord thy God, is the One

---

175. MDB: Acts 9:30.

176. [ERH must have been acutely aware of how Paul's *readmission* prefigures FR's reversal of that step, at the opening of a new millennium of realigned truths.]

and Only One.' We should try to see the tremendous danger of a watering down of the height of the pure faith of the Rabbis in weaker hands; then, the gospel of Luke assumes the gigantic proportions of Paul's own struggle to translate the full purity of Jewish monotheism into the trinitarian open road into the world. {And then, we shall be astounded how his making by the Gentile world contained so many reasons for his gratitude.}[177]

James, Peter and Paul . . . have they emerged behind their respective gospels as the proconsuls of the Lord in Hebrew, Roman, and in Greek as the famous inscription of Pilatus on the cross postulated? {If you the Hebrew law,[178] the Roman temple, the Greek individuality} [t]hen, the miraculous synthesis of John's gospel will become visible. The brother of James, the natural friend of the Lord, the companion, aye the co-worker of Peter, all this allows John to inherit from all of them their achievements, their official date in the history of the Church. He will not loose anything they {had to} learn {and to represent} when taking up the succession.

But to these miraculous gifts[179] of inheritance he receives the fourth gift: he is allowed to see his master and friend fully vindicated. The epoch secretly initiated by the Son of Man, bursts into the open with the Fall of the Temple. Freed from any comparison, the gospel now stands on its own merits. The lean-to, Judaism, is broken off, the tree now must be planted in eternity alone, in the creation at the very beginning long before the world existed, and in the end when heaven and earth will pass away. The author of Revelation has the power of proclaiming the epoch; the new eon {in the fall of Jerusalem} is accepted by the father as the gift of the son. The most loveable and the most unpolitical and untemporizing of all the apostles is distinguished {for} the virginity of his soul; into it, the event of the outer end of the old Israel can be engraved: the end now has not to be announced, it has not to be proven, it has not to be sollicited {as in the other gospels}. It can be {presupposed}! {Its} unquestioning tone is the distinguishing feature of the gospel according to St. John. And this, in turn, is a gift of God's history, not of John's private merit. John remains the apostle of cosmic history without particularized office or bishopric; open to the event of God's coming.

With this, we have said it before, he can bring into a world of mere cults, rituals, possibilities, books, ideas, the stern fact of the incarnation as the new date in history. He can redeem the creative spirits of all the geniusses since Homer by revealing to them the higher law of order inside

---

177. MDB: Acts 21:19.
178. [1978: *If you see there the Hebrew law...*]
179. [1978: *But in addition to these miraculous gifts...*]

THE FRUIT OF OUR LIPS, OR WHY FOUR GOSPELS?   259

which even genius is one in a fellowship of all those who are illuminated by the Word. {Jesus made epoch; John proclaimed the epoch.}[180]

In John, the Hebrew, the Roman, the Greek form of Gospel truth, is reunited. In the death cells of Hitler, that is outside this world of James, Peter, and Paul, John's words were sought for more[181] than the words from any older gospel! {Often their own} full and free life of peace leads readers to find John overwritte[n], mystical, exaggerating. On Patmos, in the face of death, the truth has to be stated not in the three languages of this world but in the uncontaminated terms of the center of the fire.[182] John who concludes the cycle of the four gospels, is capable of starting it all over because {only} to the sceptic he seems to speak out of nowhere; the sufferer knows that he speaks from there where the divisions on this earth have disappeared. The Church ends each service with the first verse of John: In the Beginning was the Word. We now see why.[183]

{11.} The Law of Liberty[184]

If "the Four Gospels" were His lips, the lips formed themselves by Matthew going forward, motivating Marc to move into the inner sanctuary, Marc motivating Luke to look up the records from the past, Luke motivating John to move into the eternal cosmic seat of truth. And thus, these four men reached {out in four directions:} into the new world, the inner sanctum, the times of the past, the eternal truth; they reformed the cross of grammar, of which those pages had to speak so often, by forming a grammar of the cross, in which mortal men united may conceive of being yet in process of being created, of being in the crucible today. For one moment, the cross of grammar had become flesh in one living being. For this, he{is} called the Word. But this earth has no place for the absolute truth, it breaks it {up} into times

---

180. ERH: Hoskyns and Davey, *The Riddle of the New Testament*, 1931 p. [281–]282: "Those who are convinced . . . that [Jesus] can be . . . described within the framework of modern humanitarian and ethical idealism, are frankly shocked by the Fourth Gospel . . . The denial of Apostolic authorship, and even of a relation to Apostolic reminiscences is felt (by these readers and critics) to be essential." [ERH added additional capitals and Jesus' name.]

181. [Probably: *far more*.]

182. [As in *Out*, 221, ERH is consciously echoing Franz Rosenzweig's dictum in *The Star* that the Jews are the coals at the heart of the fire that is God, and the Christians the rays that reach out into the world (438–39 in the Galli translation). I am indebted to Wayne Cristaudo for locating this reference.]

183. [The 1964 German version runs in parallel again from here on.]

184. [From here on in, the typescripts's chapter headings are typed, though the numbers were added by hand.]

and situations. And the Cross was the only place where the full truth of a man's heart could be revealed at one glance. {However, lest we misinterpret the cosmic order represented by the four directions of the Cross, the Evangelists bring each one singly down to earth.}

Four great truths have been kept alive by the gospels, and even the most ritualistic clergy, the most cynical science, the most legalistic inquisition, the most superstitious mobs have not been able to exclude {these truths} from a {perpetual} hearing.[185] To the contrary, these institutions themselves had to teach the gospel truth which defied their own natural tendencies, at their own altars, in their own courts, by their own systems, during their own election campaigns. These four truths were: 1. Freedom, 2. The relativity of any law for the free, 3. The price of freedom, 4. The absolute authority of the law for those who are not free.

1. Freedom was not the freedom to think since thought can only think the law. When William James languished through four long years from being a so-called free thinker, he one day discovered that his mind could see only laws. He jumped from his sickbed and declared: "In freedom, a man must believe by his actions; it cannot be proven." This was his gospel truth. He who loves is free.

2. Freedom makes all the laws relative. For he who loves understands all laws as having been introduced to defend freedom. Marriage is the fruit of love. The Constitution is the fruit of comradeship in arms. Science is the fruit of a brotherhood of minds. That which is freedom for the founders is law for their trusting and grateful heirs. They speak the language of their fathers willingly, as laid down in the laws because they recognize themselves in the names bestowed on them by the founders.

3. The price of freedom is threefold: time, wealth, life. All three must be given freely to achieve great ends. Freedom "is" an empty word where not at least one of these three powers is given freely. Freedom's way into the world consists of the investment of these three powers in the service of a new love, a new faith, a new hope. No other incarnation of freedom is possible.

4. The relation between freedom and law is absolute. Nobody who is unwilling to pay the price, may enjoy freedom. He who is not willing to marry, cannot and can never know what {full} love {between the sexes} is. He who is not willing to suffer for the truth, can never know what the truth is. He who does not defend his country will not and shall

---

185. [1978: *from being perpetually heard.*]

never understand what freedom is. He must be dealt with accordingly, by and under the majesty of the law.

In these four truths the four names of Jesus are retranslated. They are his names in which and under which the gospels were written. Never before had a poem, a law, a prophecy, a book, pointed beyond themselves to the price which it cost to compose the poem, to pass the law, to conceive the prophecy, to articulate the book. The gospels have been abused. They have been reduced to material. And they have been exalted to sacred words in themselves. However, as long as they are the four gospels, *they protect their readers against themselves*. This, antiquity had not known. All the lips of antiquity had become idols and gods and scripture and authority, *in themselves*. To our era, then, only those processes belong which inherited the evangelical quality of being done in the heart's name, and of being said in His name. The rest remained pre-Christian even when it was enacted in 1500 or 1900. As the symbols of the four evangelists themselves were pre-Christian, and may become baptized in his name only today, so the Christian era saw numberless books on Christianity which though boasting of it, are not Christian themselves.

Gradually, in religion, in art, in science, in economics, in education, such makeshifts, books or sayings, will have to go.

They stand condemned in the light of the four gospels, as fruitless words. And we are free to live after the era of fruitless words because we are living in the pedigree of freedom of which Isaia had foretold: "I shall create fruit of lips."[186]

{12.} The Oldest Official Remarks on the Gospels[187]

Dom Donatien de Bruyne, in Revue Benedictine, 1928, gave us the restored text of four prologues to the four gospels which go back to about 160 of our era. Adolf Harnack accepted his thesis immediately (Berlin Academy, SB, 1928, 322ff.).[188] These prologues were written in defense against the Marcionite rejection of three gospels (John, Matthew, Marc), and his arbitrary editing of the fourth. For this reason, the prologue on this fourth, Luke, was the main task undertaken by the official Church, and therefore, the prologue to Luke is by far the longest.

---

186. ERH: chapter 57, 19.
187. [The following chapter was replaced in the German version. See 120–23.]
188. [Harnack, "Evangelien-Prologe," 322–341. See Appendix I, 346–50.]

Since no reader will have the text of these prologues, and since few may have heard of them, I here give them in translation. They were written one hundred years or eighty years after the gospels were written. But they were provoked by a fierce controversy which practically raised all the issues of the critics of the last 150 years.[189] The Christians were under fire all the time, from the outside as well as from Jews, Romans, Greeks, Heretics. It is in no way different today. Therefore, the arguments of the four adversaries then may well be listed. They add spice to these "prologues."

1. *The Jews*: The Jews had endless "genealogies." Paul in the first letter to Timothy (1, 4) warns against them. Our prologue to Luke mentions them. The Letter to the Hebrews, on the one hand, concurs with Matthew and Luke in freely quoting the genealogy of Joseph: "It is undeniable that our Lord sprang from the tribe of Judah" (7, 14). On the other hand, the *same* Letter says that Jesus as THE WORD was without a father or mother, and "without a genealogy."[190] The Jews of course concentrated their attack on the illegitimate birth of Jesus. In the first volume of the Acta Patrum Orientalia,[191] we have a very humorous account of a discussion between a Jew and a Christian on this subject, the reading of which can be highly recommended.

2. *The Greeks*: The Greek argument were collected by Celsus who wrote at the time of our prologues. (See my book, "The Christian Future," on this.)[192] But the simplest access to the Greek attitude is in Acts, at the occasion of Paul's defeat in Athens, on the Areopag.[193] To the Greeks, the Resurrection was the stumbling block. They were the people of genius, and genius means the cult of eternal new beginnings, the right of every newborn man to act as a child of nature, to behave as though nothing before had been thought or done. The Resurrection means that we all come after Christ. It is our first technical expression for the Christian Era. By our faith in his Resurrection, Jesus becomes the

---

189. [Harnack dates the prologues to between 160 and 180. His (and ERH's) dating has since found an unwitting echo in J.A.T. Robinson's *Redating the New Testament*, available online, and from Wipf & Stock. See the Introduction, 16–17.]

190. ERH: On this see Leisegang, Logos in Pauly-Wissowa, Real-Encyclopädie, 1079.

191. MDB: The 'Oriental Acts of the Apostles,' an apocryphal book of the early Eastern Church, translated from Ethiopic MSs. [The book cited appears nowhere on the internet. ERH may have meant to cite the *Patrologia Orientalis*, a collection of early writings from the Eastern churches similar to Migne's *Patrologia Latina*; the two works are shelved side-by-side at Dartmouth's Baker-Berry Library.]

192. [No page number is given.]

193. MDB: Acts 17: 22–34.

THE FRUIT OF OUR LIPS, OR WHY FOUR GOSPELS? 263

Roadblock, id est, the Word, under whose impact every one word of the earlier languages is reilluminated and retranslated and filled with new and deeper meaning. The term of a Christian Era was formulated in 530 of our era first, by a monk who was tired of quoting the Roman emperors for his history. This man, Dionysius Exiguus, said for the first time: Anno Domini, instead. That is, he applied the inner Christian vision of the new Aeon, to the outer world. Anybody today who says A.D. exploits the original term "resurrection," in its secular application. In other words, our modern academic world no longer is Greek, for this one reason that it believes, for all practical purposes, in the beginning of a new era, by the resurrection.

But the Greeks of Paul's days lived from Genius to Genius, or as Luke said, "to the latest new thing" (Acts 17, 21). The Apostle Paul tried to accommodate them by making a speech in which he politely stressed all the agreement between him and the Athenians first, and mentioned {the ridicule and scandal, the} resurrection in the last sentence only.[194] Whereupon, as might be expected, they scoffed. In the {first chapter of the first} Letter to the Corinthians,[195] Paul reviewed his mistake of concealing the conflict to the last and promised to come out with this fundamental difference boldly, from now on. Modern criticism, of course, has denied that Paul could have made this speech. In a monograph of 1939 by Dibelius (Heidelberg Academy) on Luke,[196] this Athenian world has left a lasting monument of its truly Greek faith and incapacity to understand the very meaning of the resurrection. Any reader who wishes to learn about the method and the right[197] of Biblical Criticism, should try to read Dibelius' argument; it should be translated and made a textbook study in Sunday Schools. It is a shining example of the Greek mind. This is its logic: Paul has not made the speech. It is too cleverly composed. Luke has invented it and composed it. And—O wonder—the speech was not a failure and a slip as we all have thought, but it was—because it was so truly Greek—a great success! Paul did not change his mind from this experience with the so highly recommended "adjustment" to one's audience. So, Dibelius, on the one hand, construes an invention by Luke, Paul's truest disciple, and on the other—a success of this "invented" speech, in real history!

194. [This passage is in the 1954 typescript, but not in the 1944 typescript, so it is probably an addition from 1946.]
195. MDB: 1 Cor 1:22–23.
196. [Dibelius, "Paulus," 3–56. See Appendix I, 323–24.]
197. [Perhaps: *rightness*.]

This is very Greek because the Greeks live by literature, by thought, and all the time they evaluated[198] "ideas" more than successive and consecutive progress. They played with everything, to the point where young men served as girls to their teachers. The love of man and man, woman and woman, was transferred from the mind to the bodies, in Greece quite logically since ideas were more real to them than any other order. When Ideas reign supreme, we forget ourselves. In the realm of ideas, a man may have motherly or bridal feelings or thoughts. In fact, we all have. But in the realm of reality, this is perversion. The Resurrection by which THE WORD sacrificed his genius to his obedience, made these Platonists and Alkibiadesses furious. {Mr. Dibelius is their offspring. He does not understand that Paul recognized his "Athenian" style as a mistake.}

3. *The Romans*: The Romans although helpless against the Greek and the Jewish arguments, allowing for homosexuality among the educated with a shrug, and believing in the lasting divisions of the clans, as the Hebrews, had their own grudge against the new faith: The destruction of their Sky World, of their Augustus as the Center of the Cosmic Order. The Christians were rebels. They did not worship the Gods of whose various cults the cult of Caesar was the coping stone. The Christians rejected any such visible coping stone. Instead, they worshiped their corner stone. That is, they began exactly on the opposite end from where the worshippers in the temples started. The cornerstone is down in the crypt; the coping stone hangs high up in the center of the vault, above us. Virgin birth, resurrection, keystone, were and are the stumbling blocks for the Jewish, the Greek, the Roman faith.

4. *The Heretics*: The Heretics from within were impatient. They were loathe to be reminded of the past dark ages. They felt superior to Jews, Greeks, Romans. They were sure that the meeting with the WORD, the RISEN, the CORNERSTONE, had given them a completely new nature. The Heretics were sure that they never would fabricate genealogies of "daughters of the Revolution," or "Royal Descent"; they were sure that they never would, from idealism, transgress the ten commandments; and they saw no difference between the invisible cornerstone in the crypt, down in the catacombs, in humiliation, and the visible coping stone of the Church Triumphant, high up in splendor and power. The one hundred percent nationalists, the André Gides and Prousts, the People who equated Christ and Hitler—all these types of naïve progressives were the heretics. They were trapped by their naïve

198. [Perhaps: *valued.*]

conviction that they themselves no longer had to fear a relapse into the shortcomings of clannishness, {of} Genius, and {of} the cult of *success*.

Against the genealogies, the geniuses with their ideas, the power politicians, and the naïve believers in progress without the risk of relapse, the prologues reiterated the necessity of the four gospels. For they showed that they all knew of each other and intended to create a "series." The prologue of Marc calls this creating of a series quite literally "adseruit," "he formed a series," Marc added the second link of the chain. Hence, we have proved that our oldest tradition conceives of the gospels not as rivals but as a *series*.[199]

That this series is in process, and emerges, in every one of its links or members or cells, from the very depth of the error which it overcomes, we have seen. This "series" character of all four gospels together permeates, as a living movement of progress, each gospel, with every one of them beginning at a different angle and proceeding from there to its opposite pole. This could not be recognized as long as the progress in John's book was not admitted; the progress from the word into the flesh, though clearly stated as the topic by John himself was overlooked in favor of some Buddhistlike admiration for the famous first chapter of John. Against this fatal worship of first lines, we related the first chapter to the last chapter and marvelled that the same Eternal Word which was with the Father in the Beginning, had become the man Jesus whose name would fill the libraries of the universe.

Once, the mere awe before the first chapter of John, gives way to an acceptance of the inner movement of this book, it is not at all separated from the three other gospels, in its method. It moves in exactly the same manner from one extreme to the other. Because the extreme opposites coincide in THE WORD: The genealogies prove Jesus to hail from the tribe of Juda; yet he is without father or genealogy. The sayings prove him to be a genius; yet he gives back his genius for the comprehensive Spirit of the Church. The miracles prove him to be a *cosmic force*; yet this cosmic force does not dominate but serves. And the prophecies prove him to be the *Fruit of the Lips* of all the peoples of the world; yet he is *a person, a man in space and time*, the personal friend of John.

---

199. [Harnack praised and seconded De Bruyne's demonstration that these prologues were unique second-century texts. See Appendix I, 346–50. Harnack and De Bruyne's agreement settled the matter for ERH, to whom second-century witness was indeed "proof." Many current editions again date the prologues later, ignoring both de Bruyne and Harnack. See Appendix I, 315.]

And now, the reader may enjoy the old texts, the first authentic statement of the slow, sober, realistic and reluctant birth of the "Four Gospels," the statement of 160 Anno Domini.

Texts:

On Matthew: "Matthew wrote his gospel among the Jews in their language, and he was the first gospel writer."[200]

On Marc: "Marcus followed in the series, he was called the stump-fingered, simply because in relation to the big size of his whole body, his fingers were extravagantly short. He was interpreter to Peter. After the passing away of Peter himself he wrote down this very gospel of his in the province of Italy." ("And with this gospel, he proceeded to Egypt and became the first bishop of Alexandria" but this last sentence seems to be of a later vintage.)

On Luke: (This prologue begins differently because Marcion used the text of this gospel and, at the same time, he said it had fallen down from heaven and was not written by Luke. Hence, the first word is *"Estin"* this Luke," that means *"The facts about Luke are these*: This, then, is the text of the lengthiest prologue which had to contradict the rather flattering contention of the heretics that the gospel according to Luke was not written by a mortal man.)

"The facts about Luke are these: He was from Antioch and a Syrian, a physician in his profession. He had become a student of the apostles and later accompanied Paul, until Paul was martyred, a servant of the Lord with singleness of purpose, unmarried, without offspring in his eighty-fourth year falling asleep in the province of Boeotia, full of holy inspiration.

"This man Luke found already gospels in existence, one which Matthew had written in Palestine, the other by Marc in Italy; moved on by the holy spirit he was living in Achaia when he composed this whole gospel. And he himself made this clear in his own prologue that before him others had been writing and that it was necessary for the faithful of Gentile descent to put forth the precise narrative of the economy of salvation, for their protection lest they be led astray by the mythological

---

200. [ERH reconstituted this prologue according to Adolf von Harnack's supposition. See Appendix I, 357-58. MDB referred readers to Robert M. Grant's *Second Century Christianity* "for a translation," even though this essay includes one, however personal; Grant does not use De Bruyne's version of the text, which Harnack praised. See Appendix I, 347.]

tales of the Jews or deceived by arbitrarily selected and baseless speculations miss the truth. As the most necessary element therefore we read in Luke the birth of John the Baptist as John is the beginning of the Good News. For, he became the precursor of the Lord, participated in the organic unfolding of the Good News, in the institution of baptism and in the communication of the spirit. And this order of the economy (of salvation) one of the twelve prophets had foreseen." (This secured the unity with the Old Testament.)

"And so later on the same Luke wrote the Acts of the Apostles. Later John, the apostle, one of the original twelve, wrote "Revelation" on the island of Patmos and after that, his Gospel."

On John: "The gospel of John was published and given to the churches by John still in his lifetime, as Papias, a beloved disciple of John has reported. And the gospel was written down under the dictation of John, and it was written down correctly."[201]

The Word Himself

We are not studying the history either of the Church or of the world. We are laying the foundations for a history of the human spirit.

The spirit had moved the chieftains and the priests and the poets and the prophets; however, they all were driven by this power without being able to account for this driving power. For this reason, men had been driven by the spirit to cross purposes. And the confusion of tongues, and the incessant war between these tongues had become dominant.

This was changed by the Man who paused. He halted the mere flow of talkative, newsmongering, mystical, or practical humanity. So what? He saw that in separation, they were evil and poisonous even though in themselves they were highly elaborate and efficient. Jesus did not say that poetry or magic or ritual or prophecy were not excellent. He knew that they were, and how well he knew, he proved by his creative inventiveness of new ritual, his poetical genius of the parable, his effortless superiority to obsessions and demonies, his prophetic insight into the future of the world's history. But with all these four rivers of speech filled to the brim, he emptied himself of

---

201. [ERH's translation follows de Bruyne in most respects, Harnack in some, and at times departs from both.]

all of them.²⁰² He, the harvest of all times,²⁰³ decided to change into the seed of a future completely protected against mere times. The old dividedness of the human soul by these canyons wrought in us through the flow of these rivers of speech was to cease.

He placed himself between the era of these canyons and our own lives lest we too were swayed by the avalanche blasts, the obsession which drives all unbelievers unknowingly forward by the mere inertia of their particular jargon of thought.

To this day, we have nothing to carry us but namegiving speech, and cosmic writing, natural poetry, and prophetic vision. We may call them the mores and science, and the arts, and politics. But this is only a slight difference in terms, compared with antiquity in which the mores were tattoos enounced at the tribe's assemblies, the science carved as "runes" in the temple's cosmic body, the art consecrated by one of the muses, and political progress and change prophesied in danger of life.

The "time-cups" formed on these four wavelengths, of the "oyez," "harken," "listen, be silent," in all law giving assemblies of the "contemplate," "measure," "enter," "ascend" of all the cosmic temples, the "sing, tell, say, adorn, glorify," of all the nine muses, the "thou shalt tell them, warn, flee, expect, fall, prostrate, emerge, promise, hope," of all the prophecies, these times were merged by Jesus. For this reason, the Liberals could define him as an artistic genius, the psychoanalysts, a tribal ritualist, the Jews, a prophet, the Fundamentalists a cosmic force, during the last century of critical dissection. The mind's anatomy could find those elements within him, of course. As he had to atone the division of these four "offices" of human speech, he obviously must master them, himself. But all were simply the abutments against which he pressed the new life. He rejected his four offices in as far as they were the dead ends of ancient ritual, cult, prophecy, poetry.²⁰⁴ Having demonstrated that he could heal, rule, teach, sing, he dismissed all this as not good enough. And in this dismissal of his own role of harvest, he made the end into the beginning. His whole life is like an unconquerable wall, inscribed: Never again. The blind avalanche of single-track reasoning lost its momentum by his intervention.

The humanity of the final man is in our four offices as solons, scientists, artists, prophets. Our divinity is in renouncing every one of these offices

202. MDB: Phil 2:7-8.
203. MBD: 1 Pet 1:23.
204. ERH: {"a biography of Jesus cannot be provided... He was bringing into being a new order and working out a purpose—in complete isolation... The future order, which it was the purpose of Jesus to bring into being, depended upon what he said and did, and finally upon his death." Hoskyns and Davey, *The Riddle*, p. 248f.}

when they separate mankind. Jesus gave up his own spirit lest anything pre-Christian, preceding him, should enter the new creature. He placed himself between the past and the future, and nothing of the man Jesus was allowed to enter the new order of his second body, the Church. People who speak of his sacrifice, often do not understand this. He interposed his whole life, from beginning to end, and not just his last day, between the past and our era. His own life was used up in the house-cleaning. He volunteered to have his own flesh belong to the old eon. For this reason, it is appropriate that we speak of the risen Christ as the first cell of the New Body of our own humanity.[205]

Jesus is the first name of a new language of mankind. Our sacrifice of our own private, professional, accidental nomenclature is our contribution to the common and universal and single and unanimous new tongue founded on and in his name. The Letter to the Hebrews simply says so: "your sacrifice consists in your admitting that his name precedes all other words of your vocabulary."[206] Now, the crux of Christendom, in our days, is its denominations, its splits, sects, churches, schisms, confessions, religious squabbles. Neither Mr. Rockefeller nor I nor anybody else can see anything good in these fissions. At best they seem Donquichotic, at worst, hateful and baleful. But behind the denominations there looms a bigger issue, the issue of all speech of our era. It is one thing to repudiate the denominations, and a second step to refuse the name of a Christian. The Word cannot come into the world unless it is ushered in by us, into our native tongue and locality, in each age.[207] And this acceptance of the Cross is a scandal and is ridiculous, each time. All natural minds, the Greek, and the Roman, and the Hebrew, and the Gothic, hate the idea that a new language should start right here and now, a new tongue which empties their great literatures and codes and manuals of science, and Emily Posts, of their ultimate value. Since this is exactly what the new name "Christian" at our letter head does, the four "anti-gospel" parties all declare the very mentioning of the name of Jesus Christ to be bad taste. As we have seen, it is bad taste; they declare it to be unscientific; as we have seen, it is unscientific; they declare it to be blasphemous. As we have seen, it is blasphemous. And they declare it to be inconsistent; as we have seen, it is inconsistent as it is preached in a new tongue every day and every year and every century.

---

205. [The earliest typescript, probably from 1944, ends here. In the 1954 typescript, a typed heading, "Revelation," was added over the following section, but later crossed out.]

206. [ERH: 13, 15.]

207. [The 1964 German version does not include this passage on the denominations.]

The name of the Word is our sacrifice. And if we are too timid to mention this name for the sake of taste, of science, of good feeling, of systematic consistency, we exclude ourselves from the new eon and from the crucial language of free men. We prefer to be B.C., and we soon will boast that there is no A.D.

The present-day crisis, then, is between the deep longing of all of us to drop the denominations and the high necessity to confess the scandal and the ridicule of the Cross. The Word of Mankind will remain a helpless stammering and a vile repetition of dead words if we, for the sake of taste, manners, science, system, decline to respond to our sponsor, to understand his stand, and to dare the world by the disreputable Words, Christ, Christians.

If Jesus is the "*Logos*," the Word, we must become, as the Greeks called it, "*homo-logos*," which means of the same Word. We must revamp our words by making him explicitly the Keyword of all our own words—and everybody must do this, in person. The simple reason for this iron law of speech in our era can now be stated; when people speak or act, the fruits of their words and acts are hidden from them. We all, in weak moments, think that we can get away with empty or lying or conventional phrases. And we like to imagine that such words or deeds have no consequences. We say: "I was driven to say this; I was motivated by fear or self-interest or pity." And this explanation seems to excuse us. But what do we actually aver, by those statements? We aver that we are mere cogs on the wheel of blind fate. For all these three common explanations of our ways of talking connect our sayings with some "reason," some cause or motive which hails from the past.

All our excuses are facing backward. Jesus' sayings are all forward-looking. Every one of them made sense solely in the light of the future. Not one of them was "caused" by any precedent, convention, excuse, cause, reason, motive; to the contrary, all his antecedents advised against every one of his acts and sayings. He said so and he did so because he could not help creating a future different from the past. As Ambrose Vernon has put it: Jesus went to the cross because he could not help it.[208] "By their fruits, ye shall know them" is not true of us, but of our Lord. Now in his crucifixion, the clash of backward justification by precedent, motives, environment, piety, with the "forward" love, is totally visible. He who lives under the cross knows that he is not excused by all his rational, social, natural, physical propensities. He knows that of course, man is a coward, man is a conformist, man is patterned and conditioned. But after Christ, he also knows that this is one half of the ledger only. The heavier the pressure of conditions and prejudice and tradition and nature, the more necessary that we should feel

208. [See note, 127.]

THE FRUIT OF OUR LIPS, OR WHY FOUR GOSPELS? 271

provoked to break these chains of mere causation. Now, people have made Spartacus rebellions, and nasty doggerels, and psalms of repentance before Christ. The new law which he proclaimed was that one's own life and words were the *starting places* for a new incarnation. Facing forward, every one of his acts was a seed to bear fruit in unending times to come. Not one of his acts could be understood as well by his contemporaries as it can by us who see all the implications.

Implications become explicit through the lapse of time. And Jesus was the first man to prove this by not giving in to any one temptation to reap the harvests of the past as the tempter offered him to do.[209] We all can skim the milk for the cream in our time. We all can get big salaries if we take the jobs which are organized already and therefore paid. But man's life as God's poem, or society's scapegoat, or the earnest of the spirit, as Paul called it,[210] has no place in the budget or any going concern of society. Any man who is a child of God is supernumerary. There is no place for him in the surveys, questionnaires, statistics, because he is so unlabeled as the child in the manger for whom the innkeeper had no room. How could he? Jesus was unforeseen, unpredictable. Yet, get this well, he was foretold and visible. The ordinary coward wants to be told by going to the quacks of the soul that he is predictable, and yet he does not wish to be looked through[211] by his neighbors. He is secretive and superstitious at the same time.

> Unforeseen, yet foretold,
> visible yet unpredictable,

is the man who lives in our era.

> Predictable yet concealed,
> Not promised yet foreseen,

is the sterile life.

Now the reader although unaccustomed to do so in our world of speechless thinking, may by now be ready to analyze the four terms in this "fork"[212] by which we predicate some general truth about speech and the power of speech over our lives. One term is "foretold," the other is unpredictable, in the Christian life between past and future. The other "fork" is "predictable" and "unpromised." The dead soul, to take up the latter "fork"

---

209. [Perhaps: *the tempter offered him.*]
210. MBD: Eph 1:14.
211. [Perhaps: *seen through.*]
212. [Perhaps: *in these forks*, plural as in the following sentences).]

first, is easily understood. He follows the line of least resistance. The psychologist whom he consults, comforts him by saying: "Well, your behavior is natural. You are afraid. You are sexually restless, etc. etc." The client is glad to hear that anybody would act like him, under the circumstances. *This man is predictable.* If you knew his pressures and urges, you would always know what he will do next. He is, however, so repetitive that he is not expected or promised or heralded because no new contribution can be hoped for from him. We know this type of a man since the days of Adam. He is, therefore, very anxious to remain unknown to us, in his private religion, private opinions, private affairs. People like to call this "privacy," their "personal life"—or they lisp the formula, "On the personal level."

Of course, this is a mere way of divorcing the potential powers for doing unpredictable deeds and saying unpredictable words, from our highly predictable actual behavior. This phrase "on the personal level," is a wonderful way of cheating oneself. A person is a man who as far as he is personal, lets the truth shine right through him. The term "person" means to let shine through, to become transparent, to stand revealed and to be representative. Eisenhower has no life on the personal level because he represents the American G.I. There his person is, stands, lives, comes to realization—and nowhere else.[213]

The constant abuse of the term "person" for unused freedom, concealed opinions, private affairs, forces us today to avoid the word. It is sick. It means solely, to most people, that they have some secrets to themselves. This is their balm and comfort; for it means: "although we are predictable and although we do follow the law of averages, yet you do not know everything about me. Hence, you are not totally my master and boss." A man who was both, completely known and completely predictable, would be obviously, in the hands of the psychologist and demagogue one hundred percent. The predictable man must at least feebly try to remain unknown.

There is, however, another way. You may be one hundred per cent known, for all your handicaps, disadvantages, as Jesus was, and yet remain free and unpredictable. He clearly could be seen to be without office, without beauty, without power, and without family. And he deceived them, not because they did not know him on a personal level, but because they did not believe that he, of all people, was the promised one, the one man whom the sages had foretold as the one truly free man who could be nothing but seed of a future, first word of a second incarnation.[214] Jesus was not invisible but he was foretold, promised, as the harvest of all the sighs of all men of all

---

213. [Perhaps: *comes to actualization*, or *becomes real*. 1964: *From 1942 to 1945 Eisenhower had no 'private life.'* See 128.]

214. [1964: *Isa 40–57.*]

THE FRUIT OF OUR LIPS, OR WHY FOUR GOSPELS?   273

ages in their caves of predetermination, fate, scientific predictions. He was a person in that he let the spirit become transparent. And on his face, the reflection of God's freedom to create the world outshone the blood, sweat, and tears which the mortal man expired.[215]

We speak of the three persons of the trinity because they are the three ways by which the full power of God is reflected and leaves their mark on us. "Three persons" are not three disconnected individuals. The three persons of the trinity do not have to be found on any "personal level." {They are the three faces on which God shines forth.} They are the father, the son, and the spirit. And in the son, God conquers the death of our soul by which she {would have to} live predictably and concealed. In the son, God stands revealed and promised.

The Son restores then the proper order between words spoken and lives lived. Words should be orders given, promises made. Lives should be orders carried out and promises fulfilled. This, we saw, had been the essential aim of all speech and ritual, since man spoke. The purely indicative usage of our textbooks and "thinkers" is mere grave-digging or after-thought, after the events made possible by speech. Jesus showed that all words spoken before him had challenged him, ordered him into existence in as far as they were real prayer, real longing, real prophecy, fruitful imagination. And so he fulfilled them all. He revealed what we do when we speak: By speaking as it requires listening,} we believe in seed and harvest, promise and fulfillment, command and report. We believe that in the beginning was the Word, and in the end, there shall be incarnation.[216]

{And this we believe [. . .] by opening our lips, by speaking at all. Anybody who enters upon the ocean of speech has believed in the truth. We have believed before we speak. That we speak is the fruit of our faith in the Word which comes forth out of the mouth of the Godhead; we need [*not ask for*] denominations and their accounts of doctrine. Many believe [*who decline to be*] labeled as believers. But it is true that the many do not think that they believe. The veil is not lifted for most men; they do not see what they do when they speak. They speak *about* God and ignore the fact that God must have spoken from the beginning if their own words shall make any sense. Scientists, especially, are ignorant of the man-creating, peace-creating, science-creating character of speech. Their inveiglement is responsible for the crucial sacrifice, for the necessity of placing the name of Jesus in front and ahead of our own words.}

215. MDB: 2 Cor 4:6.
216. [The following section is partly illegible, written in smeared pencil and then in ink.]

117   EPILOGUE

F A I T H   a n d   T I M E.

11/15/65 — Note- This section not in basic set when handed to me but in a separate folder. Also not in German text. ccc

Since the New Era and in as far as we enter upon it, ~~XXXXXXXXXXXXXX~~ we know again that which the kings, the priests, the prophets, the poets had forgotten and do forget time and again: that to speak also measn to hear, that to think also means to thank, that to call names also means to be called names, that to create also means to be created.

                    The complete equilibrium between my commandeering and my obeying position in the universe is destroyed by all those who crave power or science or art or authority for their sake. In our era, the king never is without the slave, the judge never without the culprit the scientists never without their consciences, the priest never without his own layman's soul. In our era, man is not without wife, hoary head not without child in his heart, for the cruxified one always has spoken to us before we have thought, always has suffered before we have made suffer, always has obeyed before we have commanded, always has been a song before we have opened our mouth to sing.
Man no longer is alone . Well , this would be an empty logical statement if this pagan word "Man" in its abstract singular of One Man was not exploded in the "Ichthys", the Son of Man of the old covenant and the King of the new covenant, the lowly one , Jesus and the exalted one, Christ, disproves that God created single atoms, called with the abstract collective M A N. We are not all General Issue of one animal species. We are every one of us a species and together we do constitute/~~this~~ a species out of innumerable species, species specierum.~~this~~; this is not a specious pun. No, it is the simple fact that outside the Christian era, we are particularized into the shabby halfness of one sex, one generation one place, one class, one intelligence, one individual separatedness. Inside the Christian era, every one hearer of the word who links up with one

Epilogue: Faith and Time[217]

Since the New Era, and in as far as we enter upon it, we know again that which the kings, the priests, the prophets, the poets had forgotten, and do forget time and again: that to speak also means to hear, that to think also means to thank, that to call names also means to be called names, that to create also means to be created.

The complete equilibrium between my commandeering[218] and my obeying position in the universe is destroyed by all those who crave power or science or art or authority for their sake. In our era, the king never is without the slave, the judge never without the culprit, the scientists never without their consciences, the priest never without his own layman's soul. In our era, man is not without wife, hoary head without child in his heart, for the crucified one has always spoken to us before we have thought, always has suffered before we have made suffer, always has obeyed before we have commanded, always has been a song before we have opened our mouth to sing.

Man no longer is alone. Well, this would be an empty logical statement if this pagan word "Man" in its abstract singular of One Man was not exploded in the "Ichthys," the Son of Man of the old covenant and the King of the new covenant—the lowly one, Jesus, and the exalted one, Christ—disproves that God created single atoms called with the abstract collective M A N. We are not all General Issue of one animal species. We are every one of us a species and together we do constitute a species out of innumerable species, *species speciorum*. This is not a specious pun. No, it is the simple fact that outside the Christian era, we are particularized into the shabby halfness of one sex, one generation one place, one class, one intelligence, one individual separatedness. Inside the Christian era, every hearer of the word who links up with one single underdog, any one team composed of speaker and listener, of battered victim and baptized good Samaritan, together make epoch.

To give a very simple example. If every judge in our courts would only judge one single criminal case and solve it by living with the culprit as long as it was necessary, our prisons would be replaced by an "eschatological" substitute. Now this sounds ridiculous. And yet, our attempt of probation points precisely in this direction. For, probation obviously does not work—all reports agree on this—unless the condemned person is able to move into a changed environment. At least, one person, from now on, must be seen by

---

217. [A hand-written note by Clinton Gardner dated 11/15/65: *This section was not in the basic set when handed to me but in a separate folder. Also not in German text.* CCG However, the last page of the 1954 typescript is numbered *116*, and this section is headed *117*. See 184.]

218. [Probably: *commanding*.]

him he did not meet before, and probably, at least one person whom he used to meet before, should be expunged from his daily routines. Thus, though the judge himself may as yet remain on his bench, he in fact whenever he passes sentence, does expect that somewhere in our society somebody will join the culprit and make his probation period meaningful. But when this actually happens—and I do not speak of our overburdened officials of probation but of good Samaritans who do this once but with their whole heart—when it does happen, it does make epoch.[219] Why? Because one man has conceived of this crime and this trial as addressed to him in person, and to nobody else. That is he will not speak of "society" having to foot the bill; he will not plead with the City Fathers, he will say: this means me.

Has this anything to do with the history of the human race through the Christian era? It has indeed. For, 900 years ago, this program was outlined. Then, the Church entered the world and made epoch by changing all our criminal law for the first time. And the motto simply ran: A judge cannot be a judge unless he discovers in his own heart the wrinkle from which he, too, might have become guilty of the deed confessed to him by one repentant soul.

My proposal about probation hails right from this sentence of the Great Confessional of 1050.[220] And of course, this book's wisdom comes right down from the New Testament as here all men receive their individual character in due time out of the whole process of creating the One Man out of us all. Who knows his tomorrow? We shall be who we shall be, is the truth of men led by their creator through the night of their own preconceptions about themselves. Certainly it is a terrifying truth that we shall be like HIM who shall be who he shall be, in the Old Testament's terms.[221] Therefore no man can face up to this "We shall be who we shall be" to this endless freedom unless his bond with all men holds firm unless inside his bond with all men holds firm, inside one era, one creation, one communion of mutual commitment and mutual reliance.

No one alone has the capability of saying "I shall be who I shall be," without being ridiculous, or the devil who is so many forms that he has to call himself "Legion."[222] Yet, if he says that we all together are the Son

---

219. MDB: This is not as farfetched as it may sound, for some years ago, the victim of an attempted robbery and shooting, a professor in a theological seminary, took the convicted assailant into his home.

220. MDB: *Out*, 515–66.

221. [Franz Rosenzweig's and Martin Buber's translation of the tetragrammaton *YHWH* (Exodus 3:14).]

222. ERH: This treacherous search for many forms is described in my book *The Multiformity of Man*. MDB: Mark 5:9.

who shall become as divine as the Father, he will find inside this history his own line which just he and he alone is asked to speak. The "We" who shall be who they shall be, do not consist of dumb animals. These "We" cannot contain anybody who remains just anybody. Everybody must enter inside and into the we in his appointed hour, in his power of becoming somebody, this definite person. This strange composition of the unified Man out of persons was described by Augustine in his commentary on Man's creation (de Gen. ad lit. I, 10) as "the breath of one's calling by which in secret the divine Wisdom speaks to that creature whose principle consists in having to turn around and to face about."[223]

When the man faces about, he sees the woman inside himself; when the judge faces about, he sees the criminal inside himself. When the king faces about, he sees the slave inside himself. All this is obscured among us as today, the servant has to face about to see the boss inside himself, the public has to face about and see the government inside itself. Aye, even the children fall prey to modern education unless they face about and discover the teacher inside themselves.

We have seen the gospels as phases in the process by which this gospel of the perfect man marched to the tribes first, to the Romans second, to the Saints third, to the Greeks last. And because it went through four different forms, it became free from any one of them, as {free as} their Lord, as the GOOD NEWS itself, {had been free.}

In a book written at that very moment, the achievement of the four gospel writers was declared impossible, and we {have} quoted the paragraph from the Book of Henoch as this question of writing books, in matters of life and death, is our question, and the trouble of any age. The Evangelists {were} condemned {in advance} in these words: "Men were not created [...] to give confirmation to their good faith with pen and ink."[224] That is {an impressive} statement. And all the critics who have reduced the gospel to one source would make out the writer of this "Source" {of our gospels} as a fallen angel indeed.

I would side with the Book of Henoch if we had one gospel only. But we have four. And we have four as relay runners in the race of the gospel from its Marathon, from the Cross, to {our} Athens, {id est, into} the world of men. In its fourfoldness, the written gospel is the luminous track left in the dark from Christ on Golgotha to the Church of James in Jerusalem, to the Church of Peter in Rome, to the Churches of Paul all over the Gentile

---

223. [The Paulist Press issued the first English translation of *De Genesi* in 1982; the text may be downloaded at: https://bibleandbookcenter.com/read/genesi-ad-litteram/.]

224. ERH: Henoch 69:10. [ERH probably owes this citation to Edgar J. Goodspeed. See note, 214, and Appendix I, 324–25.]

World and {finally to John and} to the Island of Patmos, this eternal exile of any coming Christianity within the world {if} it just is {as of} today. The four gospels form a line and the single gospel is one point on that line which begins beyond all of them, and {which} ends at a point, Patmos, which points beyond all organized Christianity of its own times.

It is at this moment that we understand the full meaning of the emphasis given by the evangelists to {their} servicing[225] the Word, at the specific hour: They have never said: written by John, Marc, etc. We to this day are required if we are not cynical, to say "according to St. Matthew," "according to St. Marc." This, I well know, is not much respected today. To me, it seems to bear out all the principles of our undertaking. First the gospel is Jesus himself. But {he} is so compelling that rivers of life stream from him and compell men to write down the Good News. Four men in a succession of fourty years"accord" and this according is the premise for any one of the four gospels. He who because of his literary or philological erudition begins from one of the four {only}, must end by denying that there ever was any gospel. For the gospel proves itself simply by moving four evangelists through four decades. If only one man wrote a book, he would be the fallen angel of the Book of Henoch. The membership of all four writers inside this Body of Time—which with a dusty name we remember barely as a living Body because we think of it as an organisation in space—this Body of Time consists of a great poem, of which Christ is the first line and the gospel writers are the next lines. But it is all one song.

In the new Era of Christianity, men are hours, and the bricks of the temples of old now have become days or hours represented by living souls and peoples. This vision of a Body through Time seems to transcend the logicians' logic. Fortunately, we live by it every one of us, just the same. We constitute, all the faithful, Christ in our own time, or there never has been any Christianity. But if this is so, then the gospel-writers did not write books by themselves or as individuals, but they relayed the message at the hour in which they were called. Because time was of the essence, the ink was purified and the paper was vivified. By the term "according," the symphony of all the voices explained each individual writer's movement.

If you hold that Dante's *Divine Comedy* was written verse after verse, and no verse {in it} related to the end and from the beginning, then you must judge the gospels as separate entities. However, you then must forgive me if I am not interested in your views, because you prove yourself a complete barbarian in matters of creation. A great symphony first exists as

---

225 [Probably: *service to.*]

a whole and later it unfolds in its single movements. Quacks may patch four movements together; that, however, entitles us to call them quacks.

The whole test of Christianity is that it binds all the times together. Hence, the four gospels first are one before they are distributed over Fourty years. You may laugh at this proposition. But this is the faith of the Founder of our Era; it is the faith of the four evangelists and it is the only faith deserving the majestic name of FAITH at all.

We are sown into one field of force which is time. And the runners of the Marathon, the torchbearers in this relay race, break through the iron ring of each cycle of culture, each epoch of a civilization, each period of one partial environment. By their fruits, ye shall ye know them, and by nothing but their fruits. Sown in an incredible and incredulous situation, by their fruits they outgrow this given situation and stake out the wider heaven of one race through all epochs and all times. Thus, the millennia of Spengler, the 20 odd civilizations of Toynbee, the parts of the *Cambridge Universal History*, are transformed willy-nilly into the Chapters of One book, into mile-stones of one Road. But without the {gospel}, there would be neither one book nor one road. For at every moment, the men of their own times and their own civilization and their own culture or their own revolution delight in their self-importance and scorn any idea of getting outside one's own time, as an insult to common sense. The gospel always is the common sense of tomorrow, never the common sense of yesterday.

But, for the same reason, there is only one gospel at all times. If you travel through the four decades of the four gospels, you have identified the unity of the gospel and when {after that} you meet the people who live and die to their own times only, you may not convince them that there is a Christian Era, but you may know that there can be.

Appendix F
Jesus the Illiterate
(1963?)

{TO [SECTION] IV, FRUCHT *der Lippen* (*Fruit of the Lips*), last piece}

A WELL-KNOWN BIBLICAL CRITIC has promoted the theory that Jesus could neither read nor write. He "proves" it by the story of the woman taken in adultery, in which the Lord writes with his finger in the sand. This gesture, in Goodspeed's opinion, was invented to overcome the embarrassment over the fact that Jesus had left nothing in writing; thanks to this story, people were able to say, "You see, he did know how to write!"[1]

Even for a biblical critic, this is a record-breaking achievement. Yet in a negative sense, I quite agree with him: our Lord neither wanted to write, nor should he have written. Though there is no need for us to make excuses, there is no harm in an explanation—and one thing is easy enough to understand: his four gospels are the fruit of his unspoiled nature. The disciples knew that he would only come to life again *in them*, not in parchment or papyrus. That is why we may now take the liberty of connecting the Lord's faith that this knowledge would force them to eternalize him, with their knowledge that he himself believed categorically that he must remain oral.

So for a few minutes, I beg my readers to seek Christ's greatness not in his lordship over the Apostles (and over us), neither in his life nor in his death, but rather in his wisdom in allowing the twelve to praise God in His temple from the crucifixion to the Apostles' council in Jerusalem. This faith of Jesus' in the future perseverance of the disciples is far greater than his own path to the cross, and we rob ourselves of his *doxa*, of his true glory, when we speak of the evangelists Matthew, Mark, Luke, and John, instead of Jesus' One Gospel from the mouths of his various disciples. Of course the four evangelists are innocent of the modern abuse which claims that they are authors with Suhrkamp, Rowohlt, the Württemberg Bible Institute, or any other publisher. The word "gospel" is in the singular in all of them and only the one addition "according to Matthew," "according to Mark," and so on, differentiates the editions; it is one and the same gospel. Biblical criticism has torn the One Gospel from both Jesus and the evangelists and made

---

1. [*It was probably introduced into John at this point (7:53) to show that Jesus knew how to write, a thing the Jews had questioned his ability to do in 7:15.* Goodspeed, *Problems*, 108.]

five school-books out of it: first a sermon by Jesus, and then four different books. The only alternative we have as orthodox believers is to recognize the womb of speech from which the "gospel" sprang some 1,900 years ago.

When the Lord said, "Stay, do not scatter!" something happened that we must somehow comprehend as the tilled soil of the Word; it may help to compare that "something" to events at Karl August's court at Tierfurt, Henry the Lion's at Braunschweig, and Augustus's at Rome.[2] Eleven men between the ages of twenty and forty were condemned (called, chosen, selected, appointed, or damned) to live together from the day of the crucifixion to some distant, unknown date. They were given no mandate to convert India, China, England, or Spain; they were to remain in Jerusalem, bored stiff, and be subject to the hate of those who had persecuted Jesus. It is hard to imagine anything harder to understand, and yet this heavy load was lifted only with the Apostle's Council in something like 42 A.D.—at least a decade after Golgotha. After that, the majority of the Apostles were allowed to leave Jerusalem for the first time.

Their suffering in Jerusalem, for a period that was three times as long as the earthly activity of their Lord, would have been senseless had it not been necessary for salvation. But if it was in fact necessary for salvation, it deserves our attention. God demands no meaningless suffering, although it is true that suffering is a prerequisite for all unhoped-for fruits of faith; the cross treads a fine line between animal cruelty and divine redemption. So we may be sure that we must spend as much time reflecting on those nine years from the crucifixion to the first church council as it takes for the truth of redemption to radiate from those pains.

The Lord's command created in the disciples the leisure, the thoughtfulness, the freedom, the time spent in expectation, to be transformed into the womb of a new birth. Who was in Jerusalem then? I need mention here only the sons of Zebedee, Peter, Andrew, Jesus' family, Mary Magdalene, and Thomas. The hearts of all burned to proclaim the Lord of all their hearts. While the most recent "scholar"[3] has the first gospel composed in 84 AD in a Jewish community of the diaspora,[4] no scholarship is necessary to see that

---

2. [Karl August, Grand Duke of Saxe-Weimar-Eisenach (1757–1828), and Henry the Lion, Duke of Saxony and Bavaria (1129–1195) were, like Caesar Augustus, noted for the artistic and intellectual brilliance of their courts.]

3. ERH: Gilpatrick. [David Bade suggests that ERH refers to George Dunbar Kilpatrick; the 1946 edition of his *The Origins of the Gospel according to St. Matthew* is still in Dartmouth's Baker/Berry library.]

4. ERH: Chapman called this the greatest aberration imaginable of all biblical criticsm's aberrations. At least the confusion does us the service of interpreting Matthew's setting and audience pretty well, even if it sets it 50 years too late.

between the crucifixion and the council, in that long night when God was far from them, the fierce blaze in the believers' hearts raised a column of fire for Christ: the Hebrew plea from Old Testament references, which we know in its Greek translation as the gospel according to Matthew. Matthew was the first to say what Sidney[5] cried out to writers 1,600 years after Christ—"Look into your heart and write"—because the Lord had created his heart anew and created it to fulfillment. Judas Iscariot having been provisionally replaced, Matthew was one of the Twelve, so his scriptorium and quill stood under the aegis of his co-disciples, most of whom were stronger in spirit, however much weaker they may have been in script. His gospel clung to the old Bible in that he patterned it after the five books of Moses and wrote it in Hebrew.[6] But it looks into the heart of the future by placing Jesus at the end of the times since Abraham and at the beginning of a vast expanse of time.

In the face of the simply childish claim that the first Christians expected the imminent end of the world—a prank that has allowed theologians from 1892 until today to portray the Apostles and their time as dim, dumb, and superstitious—we must emphasize the form of Matthew's gospel. He read the slow foundation of God's people Israel in the five books of Moses, and in five parts his gospel testifies to the appearance of the Son of God, the head of the New Israel. How could he have made that claim five minutes before the end of the world? The early believers and the believers of today are always in exactly the same position of believing the end of the world possible, even probable, if the nations continue as heretofore.

It is only *because* of Jesus' crucifixion, *because* of the stoning of Stephen, *because* of the beheading of Paul that the world still goes on. Only sacrifices rescue the world. 146 years before Christ's birth, the great Scipio wept at the fall of Carthage because he foresaw the future fall of Rome; compared to him, people so intoxicated with the idea of endless duration as to declare the suicide of the white race or of Europe impossible, are just windbags.[7] Those suicides already lie far behind us! The trumpets of nationalism sound only in cemeteries while a new humanity is assembling—that is, if humanity will only listen to the doctor who explains the gravity of her current disease.

Like their Master, the early Christians scented the signs of the world's downfall; it was avoided—and only by a hair's breadth—because of those same first Christians! They also tell us that now it's our turn to prevent it. The overwhelming aspect of the church's faith is just this: the incredible depth and

---

5. [Sir Philip Sidney, whose 1591 sonnet "Astrophel and Stella" ends with the words 'Fool,' said my Muse to me, 'look in thy heart and write.']

6. [See the excerpt from Jehoshua Grintz's article in Appendix I, 325–27.]

7. [ERH names the windbags *Bramarbas*, after the braggart soldier in Ludvig Holberg's play, *Jakob von Tyboe*.]

breadth of its sermon and the indescribable patience of its silent expectation. Matthew speaks to you and me today. The time of expectation in Jerusalem is the first attempt to balance the books on the daring attempt to proclaim a new age, and the literary form Matthew chose for his role testifies to the same faith. For him it was worth the effort of invoking centuries of time, a new eon that would be able to compete with all of Jewish history so far.

So it is possible to prove even more conclusively than before that none of the Apostles other than Judas Ischariot expected an Anabaptist kingdom on earth. How does Matthew begin? First he tells of the passage of the emblem of the dove from the people of Israel to Jesus; after that comes the calling of the disciples. The head of a new people not formed by blood descent is appointed. The epoch from the Exodus to John the Baptist, guaranteed by flesh and blood, gives way, with Jesus' baptism in the Jordan, to the people of the dove of the spirit. Ben Gurion, Herzl, and the other Zionists are Christians; they owe their new state of Israel to the dove of the spirit.

The state of Israel replaces the priestly church-state as the proof of the truth of Matthew's vision of history. That is the meaning of Jesus' refusal of Lucifer's suggested program for immediate success, with its three points to solve all social problems. Matthew sets the path from the Lord's mouth to the ears of all believing passers-on through the millennia, the "revealed" continuation of the Good News lived by Christ along which each believing soul is to become a milestone, right at the very beginning of Jesus' ministry. With the fourth chapter of the gospel, the Good News is established for the peaceful Apostles of the first decade (despite the apparent truce, their lack of visible deeds, and their faithful praying in the Temple) as one and the same through the endless length of time. With this chapter, probably begun somewhere around the year 40, Matthew himself indicates that his words will have to be replaced by other versions, other languages, other forms in other places at much later times.[8] The fourth chapter of Matthew has been of interest to biblical critics largely because of the question whether or not the angels actually served Jesus. Those critics shall "have their reward" indeed.[9]

For us this chapter achieves the unity of the history of creation within which the Apostles and the writer Matthew found themselves—and knew themselves to be located! An almost unimaginably long time had passed between Adam and John the Baptist. If the Devil had tempted Jesus successfully, an Anabaptist kingdom like that of Münster would have followed the baptism in the Jordan and have cast its spell for a few years. Matthew, however, makes Jesus' time measurement his own and the Apostles allow

8. [Matt 4: 1–11.]
9. [Matt 6:5, 6:16.]

him to establish the following: at the baptism by John, the same dove that until then had been the emblem of the people of Israel becomes visible over Jesus. He *takes the place* of the people of Israel; his issue will last into the farthest future, just as the people of Israel had existed for at least 1,800 years by then.

With the temptation in the desert this anticipation of immense time becomes the blue-print for Jesus' actions. He may not stoop to magic by weighing, inspiring, or invoking the things of the world; he must instead leave his word free rein to enter the hearts of his listeners. Matthew makes this decision the cornerstone of his Good News. The News is only Good because now every soul is given the freedom [of "*Froh*" and "*Frau*,"] of lords and ladies. The *Dominus* or *Kyrios*—which is what the German word "*Froh*" means—makes all his servants masters. Thanks to Matthew 4, the "servants of the Word" are made equal to their master in the Word. For only the Word shall be his equal as the firstborn of the New Spirit; everything else is the devil's work.

In 1949 Erich Fascher dedicated his *Jesus and Satan* to the fourth chapter of Matthew. That was the time between Hitler's suicide and the "economic miracle."[10] In those four years, during which the scholars and the theologians stopped denying the existence of the devil,[11] it was even possible to talk sense to them—but alas! since the revaluation of the [German] mark[12] the value of the devil has plummeted again. In that four-year Olympiad of Truth from 1945 to 1949, however, Jesus and Satan were once more recognized: the former with his answer of eternal life out of Isaiah 40, and the latter with his word-deed-word-deed-word-deed-word-deed-action-program for the twelve years of a "thousand-year empire."

Hitlermania worked through the temptation in the desert from beginning to end; in every Anabaptist attempt like the one that ran from 1933 to 1945, Christ is replaced by the Antichrist. In 1933 a hundred years had passed since Goethe's death. In Mephisto, Goethe had subjugated the Faust within himself; Mephisto and Faust twine through Goethe's entire life. But after his death Goethe froze into an Olympian and since Goethe, educated readers of *Faust* have laughed the poor devil to shame. Germany's educated classes had been summoning Hitler ever since the moment it became good form to proclaim Jesus' temptation in the desert a myth—it was the very people who proclaimed it a myth, who had abolished the devil, who went

10. [Germany's *Wirtschaftswunder* of 1949.]

11. [Cut here: *just as that scoundrel von Camphausen does now—the one who, as a professor of theology, edited a new edition of Luther's anti-semitic writings after Christallnacht* [sic].]

12. [June 30, 1948.]

and helped Satan himself into the saddle. The devil's fundamental victory lies in your denial that you may fall prey to him again yourself at any moment. So I will let Erich Fascher's own words stand here:

> Satan . . . has us by the collar when we think we have done away with him. Modern thinking is no help at all in preventing it— only the prayer of our Lord.[13]

That is why all physical ties fall away from our Lord and his own earthly life remains in the old covenant. Only his new name bought with blood may pass over into the new era! And with that we establish that the Apostles knew how long, how far-flung, and how patient the New Way would have to be, but also how lordly, how ground-breaking, and how meaningful it would be. The Devil and the Lord take such different paths that the Apostles of the year (let's say) 35 A.D. already stand within a new time-reckoning, and we can read it in the dry words of Matthew. That means that Matthew too understood himself as only a book of hours, a milestone on the long road of the Word's further incarnation. By including the fourth chapter in his gospel, Matthew already foresees the surrender of his language, Hebrew, and his place of publication, Jerusalem. If it was the Apostles in Jerusalem who wrote through Matthew rather than the Lord who had spoken before, then the writing of the Apostles is also only a way-station and an invitation to go on writing, to continue passing on the story.[14]

This was something new compared to anything written earlier; earlier writings had all followed older writings. This gospel, however, necessarily precedes later writings; they were absolutely anticipated, absolutely necessary, and absolutely still to come. Matthew already anticipated the gospel of John when he wrote his own. That is the real time-revolution of the Christian faith, the true faith in progress, faith in the future's ability to change the past. Jesus had re-created the patriarchs in Abraham's bosom! We are only Christians if we think and speak and act backwards from the end. Matthew knew nothing of Mark, Luke, or John. We know just as little as he what we will have to do or say in fifty years' time. And yet we live as Matthew and his Eleven did in Jerusalem. Even the Borgia popes lived a *papa male informato ad papam melius informandum*.[15]

---

13. ERH: Of course the "myth-makers" don't cite Erich Fascher. [Fascher, 42: the last sentences of the pamphlet.]

14. [This was also the understanding of Joseph Wittig, whose 1926 *Leben Jesu* tells the story of his own life to illustrate passages from the gospels.]

15. [*From an ill-informed pope to a pope one may better inform*, the language of Luther's appeal of 1518.]

Christian time-reckoning isn't merely aware of the crazy claim that the times are repeating cycles and so only a rattle-trap sequence of conjunctures, of pasts and presents. No, the first word of gospel speech embarks into the fullness of time. This time—made up of the day after tomorrow, the day before yesterday, and today—is open at both ends, for looking backward no human people (whether Bushman, Hottentot, Jew, Scythian, or Greek, man-fox, or werewolf) is left behind, and looking forward, no human peoples to come are denied access.

Matthew is the first speaker, the first writer of all of Christian time and he conquers it for all of us by telling us how the Lord gave the devil his walking papers. When Matthew wrote, about ten years had passed since Jesus' three temptations in the desert. It is one of the most marvelous imponderables that we know about these temptations at all. Did the Lord tell Peter—or John and James, or Matthew—about them? Thanks to the first gospel they are the visible foundation for all our knowledge of the devil and our faith in God, but because of them this very first Christian document no longer has the character of a scroll written in the *indicativus narrativus*. At the first church councils the gospels were enthroned on chairs before the gathered bishops, as the lords of the council; only they made it possible. Even today, no one can bypass them to approach Christ, for they preach time as open to us, closed neither backward nor forward. Literature entertains us; books kill time for us. The word of God does the opposite; it provides us an exit from our own time instead of entertaining us; it lets us live the time of true salvation, instead of merely killing time.[16]

It is certainly no accident that the most important years of human history, the years from 33 to 42 A.D., remain empty in both secular and church history books. Biblical criticism would never have had to tie itself in the knots it has made, if respect for the womb of language, for the suffering expectation of the Apostles in Jerusalem, had pointed the critics toward the majestic origin of the New Testament. What a day it must have been when the Apostles, returning from the Temple, found their innermost thoughts written down in the holy language, and their reader read them the five new books of the Torah that had been made flesh.

When Goethe heard his own "Pandora" read aloud to him, he burst into tears and said, "Ah, we melt even in the heat of the coals we made ourselves!" Why is it that biblical criticism never speaks of the tears of joy or the tears of grief that watered the kingdom of the New Testament in those days of expectation? Did the early Christians not consider tears to be baptismal

---

16. [*Es überhebt uns der eigenen Zeit statt uns zu unterhalten; und es treibt uns in die wahre Heilszeit hinein, statt uns die Zeit zu vertreiben.*]

holy water, just as they still elevated martyrs above bishops? The Apostles' patient expectation in Jerusalem is the greatest event in the early history of Christianity, for they sat waiting although their hearts were ablaze. It is because of this contradiction that their blaze was allowed to become word, for only in the cooperation of previously irreconcilable enemies does faith bear fruit. The gospel is the love of enemies, because that is what transforms the earth into heaven.

The symbols for the evangelists that the ancient church established denote this triumphal way, this Calvary, of enemy love. The dove of the spirit crowns the Lord himself. Matthew is the bellicose advocate of the new event, surrounded by enemies. Learned scholarship may objectify it with the word *kerygma*, but we are happy to let the herald, the *Kyrios*, stand and so remain closer to the gospel's humanity.

Where Matthew had defended the dove, Mark's lion goes on the attack, taking on the heavenly worlds of the astrological empires. With an ox's patience, Luke plows the fresh ground of faith in the wide world, liberated thanks to the lion. At the last, John enters that place which the Lord himself had occupied, when he was with the Father, before he stepped forth from his Father's silence as his Word.[17]

The descent of Jesus and the lips of the gospels are the necessary scaffolding of the eternal. The "life of Jesus" and biblical criticism are nasty attempts of a minute-and-second-obsessed mankind to bilk us of our status as children of God. Jesus' fertility, his power of soul, called forth a family tree of faith for the new people of God, and we descend from it. So whoever tears the life of Jesus and the four gospels apart, declares Jesus impotent and the first Christian communities undermined by so-called "parish theology"— or in plain English, spirit- and God-forsaken. No one can stop anyone else from committing suicide, but when whole schools of theology try to force all believers to join their suicide pact—they go too far.

The dove, the fighter, the lion, the ox, and the eagle live in us all as stations of our full humanity. They only come to life when the time before us and the time after us become as alive to us as this shadowy moment of existence we call "our own."[18]

And yet the criticism, the enlightenment, the analysis, the research into myths, in which these creative stages have been crushed for the last two hundred years, has not been in vain. Rather we shall attempt to take

17. [Ignatius, "Letter to the Magnesians." For an online source, see 316.]

18. [Cut here: *By the way, we may do well to transpose these emblems of the old church into men standing, kneeling, sitting, and lying down, for our postures are spiritual forms of expression, as I have shown elsewhere. The old symbols, true though they may be, may be allowed to die out.*]

a proper leave of the speech of mankind by gratefully holding up to those critics their own positive achievement, even if they only become receptive to it with the passage of time.

The evangelists were privileged to become the lips of the Word, and the church fathers gave them their symbols of the dove, the eagle, the angel, and the lion. But the man Mark and his lion are two different things. The symbols of the evangelists are themselves pre-Christian; all four are still attributes whose names root in the ancient world, before the rebirth of the Word. And the evangelists have the same right to claim a Christian naming of their four-limbed incarnation as you and I do. The little dove is still good for love stories, the ox for the classroom, the eagle for military parades, the angels for confirmation classes, and the lion for Venice. Mark, Matthew, John, and Luke, and the Lord himself, demand a Christian naming. The crucified One received his long ago, for things did not stop with the dove at his head. Since he yielded up his spirit into his Father's hands on the cross, he is God's son, without the dove, as the elevated, crucified One who draws everything to himself.

But since Christ's birth, the Word must also shape the body in which the Creator formed us. Our love will also think of a spiritual form for the lips of the Word, the four evangelists; we may become carriers of the spirit in our various postures. It is strange enough that we officially know nothing of the fact that we assume various postures depending on whether we teach or dance or pray or fight or receive new truth atremble, and yet we experience it every day. Matthew appeared before the synagogue in fighting trim before he left Jerusalem. Standing against the scribes of the Old Testament, he fought for the New Testament's claim to the name; as intercessor he stands before us. His joy at being the priest-bishop Peter's deacon and amanuensis cast Mark in a kneeling position. Luke taught the next generation and so he "holds a chair" while below him his listeners listen. And John on Patmos, as Revelation explicitly says, lay like one dead, for it is the dead man whom the Lord appointed to view, and withdraw the veil from, His perfected form. So standing, lying as dead, sitting, and kneeling are the portions granted the four evangelists in the Word's becoming flesh.

The New Covenant and its artists, painters, sculptors, singers, and liturgists will only have renewed the evangelists' honor at the altar when ox and eagle, lion and angel are left behind and the evangelists are assigned the body in which they let us take part in the spirit:

standing	like Matthew,
kneeling	like Mark,
seated	like Luke,
lying „dead"	like John

Matthew fought for Jesus' Davidic rank and his faith's full equality with Abraham's. Mark secured His rank in worship by receiving his own body and the Word on his knees. Luke knitted the chain of generations to the creation of a spiritual people of God, seated and teaching. But John, the unpredictable man without an office, is so overwhelmed by divine omnipotence it throws him to the ground. This position, lying overwhelmed and prostrate, allows the entry of the enduring truth: the Word will be at the end as it was at the beginning, and as it was when it was once allowed to take on flesh for the sake of our unbelief.

Whoever can believe in the spiritual postures of human bodies has no need of the ancient emblems of lion, ox, dove, and angel to find his way in the economy of salvation. In him the fruit of the lips has flourished again to form the speech of the third millennium after Christ's birth, since for him the Holy Spirit glows in the very limbs of our body. When it does, he partakes in the speech of mankind, in that speech which breaks the spell of the Babylonians, who know only the languages that followed the confusion of tongues.

Genesis uses an odd phrase for our condition before the construction of the Tower of Babel: "they had one lip."[19] The crucified one, however, the fruit of the lips of all devout believers of prehistory, *required* all four evangelists, and we need them all to protect us against remaining mired in the Babel of tongues. I may no longer know of the age of the one lip, for we have been bitten once, and we must be careful to be shy. Whoever promises that mere chatter of any variety will make us like God is indeed the devil, the father of lies. Our life may not be summed up in any slogan; on the contrary, the sensible progression though the healing postures of the spirit must take hold of us in turn throughout our life.

He whom the Word cannot move to stand fast, to kneel, to throw himself down, and to take his seat, is no man, for man is the transmitter of the Word and for this office he requires these four postures in rotation. When, in the first volume, Richard Koch's discovery[20] helped me to discover and find the "transmitter" in our very body itself, light fell on the perfection of the Son of Man and there already the reader will find the statement that in the fourth chapter of Matthew, Jesus assumes for us all the office of passer-on of the Word. Here at the end of the second volume the same fourth chapter of Matthew illuminates us; in our struggle against our own mendacity,

19. [Genesis 11:1 KJV: *The whole earth was of one language, and of one speech.*]

20. [Koch was Franz Rosenzweig's doctor. He fled to the Soviet Union in 1937 and contacted ERH after the war from Essentuki. Their correspondence on the *corpora quadrigemina* as the possible time-organ of the human brain is reprinted in "Das Haupt beim Sprechen," *Die Sprache* I, 295–311.]

our own tendency to get mired in one phase, one posture, one disposition, our Lord converts us to passing on, to the change from one spiritual posture to the next.

You may have grown up a faithful Church member, German, and fully entitled to a pension.[21] But we are all made free by speech, made brothers of the Lord, made treasurers of the Divine Spirit only if the four gospels protect us from backsliding into pre-Christian time. We started out with Jesus the Illiterate. Now anyone can see why we could never have amassed all our divine fortune, if we did not have the first-born of the Word. There is no need for us to reach down to lift up the Illiterate; on the contrary, we must fortify him in his illiteracy. If Jesus had not voluntarily distanced himself from the alphabets of the scribes, we would still elevate the written word above our bodies as the Chinese used to do, and the Alpha and Omega of mankind, the Fruit of Lips, could not be divided among us anew each day as the bread of our life.

When the Word of God became flesh, the people of God escaped the fate that would ensnare the Chinese today, had they not become Communists, for their written characters would have bound China in eternal chains. Man's mouth is eternal, because it is transitory. God made only mortals his equals.

---

21. [or: *a church-going all-American citizen, fully qualified for full Social Security benefits.*]

Appendix G
Descent and Assent
(1964?)

{PLANNED AS THE ENDING of 'Fruit of Lips'}

HE, THE WORD MADE flesh, gave his fleshly life to the Apostles and to all of us, so that a truly human race[1], instead of merely having descent only from a mother's womb,[2] might now be able to assent to an unspent womb of language. Our body is taken from our mother's womb, but the spirit is redeemed into the womb of the Resurrected One. So what is this assent?

If we were [*merely*] mammals, our embryo would receive its due in a pregnancy that was eleven to thirteen months longer: even a horse is carried [*a full*] eleven months. But man leaves his mother's womb after nine months, and it is only out in the open that the suckling babe develops his organs of speech: [*he spends*] the first two years in the womb of society. That is why you and I didn't learn to speak Gothic, but modern German. We are historical, that is to say, newly occurring, beings and in 1963 we no longer need to give voice in a language heard in 500 BC. Animals must give voice to the same old song. So our humanity depends on our assenting to articulated speech rather than to sounds that remain the same. But how is that possible? If we are not to give voice to the same old song, but each one of us is to sing his own song because he is destined to become his own note on God's harp, then old age and childhood must be given tasks that do not exist in the animal kingdom.

Society today, which wants to descend from the apes, cannot find appropriate tasks either for children or for the aged. It can only discern the so-called "grown-ups," the wage-earning man and the mother animal. The "natural" man is supposed to work and indulge in sexual pleasure, while she does the same and so also bears children.

But children and the aged have more important things to do than work. The mouth and teeth we use to speak and the ears we use to hear, the body as "all mouth" in the aged and the body as "all ear" in the child, must both be formed to fit the year of their salvation. That is denied today, and the last people who would have a clue about it are the experts on language. They

---

1. [*Menschengeschlecht.*]
2. [*the womb of one giving birth.*]

think that all speech is just a means to understanding—the Anglo-Saxons maintain that "it's all communication."

These speech-animals can't even count to three, or they would see that the means of communication that steer us are not the words alone, but [*the fact*] that what we are supposedly communicating has already been determined in advance by you and I being called "you" and "I"—that before we speak ourselves, we have already been named.[3] So we are ruled by a higher power, and it is speech-currents that steer us. But what if they are devilish? How could these witch-doctors of speech ever know what it is about words that infuse us with comfort, strength, and courage, or with misery and fear? The aged must already have weeded out the deviltries that proliferate in the workaday world of grown-ups (curses, hatreds, contempt, indifference, boredom, cowardice, and routine) because children must reach the future halls of powerful speech, and must by-pass the grown-ups to do so.

Today the aged, the grown-ups, and the children all appear to exist "naturally," so that the aged are thrown as fodder to the geriatric specialists, which is to say the doctors of the body only, and children are imprisoned in a child's paradise that is a true hell, for in it they are not allowed to absorb any wisdom the aged have to offer, but must just be "young." Nothing restricts a child more terribly than not being allowed to long for the wisdom of age. In the same way it is the most dreadful humiliation for the elderly to have to occupy themselves with their own bodies instead of with the renewal of language among men. But how could the ruling natural scientists of language even conceive of such things, when they are not even aware that we create a new body of language in each generation?

Only he who is capable of laying aside in old age the specialty that made him a grown-up takes part in this creation. As the Letter to the Ephesians puts it (3:2),[4] only he is empowered to create a new voice, to give names, to found a language, who breaks away from his specialization and crosses over into our undivided life, into the full idea of our being that our Father expressed when he let us know his life through his Son.

The reconquest of the content of old age and youth, the counterattack on the work-drunk busyness of the 20 to 60-year-olds, is in a sorry state—at least when it comes to old age, though a first loving advance for

---

3. [This passage is obscure in the original, so must remain obscure in translation: *Sonst würden sie sehen, dass ja die Mittel der Verständigung nicht die einzigen Worte sind, die uns lenken, sondern das worüber wir uns angeblich verständigen, bereits vorweg dadurch bestimmt ist, dass Du und ich heissen und das bevor wir selber sprechen, wir bereits benannt worden sind.*]

4. [Given the traditional translations of Ephesians, the reference is unclear—perhaps 3:20?]

children has been made in Adolf Portmann's writing on how our infancy differs from that of animals.

Portmann discovered in the shortness of a woman's nine-month pregnancy our opportunity to become carriers of a changing history. As a zoologist he was not concerned with the provenance of the things a baby learns in 1963. But who has the authority to deny these suckling babes the life forms of 1000 BC and 1000 AD? Who prepares the new hive for our newborn? And by what authority do they do so? Why must the newborn be protected from the looming influence of antiquity by an explicit break? How are we to measure how much of an upheaval is suitable? The content of our time-reckoning[5] consists in nothing more than the achievement of a measure for the allowable degree of innovation that may receive and surround the newborn. Since Christ we have known that innovation is necessary; that is what he died for. He fixed the conditions under which innovation is allowed: at least one person must believe in it and at least one person must be willing to die for it, so that the death of a tradition is inserted between that tradition and the newborn. We Men must die—learning that required no revelation. But the mortality of each of our eternities is something that had to be won.

Now the reader will understand the fulfillment that had been eagerly desired from the beginning of history. It was the *transitory aspect of our laws* that had to be achieved and made our own in addition to Adam's mortality, and this is the gift we receive from the Lord and his Apostles: He made possible the death of the law. The ancient world never managed, was never allowed, to abolish a single cult or superstition; we do, and may do so, because our Lord inserted his death before the lives of the Apostles; that insertion became what allowed the Apostles to set David before Saul, the still-impending destruction of Jerusalem before their own lives that apparently preceded it. In this anticipation the times were reversed, so that an earlier event was made part of the future and a later one made part of the past. And that makes us God's co-creators, the continuing stewards of numerous times. To this day the Jews do not understand the meaning of the death on the cross: Weren't millions of Jews killed? what's so important about a single crucifixion?

It is the reversal of direction that was "worth a mass."[6] It takes people who were merely racing blindly through the half-times of youth and old age, through the *k'atuns* of the Maya,[7] which chase each other without end,

---

5. [The Christian era.]

6. [On deciding to convert to Catholicism in order to be acceptable as king of France, Henri IV is said to have remarked *Paris vaut bien une messe*. (ERH, *Out*, 156.)]

7. [20 *tuns* or 7,200 days.]

and grants them lives as Apostles whose eyes were opened by their Master's death, so that they are no longer automatically young- or old-minded.[8] The death that opens the eyes of the survivors, perhaps even the eyes of the executioner, is the seed of a future proclaimed by the lips of the dying; as such it is liberated from the mere busyness of grown-ups and becomes a future to which [*all*] our newborns may lay claim. So no one need fall prey to his own time any more—thanks to Christ there no longer need be Nazis, for instance. Because the Jews may not change their law, but can at best ignore it, Christ's death remains incomprehensible to them. He was not meant and did not want to become the martyr of a faith; instead he became a blood witness of our need to shed the garment of any one eon, to let all our little eternities to die.

That is why the new state of Israel is a Christian state; as an Old Testament state it would not endure a day. The new state took on the mutability of its laws and the secularity of its constitution from Christianity: it is under the reign of Christ that worldly states arose who glory in the transitory nature of their spirit, and only under that reign that such states are possible. Just as Jesus was the fruit of the lips of all believers since Adam, we are the fruits of Christ's death. He embodied the death of the Word, so that we could call out a new word to each new generation, and so allow them to inherit newly acquired attributes.

Children and the aged must be called anew to their right to give names, to their authority to name. It is neither the bourgeois, the man of 45 to 60, nor the proletarian, the lout of 18 and up, who renew the Holy Spirit; that spirit flows where the times are so intertwined that the youngest and the oldest can speak jointly. We may have our descent from the past, but we must assent to our future; the body is produced at birth, but the spirit is produced by death. It is not because he died that our Lord's name is raised above all other names. There is salvation in no other name because only he took on the task of giving us the voice thanks to which we mute creatures are granted the human office of constantly changing assignments, and may practice it for eternity.

Passer-on Adam, Reassigner Christ: each of us children of man is born and reborn of them: Eve and Mary as much as Abel and John [*the Evangelist*]. It is only recently that the scope of our marching orders, the breadth of our listening space have suddenly become gigantic. All the more honestly do we need to honor the very small, by listening and speaking in whispers, and so honor the tone, so hushed as to be almost inaudible, in which each New Assignment will first sound to us humans before it may take visible form.

8. [Cut here: *Robert Frost expressed our Christian liberation this way: 'I never dared to be radical when young for fear it would make me conservative when old.'* Frost, "Ten Mills: Precaution," *Poetry* 48:1 (1936) 3.]

Appendix H
A Reflection on the 1916 Correspondence between Rosenstock and Rosenzweig

Franz Rosenzweig and Eugen Rosenstock-Huessy, around the time of their correspondence. The photo below is supposed to have been taken in Leipzig in the summer of 1913; if so, it may have been taken at Rudolf Eherenberg's house.

IN 1968, ROSENSTOCK-HUESSY WROTE that "much nonsense has piled up about this 'existential correspondence.'"[1] The last forty-five years have changed little in that regard—and high on the pile is the often repeated contention that in the correspondence, Rosenstock-Huessy sought to convert his friend to Christianity. That claim stands the overwhelming shared experience of the two men on its head.

Insofar as there was any attempt at "conversion," it was made in July of 1913, not in the correspondence, and it was an attempt to convert Rosenzweig from his "religious faith in philosophy"[2] to a view of the world based in revelation. Because Rosenstock-Huessy argued for revelation as a Christian (he would later say "I melt down German and Jewish gifts and possessions in the attempt to become a Christian,")[3] his arguments for revelation were those of a Christian. The arguments must have been persuasive, as Rosenzweig likewise planned to convert to Christianity. But after the four months of struggle that he himself characterized as "breakdown,"[4] Rosenzweig could write his cousin Rudolf Ehrenberg (who was raised a Christian) that he had decided to remain a Jew—or as Rosenstock-Huessy later reminded his wife, Margrit, to "become a Jew."[5]

Rosenstock-Huessy did not hear of the effect of his arguments until early 1916, when Ehrenberg told him of Rosenzweig's decision and urged him to write Rosenzweig; that evoked the first of the "foxhole letters" that have been called "the purest form of Judaeo-Christian dialogue ever attained, perhaps even for ages to come."[6] It bears repeating, as Harold Stah-

---

1. [*Despite*, 71. By 1966, Edith Rosenzweig Scheinmann no longer knew where the originals of the war-time letters were. They are not in the Rosenstock-Huessy Archive at Dartmouth, nor are they not among the Rosenzweig letters at the Leo Baeck Institute in New York. They were apparently last seen at Schocken's Berlin offices in 1935, and may have been destroyed there during the war-time bombing of the city.]

2. [*Philosophiegläubigkeit*. FR, *Briefe*. 639.]

3. [FR, *Briefe*, 664.]

4. [Letter to his earlier professor Friedrich Meinecke dated August 30, 1920 in FR, *Mensch*, 679.]

5. [Unpublished letter dated June 21, 1918.]

6. [Schoeps, *Argument*, 130. Manfred Vogel preferred Schoeps's work to that of Jacob Katz and James Parkes. See Vogel, "Dialogue," 131-36.]

mer said long ago, that it was the testimony of a Christian that prompted Rosenzweig to commit to living as a Jew. That testimony and that commitment both preceded the letters; what the letters themselves actually contain is the dramatic discovery of a united front based on the two men's common faith in revelation.

The events unroll just as described in "*Ichthys*,"[7] as a drama in several acts, each of which is complete in itself and yet builds up the meaning of the whole. In the first two acts, it is Rosenzweig who changes: in the first, he is confronted with the claim of revelation, and after a period comes to accept it; in the second, having decided to convert to Christianity, but as a Jew, not as a philosophical "pagan," he then realizes that for him, conversion is no longer necessary. In the third act, it is Rosenstock-Huessy who must accept the fact that his friend can accept the premises of his view of revelation and Christian history but draw completely different conclusions from them, and they agree that they can form a united front in spite of their differences. In the final act, they are enough "at home" in their "*terra nova*" to feel free to make their unanimity public.[8]

The process exemplifies both the conjugation of life experience Rosenstock-Huessy called the cross of reality, as well as his dictum on the movement of the spirit in the Christian era—the ability through a "yes, but" position to make common cause in spite of disagreement in detail.[9] And Rosenzweig's final position is surely the source of Rosenstock-Huessy's commitment to "*respondeo etsi mutabor*," however much the idea of the necessity of truth being incarnated in social reality may predate it. The cataclysmic changes wrought in both men oriented them for the rest of their lives. In 1916 Rosenstock-Huessy wrote that "revelation is orientation" and was "more and more an immediate here-and-now reality."[10]

The first act opens on a Monday afternoon, the day after Rosenstock-Huessy's twenty-fifth birthday. Ehrenberg, in whose Leipzig home they met, had recently published a commentary on the Letter to the Hebrews, which must perhaps be viewed as a prologue, and may also be the reason that the conversation, which went on through the evening into the night, turned on science and religion. Wolfgang Ullmann has said that the discussion "heralds for the first time an epoch where the equation of God and Nature that had ruled ... since the 18th century, encounters a consciousness of reality, in which the difference of God, man, and world became evident in an

---

7. [See "Ichthys," 15–17.]
8. [I am aware that ERH himself broke the sequence differently.]
9. [See "The Fruit of Our Lips," 89 or Appendix E, 225.]
10. [FR, *Briefe*, 663.]

utterly new way."[11] What they were discussing was the last chapter of Selma Lagerlöf's *The Miracles of the Antichrist*, and its last sentence in particular. Looking back over fifty years later, Rosenstock-Huessy would write that

> Eugen has not seen the novel since that night, and yet the last sentence of this book—on the miracle-working effigy of the Madonna in a Sicilian church—still reverberates in his mind. It reads, or it read in 1913: "Nobody can redeem men from their sufferings, but much shall be forgiven him who re-encourages them to bear these sufferings."[12] This sentence is full of faith and full of skepticism, both, and on that warm evening its thesis was chased around and around. . . . Franz, a student of philosophy and history for eight years by that time, defended the prevailing philosophical relativism of the day, whereas Eugen bore witness to prayer and worship as his prime guides to action.[13]

His friend's defense of revelation against relativism plunged Rosenzweig into crisis. His next three or four months of internal struggle are the second act of the drama.

> [Eugen's] outburst in the Lagerlöf debate had shaken Franz' agnosticism to the extent that in the months from [July] to September 1913, Franz was resolved to become a Christian, and to confess as radically as Eugen had to a faith in the revealed, living God. But in September 1913, Franz attended services of the highest Jewish holidays, and his participation in this act of divine worship convinced him, much to his own surprise, that he could remain, that he would *have to remain*, a Jew—but on a different basis than before.[14]

On the last day of October and the first day of November 1913, just three weeks after the Yom Kippur services, Rosenzweig wrote Ehrenberg the long letter in which he reminds him of the course of their July conversation, and lays out the reasons and reasoning for his own final decision.

---

11. [Ullmann, "Entdeckung," 148. Ullmann also returns Ehrenberg to his rightful place as the third and equal participant in the conversation.]

12. [This quote from memory comes amazingly close to the actual words of the English translation, although in recall, the novel's image of the Christ-child has become a Madonna. (Ullmann in turn cites the old pope's words as addressed to God, rather than an itinerant friar, "Entdeckung," 152.) For an excerpt from Lagerlöf's last chapter, see Appendix I, 331–33.]

13. [ERH, *Despite*, 73.]

14. [ERH, *Despite*, 74.]

In our conversation that night in Leipzig, when Rosenstock[15] forced me out of the last relativistic positions I still held, step by step, and forced me to take an un-relativistic position, I was outmatched from the beginning because I myself had to recognize the correctness of his attack. . . . [I thought] that I had conceptually Christianized my Judaism, that I shared a community of faith with you. . . . That is why I was already, immediately disarmed by his simple confession, which was only the beginning of Rosenstock's attack. That a man like Rosenstock could consciously consider himself a Christian . . . threw all my ideas of Christianity, but also of religion in general and of my own religion, right out the window.

We are in agreement on what Christ and his Church mean in the world, that no one comes to the Father except through him. No one *comes* to the Father—but it is quite different when one no longer needs to come to the Father, because he already *is* with the Father. And that is the case of the people of Israel (if not of the individual Jew). . . .[16]

And yet, since the sufferings caused by the Synagogue's denial of the world are incorporated in the same final hope as the sufferings caused by the Church's affirmation of the world . . . [and] the roots of that hope, the God of all *time* here and there, spring from the same source, the revelation of the Old Covenant that we hold in common, Church and Synagogue have no choice but to rely on each other. The synagogue, immortal, but with her staff broken and eyes bound, must herself forego all work in the world . . . She stares fixedly at what is yet *to come*. And the Church, with her unbreakable staff, her eyes open on the world, the warrior sure of victory . . . the power of faith commands her to look around herself and to do the work of love in the *present*.[17]

Ehrenberg's visit to Rosenstock-Huessy set off the third act. Rosenzweig writes in defense of his decision, but Rosenstock-Huessy writes with respect for it:

You overrate the Christian in me. I am not Paul of Tarsus, sad to say; my mission comes to a halt before you. You are the human individual whose particularity I acknowledge despite its anti-Christian character. I see Judaism exactly as you demand

---

15. [FR, *Briefe*, 71–72. Rosenstock did not legally hyphenate his name until 1925; he published as Eugen Rosenstock until he left Germany in 1933.]

16. [FR, *Briefe*, 73.]

17. [FR, *Briefe*, 75.]

that "the Church"—and you yourself?—see it, the way all God's revelation in the world from day to day becomes more and more an immediate, here-and-now reality, rather than a metaphorical abstract concept in the background.[18]

And he answers one of Rosenzweig's more defensive letters by saying that "you end with what I tried to make my beginning: I must, and am to, let you stand."[19] None of that keeps them from arguing about the principles involved. When Rosenstock-Huessy wrote that "Abraham sacrifices what he has, Christ what he is" and likens Israel's pride to that of Lucifer, Rosenzweig retorts:

> what the two sacrifices on Moriah and on Golgotha, have in common in distinction to all pagan sacrifice is that in them nothing was *achieved* (since it is only what was sacrificed that is found again) and that the sacrifice *itself* becomes what faith retains, and thereby all that is retained at all. . . . perhaps the antidote closest to hand to this mutual declaring the other pagan, if not the most correct one, is to reflect on the common possession of the one *book*.[20]

Each asks the other for a statement of how his views have changed since 1913. That elicits a torrent from Rosenstock-Huessy, full of statements that echo on fifty years later:

> Today Christianity has a new Old Testament in place of your old one. The Old Testament that lives today is church history itself, in the legends of the saints and the calendar of feasts . . . The Western world has come so far today that it may forget the Old Testament, the Greeks, the Romans, the Jews, and the Persians, because there are Englishmen, popes, Germans, etc. And what is worse, my poor ben Juda, it *will* forget its Old Testament. . . . Do you believe Zionism is a coincidence? Israel's day as the people of the Bible is over. The Church [itself] . . . is the Synagogue of today! . . . Christ has enough people to crucify him in his own Church. . . . The Jews no longer crucify, judge, or sentence any more at all. Today there are states and the Church, where before there were the peoples and the Synagogue.[21]

18. [FR, *Briefe*, 662–63.]
19. [FR, *Briefe*, 694.]
20. [FR, *Briefe*, 690. This also in distinction to Islam, which made substantial changes to the Jewish and Christian stories it incorporated into the Quran.]
21. [FR, *Briefe*, 695–96. The European nations as the new "Old Testament" is the hidden theme of *Out of Revolution*.]

If Zeus and Wotan are too weak to be dangerous today, the ghosts that rule ... in their stead are all the "isms": culture, German religion, "natural" Christianity. With them, against them, we must *speak*. . . . What has replaced the problem of the Babylonian confusion of tongues is the problem of *translation*, that is, of healing the former confusion, even if doing so causes new confusion. Luther, who is so magnificently right as a translator and Germanizer, becomes a criminal in letting everything Catholic fall by the wayside. The true and enormous tension today is whether or not the *translation* of Christianity, and thereby of Christ's *name*, for the fourth estate will succeed or not.[22]

The men struggle towards recognition both of each other and of their unanimity, and it is that struggle that characterizes the correspondence. Rosenstock-Huessy said that they "stumbled toward each other."[23] Rosenzweig responded to the first quote above with this:

... you are quite correct to say that the early, real epochs, church history itself, acquires the meaning of an "Old Testament." The proof of Christianity's effectiveness already lies *behind it*.

Early on, Rosenzweig writes that "we crucified Christ, and believe me, we would do it again at any time, we alone in the wide world,"[24] to which Rosenstock-Huessy returns towards the end of the exchange with "Dear Franz Rosenzweig . . . *you* would certainly not crucify Jesus of Nazareth, you alone in the wide world. Believe you *me!*"[25] At one point Rosenzweig responds to a letter from his friend with "I asked myself this morning, 'Did I really not write him all that myself yet, that *he* writes it to *me*?'"[26] Rosenstock-Huessy writes in turn:

We are indeed completely of one mind. And our monologues are the nicest possible dialogue between "school" and "home." (Finally we have a label for our roles: you talk like a schoolmaster, and live "at home" (*quo ad intentionem*); I talk the way a

---

22. [FR, *Briefe*, 698–99. As in Fielding, the *fourth estate* here refers to the proletariat. The urge to *translate* is the root of ERH's decision to go to Daimler-Benz (then in the grip of a debilitating strike) and to found the Academy of Labor. His work in adult education continued until he left Germany in 1933.]
23. [FR, *Briefe*, 638.]
24. [FR, *Briefe*, 670–71.]
25. [FR, *Briefe*, 699–700.]
26. [FR, *Briefe*, 685.]

housewife or a child does at home, and live on the podium, *in publico*.²⁷

That "monologues of dialogues" returns in Rosenzweig's wonderful statement, perhaps the highpoint of the third act:

> I believe that there are moments in the life of every living thing, perhaps even only one moment, in which it *speaks* the truth. So perhaps it is not even necessary to speak *about* any living thing, but only to await the moment in which it expresses itself. The dialogue of these monologues among themselves . . . is what I consider the *whole truth*.²⁸

The final act involved Rudolf Hallo, whom Rosenzweig had made his deputy at the *Jüdisches Lehrhaus*:

> A third man . . . under the influence of Eugen, had toyed with baptism for himself, but with Franz' help . . . re-establishes his Jewish identity. But now he plagues Franz with outbursts of his too violent, even fanatical, return to the Jewish fold, and Franz has to put his foot down, insisting that the community of all those who confess, against those who merely think timelessly, embraces all believers.²⁹

Rosenzweig wrote Hallo [the passage Rosenstock-Huessy quoted appears in square brackets]:

> Then I went and engaged myself to Edith Hahn . . . I no longer did it because, but rather although, she is entirely Jewish. It was only that afternoon that I really realized that I would now be able to lead a Jewish life, would have to lead one, for love of her—that Jewish life into which you had wanted to thrust me like a ghetto. But I demand that you believe me, not because I will lead a kosher life at home, but because outside my home I will not feel bound by it in the least. Or if you prefer, believe me because of both. But not, never, for the first reason alone. [Those walls have fallen. Where Eugen and I met, where Rudi and I . . . met, no such dilapidated walls separate people from each other. . . . You can no longer set yourself outside our common world, what we have in common. . . . What has happened to us, to Judaism, to Christianity, to creation (it doesn't matter! perhaps to all three together!) is the only thing that retains life,

27. [FR, *Briefe*, 701.]
28. [FR, *Briefe*, 711. The motto for *Die Europäischen Revolutionen*, 1951.]
29. [ERH, *Despite*, 75.]

and only out of that vital life, which we may not weigh down with mere orthodoxy, can the call to resurrection ring out over the charnel house that is European and German existence. What form this earthly existence will take then, I don't know, but that is not up to us; rather than worrying about what has died, what we have to do is to live life.]³⁰

"To live life" meant a profound commitment to support any new life, any love from which new life might spring. It was never easy; one might describe it as a commitment beyond pain and suffering.

It extended well beyond Franz Rosenzweig's all-too-short life and beyond the two men. Margrit Rosenstock's family had practically adopted Franz when he first appeared as Eugen's friend, and both Eugen and Margrit went on corresponding with Franz's mother until shortly before her death. Eugen not only came to accept that his best friend could say that "*The Star* is based entirely on the single premise that Christianity is a lie,"³¹ and that he found Christians "physically nauseating,"³² but also to accept Franz's great love for his wife, Margrit, which began shortly after the last of the "foxhole letters" were written. (Rosenzweig wrote her every day for years, even on his honeymoon.)

Eugen found his limits, however: when Franz wrote Margrit, in full knowledge that she shared her letters with her husband, that her mother-in-law had always reminded him why some people become anti-semites, he broke down—but in the end he overcame that, too.³³ The suffering was by no means all on one side. After Franz's A.L.S. progressed to the point that he himself could no longer write, type, or speak, Margrit was one of only three people who could interpret his dictation signals. Her visits to take over the task from Edith Rosenzweig, who also had the house and her young son Rafael to look after, cannot have been pleasant for Edith.

Rosenzweig had elaborated on his response to Rosenstock-Huessy's letters in *The Star of Redemption*. Rosenstock-Huessy responded to *The Star* by insisting on the importance of the incarnation in "*Ichthys*" (which he included in his church history, *Das Alter der Kirche*). He seems to have based much of his take on the French revolution and its meaning on Rosenzweig's essay on Schelling and the years 1796–1800. And he went on to work

---

30. [FR, *Briefe*, 381–83. ERH's translation is markedly different, but he is surely right to accent "resurrection." See ERH, *Despite*, 76.]

31. [Letter to ERH in the "Gritli Letters" (July 2, 1919).]

32. [Töpfer and Wiesling, *Richard Koch*, 112. See Cristaudo, *Religion*, 142.]

33. [Letter to MRH in the "Gritli Letters" (May 4, 1918). Published in Huessy, "Rosenzweig Studies," 111.]

with others in what he called "fruitful opposition."³⁴ For the rest of his life, Rosenstock-Huessy went on citing Rosenzweig (he is named or quoted in almost every book he published in German) and arguing with him as well. At 75, he was still insisting that

> we men must die—learning that required no revelation. . . . It was the transitory aspect of our laws that had to be achieved and made our own in addition to Adam's mortality, and this is the gift we receive from the Lord and his Apostles: He made possible the death of the law. The ancient world never managed, was never allowed, to abolish a single cult or superstition; we do . . . because our Lord inserted his death before the lives of the Apostles . . . the times were reversed, so that an earlier event was made part of the future and a later one made part of the past. And that makes us God's co-creators, the continuing stewards of numerous times.³⁵

---

34. [ERH, *Ja und Nein*, 103–04. (FR appears over and over again in this little book from 1958.)]
35. [Appendix G, 299.]

Appendix I
Sources and Commentary

IN THE 1978 EDITION of *Fruit of Lips,* Marion Davis Battles raised numerous questions about Rosenstock-Huessy's use of sources. There is no question that he was less than careful with some of his references (his obvious lack of concern for citing the exact year a work was published is only one example). What I found on consulting the sources myself, however, is that Mrs. Battles did not dig very deep before making some of her tart remarks. So I thought it fair to reprint excerpts from the sources cited, including excerpts from the articles which appeared in *Studia Evangelica* in 1959.

All appear alphabetically by author, except for the articles by De Bruyne and Harnack, which should be read together and in order; they begin on page 337. I have included lengthier extracts from those two articles since neither has appeared in English before. Rosenstock-Huessy clearly considered their unanimity conclusive evidence for the dating and authority of the "primitive" anti-Marcionite prologues, and hence of the gospels.

He often implicitly credited the judgment of authors (like Joseph Wittig) whom he had come to trust for other reasons, which has been a stumbling block to many; with De Bruyne and Harnack, he was clearly more selective. What impressed me about their work was the clarity of the prose and argument in their articles; a century ago, the knowledge of ancient languages was sufficient in and of itself to differentiate the educated from the masses. In order to establish the same distance today, academics (many of whom cannot in fact read any language but their own) create the distinction through the use of jargon incomprehensible to those outside "the field."

De Bruyne's dating of the prologues and Harnack's enthusiastic agreement to the arguments for it have since been eclipsed. Ernst Haenchen and Helmut Koester are only the most recent specialists to follow Jürgen Regul, R.G. Heard, and Engelbert Gutwenger in over-ruling Harnack and de Bruyne. Online, therefore, the prologues are often dated to the fourth century again and the name "anti-Marcionite prologues" goes about in quotation marks. Given established academic cycles, however, de Bruyne and Harnack may yet come out on top again.

The article by Grant cited by Mrs. Battles in addition to Harnack and De Bruyne is not included—it contains some useful information for non-scholars, but it offers different texts of the prologues, and ignores many of the findings of both Harnack and De Bruyne.¹ Grant used the Latin text to correct the Greek (which De Bruyne refused to do, to Harnack's satisfaction) but appears to present much of De Bruyne's research and many of his conclusions without crediting his source.

Online sources (accessed accessed May 20, 2020) include:

The Migne *Patrologia Latina* (including Augustine's *De Genesi ad litteram*, Vincent of Lerins' *Communitorium,* and Ignatius's *Letters*) and the *Patrologia Orientalis* are both available, in Latin, at http://www.documentacatholicaomnia.eu. English translations of most of the cited patristic works may also be found at www.newadvent.org/fathers. The entire collection may be downloaded for a fee.

Another English translation of De Bruyne's edition of "The Oldest Gospel Prologues" may be found at: http://www.tertullian.org/fathers/anti_marcionite_prologues.htm. A substantially different edition is to be found at: http://www.textexcavation.com/latinprologues.html.

The only complete and unexpurgated text of Franz Rosenzweig's "Gritli Letters" may be found at: http://www.erhfund.org/the-gritli-letters-gritli-briefe/. They have not yet been translated into English.

William R. Farmer on the history of the argument for the primacy of Mark may be found at: http://www.churchinhistory.org/pages/booklets/farmer(n).htm. Some of what he says on Rosenstock-Huessy should be taken with a grain of salt.

W. H. Cadman, "The Raising of Lazarus," *Studia Evangelica*, 423–434.

After a lifetime spent defending the truth and continuing importance of the Christian tradition, Rosenstock-Huessy could write that:

> honesty demands that I myself be as modest as those reporters when it comes to the raising of Lazarus. Like any Greek I have not yet understood this pericope unique to John, but it is obviously at the heart of the gospel.

In the footnote he adds that "I have come to the first traces of understanding thanks to W.H. Cadman's 'The Raising of Lazarus.'" The phrase

---

1. [Grant, "Gospel Prologues," *ATR* 23 (1946) 231–45. Later editions of Grant's book do not include the *primitive* prologues at all.)]

"first traces of understanding" stopped me in my tracks: what could Cadman possibly have said to trigger such a statement? Aside from a polite rejection of Bultmann, the article appears to be "as modest as those reporters" itself:

> The questions considered in the following pages are primarily (a) the meaning of the terms *doxa* and *doxazo* in 11:4 and 40 . . . (b) the interpretation of the saying *ego eimi e anastasis kai e zoe* in vs. 25; and (c) what may be learnt from the chapter about the content of Johannine belief in Jesus. . . .

I suspect that it is (c) that evoked those "first traces of understanding":

> [Lazarus'] illness was to lead to the "glorification" of the Son of God. Yes, for His raising of Lazarus from the dead would bring Him to the Cross, and at and because of the Crucifixion, He would be "glorified," be given "glory," *doxa*. . . .
>
> "Glory," *doxa*, in what sense? In 17:22 the gift made by Jesus to believers, by which they become sharers of His own union with the Father and are bound together in union with one another, is called His "glory," His *doxa*. . . . The works of Jesus include the "signs" wrought by Him, and the "signs" are held in St. John to be revelations of His "glory," his *doxa*. . . . It may be said in brief that just as *doxa* is a Johannine term for the love-relation between God and the Logos "in the beginning" (1:1), so it is for the union in love of the Father and the Logos incarnate. His "glory" in this sense—His communion with the Father, His oneness with Him, His union with Him in love—Jesus revealed in His public ministry. "We beheld his glory" (1:14). . . .
>
> The claim of Jesus to be the *anastasis* has all this future, as well as the present reference in it. . . . In vs. 26b Martha is asked if she believes what has been said to her in vss. 25 and 26. "She saith unto him, Yea, Lord: I have believed that thou art the Christ, the Son of God, even he that cometh into the world." . . . There is no hint that enough has not been said. . . Her understanding of what Jesus had said then about the significance of His own Person for believers who die, the faith to which she had then risen, would enable her now to see the "glory" of God. Only because she had this faith would she be able to see it; not otherwise, nor would anyone else, though all present would see Lazarus come forth from the tomb. . . .
>
> The utterance of Jesus "*ego eimi e anastasis kai e zoe*" (vs. 25) discloses a consequence when God and the incarnate Logos are in the relation of "glory" or "love" in which God dwelt with the Logos "in the beginning" (1:1), "before the world existed" (17:5). If Martha had grasped and accepted this consequence of

the love-union she will discern in the raising of her dead brother a revelation of the union itself.

John Chapman, *Matthew, Mark, and Luke*, 1–8, 38–53, 187 n2.

(The copyright to Chapman's work is held by the Downside Abbey General Trust; this excerpt is reprinted by generous permission of the monks of Downside Abbey.)

[Before 1916] I held, rather dogmatically, that our Greek St. Matthew depends on St. Mark, and (with somewhat less certainty) that Q, the matter common to Mt. and Lk., was the other source; so that I roughly believed what is called the "two-document" theory.... I was not only quite certain that Mt. depended on Mk., but I was extremely anxious to hold that Mk. was an independent Gospel, and not merely, as St. Augustine held, an abbreviation of Mt....

My sudden conversion, by a regular knock-down blow, took place during the war.... I started thus, "It is never good to assume one's own opinion to be infallible.... Therefore I must assume it as possible that tradition really meant that St. Matthew's Gospel was written ... before St. Mark, and that St. Mark's Gospel is actually an extract from it, and must see whether this can be quite easily disproved." ...

The ordinary bases of the "two-document" theory are just as consistent with the view that Mt. was first and Mk. second, provided Lk. is third.... Mk. is often longer than Mt. in descriptions, is more vivid, and is not so good in style; in all this it seems obvious at first sight that Mt. is a corrector of Mk., who is more primitive. But ... all these characteristics are just what tradition leads us to expect in Mk. since it is said to consist of lectures delivered at Rome by an eye-witness of the events, the impetuous St. Peter. If he took St. Matthew's work as a basis, he would retell it just in this way, amplifying and enlivening, and making somewhat haphazard statements, which might be easily misunderstood, and are in fact carefully toned down by St. Luke, who has a very strict regard for propriety.

Therefore the arguments which are usually given to demonstrate the dependence of Mt. on Mk. are perfectly compatible with ... the dependence of Mk. on Mt. I saw this clearly; I had never seen it before.... What argument would finally dispose

SOURCES AND COMMENTARY 319

of [the traditional sequence] and set firmly on its feet the "two-document" hypothesis which was so simple and satisfying and ... so clearly true?

I hit upon an easy test, and one that would be perfectly conclusive: If Mk. abbreviated Mt., omitting much, adding next to nothing ... wherever it makes long omissions we shall find some sign of the gap—perhaps merely want of sequence, for Mt. is very systematic, or even illogical sequence. If there are no such signs—and there cannot well be, since nobody has noticed them—I shall conclude quite securely that Mk. is indeed prior to Mt. Here was a practical test, and I applied it at once. . . . I started with Mk. 4:1 which is parallel to Mt. 13:1, where our Lord teaches from a boat.

Here is what Rosenstock-Huessy found such irrefutable proof (5-8):

St. Matthew gives a series of parables and explanations, given in private to the disciples. . . . Mk. has three parables and one explanation, against the seven parables and two explanations of Mt. Does Mk. show any sign of having omitted anything? He does. Twice. [Mt. 13:3 has] "And He spoke to them many things in parables, saying . . ." [where Mk. 4:2 has] "And he was teaching them many things in parables, and he was saying to them in his teaching . . ." Here Mt. has *pollá*, and proceeds to give actually many parables. Mk. retains *pollá* and intends to give only three parables, so he adds, "And in the course of His instruction He said. . ."

Can one conversely assume Mk. to be the original, and then explain that Mt., in using Mk, noticed the statement that Christ "taught many parables, and among them said . . .," so that Mt. thought his was a splendid place for interpolating a number of additional parables and a couple of O.T. quotations, altering Mk.'s . . . passages which implied that many parables had been omitted?

. . . I had imagined, I suppose, some illogical sequence at most, and I expected to find nothing all; and I found (apparently) two definite statements by Mk. that he had omitted some outdoor parables and indoor explanations. This was astounding. I did not wait. I went on in haste to another passage.

Mt. 23:1-39 contains a long discourse of Christ against the Pharisees and the scribes, ending with an appeal to Jerusalem, which had slain the prophets. Of these 38 verses (2-39) Mk. has two and a half only, very freely and pointedly given. The chapter was of great importance in Palestine; but at Rome it was valueless, except as a moral lesson against vanity and ambition. Now let us see how it is introduced: [Mt. 23:1 has] "Then Jesus spoke to the crowds and to His disciples, saying..." [where Mk. 12:38 has] "And in the course of His teaching, He was saying..."

This... completely bowled me over. No reply is possible. Mk. tells us once more, "In the course of His teaching, He was saying." What teaching? Look at Mt.; there it is, shoals of it. In the course of the same half hour I turned to another important passage, the one long discourse in St. Mark, ch. 13, mis-called "the little Apocalypse," and there I came upon another yet more unmistakable example of Mk. indicating omissions.... Since 1918 I have not changed my mind, but I have now and then turned back to the subject and added to my notes, especially with regard to St. Matthew's character and origin. Having once recovered the right point of view, confirmations have forced themselves into view. I now see that any form of the "two-document" theory is a paradox, unworthy of support. I am much ashamed of having held it probable.

Chapter 4 of Chapman's book (38–43) opens with this statement:

> If we compare Mk. with Mt. as the part with the whole, the chief characteristic of Mk. is seen to be this, that Mk. contains nothing but what St. Peter saw and heard, and might easily remember. Thus he omits all the long discourses save one, but preserves short and pithy sayings of the kind that would be easily remembered, and a few parables. He omits all incidents at which Peter could not have been an eye-witness. He also omits all incidents which are to the honour of Peter. (38) ... Mk. is Mt. retold by an eye-witness and ear-witness, who omits all the incidents at which he was not present and leaves out *in just the same way* all words of Christ which his memory had not clearly and verbally recorded.... That Mk. is an eye-witness's report is a commonplace which need not be proved here (43).

Chapter 5 (44–53) begins by listing twenty cases in which "a comparison of Mk. with Mt. suggests that Peter was the source of Mk.'s words [and] seven places in Lk. where he adds to Mk. further information about Peter" and argues that "the view that Mt. like Lk., used Mk. and added much about Peter is untenable."

> Jo., like Lk., is careful to add to our knowledge of St. Peter.... he gives us the touching story of Peter's three-fold protestation of love, making up for his threefold fall, and his reception of the promised office of chief shepherd; and lastly, the prediction of his

martyrdom. All this familiar evidence shows that Mt., Lk., and Jo. make much of St. Peter, whereas Mk. does not: just as (and these points have been noticed from Origen and Eusebius onwards) Mt. alone speaks of Matthew the publican, Lk. never mentions himself in Acts, and John never gives his own name. (52)

Rosenstock-Huessy himself cited Chapman's footnote (187) in which he expresses his bafflemnt at the state of 20th century German criticism:

> In 1910, Bernhard Weiss wrote a small book [*Der Hebräerbrief in Zeitgeschichtlicher Beleuchtung*, Leipzig] to show that "Hebrews" was addressed to Hebrews, because the contrary was the unanimous view in his country. I do not know whether the paradox survives. But common sense suggests that Hebrews was written in Aramaic and was very well translated, as Mt. and James were well translated.

The rest of Chapman's book was clearly just as important to Rosenstock-Huessy; he seems to have based his stance on the Greek text of Matthew being a translation from the Aramaic on Chapman's thorough argument—at least, until he met Grintz's argument for Hebrew. Chapman's chapter on the "impossibility of Q" (95-99) deserves to be read, if only for the pleasure of the sarcastic turn to Chapman's logic.

G. K. Chesterton, *Orthodoxy*, 299.

> Joy . . .the small publicity of the pagan, is the gigantic secret of the Christian. And as I close this chaotic volume I open again the strange small book from which all Christianity came; and I am again haunted by a kind of confirmation. . . . The Stoics, ancient and modern, were proud of concealing their tears. He never concealed His tears. . . . Yet He concealed something. Solemn supermen and imperial diplomatists are proud of restraining their anger. He never restrained His anger. . . . Yet He restrained something. I say it with reverence; there was in that shattering personality a thread that must be called shyness . . . something that He hid from all men when He went up a mountain to pray . . . something that He covered constantly by abrupt silence or impetuous isolation. There was some one thing that was too great for God to show us when He walked upon our earth; and I have sometimes fancied that it was His mirth.

Albert C. Clark, *The Acts of the Apostles*, xxiii.

Rosenstock-Huessy's footnote refers to Clark's citation of James Hardy Ropes' argument in *The Beginnings of Christianity* (London, 1926):

> [Ropes] draws attention to the fact that [Acts] contains a number of Hebraisms and certain agreements with the Hebrew Old Testament as against the Septuagint. His conclusion is "that the 'Western' text [of Acts] was made before and perhaps long before the year 150 by a Greek-speaking Christian who knew something of Hebrew, in the East, probably Palestine (ccxliv)."

Rosenstock-Huessy states that "Clark thinks that this proves Luke to have been a Jew himself"; Mrs. Battles remarked tartly that "in checking the reference to Clark, the editor finds that Clark is quite discreet in his statement." She should have read the rest of the book—in Appendix III ("Authorship of Luke and Acts," 393–98), Clark writes:

> It is allowed by those who are most emphatic in declaring that Luke was a Greek that both the works attributed to him are full of Hebraisms. Thus Plummer says . . . "In construction even Matthew, a Jew writing for Jews, sometimes exhibits fewer Hebraisms than this versatile Gentile." I find this theory of the "versatile Gentile" unconvincing. Greek was the literary language of the East and known to all Jews with any claim to culture. It is easy to see that a Jew when writing Greek would from time to time use native idioms and constructions. It is difficult to conceive the case of a Greek who became so saturated with Hebraic idioms as to use them when writing in his own tongue. If, therefore, the meaning of Col. 4:10–14 is that *Loukas* was a Greek, it is hard to suppose that he wrote either of the works attributed to him.

That is hardly a "discreet statement."

Hubert Cunliffe-Jones, "The Fourfold Gospel, a Theological Problem," *Studia Evangelica*, 14–24.

Cunliffe-Jones admits his title is an adaptation of the title of Oscar Cullmann's 1956 essay, "The Plurality of the Gospels as a Theological Problem in Antiquity," but posits the question for our own time.

SOURCES AND COMMENTARY   323

Professor Cullmann's main point is: if they were biographies they could be harmonized; as they are Gospels they must be set alongside one another.

Cunliffe-Jones cites several statements of C.H. Dodd's in support of this proposal:

> I believe that the course which was taken by *Leben-Jesu-Forschung* ("The Quest of the Historical Jesus" . . .) during the nineteenth century proves that a severe concentration on the Synoptic record, to the exclusion of the Johannine contribution, leads to an impoverished, a one-sided, and finally an incredible view of the facts—I mean, of the facts, as part of history.

as well as:

> The kind of interpretation I have in mind will in one sense reverse the main direction in which New Testament studies moved for a century . . . These writings have come down to us in the form of a Canon, representing the judgment of the early Church—of those best qualified to judge—that in them the Christian religion as a whole received authoritative expression, under a diversity of manifestations, but by the same Spirit.

Later on, Cunliffe-Jones adds that "the common conviction of all four Gospels is more important their divergences." And he closes with this:

> I hope that the conception of a fourfold Gospel is a valid concept for the twentieth century, and that others abler than I am may show how with continuing research into the differences between the four Gospels, we may still, with complete integrity, think together their witness in a way that is fruitful for theology, preaching, and private devotion.

Martin Dibelius, "Paulus auf dem Areopag," *Sitzungsberichte* (1939) 3–56.

It is hard to imagine the Sunday School which would adopt Rosenstock-Huessy's proposal to adopt Dibelius' essay as a teaching tool. Its 136 footnotes threaten to overwhelm the 56 pages of very small type larded with Greek, all of which contrasts starkly with the nine short verses of Paul's own speech. Dibelius claims that Paul's speech was a sufficient and complete argument in the terms of, and attempting a synthesis with, Greek philosophy. He laments the victory of "Luke's" Greek synthesis, over Paul's work in the

Epistles. And yet Dibelius redefines all the words used in the speech to conform to Greek usage of "Luke's" time and, interestingly enough, denies that *kairoi* refers to periods of time, just as Michaelis did with *aion*:

> It is more difficult to understand *kairoi* in this context. Some see it as representing "the appearance, blossoming, and disappearance of the nations," "*les saisons de leur prospres saisons de leur prospérité*," while others remind us of the use of *kairo ethnon* in Luke 21 and 24. But this expression is an eschatologichal term, which designates the time between the destruction of Jerusalem and the in-breaking of God's kingdom. There is no mention of any of that here.

Dibelius exemplifies both his guild's late dating of the N.T. canon and its denial that time and timing are central to it. The essay is a triumph of self-aggrandizing academic argument.

Edgar J. Goodspeed, "Greek Idiom in the Gospels," *JBL* (1944) 87–91.

Rosenstock-Huessy expresses deep gratitude for Goodspeed's later championing the apostle as "the author of Matthew" (107), and I suspect that Rosenstock-Huessy's citation of the Book of Enoch is drawn from this article of Goodspeed's. On 90 and 241, however, he cites its author as one of the scholastic blind leading the blind: Goodspeed is eager to prove that the gospels did not have Aramaic but Greek origins.

> [T]he Book of Enoch declares that the fourth of the Fallen Angels was the one "who instructed mankind in writing with ink and paper, and thereby," it goes on, " many sinned from eternity to eternity and until this day. For men were note created for such a purpose, to give confirmation to their good faith with pen and ink" (69:9–10). Such was the Jewish point of view in the first century before Christ. It would be hard to put the wickedness of literary composition more bluntly....

Goodspeed then proceeds to list examples of Greek idiom in the gospels which make no sense if translated back into Aramaic or Hebrew:

> 8. The gospels also have ways of speaking which can hardly be reconciled with an early Judean origin. "The Jews" are spoken of more than sixty times in John in contradistinction from Jesus and his disciples; though these latter were just as truly Jews as his opponents were. This can hardly be thought a Jewish form

of expression. It shows plainly that a Greek-speaking Gentile is writing—and at a time when, and a place where, Church and Synagogue were at war . . .

After the paragraph (#11 in Goodspeed's list) which Rosenstock-Huessy quotes at length, Goodspeed says that John "identif[ied] the Logos with that divine Wisdom" which was with God in the beginning, referring to the Book of Wisdom. Goodspeed closes by saying "one might as well deny Greek idiom to Homer," but does it not seem odd that a Gentile Greek "fourth evangelist" should be so familiar with the Book of Wisdom?

Jehoshuah M. Grintz, "Hebrew as the Spoken and Written Language in the Last Days of the Second Temple," *JBL* (1960) 32–47.

> It is the prevailing view that at the time of the Second Temple, Aramaic was the only popular language of Palestine. Even when contemporary sources attest to the actual use of "Hebrew," this is taken as a reference not to Hebrew itself, but to the Aramaic dialect current in Palestine. Our intention is to demonstrate that this opinion . . . dominant for about a century and a half, is quite erroneous and should be discarded . . .

Grintz cites the concurring work of M.H. Segal and E. Ben-Yehuda, "who based their arguments upon the mishnaic literature, the most important Hebrew monument of those times." He himself argues from the Gospel of Matthew and Josephus' *Bellum Judaicum*, and his argument on Matthew derives from phrases which differentiate it from the other Gospels, particularly in parallel passages:

1. Matthew renders the name of Jewish people or land of Palestine consistently as "Israel," whether the speaker is Jesus or the evangelist himself. Only when the speech is put into the mouth of a Gentile does a variation occur, and instead of "Israel" we have "Jews." Such a consistent usage is hardly conceivable in any language other than Hebrew. . . .

2. . . . we have a parallel usage with foreign people: Gentile(s)—*ethnikos, ethnikoi, ta ethni*, a designation foreign to Aramaic but familiar in Hebrew, being an accurate translation of the old collective noun [*goyim*]. . . .

3. In Matthew 15:21 we read: "Jesus . . . departed into the coasts of Tyre and Sidon; and behold a Canaanite woman (*gyne xananaia*)" came

out to ask mercy for her "devil-vexed" daughter. "Canaanite" is a term commonly used in Hebrew for "Phoenician," but not in any other language. In Aramaic or Greek it is simply devoid of meaning. . . .

4. Another significant usage is the combined term "flesh-and-blood" (*sars kai aima*) for a "human being." This expression is quite common in Mishnaic Hebrew (in the Talmud—B. Tmura xxi:2—it is taken as one word), but altogether unknown in Aramaic. . . .

5. Two other instances which attest to the Hebrew origin of Matthew are the compounds: *Basileia ton ouranon*, "kingdom of the heavens," [sic] and *patyr mou o un teis ouranois*, "My (or Our) father who is in the heavens." . . . In the other gospels they are virtually non-existent. The two phrases using the word "heavens" are characteristically Hebraic but do not occur in any other language. . . . That the word for "heaven" in the Greek Matthew is always written in the plural is another striking example of a very literal translation from Hebrew. . . .

6. In Matthew 12:42 the queen of Biblical "land of Sheba" is called simply: "queen of the south," *Basilissa notou*. . . . Neither in Greek nor in Aramaic could the term for "south" be used as an equivalent of Sheba. It is only in Hebrew that the archaic biblical name for south. . . acquired in time this specific meaning. . . .

7. For decades scholars have been trying to demonstrate the existence of an Aramaic substratum of the gospels in general, including Matthew, yet . . . not a single case supports this contention as regards Matthew. On the contrary, Matthew is replete with Hebrew phrases . . . this gospel, unlike the others, which in general are addressed to the external world, is always directed at a Jewish audience. . . .

8. The book as a whole seems to be written as a counterpoise to the Books of Moses. Jesus' birth like that of Moses (according to Aggadic sources) was foretold by magicians, i.e., astrologers. Like Pharaoh on the eve of Moses' birth, so Herod at the time of Jesus' birth commanded the execution of children. . . . Jesus, like Moses, was called out of Egypt and like Moses the divine Spirit descended upon him. He too fasted for forty days in the wilderness, went up a mountain, preached his sermons in five divisions (as against the five books of the Pentateuch) and performed ten miracles (as against the ten plagues in Egypt). . . . Nor should we overlook the testimony of Papias and the Church Fathers to the effect that there was a Hebrew gospel. The Church Fathers even cite Hebrew expressions. . . .

9. Taking into account all the evidence adduced, one can assert that the original language behind the Gospel of Matthew was Hebrew. . . . The vast treasures recently discovered at Khirbet Qumran . . . are a pertinent example of the living force of Hebrew. . . . To this alone we can attribute the fact that the new sect of "unlearned and ignorant men" (*anthropoi agrammatoi kai idiotai*) [Acts 4:13] set out to write its main book, intended for its Jewish members, in this language.

Hilarius Isaac, "Quaestiones de Novo Testamento," *Corpus Scriptorum* 50, 430.

Mrs. Battles correctly cites Rosenstock-Huessys' friend Joseph Wittig as the reason he accepted "Hilarius Isaac" as the author of the "Questions on the New Testament." By 1905, Dom Germain Morin and Alexander Souter of Oxford had proven to general satisfaction that the author of the "Questions" had also written a famous and respected fourth-century commentary on Paul, long attributed to Ambrose (hence the nickname "Ambrosiaster.") In 1899, Morin had proposed the Jewish convert Isaac as author of both, but in 1903 he abandoned Isaac in favor of Decimus Hilarianus Hilarius, a Roman proconsul in Africa; Souter accepted Morin's second identification later that year.

Wittig had published his "inaugural" doctoral thesis on Isaac's enemy, Pope Damasus. His 1905 essay "Der Ambrosiaster Hilarius" argued eloquently for Morin's first theory against the second, tentatively ascribing a number of other works to Isaac and reconstructing a life of Isaac that fit what was known about "Ambrosiaster." He wrote of Isaac's skills and weaknesses with deep insight and appreciation, but the essay apparently caused a critical fire-storm. In the introduction to the 1909 volume containing a second Wittig essay on Isaac ("Filastrius, Gaudentius, und Ambrosiaster"), his mentor Max Sdralek defended the precocious young scholar, quoting high-placed professors in his defense (though several were unwilling to have the quotes attributed to them in print):

> his observations and conclusions were recognized as 'decisive' in Germany by [Munich professor Carl] Weymann, and met with such success in England that even A. Souter (of Oxford, who had accepted Morin's first thesis, then abandoned Isaac and, along with Morin, set Decimus Hilarius Hilarianus in the place of honor) reverted to considering Isaac the author.

(In his 1908 edition of the "Questions" Souter does indeed name Isaac as author, but without crediting Wittig. In his preface to his 1927 edition of Ambrosiaster's commentary on Paul, Souter does cite Wittig—but not for changing his mind in 1905. The academic wheel keeps turning: in 1914, Morin proposed Evagrius of Antioch as yet another candidate for "Ambrosiaster's" place and Morin's new proposal was, inevitably, also accepted by Souter.)

In his second essay, Wittig begins by retreating on the question of identification, but then argues that Isaac/Hilarius was probably identical with the Gaudentius who succeeded Filastrius as bishop of Brescia, as "Isaac," his baptismal name "Gaudentius," and his pseudonym "Hilarius" all share the same meaning; Wittig examines the clear parallels between Filastrius' responses to Gaudentius the man and to "Hilarius" the author. Though his enemies had accused Isaac of reverting to Judaism, Wittig argues that he remained a devout Christian, though one with little investment in the hierarchy of the Church Visible—an accurate description of Wittig himself, at least at the end of his life. Indeed, Isaac's banishment to Spain and the subsequent reconciliation with Pope Damasus (for which Wittig argues) eerily prefigures Wittig's own 1926 excommunication and 1946 reconciliation with Rome. Wittig ascribed Isaac's interest in calendars (a trait he certainly shared with Rosenstock-Huessy) to his being a Jewish convert, or from a converted Jewish family. In which light, it is interesting that in his translation, Rosenstock-Huessy lets "Hilarius Isaac" speak of "the plenitude of times."

Adolf Hitler, *Reden des Führers am Parteitag der Ehre* 1936, 37.

I am grateful to Bruce Walker and Jonathan Huner for their help in finding this text. This is not quite the "smoking gun" I had hoped to find for Rosenstock-Huessy's claim that Hitler had actually said the "solar constellation of Christianity" had ended, but it is the only similar statement I have found so far. What Hitler actually said here is also not quite what Landau reported, though the claim is certainly implied. (The text of the second paragraph is given violent emphasis in the original.)

> *So kann in einer solchen Zeit auch nicht die Kunst- und Kulturentwicklung den Auffassungen des einzelnen Individuums nicht ausgeliefert sein. Denn diese Auffassungen ermessen nicht den Sinn einer Gemeinschaftshaltung, sie glauben nur zu oft entbunden zu sein von den Verpflichtungen dieser Gemeinschaft*

SOURCES AND COMMENTARY 329

und von den besonderen Aufgaben, die sie stellt. Dies ist aber ein kapitaler Irrtum.

Ein christliches Zeitalter konnte nur eine christliche Kunst besitzen, ein nationalsozialistisches Zeitalter nur eine nationalsozialistische. So wie der nationalsozialistische Staat die Aufgaben stellen wird und sie heute auch auf kulturellem Gebiet bereits gestellt hat, so wird er auch über die grosse Tendenz der Erfüllung wachen. Daher ist die Periode der bolschewistischen Kunstvernarrung in Deutschland nunmehr abgeschlossen, denn diese bolschewistische und futuristische Kunst ist eine anarchistische Zurückentwicklung.

In such a time the development of art and culture may not be abandoned to the perceptions of the lone individual, either. For those perceptions cannot fathom the meaning of a community's position—they only too often believe that they have been delivered from all responsibilities to that community and the particular tasks it sets. But that is a fundamental error.

A Christian era could only have Christian art, a National-Socialist era can only have National-Socialist art. Just as the National-Socialist state will set the tasks, as it has already set them in the cultural area today, so it will watch over the larger trend of its fulfillment. That is why the period of Bolshevik idolatry of art is now over in Germany—this Bolshevik and futurist art is an anarchistic atavism.

Hitler goes on to say that democracy necessarily leads to anarchy, though his worst is saved up for the Bolsheviks—a lot of the language prefigures Cold War American rhetoric altogether too closely for comfort. On the other hand, he describes bourgeois democrats as singing "Who's afraid of the big bad wolf?" while the Bolshevik threat mounts around them. Disney's "Three Little Pigs" came out the year Hitler came to power, but who would have thought he had seen it—let alone seen fit to quote it?

Hoskyns and Davies, *The Riddle of the New Testament*, 137–38.

Mrs. Battles accused Rosenstock-Huessy of distorting this quote through his ellipses, but the point of the citation is in the final sentences. Here is the entire quote, with the "missing" sections in brackets:

> In the Marcan gospel Jesus is isolated and wholly misunderstood [not only by the crowds and by the Jewish authorities, but

also by his family or kindred, and] by his chosen disciples. In Mark this is of vital importance because [it is precisely in this complete humiliation and isolation that the revelation of God takes place.] The salvation [of men] is wrought [out as an *opus operatum* by Jesus] in complete isolation. [The gulf which separates Jesus from the Jews is hardly greater than the gulf which separates him from his disciples.] Both the Editors are unable to preserve this isolation with the staggering brutality of Mark. [To them this terrible misunderstanding seems derogatory to the Apostles, to the family of Jesus, and even to Jesus himself.]

The above text is from the first edition; in later editions, the "staggering brutality" became the "consistent rigour."

Gottlieb Klein, *Ist Jesus eine historische Persönlichkeit?* 28, 40–43.

I am indebted to the work of Pinchas Lapide for the discovery of Klein's work. Like Grintz, Klein argues for the historicity of the gospel accounts of Jesus exclusively from Jewish sources, including Hillel and Gamaliel, putting Jesus' words to the priests, Pharisees, and Sadducees, in context.

> Here we have an account which can be verified. The background is so thoroughly Jewish, the smell of Palestinian soil clings to it on all sides so strongly, that only unbridled fantasy could seek to turn this historical Jesus into a myth. . . .
>
> According to the sources [Jesus' sentence] followed an accusation of blasphemy. But nowhere are the grounds for this accusation to be found . . . . If anything is suited to settle the historicity of . . . the simple fact of the judgment [against him] . . . it is Jesus' conversation with the high priest—assuming it is correctly understood.
>
> In the Mishna (Sukka IV:5), the procession around the altar at the Feast of Tabernacles is described: every day of the festival, they went around the altar in procession saying the prayer: "O Lord, deliver us!" (Psalm 118:25) Rabbi Jehuda says: "They prayed, *Ani-we-hu*, O help us!" In this *Ani-we-hu* I find the "hidden name of God" . . . which, according to Jewish tradition, God was to reveal to all in the messianic age. One teacher of the Mishna explains it this way: "*Ani-we-hu* = he and I = I want to be like Him." . . . The content of the name of God . . . is kept secret; it contains within itself the deepest secret of religion, the *unio mystica*, the challenge to become one with God.

Jesus appears in order to reveal this secret to the world. When he pronounces the mighty word misunderstood by most people, "The father and I are one" [John 10:30], he is expressing the content of the hidden name of God, *Ani-we-hu*. This teaching is to be found throughout the entire fourth Gospel: John 9:15; 5:19ff.;14:10ff.; 17:6ff.

I maintain that Jesus' opponents had cause, fully justified in their own eyes, to accuse Jesus of the sin of blasphemy. For it is on account of his pronouncing the "hidden name of God" ... that he is treated as a blasphemer. And the statutes in the Mishna (Sanhedrin VII:5) on blasphemy state: "The blasphemer is only guilty when he pronounces the hidden name of God ... When the verdict is pronounced ... the judges are to rise and tear their clothing and never to sew [it] together again."

Mark 14:61 contains the following description of Jesus' conversation with the high priest: "Again the high priest questioned him: 'Are you the Messiah, Son of the Blessed One?' 'I am,' said Jesus.'" In all probability, the answer in the Hebrew original was: "*Ani-we-hu*." The next part of the account bears witness to it: "Then the high priest tore his robes and said, 'Do we need further witnesses? You have heard the blasphemy.'" Now the tearing of clothes was *only* to follow on the pronouncement of the name of God, so Jesus must have spoken it, and the high priest received his apparent justification for his verdict.

Selma Lagerlöf, *Miracles of the Antichrist* (1911) 373–378.

(The book was first published in 1897 and first translated into English in 1899. Lagerlöf was awarded the Nobel prize for literature in 1906.)

Looking back on the slaughterhouse that was the 20th century, both the last chapter of *The Miracles of the Antichrist* and its last sentence (which offers a historical amplification of "her sins, which are many, are forgiven, for she loved much" in Luke) seem prophetic. Set amid the battle between socialism and traditional Italian authorities, the novel concerns on the one hand the love of a devout young woman for a young Socialist, and on the other the discovery that the figure of the Christ child in the church of their small Sicilian town can work miracles. The figure is stolen by a rich Englishwoman and replaced with a copy—which, as the miracles continue, an itinerant monk decides to burn as a false god. The novel ends by ascribing the (otherwise not very astonishing) claim that false religion should be tolerated, even welcomed, as a path to true religion, to the wisdom of an aged pope—perhaps a nod to Leo XIII.

A week later, Father Gondo was in Rome. He was granted an interview with the old man in the Vatican and told him how he had found Antichrist in the likeness of Christ, how the former had entangled the people of Diamante in worldliness, and how he, Father Gondo, had wished to burn him. He also told how he had not been able to lead the people back to God. Instead, all Diamante had fallen into unbelief and socialism. . . . The old pope, who is wiser than any one now living, did not laugh at Father Gondo's story; he was deeply distressed by it. "You have done wrong; you have done very wrong," he said. He sat silent for a while and pondered; then he said: "You have not seen the Cathedral in Orvieto? . . . Then go there now and see it," said the pope; "and when you come back again, you shall tell me what you have seen there." Father Gondo obeyed. . . . "What did you see in Orvieto?" the pope asked him. Father Gondo said that in one of the chapels of the Cathedral he had found some frescoes of Luca Signorelli, representing . . . "The Miracles of Antichrist." . . .

"What did you think when you saw that?"

"I said to myself: 'That Signorelli is not mad; he is a prophet. Antichrist will certainly come in the likeness of Christ and make a paradise of the world. He will make it so beautiful that the people will forget heaven. And it will be the world's most terrible temptation.'"

"Do you understand now," said the pope, "that there was nothing new in all that you told me? The Church has always known that Antichrist would come, armed with the virtues of Christ."

"Did you also know that he had actually come, Holy Father?" asked Father Gondo.

"Could I sit here on Peter's chair year after year without knowing that he has come? . . . I see starting a movement of the people, which burns with love for its neighbor and hates God. I see people becoming martyrs for the new hope of a happy earth. I see how they receive new joy and new courage from the words 'Think of the earth,' as they once found them in the words 'Think of heaven.' I knew that he whom Signorelli had foretold had come."

. . . "Father Gondo," said the pope, sternly, "when you held the image in your arms, you wished to burn him. Why? Why were you not loving to him? . . . That is what you wandering monks could do. You could take the great popular movement in your arms . . . and you could bear it to Jesus' feet; and Antichrist would see that he is nothing but an imitation of Christ, and would acknowledge him his Lord and Master. But you did not do so. You cast Antichristianity on the pyre, and *soon he in his turn will cast you there* [emphasis added]. . . . We do not fear him. When he comes to storm the Capitol in order to mount the throne of the world, we shall meet him. . . . You do wrong," he continued more mildly, "to hate him. You must have forgotten that the sibyl considered him one of the redeemers of the world. . . . Father Gondo, you will permit me also to tell you a Sicilian story. . . .

"[W]hen Our Lord was busy creating the world, He wished one day to know if He had much more work to do. And He sent San Pietro out to see if the world was finished. "When San Pietro came back, he said: 'Everyone is weeping and sobbing and lamenting.' 'Then the world is not finished,' said Our Lord, and He went on working. Three days later Our Lord sent San Pietro again to the earth. "'Everyone is laughing and rejoicing and playing,' said San Pietro, when he came back. 'Then the world is not finished,' said Our Lord, and He went on working. San Pietro was dispatched for the third time. "'Some are weeping and some are laughing,' he said, when he came back. 'Then the world is finished,' said Our Lord. And so shall it be and continue," said the old pope. "No one can save mankind from their sorrows, but much is forgiven to him who brings new courage to bear them."

Bruce Marshall, *The World, the Flesh, and Father Smith*, 82.

Father Smith is a preternaturally humble priest—always on the verge of standing up for himself but never quite able to do it—who dies as humbly as he lived. When he returns from duty as a chaplain in the Great War, he is sent back to his old parish, only to find that he is no longer in charge.

> "I am afraid, Father, that you'll find that I have made some changes since you've been away," Father Bonnyboat said at length. Father Smith was silent. He thought that he knew what was coming. Father Bonnyboat was a liturgical scholar and knew exactly how a Benedictine abbot should sing Pontifical High Mass on a double of the second class in the presence of a Cardinal Archbishop of the Ambrosian rite. He himself had never been any great shakes at liturgy, although he had tried to be because he knew that liturgy was only another name for Almighty God's table manners; but both his build and his voice had been against him, and he knew that there was all the difference in the world between a monk from Solesmes singing Mass and himself singing Mass, and he never could remember whether the Feast of the Holy Innocents was red or violet when it fell on a Sunday.

Wilhelm Michaelis, *Die Apokryphen: Schriften zum Neuen Testament*, 316.

Rosenstock-Huessy's citation refers to a footnote to a passage in the *Acts of Paul*: in order to hear Paul preach, Nero's beloved slave Patroclus climbs through a high window in a barn and falls to his death; Paul and his companions pray over him, and he returns to life. Back at the palace, Patroclus is asked by Nero (in my translation of Michaelis, with my italics):

> "Who has brought you back to life?" The page, moved by the spirit of faith, replied, "Jesus Christ, the Lord of the Eons." The Emperor took fright and said, "So he is to be Lord over the Eons and destroy all other *kingdoms*?" and Patroclus answered him, "Yes, he will destroy all *kingdoms* under heaven, only he will remain in all eternity, and there will be no *kingdom* that shall escape him." [The emperor] struck him across the face and said, "Patroclus, do you also fight for this king?" but he said, "Yes, [my] Lord Emperor, it was he who awakened me when I was dead."

Michaelis' footnote refers to the translation of "eons" and reads as follows:

> The expression "Lord of the Eons" comes from I Timothy 1:17, where it refers to God; however, perhaps here "eons" is meant to refer not to periods of time, but to *kingdoms* of this world.

Michaelis admits distorting the text because it made no sense to him as written; M. R. James, who translated the *Acts of Paul* into English, turned "*aionoi*" into "kingdoms" as well, but without footnoting it. You have only to reread the passage, restoring "eons" for "kingdoms," to see its appeal to Rosenstock-Huessy. What is less clear is why he would cite an apocryphal text, known to be a fraud since the time of Tertullian, as a source for the opinion of the Emperor Nero.

Eugen Rosenstock-Huessy, statement made August 24, 1929. *Conference Report of the World Association of Adult Education* (1929), 179–180.

> We have to deal with small numbers in adult education, not because there are not millions longing for adult education, but because the real wants of adult education can only be answered by grouping people in very small sections or fellowships....

The structures of Church and State have become enormous and gigantic; today, the average individual can no longer discover the mirror of the life of the social universe in his own spiritual experiences. [The quote from 6 falls here.] . . . Cultivating this natural and secular method will enable and empower the stunted, drugged members of modern society to rediscover the Eternal Truth. The great world-wide institutions, churches, and empires cannot endure if they are not reflected every day in the small cells and smallest groups of human beings, who spell out afresh in their own tongue the eternal secrets of humanity and Christendom. I am convinced that the cancer of speed, which is destroying the spiritual life and the functioning of these smallest cells, could be overcome by the safety-valve of these new forms of adult education.

Rosenstock-Huessy, Werner Picht, and Wilhelm Flitner were personal friends as well as colleagues in adult education. Flitner was co-founder of the *Volkshochschule* Jena (Community College of Jena); Adolf Reichwein, who later took part in the Löwenberg work-camps and Helmuth von Moltke's "Kreisau Circle," was his successor. Flitner also co-founded the "Hohenrodter Bund," in which he worked with Rosenstock-Huessy, Picht, and Robert von Erdberg, among others.

Rosenstock-Huessy, "Andragogik" ("Andragogy") in Picht and Rosenstock, *Im Kampf um die Erwachsenenbildung*, 193–219.

Claiming that discussion was made sterile by any "natural" homogeneity of the participants—Rosenstock-Huessy termed schools that catered to a single class or social group "incestuous"—he explicitly defined the kind of "teacher" true adult education required: someone who is political "in the broader sense," that is, passionate about creating community, and therefore willing to sacrifice his own expertise to the common goals of the teaching community and his students' interests.

Without . . . "truth" being cleansed of the fetters of individuality, one age cohort, one generation, can never connect to another. [We must] understand the enormous difference between truth and doctrine. . . . Scholasticism once sacrificed truth to doctrine; modern science sacrifices doctrine to truth. . . .

All adult education, if it is to achieve anything original, anything that shapes men . . . will have to proceed from the suffering which the lost war has brought each one of us personally and economically... and from the catastrophe it means for Europe.... Schools for men which do not give the country men would be a luxury. Schools for men which did not give them to the whole country would be a danger. The school of suffering and disaster... is a School of Events, and a school for those who have undergone those events... [The quote from 7 falls here]

... Theory becomes practical deed in the responsible word; in the crucible of necessity, practical deeds become the basis of theory. So the division between Aristotle and Philip, or Machiavelli and Descartes, breaks down. Even in its own time it was only an apparent division. Philip's son Alexander did what Aristotle had taught him: that already expresses better the truth of the relation of theory and practice.... Paul is the philosopher of the cross that Jesus lived; he himself lives what Jesus taught. Only in the new situation of such a school will the fate which has befallen our generation be able to become historical doctrine; without such doctrine, what has befallen us would have happened in vain...

Rosenstock-Huessy, "Ehrlos—Heimatlos," ("Honorless—Homeless," 1920) reprinted in *Die Sprache* II, 85–115.

We are in night, and only in night; one o'clock has already come and gone, and it has become quite hopelessly quiet and silent. Boundless fears will drive many Germans in the coming decades to seek revenge, to attempt a restoration, and to violent indignation. We will have to suffer through the attempt to establish an "Empire of lies," because these forces will not rest until they are proved wrong.

So this tiny perch for all the German churches, parties, and tribes will be made a hell. We however, who are now without honor and without a homeland in the Babylonian confusion of tongues that was the war, we who voluntarily take on ourselves the double curse of the pagans of Germany and of the League of Nations, receive in this hour, as it becomes more and more silent, the law of eternal life, which points from evening toward morning....

Their double curse will allow us to hate nothing that retains life; our hate may target only what is dead and rotten. Any living spirit may command our love, no matter in what shape it may come to us.

Lukas Vischer, "Die Rechtfertigung der Schriftstellerei in der alten Kirche," *TZ* 12 (1956) 320–336.

Vischer writes that the Church Fathers all felt the tension between the pagan "art of rhetoric" and the Christian belief that the spoken or written word should draw attention, not to itself, but to God.

> The negative stance toward writing has its roots in the New Testament itself. There is no explicit ban on writing, and artistic composition is nowhere explicitly attacked. The rejection is explained only by the peculiar nature of the Gospel itself[: it] . . . is a message which must be proclaimed; it is no common truth to be handled in the common way.

He cites the introductions Irenaeus, Theophilus, and Clement of Alexandria composed for their works. Clement remarks that when teaching students you could see, you can gauge their understanding and reformulate statements if necessary; writing for unseen readers risks misreading and misunderstanding. Irenaeus asks his unseen readers to "receive with love what [was] written in love." By the time Augustine wrote *De Doctrina Christiana*, however, he could address this tension and propose a way to use rhetoric without succumbing to it, citing both Paul and the prophet Amos as examples. Vischer closes with this statement:

> Christian literature can only exist in constant tension with the New Testament. For only in denying itself in part can it lift into the light that what really matters is the Gospel proclaimed.

Donatien De Bruyne, "Les Plus Anciens Prologues Latins des Evangiles" ("The Oldest Latin Prologues to the Gospels"). 193–214. Excerpt translated and reprinted by generous permission of Paul Bogaert of the *Revue Bénédictine*.

De Bruyne's essay appears here in translation and drastically abridged. As a person of "little Latin and less Greek," I have not included the Greek text of the prologue to Luke; as a layperson, I have not included De Bruyne's learned footnotes.

> These prologues are not unpublished and have not been neglected by the critics—quite the opposite. However . . . if we can establish that these prologues predate the famous Monarchian Prologues, that they were collected together in the same

manuscripts, that they are never found except in Biblical manuscripts, that it is unlikely that anyone would write a prologue for one Gospel only, leaving others without prefaces, that it is supremely unlikely that three different authors wrote three prologues independently, one for Mark, another for Luke, and a third for John, one must acknowledge that these prologues make up a series....

It has been twenty years since I began to collect the many Latin Biblical prefaces, published and unpublished, and I have never doubted that these three are by the same author. The prologue to Matthew is irretrievably lost.... I even believe that it had already disappeared when the Monarchian Prologues were written in the 4th century, and the undeserved popularity that those new prefaces enjoyed ... is probably due to their being a complete series....

De Bruyne sets out the existence of "three texts: 1) the Greek prologue to Luke, 2) the Latin series of prologues to Mark, Luke and John, 3) the corresponding passages of the Monarchian Prologues" and then details at length the forty MSs which contain the "primitive" prologues (and their printed editions). The earliest is "ff," a 5th century MS from Corbie. Harnack applauded De Bruyne's edition of the texts, saying he "was right to avoid premature correction of the Latin tradition based on the Greek."

II. Texts

Mark: Primitive
... Marcus adseruit, qui et colobodactylus est nominatus, ideo quod ad ceteram corporis proceritatem digitos minores habuisset. iste interpres fuit Petri, post excessionem ipsius Petri descripsit idem hoc in partibus Italiae euangelium.

Mark: Monarchian
Marcus ... petri ... in diuino sermone discipulus ... euangelium in Italia scripsit ... Deinde amputasse sibi post fidem pollicem dicitur.

De Bruyne's edition of the Greek prologue to Luke is not included here.

SOURCES AND COMMENTARY 339

LUKE: PRIMITIVE
Est quidem Lucas Antiochensis Syrus, arte medicus, discipulus apostolorum; postea vero Paulum secutus est usque ad confessionem eius, serviens deo sine crimine, uxorem unquam habuit, filios numquam procreavit. octoginta quat-tuor annorum obiit in Boeotia, plenus spiritu sancto. Igitur, cum iam descripta essent evangelia—per Mattheum quidem in Iudaea, per Marcum autem in Italia—sancto instigatus spiritu in Achaiae partibus hoc descripsit euangelium, significans per principium ante suum alia esse descripta, sed et sibi maximam necessitatem incumbere Graecis fidelibus cum summa diligentia omnem dispositionem narratione sua exponere, propterea ne Iudaicis fabulis desiderio tenerentur, neve hereticis fabulis et stultis sollicitationibus seducti excederent a veritate. itaque perquam necessariam statim in principio sumpsit ab Iohannis nativitate, quae est initium evangelii, praemissus domini nostri Iesu Christi, et fuit socius ad perfectionem populi, item inductionem baptismi, atque passionis socius. cuius profecto dispositionis exemplum meminit Malachiel propheta, unus de duodecim. Et tamen postremo scripsit idem Lucas Actus Apostolorum; postmodum Iohannes apostolus scripsit Apocalypsim in insula Pathmos, deinde euangelium in Asia.

LUKE: MONARCHIAN
Lucas syrus, natione antiochensis arte medicus, discipulus apostolorum, postea paulum secutus usque ad confessionem eius, seruiens domino sine crimine.
Nam neque uxorem umquam habens, neque filios LXXXIIII annorumobiit in bithynia, plenus spiritu sancto. Qui cum iam descripta essent euangelia, per mattheum quidem in iudaea, per marcum autem in italia, sancto instigante spiritu; in achaiae partibus hoc scripsit euangelium, significans etiam ipse in principio ante alia esse descripta. Cui extra ea quae ordo euangelicae dispositionis exposcit, ea maxime necessitas labris fuit ut primum graecis fidelibus, omni perfectione uenturi in carmen dei manifestata, ne iudaicis fabulis intenti in solo legis desiderio tenerentur, neun hereticis fabulis et stultis sollicitationibus seducti excederent a ueritate elaboraret, dehinc ut in principio euangelii, iohannis navitate praesumpta . . .
Cui lucae non inmerito etiam scribendorum apostolicorum actuum potestas in ministerio datur. . . . Hoc autem euangelium (iohannes) scripsit in asia, posteaquam in pathmuos insula apocalypsin scripserat. . . .

JOHN: PRIMITIVE
Euangelium Iohannis manifestatum et datum est ecclesiis ab Iohanne adhuc in corpore constituto, sicut Papias nomine Hierapolitanus episcopus, discipulus Iohannis carus, in exotericis suis, [id est in extremis] quinque libris retulit, descripsit vero euangelium dictante Iohanne recte; verum Marcion hereticus, cum ab eo fuisset inprobatus eo quod contraria sentiebat, abiectus est ab Iohanne. Is vero scripta vel epistulas ad eum pertulerat a fratribus qui in Ponto fuerunt.

III. Relations between the Texts

A. *The Greek is the original text*

Whoever closely examines ... the prologue to Luke will have to conclude, as Zahn did, that the Latin is a translation of the Greek.... If the prologue to Luke is a translation and if the three prologues are by the same author, one must acknowledge that the prologues of Mark and John are also translations. We have long suspected that the prologue to John was a translation, and in the prologue to Mark, the use of the word "*colobodactylus*" clearly suggests a Greek origin.

B. *The Monarchian Prologues depend upon the shorter prologues*

Here, again, we begin with the prologue to Luke where the connection is more marked. Everyone who has studied the Monarchian prologues ... has noted two most characteristic traits: first, a pompous and almost unintelligible style, and second, an odd and heretical theology.... The obscure style and the heresy appear only where the Monarchian prologues abandon their source, i.e., where they are original.... [They] betray their later origin at every point. This dependency has been acknowledged and demonstrated by

Zahn, who also noted that the Monarchian prologues are based on the Latin translation and not on the Greek original.

C. The unity of the three shorter prologues

In my written account of Harnack's *Marcion* . . . I expressed my conviction, even then of many years' standing, that these three prologues are by the same author, and I had the pleasure of seeing in *Neue Studien zu Marcion* that Harnack did not hesitate to accept it. One must nevertheless give the arguments that demonstrate it:

1. The prologues are together in the two principal branches of the manuscript tradition. . . .
2. Mark and Luke have an identical phraseology: *descripsit idem hoc in partibus Italiae euangelium* and *in Achaiae partibus hoc descripsit euangelium*.
3. Mark and Luke were both used in the 4th century by the Priscillianist who drafted the Monarchian prologues.
4. Luke and John both have an anti-Marcionite tendency, explicit in John and certainly implicit in Luke.

IV. The Prologue to Mark

Qui colobodactylus est nominatus. This . . . is a harmless nickname bestowed on [Mark] because of a physical defect of his fingers . . . likewise, we find in the *Acts of Paul* (ed. Lipsius, 108, 13) a Justus "with flat feet" and in Mark 15:40 James "the short," he whom we normally call "the lesser," which is more respectful toward the apostle, but less precise. . . . These are things no one would invent. The memory was preserved in Rome, where Mark had lived. The author of the Monarchian prologue gives a completely different, and rather romantic, explanation. . . .

Iste interpres fuit Petri. On this point tradition is unanimous. . . . Our prologue is Roman and . . . yet, in Rome the Jews . . . many slaves, and the ruling class spoke Greek; Greek was the language of liturgy and of preaching. . . . Doubtless, poets were sometimes called the "interpreters of God," but that is only a metaphor. Here we must take the word . . . in its natural and literal meaning. Luke wrote his Gospel after being Paul's companion and no one has said, as far as I know, that Luke was Paul's interpreter. . . .

Post excessionem ipsius Petri descripsit idem hoc in partibus Italiae euangelium. This important passage wants to localize and date the second Gospel. *In partibus Italiae* does not exclude Rome. . . . The most accepted tradition agrees with the prologue, and internal criticism seems to support it. . . . The prologue does not depend upon Irenaeus. . . . It is Irenaeus who depends upon the prologue. . . .

We have examined what the prologue says. Let's look at what it doesn't say.

1. Today's common opinion identifies Mark with John, nicknamed Mark (son of Mary and cousin of Paul's companion Barnabas). . . . Ancient tradition knows nothing of this identity. . . .

2. Mark's voyage to Egypt is a little better attested, but . . . I consider Mark's voyage and his episcopacy in Alexandria a legend. This little story is found in the Monarchian prologue: *Alexandriae episcopus fuit.*

3. . . . Some fathers say that Mark wrote during Peter's lifetime (Clement of Alexandria) or even that Peter approved the Gospel (Eusebius and Jerome). Others, like Irenaeus, place the Gospel after the death of Peter. The . . . argument is simple, purely historic and without any apologetic tendencies, and I cannot but add that this too speaks for it.

V. The Prologue to Luke

Printed in 1749, this prologue had fallen into complete obscurity until Zahn commented on it recently, both with his customary erudition and with a less familiar open-mindedness. . . . Luke's age is given as 84, not only in our prologue, but also in the Monarchian revision. . . .

Our prologue says:

1. that Luke followed Paul *usque ad confessionem eius*, so he was in Rome around the year 66, at the time that Paul was martyred;

2. that Luke wrote his Gospel, and later Acts, in Achaia ;

3. that he died in Boeotia, which is a part of Achaia. . . . Isn't it odd that our author, so poor in information on Mark, who lived so nearby, is so well informed about Luke, who lived so far away?

. . . [T]he anti-Jewish polemic was commonplace; it is the anti-heretic polemic which deserves all our attention. The heresy is not named, but it is revealed in the next sentence. *Itaque,* that is to say, to dispel this heresy, Luke begins his Gospel by telling the story of the birth of John the Baptist. This story is called *perquam necessaria*, it is an . . . absolutely necessary part, as is demonstrated by the high praise given John the Baptist, in a tone which the fourth Gospel carefully avoids. . . .

There is only one possible explanation. . . .The Prologue to Luke combats the Gospel of Marcion; it is probably the same motivation that leads the prologue to say that there are three other Gospels—Matthew, Mark, and John—because Marcion had rejected them. This prologue, which is probably the oldest evidence of the Gospel of Marcion, is missing from the beautiful book which Harnack just published. The Monarchian prologue dropped this anti-Marcionite polemic, another trait which suggests a later period.

VI. The Prologue to John

The prologue to John is the best-known, the most discussed, and also the most obscure; I would say that it is also the one whose text leaves the most to be desired. . . . We do not have, as we do with Luke, a 5th century manuscript. . . .

Our prologue has also been accused of error for calling *Papias discipulus Iohannis carus* and many assumed that he borrowed this expression form Irenaeus . . . but Irenaeus does not cite Papias's evidence. . . . The more our author is removed from John in time and space, the more mistakes he makes. It seems to me that he wrote in Rome in the second half of the 2nd century; he could have known that others had had some part in the edition of the fourth Gospel . . . [and] might have expressed this tradition by saying that Papias wrote at John's dictation. We are all in agreement that he is mistaken, but it is a harmless error. . . .

Let us move on to the history of Marcion, where the difficulties are so large that we must seek some solution. The sentence, as it reached us, tells us that because of his errors Marcion was condemned by Papias, and later rejected and excommunicated by John. . . . Which word is the impossible one? I reply: *ab iohanne*. First, there are a lot of *iohannes* in our prologue: five times in five lines—that's too many. Secondly, Papias seems rather too emancipated a disciple to me. . . . Next, and the anachronism is a violent one: who could have believed that John was still alive in Marcion's time?

. . . According to Tertullian, it was in Rome that Marcion presented his letters and our prologue says the same thing, without depending upon Tertullian. We understand, then, the mention of Papias: John was dead, Marcion was condemned in Asia by a disciple of John's (rightly or wrongly, our author says it was Papias). . . . In the explanation I have just proposed, however, there is still a great difficulty to which I have no answer: why in a prologue to John, do they mention Marcion at all, if John was not mixed up in this affair? . . .

VII. The Origin and the History of the Prologues

Where and when were our prologues written in Greek? Where and when were they translated into Latin?

1. It is in Rome and only in Rome that Mark was known under the sobriquet *colobodactylus* (Harnack, *ZNTW* 3, 1902, 164).

2. The prologue to John was written from the Roman point of view. Speaking of heretics and the fourth Gospel, it mentions neither Cerinthus nor Ebion, whom we might expect to encounter, but Marcion, whom no one would have expected. The reason . . . is no less strange than it is simple: Cerinthus and Ebion were only of interest in the Orient, whereas only Marcion had just provoked sharp crisis in Rome. . . .

3. If we accept my explanation above, the prologue to John finishes by telling of the events that took place in Rome.

We have the following facts to help us date the prologues.

1. They were written when the Roman church still spoke Greek.

2. They date from a period where they still had information on Mark and Luke that, on the one hand, conform to the oldest traditions and, on the other, are neither improbable nor tendentious where they cannot be verified.

3. They occur after the Marcionite crisis, but not by much.

4. They are notably older than the Monarchian prologues. . . . It does not seem reckless to situate their composition to the second half of the 2nd century.

5. Literary dependency can help us date them even more precisely: the prologues borrow from Papias. . . . There is probably a literary relation with Irenaeus, but it seems to me that it is the Bishop of Lyon who is the borrower.

De Bruyne then lays out his arguments for the African origin of the Latin translation.

VIII. The Marcionite Bible and the Catholic Bible

A. The Catholic Edition of the Four Gospels

We have seen that our three little texts were written in Rome after 150, and that they were directed against a sole heretic, Marcion. . . . The inevitable conclusion is: the prologues were composed for a Catholic edition of the four Gospels, provoked by the Marcionite edition of the lone "Gospel." This dangerous heretic falsified one Gospel and rejected the three others. . . . The Roman church had to issue an edition of the four Gospels to refute him.

B. The Catholic Edition of the (ten? thirteen?) Epistles of Paul

Marcion had . . . published ten letters of St. Paul, though he distorted their text. So Rome also had to publish the Epistles of the great apostle whom Marcion had exalted. . . . The Catholic edition had to have prologues. . . . Were they lost? I doubt it, and here I dare to propose a hypothesis that would have frightened me in 1907. . . . It was no ordinary Marcionite that composed the Marcionite Prologues, but Marcion himself. . . . The Catholics saw, above all, useful geographical and historical information in the Marcionite prologues. It may have been the little prefaces that gave them the idea—then new—to write similar ones for the Gospels. I note a curious difference between them: where Marcion always indicates the city where Paul wrote, the Catholics mention only the country where the Gospel was written. . .
. Marcion, for dogmatic reasons, had reordered the letters, putting Galatians in front. . . . There was also a very old order, probably introduced in Corinth, that put Corinthians first. In the anti-Marcionite edition made in Rome, did they not place the Romans in front?

De Bruyne compares the ten letters to individual churches and the general pastoral letters, whose prologues he sees as of Catholic origin.

C. The Other Writings of the New Testament

Last question: does this Catholic Bible, issued by Rome in opposition to that of Marcion, include other writings? ... Our prologues to the Gospels speak of Acts and Revelation and put them on a level with the Gospels. ... It does not follow that the Catholic edition also included Acts and Revelation. ... It sufficed for the moment to offer all the Gospels and all Paul's letters. This opinion is confirmed by the fact that there are, I believe, no prologues that resemble those for the four Gospels or the thirteen Epistles for the rest of the New Testament.

What has held me back from publishing the three prologues to the Gospels was that they are anything but "unpublished." If the texts were known, however, they were not esteemed. ... I am convinced that they are Roman, anti-Marcionist, and of 2nd century origin. If so, they are important evidence in the continuing controversy over the date of the Gospels. They also throw new light upon the history of the New Testament canon. Harnack, *Die Entstehung des N.T.* 1914, has shown that the Roman church gave the decisive impetus for the creation of a complete New Testament, but that Marcion also played an important role. On these two points, my studies confirm Harnack's conclusions. I hope that on certain secondary points they clarify and correct them.

Adolf von Harnack, "Die ältesten Evangelienprologe" ["The Oldest Prologues to the Gospels"], *Sitzungsberichte* (1928).

Harnack's review article is presented here in translation and drastically edited I have not included Harnacks' copious and learned footnotes.

We now know what introductions the Pauline Letters received as early as the 2nd century and what part Marcion played in the process, and the merit of the discovery goes to [Peter] Corssen and [Dom Donatien] De Bruyne. The latter has turned his attention to the phenomenon of Gospel prologues in the church for several years, combing through the libraries of Europe to this end. ... Now he has brought this research to a conclusion. ...

Harnack reports at length on the arguments and conclusions made in De Bruyne's article (perhaps supposing that no one else had, or could have, read it in French). In a note he adds:

I leave aside what De Bruyne has laid out as to the secondary character of the Monarchian prologues . . . because as far as I am concerned there is no longer any controversy about the matter. Their dependence on the prologues discussed here is so evident that a proof is superfluous.

III. Critique of De Bruyne's Research

The edition of the texts

I have nothing to add on the subject of the prologues to Mark and Luke, aside from the retention of "*in Asia*" in (the ending of) the prologue to Luke from the Latin translation. De Bruyne was right to avoid premature correction of the Latin tradition based on the Greek. . .

The Unity of the Three Prologues

A Greek original . . . may certainly be assumed for all three prologues once the unity with [the prologue to] Luke has been established . . . [and] De Bruyne's proofs establish it. . . .

The carefully constructed [Catholic] prologue to Luke is in truth a strictly anti-Marcionite prologue to all four Gospels, Acts, and the Apocalypse, and mentions in which order they were written (Matthew, Mark, Luke, Acts, the Apocalypse, and John). After the author composed this prologue, he must have thought it only fitting to provide the other Gospels with prologues as well. . . . But he . . . settled for doing the necessary minimum—which has come back to haunt him, for while the prologue to Luke has survived at least 31 or 32 times, and has survived even in the Greek original, so far only 12 copies of the prologue to Mark, and only 10 of the prologue to John, have been found. . . .

The disappearance of the prologue to Matthew requires a particular explanation. . . . We must assume that it must have been markedly inferior to the prologues to Mark and John. That is no surprise; aside from the tradition that Matthew wrote in Judaea, which the author repeats in the prologue to Luke, there is no tradition in the Empire aside from the unsettling assumption (or was it truly a tradition?) that the apostle wrote his gospel in Hebrew. . . . It is not improbable that the author had to settle for introducing the Gospel with the single sentence that it had been written in Judaea (and in Hebrew?). That such a "prologue" has not survived is no surprise.

The prologue to Mark:

"*Colobodactylus*" indicates Rome, which parallel accounts confirm. . . . It is also a sign of the prologue's antiquity that it treats the designation merely as *signum* and leaves it at that, in contrast to the later explanation. . . . According to the prologue, Mark wrote the Gospel after Peter's death ("*excessio*"): since the same word is to be found in Irenaeus . . . it must depend on the prologue. Here accident is quite improbable; equally improbable is the assumption that the prologue could be the dependent text. . . . We must simply accept the prologue's statement that the Gospel did not exist during Peter's lifetime, as long as there no opposing evidence can be produced. . . .

The prologue to Luke

De Bruyne's great achievement is to have exposed this main prologue as strictly anti-Marcionite—which even Zahn did not recognize. . . . The sharp anti-Marcionite tendency together with the simplicity and the sober clarity of the prologue both guarantee its antiquity (2nd century) and its trustworthiness. It cannot be later than Eusebius (contrary to Zahn)—let anyone produce an even vaguely similar text from the 4th century—and it was probably already used by Irenaeus. . . .

The prologue to John

The first sentence says that as Papias, the trusted student of John, reports in his five exegetical books, the Gospel of John was proclaimed and given to the Asian churches by John himself while "he still lived." Papias cannot really have said that, but it does not necessarily mean that it is not true. . . . The author connects it with the . . . report about Papias and Marcion: Marcion had brought written recommendations from the brothers in Pontus to Papias, but the latter rejected him based on his conflicting beliefs. . . .

The connection of the two reports is best understood in light of the prologue's intent: not that John had said false things in the Gospel he dictated to his beloved student Papias, as Marcion said, but rather that this same Papias had stigmatized Marcion as a false teacher. . . . If we understand the text in this manner, we can understand the otherwise peculiar mention of Marcion, who according to the prologue to Luke was the church's chief opponent at that time, and De Bruyne's careful question as to how Marcion ever entered the prologue to John, appears to be answered. It also takes care of the *metabasis eis allo genos* which De Bruyne attempts. . . . De Bruyne ignores the fact that the report of Papias and Marcion has an excellent parallel in Asia and so there is need to leave Asian territory. The heretic, already driven out of the community in his hometown of Sinope, turned to Polycarp in Asia, and then also to Papias in Phrygia, for recognition. Both denounced him. . . .

Not only can our prologue to John (which is strictly anti-Marcionite, is aware of Papias and his great exegetical work, knows this bishop's negotiation with Marcion, but also reports unreliable things about Papias) have been composed in the second half of the 2nd century, but becomes increasingly out of place in each succeeding period after it. . . .

Origin and history of the prologues

As far as the time of composition is concerned, I agree with De Bruyne. . . . I can be more specific in narrowing the time-frame . . . since what is said about Papias forbids anything earlier than 160, and on the other hand Irenaeus' dependence on the prologues is so likely that they must have existed by 180. These prologues are also certainly older than the Muratorian fragment, which represents the next step in the formation of the canon after them. . . .

A bishop like Dionysius of Corinth, who fought energetically against Marcion, could very well be the author of the prologues, as well as the editor of the four Gospels. But I have to concede to De Bruyne the greater likelihood of Rome, for what is said about Mark—both his nickname and the mention of the "*excessio Petri*"—does point to Rome. The knowledge of Luke's life story may have penetrated as far as Rome . . . knowledge of Papias may also be assumed, and—the most important argument—the prologues have been found almost exclusively in the West. . . . They were known in Lyons before the end of the 2nd century.

As far as the time and place of the Latin translation goes . . . so I defer to De Bruyne. . . . I concur with all that De Bruyne lays out in his summary last section "The Marcionite and the Catholic Bible," with the relative reservation on the question of Rome (see above).

De Bruyne's treatise, for all its brevity, has rescued three unrecognized or insufficiently appreciated texts from the waste basket of literature and restored them to the 2nd century. That is no small achievement in view of the meagre sources from that century! But he has done even more: he has pointed out the existence of a hitherto unknown step in the formation of the N.T. canon; it occurs at a spot which has the most need of light—between Marcion on the one hand and Irenaeus (and the Muratonian canon) on the other; it broadens and secures our knowledge of the influence that Marcion had on the formation of the Catholic canon. And beyond that, considerable information about Luke's early and later history has been gained: he was connected to the apostles before his connection with Paul; he remained unmarried, moved to Achaia after Paul's death, and died at 84 in Boeotia. And we may also accept Mark's "*proceritas corporis*" and his stubby fingers—no earth-shaking illuminations, but apart from the personal description of Paul in the "*Acta Pauli*" and of James in Hegesippus we possess no similar news of any kind on the persons of the apostles.

In closing, Harnack points out the significance of the prologues through the long centuries prior to Luther's German Bible (such that "from time to time they even seemed to merge with the books themselves"). Based on his own agreement with De Bruyne, he recaps the prologues' place in the history of the church's conflict with Marcion and the development of the canon. He ends with an imponderable question: whether the New Testament would ever have taken the shape we know, had it not been for Marcion's truncated and distorted version of it.

Bibliography

Works cited by the author

Akademie der Wissenschaften in Wien. *Corpus Scriptorum Ecclesiasticorum Latinorum.* Vienna: Hoelder-Pichler-Tempsky, 1908.
Bultmann, Rudolf. *Jesus.* Berlin: Deutsche Bibliothek, 1926.
Cadman, W. H. "The Raising of Lazarus." In *Studia Evangelica.* Berlin: Akademie, 1959.
Chapman, John. *Matthew, Mark, and Luke.* London: Longmans Green, 1937.
Chesterton, G. K. *Orthodoxy.* New York: Dodd, Mead, 1908.
Clark, Albert C. *The Acts of the Apostles.* Oxford: Clarendon, 1933.
Cunliffe-Jones, Hubert. "The Fourfold Gospel, a Theological Problem." In *Studia Evangelica.* Berlin: Akademie, 1959.
De Bruyne, Donatien. "Les Plus Anciens Prologues Latins des Evangiles." *Revue Bénédictine* 40 (1928) 193–214.
Dibelius, Martin. "Paulus auf dem Areopag." *Sitzungsberichte der Heidelberger Akademie der Wissenschaften, phil. hist. Klasse,* 1938/1939, 3. Abhandlung.
Fascher, Erich. *Jesus und der Satan: eine Studie zur Auslegung der Versuchungsgeschichte.* Halle: Niemeyer, 1949.
France, Anatole. *Le Procurateur de Judée.* Paris: Ferroud, 1919.
Goodspeed, Edgar J. "Greek Idiom in the Gospels." *Journal of Biblical Literature* 63.2 (1944) 87–91.
———. *Matthew: Apostle and Evangelist.* Philadelphia: Winston, 1959.
———. *Problems of New Testament Translation.* Chicago: University of Chicago Press, 1945.
Graffin, R. et al. *Patrologia Orientalis.* 49 vols. Paris: Firmin & Didot, 1907–75.
Grintz, Jehoshua. "Hebrew as the Spoken and Written Language in the Last Days of the Second Temple." *Journal of Biblical Literature* 79 (1960) 3–56.
Grohmann, Will. *Schmidt-Rotluff.* Stuttgart: Kohlhammer, 1956.
Harnack, Adolf von. "Die ältesten Evangelien-Prologe und die Bildung des Neuen Testaments." In *Sitzungsberichte der Berliner Akademie der Wissenschaften* (1928) 322–41.
———. "Zwei alte dogmatische Korrekturen im Hebraerbrief." In *Sitzungsberichte der Berliner Akademie der Wissenschaften* (1929) 62–73.
Holtzman, Heinrich Julius. *Hand-commentar zum Neuen Testament.* Freiburg: Mohr, 1893.
Hoskyns, Edwin, and Noel Davey. *The Riddle of the New Testament.* London: Faber & Faber, 1931.
Jensen, Adolf Ellegard. *Die getötete Gottheit: Weltbild einer frühen Kultur.* Stuttgart: Kohlhammer, 1966.
Marshall, Bruce. *The World, the Flesh, and Father Smith.* Boston: Houghton Mifflin, 1945.

Michaelis, Wilhelm. *Die Apokryphen: Schriften zum Neuen Testament*. Bremen: Schünemann, 1956.
Murray, Gilbert, et al. *Oxford Book of Greek Verse*. Oxford: Clarendon, 1930.
Pauly, August, Georg Wissowa. *Real-Encyclopädie der Classischen Altertumswissenschaft*. (I have not been able to ascertain which edition of the R-E Rosenstock-Huessy used).
Picht, Werner. *Albert Schweitzer: Leben und Bedeutung*. Hamburg: Meiner, 1960.
Rang, Florens Christian. *Shakespeare der Christ*. Heidelberg: Lambert Schneider, 1954.
Rosenstock-Huessy, Eugen. *Der Atem des Geistes*. Frankfurt: Frankfurter Hefte, 1951.
———. *The Christian Future*. New York: Scribner's, 1946.
———. *Heilkraft und Wahrheit*. Stuttgart: Evangelisches Verlagswerk, 1952.
———. "Hitler and Israel, or on Prayer." *Journal of Religion* 25.2 (1945) 129–39.
———. "Liturgical Thinking." *Orate Fratres* 23.12 (1949) 529–37; 24.1 (1950) 63–69.
———. *The Multiformity of Man*. Norwich, VT: Beachhead Press, 1948. [Also Essex: Argo, 2000.]
———. *Out of Revolution, Autobiography of Western Man*. New York: Morrow, 1938. [Also Providence: Berg, 1993.]
———. *Die Sprache des Menschengeschlechts*. 2 vols. Heidelberg: Lambert Schneider, 1963–64.
Schweitzer, Albert. *Von Reimarus zu Wrede: eine Geschichte der Leben-Jesu-Forschung*. Tübingen: Mohr, 1906.
Schweitzer, Albert. *Die Mystik des Apostels Paulus*. Tübingen: Mohr,1930.
Vischer, Lukas. "Die Rechtfertigung der Schriftstellerei in der alten Kirche." *Theologische Zeitschrift* 12 (1956) 320–36.
Weymouth, Richard Francis, and James Alexander Robertson. *The New Testament in Modern Speech*. 5th ed. Boston: Pilgrim, 1939.

Works the author may have consulted

Augustine, *De Genesi ad litteram* (in Migne, *Patrologia*?).
Chesterton, G.K. "The Ballad of the White Horse." New York: John Lane, 1911.
Frost, Robert. "Ten Mills: Precaution." *Poetry* 48.1 (1936) 3.
Ignatius. *Letter to the Ephesians* (in Migne, *Patrologia*?).
———. *Letter to the Magnesians* (in Migne, *Patrologia*?).
Vincent of Lerins, *Commonitorium* (in Migne, *Patrologia*?).
Works which may be the source of references in the text:
Augustine. *In Johannis evangelium tractatus* (in Migne, *Patrologia*?).
———. *Contra Faustum* (in Migne, *Patrologia*?).
Bornkamm, Günther. *Jesus von Nazareth*. Stuttgart: Kohlhammer, 1956.
Kilpatrick, George Dunbar. *The Origins of the Gospel according to St. Matthew*. Oxford: Clarendon, 1946.
Scharrelmann, Wilhelm. *Jesus der Jüngling*. Leipzig: Quelle & Meyer, 1920.
Stalin, Yosif V. *Der Marxismus und die Fragen der Sprachwissenschaft*. Berlin: Dietz, 1951.

Additional works cited by the editors

All excerpts from Franz Rosenzweig's "Gritli Letters" are taken from the complete text online at www.erhfund.org/the-gritli-letters-gritli-briefe/ (accessed May 20, 2020).

Rosenstock-Huessy's correspondence with Georg Müller is held at the archive of the Landeskirche Westphalen in Bielefeld; an overview of the archive may be found at: www.ekvw.findbuch.net/php/main.php?ar_id=3682&be_kurz=3&ve_vnum=0#426573742e20352e3136 (accessed May 20, 2020).

Alsberg, Dietrich. *A Witness to a Century: A Memoir*. Bloomington: iUniverse, 2002.

Butler, Basil Christopher. *The Originality of Matthew*. Cambridge: Cambridge University Press, 1951.

Chesterton, G. K. *The Everlasting Man*. New York: Dodd Mead, 1925.

Cristaudo, Wayne. *Religion, Redemption, and Revolution: The New Speech Thinking Revolution of Franz Rozenzweig and Eugen Rosenstock-Huessy*. Toronto: University of Toronto Press, 2012.

Cristaudo et al, "Introduction: Eugen Rosenstock-Huessy (1888–1973)." *Culture, Theory, and Critique* 56.1 (2015) 9.

Galsworthy, John. "Escape" in *Plays* VI. New York: Scribner's, 1934.

Grant, Robert M. "The Oldest Gospel Prologues." *Anglican Theological Review* 23 (1946) 231–45.

———. *Second Century Christianity*. London: Society for Promoting Christian Knowledge, 1946.

Heidegger, Martin. *Basic Writings from* Being and Time *(1927) to* The Task of Thinking *(1964)*. New York: Harper & Row, 1977.

Heschel, Abraham J. *The Sabbath*. New York: Noonday (FSG), 1975.

Hitler, Adolf. *Reden des Führers am Parteitag der Ehre 1936*. München: Zentralverlag der NSDAP, 1936.

Huessy, Raymond. "Eugen and Margrit Rosenstock-Huessy in 'Rosenzweig Studies': A Reflection on the Centennial of the 'Leipziger Nachtgespräch.'" *Culture, Theory and Critique* 56.1 (2015) 101–17.

Kanamori, Paul. *Paul Kanamori's Life-Story, Told by Himself*. Philadelphia: Sunday School Times, 1921.

———. *Three-Hour Sermon*. New York: Revell, 1920.

Klein, Gottlieb. *Ist Jesus eine historische Persönlichkeit?* Tübingen: Mohr (Siebeck), 1910.

Lagerlöf, Selma. *The Miracles of the Antichrist*. Boston: Little Brown, 1911.

Landau, Rom. *Hitler's Paradise*. London: Faber & Faber, 1941.

Lapide, Pinchas. *Ist das nicht Josephs Sohn?* Gütersloh: Mohn, 1988.

Preiss, Jack. *Camp William James*. Norwich: Argo, 1978.

Robinson, John A. T. *Redating the New Testament*. London: SCM, 1976.

Rosenstock-Huessy, Eugen, and Joseph Wittig. *Das Alter der Kirche*. 3 vols. Berlin: Lambert Schneider, 1927–28.

Rosenstock-Huessy, Eugen. "Andragogik." In *Im Kampf um die Erwachsenenbildung*, 193–218. Leipzig: Quelle & Meyer, 1926.

———. *Bibliography and Biography*. New York: Four Wells, 1959.

———. *The Collected Works of Eugen Rosenstock-Huessy on DVD*. Essex: Argo, 2005. ("Universal History 1957," "The Jewish and the Christian Trinity.")

———. *Die Europäischen Revolutionen: Volkscharaktere und Staatenbildung*. Jena: Diederichs, 1931.
———. *Das Geheimnis der Universität*. Stuttgart: Kohlhammer, 1958.
———. "Generations of Faith," *The Hartford Quarterly* 3 (1961) 95–111.
———. *Die Hochzeit des Krieges und der Revolution*. Würzburg: Patmos, 1920.
———. *I Am an Impure Thinker*. Essex: Argo, 2001.
———. *Ja und Nein*. Heidelberg: Lambert Schneider, 1968.
———. *The Origin of Speech*. Norwich: Argo, 1981.
Rosenstock-Huessy, Eugen, and Ford L. Battles. *Magna Carta Latina*. Pittsburgh: Pickwick, 1975.
Rosenstock-Huessy, Eugen and Martin Buber. *Die Tochter/Das Buch Rut*. Mössingen-Talheim: Talheimer, 1988.
Rosenstock-Huessy, Eugen, and Franz Rosenzweig. *Judaism Despite Christianity*. Chicago: University of Chicago Press, 2011.
Rosenzweig, Franz. *Briefe*. Berlin: Schocken, 1935.
———. *Der Stern der Erlösung*. Heidelberg: Lambert Schneider, 1954.
Schoeps, Hans-Joachim. *The Jewish-Christian Argument*. London: Faber & Faber, 1963.
Töpfer and Wiesing, *Richard Koch und Franz Rosenzweig, Schriften und Briefe zu Krankheit, Sterben, und Tod*. Münster: Agenda, 2000.
Ullmann, Wolfgang."Die Entdeckung des Neuen Denkens." *Stimmstein* 2 (1988) 147–78.
Wolf, Hubert and Klaus Unterburger. *Die Lage der Kirche in Deutschland: Der Schlussbericht des Nuntius vom 18. November 1929*. Veröffentlichungen der KfZ A 50. Paderborn: Kommission für Zeitgeschichte, 2006.
van der Molen, Lise. *Guide to the Works of Eugen Rosenstock-Huessy*. Essex: Argo, 1997. (available on the Eugen Rosenstock-Huessy Fund's website, www.ehrfund.org).
Vernon, Ambrose. *The Religious Value of the Old Testament in the Light of Modern Scholarship* at https://archive.org/details/religiousvalueooovern/page/n8 (accessed May 20, 2020).
———. *Some Turning Points in Church History* at https://archive.org/details/someturningpointo1vern/page/n6 (accessed May 20, 2020).
Wittig, Joseph. *Leben Jesu in Palästina, Schlesien, und anderswo*. Gotha: Klotz, 1927.
———. *Höregott*. Gotha: Klotz, 1929.
World Conference on Adult Education. *Conference Report of the World Association of Adult Education (1929)*. London: World Association for Adult Education, 1930.
Wren, Brian. "There's a Spirit in the Air." In *The New Century Hymnal*. Cleveland: Pilgrim, 1995.